AMERICA'S
SHADOW

Also by William V. Spanos

The End of Education: Toward Posthumanism

Heidegger and Criticism: Retrieving the Cultural Politics of Destruction

AMERICA'S SHADOW

An Anatomy of Empire

William V. Spanos

University of Minnesota Press
Minneapolis
London

A shorter version of chapter 2 was previously published as "Culture and Colonization: The Imperial Imperatives of the Centered Circle," *boundary 2* 23 (spring 1996): 135–76.

Published by the University of Minnesota Press
111 Third Avenue South, Suite 290
Minneapolis, MN 55401-2520
http://www.upress.umn.edu

Printed in the United States of America on acid-free paper

The University of Minnesota is an equal-opportunity educator and employer.

Library of Congress Cataloging-in-Publication Data

Spanos, William V.
   America's shadow : an anatomy of empire / William V. Spanos.
     p.   cm.
   Includes bibliographical references (p.   ) and index.
   ISBN 0-8166-3337-1 (alk. paper). – ISBN 0-8166-3338-X
  (pbk : alk. paper)
     1. Vietnamese Conflict, 1961-1975 – United States. 2. Vietnamese
Conflict, 1961-1975 – Influence. 3. Imperialism – United States –
History – 20th century. 4. East and West. 5. Postmodernism –
Political aspects – United States.   I. Title.
DS558.S687 2000
325'.32'0973 – dc21   99-41284

11 10 09 08 07 06 05 04 03 02 01 00   10 9 8 7 6 5 4 3 2 1

TO THE MEMORY OF
CONSTANCE COINER

Sweet Constance,

gentle but not passive comrade,

no plea from me

to flights of angels

to sing thee to thy rest

but a barbarous apostrophe:

may your specter

remain here in the place

of your labors

to haunt us all

until

the justice you struggled

in your teaching and practice

to bring to pass

with the passion

of a great soul

is realized

in this mendacious

and unjust world.

Thou art a scholar; speak to it, Horatio.

— MARCELLUS, in William Shakespeare, *Hamlet*

To Daimonion is what shows itself in pointing at what is ordinary and in a certain way therefore what is also present everywhere as the perfectly ordinary, though nevertheless never merely ordinary. For those who come later and for us...the uncanny has to be the exception, in principle explainable, to the ordinary; we put the uncanny next to the ordinary, but, to be sure, only as the extraordinary. For it is difficult to attain the fundamental Greek experience, whereby the ordinary itself...is the uncanny.

— MARTIN HEIDEGGER, *Parmenides*

As theoreticians or witnesses, spectators, observers, and intellectuals, scholars believe that looking is sufficient. Therefore, they are not always in the most competent position to do what is necessary: speak to the specter.... There has never been a scholar who, as such, does not believe in the sharp distinction between the real and the unreal,... being and non-being,... between what is present and what is not.... If we were to refer uniquely to this traditional figure of the "scholar," we would therefore have to be wary here of what we could define as the illusion, the mystification, or the *complex of Marcellus.* — JACQUES DERRIDA, *Specters of Marx*

Contents

Acknowledgments

The debts I have incurred in the process of writing this book are, as always, not only too numerous to acknowledge in a limited space; they are also too entangled in my intellectual life to be sorted out. Nothing that I have been given to think, as far as I can remember, has not had its origins in an intense classroom or personal conversation in the process of which the *question* becomes more important than the particular persons involved. But because I believe deeply that truly productive scholarship, whatever the case of the quality of my own, is collaborative, I want at least to express my gratitude to the graduate students who participated in those first seminars on the American culture industry's representation of the Vietnam War, especially Wei Wang, Lara Lutz, Cynthia Davis, and Erica Braxton. As remote as the matter of those seminars was to the historical context in which it here appears, this book had its origins in those intense classroom spaces and could not have been written without my students' unknowing contributions to the question we thought together. On the same level of exasperating generality, I want also, and as always, to thank my colleagues on the *boundary 2* editorial collective. As I have said on other occasions, my original role in my relation to these extraordinary scholars/critics was that of either mentor or provider of a space conducive to their intellectual development. But in the process of our long relationship the roles have been reversed. This is not to say that they finally "killed the father." It is to say, rather, that they collectively came to provide the ferment that has not only sustained but energized that aspect of my intellectual life that is engaged with the question of justice. And I don't say this lightly. For in this dark time of dearth, there is very little, especially in the space of the academy, that one can count on to encourage commitment in the old existential sense of the word.

I also want to thank my colleagues Christopher Fynsk, Bill Haver, Gisella Brinker-Gabler, David Bartine, Liz Rosenberg, Sidonie Smith, Carol Boyce Davis, Marilynn Desmond, and Lennard Davis, whose presence at Binghamton in a time of multiple retrenchments that conceal a reactionary ideological agenda has been redemptive. Not least, I want to express my gratitude to my graduate student Assimina Karavanta, whose knowledge about and uncanny feel for things Greek, past and present, have contributed in a fundamental way to my groping effort to think "classical Greece" against its representation by the post-Enlightenment West.

I am also grateful to Vassilis Lambropoulos, director of Modern Greek Studies at Ohio State University, and to William Murphy of the University of Minnesota Press, both of whom read *America's Shadow* in manuscript form. Vassilis, the author of the inaugural book *The Rise of Ethnocentrism,* saw immediately the importance of the question I was posing concerning the origins of the identity of the Occident and encouraged me to pursue it despite its obvious controversial tenor. To William Murphy, I am grateful for his initial and continuing support of my project and, especially, for his acutely discriminating editorial sense. His uncanny ability to single out what was superfluous in the original manuscript convinced me of the need to temper my predilections for inclusiveness. As a result, the book, in my mind, is a better one.

On a more personal level, I thank my daughters, Maria and Stephania, and my sons, Aristides and Adam, for their abiding love and for their understanding that my errancy is only a different kind of being there. Above all, I want to express my gratitude to Jan McVicker, who read all the chapters of this book with the deep care for the world and passion for justice that inform her very being. Indeed, she has been the specter that from the beginning has haunted the process of its writing. Instead of keeping her voice at bay, however, I have tried to listen carefully to its directives. I am sure that I have not entirely succeeded in fulfilling its imperative to think the "Other" in all its manifestations. But I hope that she and those she represents will recognize that I have written this book in the spirit of that care. Finally, I dedicate this book to the memory of my colleague and dear friend Constance Coiner, who was killed, along with her daughter Anna, on TWA Flight 800 in July 1996. She practiced the thought of justice to which most of us in the academy only pay lip service.

Parts of this book were presented as lectures at the University of Trento in Italy, at the University of Thessaloniki, at the University of Athens in Greece (the latter during a three-week period as a visiting lecturer in November 1995), and at the State University of New York at Buffalo. I want especially to thank Professors Giovanna Covi and Carla Locatelli of the University of Trento, Professor Georgos Kalogeras of the University of Thessaloniki, Professors Bessie Dandrinos, Aliki Halls, and Yannis Chioles of the University of Athens, and Professors Rodolphe Gasché and Joy Leighton of SUNY at Buffalo for the honor they bestowed on mc in inviting me to speak at their universities and for their kind hospitality. Not least, I want to thank the students in the Department of English of the University of Athens, who, during my stay, showed me at first hand how the *Pax Americana* works in a "developing" country.

A much briefer version of chapter 2 was previously published in *boundary 2;* I wish to thank the editor, Paul Bové, and Duke University Press for permission to reprint in this book.

Introduction

Following the "decisive" defeat of Iraq in the Gulf War and amid the American media's celebration of another instance of the validity of America's "exceptionalist" mission in the world's wilderness, President George Bush announced that the American people had finally "kicked the Vietnam syndrome." In the fall semester of 1988 and again in the spring semester of 1990, immediately preceding the Gulf War, I had given a graduate seminar titled "Re-presenting Vietnam," the project of which was to think the ideological implications of the American culture industry's inordinate overdetermination of an idea of America that resonated backward to the origins of this exceptionalist national self-image in the Puritan "errand in the wilderness." One of the central motifs that emerged in the process of examining this representational discourse — in films, documentaries, histories, autobiographies, and novels — was its insistent reference to the metaphor of "healing the wound." Its ubiquity compelled us to think the history of the representational transformations of this trope and the different meanings this history wrung from it. The tentative conclusion we drew was that, more than any other function, this overdetermination of the metaphor of the wound — the rehabilitation of the vilified veteran of the Vietnam War, for example — had essentially to do with the massive protestation of the war. That resistance was undertaken not, as it came to be alleged in this representational discourse, by political extremists, maladjusted malcontents, would-be draft dodgers, or youthful dupes of Soviet communism, but by a large segment of the general American public that had become disillusioned not simply with the Cold War discourse, but, at least symptomatically, with the idea of the America dream itself. That is to say, the study of these texts suggested that this appropriation of the metaphor of the wound was intended to serve a reactionary ideological function. It was an appropriation by the ideological state apparatuses that, in keeping with the Cold War scenario, had as its end the rehabilitation of the American national identity, which the war — its insistent misrepresentation by the American government and, not least, its brutal conduct by the United States — had disintegrated. This was the exceptionalist national image that had its origins in the American Puritans' "errand in the wilderness" to "build a city on the hill" and that Alexis de Tocqueville theorized for the global future of democratic America in the post-Revolutionary era:

> The gradual development of the principle of equality is...a providential fact. It has all the chief characteristics of such a fact: it is universal, it is lasting, it constantly eludes all human interference, and all events as well as all men contribute to its progress.[1]

If President Bush's proclamation that the American public had at last been cured of the Vietnam syndrome left any vestigial doubts about that conclusion, they were decisively allayed with the virtually simultaneous annunciation of the end of history and the advent of the New World Order by the intellectual deputies of the dominant American order in the aftermath of the "revolutions" that brought down the communist regimes in Eastern and Central Europe and the Soviet Union. For the end of the Cold War was announced not simply as the *Pax Americana,* but as the precipitate — "the good news" in Francis Fukuyama's eschatological rhetoric — of the dialectics of Universal History, a narrative that, like de Tocqueville's characteristic universalist representation of the extermination of the Native Americans at the beginning of American history,[2] obliterated the actuality of that radically contradictory event or reduced it to the status of an accident — a "remediable" mistake — at the "end" of this history.[3]

This euphoric representation of the end of the Cold War by the intellectual deputies of the dominant culture has been modified under the pressure of world events since the apparently decisive defeat of the Iraqi army in the Gulf War: the genocidal ethnic strife in the former Yugoslavia; the political instability and violence in much of central and southern Africa; the bloody struggle between the secular state and religious fundamentalists in Algeria; the continuing tensions between East and West in the Middle East, not least, the reaffirmation of Iraqi sovereignty against the United States's threat of intervention; and the emergent threat of nuclear war between India and Pakistan. Indeed, references to the end of history and the New World Order have all but disappeared from mediatic and theoretical representations of the contemporary occasion. But I interpret this modification not as a tacit admission of the illegitimacy of the end-of-history discourse, but rather as an accommodation of these contradictory events to its universalist scenario, an accommodation that, in fact, renders this end-of-history discourse more powerful insofar as the apparent acknowledgment of their historical specificity obscures its real metaphysical basis.

This accommodational strategy of representation, for example, is epitomized by Richard Haass, a former official in the Bush administration and now director of foreign policy studies at the Brookings Institution, in his book *The Reluctant Sheriff: The United States after the Cold War* (1997).[4] Eschewing Fukuyama's Hegelian eschatological structure in favor of theorizing the actual practices of the United States in the international sphere — Somalia, Haiti, Bosnia, Iraq, and so forth — Haass frames the post–Cold War conjuncture in the totalizing image of a "deregulated world" (in contrast to the world "regulated" by the Cold War scenario) and the role of the United States in the trope of a sheriff leading posses (the appropriate members of the United Nations) to quell threats to global stability and peace posed by this international deregulation. Despite Haass's acknowledgment that conflict is inevitable (which, in fact, echoes Fukuyama), the triumphant *idea* of liberal capitalist democracy remains intact in his discourse. That is, his commitment to the "laissez-faire" polity (deregulation) — to the fictional concept of the sovereign subject — continues to be grounded in the metaphysics that informed America's global errand in the "wilderness" of Southeast Asia. Indeed, Haass gives this representational framework far more historical power than Fukuyama's disciplinary discourse of political science is able to muster. For, unlike the Fukuyamans, Haass informs his representation of the United States's historically determined and determining exceptionalist mission in the post–Cold War era with the teleological metaphorics that have been from the beginning fundamental to the constitution and power of the American globally oriented national identity. The metaphor of the sheriff/posse derives from the history of the American West and constitutes a variation of the pacification processes of westward expansion. As such it brings with it the entire baggage of the teleological metanarrative of the American frontier from the Puritans' "errand in the ['New World'] wilderness" to the myth of Manifest Destiny. As the "New Americanist" countermemory has persuasively shown, this is the myth that has saturated the cultural discourse of America, both high and low, since its origins: whether in the form of the American jeremiad, which, from the Puritans through Daniel Webster to Ronald Reagan, has always functioned to maintain the national consensus vis-à-vis its providentially ordained mission to domesticate (and dominate) what is beyond the frontier[5] or in the form of the Hollywood western, which has functioned to naturalize what one New Americanist has called the American "victory culture."[6] Reconstellated into this context, Haass's more "realistic" analysis of the post–Cold War occasion comes to be seen not simply as continuous with Fukuyama's, but as a more effective imperial global strategy. The utter immunity to criticism of the Clinton administration's "humanitarian" war against Serbia in the spring of 1999 — which perfectly enacted the Haassian scenario — bears witness to this. In the following chapters of this book I will, by and large, refer to Fukuyama's version of the post–Cold War American end-of-history discourse. But I wish to make it clear at the beginning that, in doing so, I am referring not to a particular theory, but to a fundamental American tradition whose theorization extends from de Tocqueville through Frederick Jackson Turner to Fukuyama and Haass.

The announcement of the end of history and the advent of the New World Order did more than disclose the dominant culture's will to forget Vietnam. It also — and paradoxically — brought into focus the persistent and unassuagable national anxiety that the Vietnam War instigated in the American national consciousness, not the least aspect of which was its affiliation with the "Old World's" perennial imperial project, which was heretofore obscured by the myth of American exceptionalism. To invoke the countermetaphorics of this book, that announcement thematized the irrepressible *spectrality* of the Vietnam War, the degree to which its actuality haunts the very "imperial" official discourse that would bury and monumentalize its corpse in the name of a "new" beginning. And this insight into the inexorable persistence of the specter of the Vietnam War, in turn, has compelled me to ask what it was/is about the event of the Vietnam War that has evoked — and continues to evoke — such a frantically sustained will to forget it.

This book, therefore, constitutes an effort or, rather, a series of *essays* (in the root sense of the word) to answer this question. It is not simply intended to challenge the politically conservative initiative to recuperate or, to invoke the ironic language of a recent contribution to this initiative, to "reconstruct" the "America" that self-destructed in the decade of the Vietnam War[7] — an initiative to which, however inadvertently, liberal thinkers such as Arthur Schlesinger and Richard Rorty have contributed.[8] Equally important, my project is to put this unexamined question back into play in the context of the dominant culture's appropriation of the metaphor of the Vietnam syndrome for the purpose of legitimizing the end-of-history discourse and the practice presided over by the United States. I mean by this — in keeping with the *unexceptionalist* (i.e., European) imperial origins of "America" disclosed by a genealogical reading of the American canonical tradition — the *Pax Americana*.

The structure of *America's Shadow* is not intended to articulate a sustained argument. Rather, this book consists of five chapters organized in terms of Heidegger's understanding of "repetition" (*Wiederholung*).

They constitute variations on a theme, as it were, in which the "theme" is the finally irrepressible Other precipitated at the limits of the thought that informs the history of the Occidental tradition, the specter, as it were, that haunts its imperial logic.

Chapter 1 undertakes a sustained ("Heideggerian") de-struction of the metaphysical discourse of the ontotheological tradition — the tradition that informs the interpretation of actual history proffered by the post–Cold War, end-of-history discourse — in the context of the question of its relationship to European imperialism. By way of thinking its etymology — *meta-ta-physika,* "after or beyond or above *physis*" (temporality and the differences it always already disseminates) — this chapter thematizes a privileged relay of tropes inhering in metaphysical thinking that are imperial *in essence:* the panoptic solar/patriarchal eye and its light, the center and the periphery, and the seed/semen (planting/cultivation). It demonstrates that this metaphorical relay — this "white mythology," to appropriate Jacques Derrida's phrase — informs the discourse and practice of imperialism proper throughout the history of the Occident. In the process of analyzing these metaphorical systems, this chapter distinguishes between the historically specific imperial uses to which the Occident has put them. It concentrates especially on the Enlightenment's complex (re)organization of the restricted economy of the internal space of the circle (center/periphery), an organizational initiative modeled on the emergent classificatory table, that was intended to render the imperial project more politically efficient and invisible than heretofore. This naturalizing initiative, it claims, achieves its "fulfillment" in what Heidegger proleptically called "the age of the world picture": the planetary "triumph" of American technological/instrumentalist reason (the *Pax Metaphysica*) and of liberal capitalist democracy (the *Pax Americana*) in the post–Cold War era.

Chapter 2 then undertakes a genealogy of this triumphant modernity that radically challenges the received assumption about the provenance of the liberal humanist democracy that History has precipitated as the New World Order. It suggests that the origins of the modern West are not in Greek thought (the originative thinking that is the imperative of truth as *a-letheia:* unconcealment), as it has been claimed, especially since the invention of what Martin Bernal has called the "Aryan model" in the period of the Enlightenment. It suggests, rather, that these origins lie in Rome's colonization of Greek thinking: its reduction of an always open — and "errant" — inquiry to *veritas,* the correspondence of mind and thing, that is, to correctness. It further suggests that this Roman colonization of Greek thinking had and continues to have as its fundamental project *eruditio et institutio in bonas artes* (scholarship and training in good conduct), that is, the production of a dependable *manly* citizenry for the purpose of establishing, legitimating, and aggrandizing the Roman Empire.

After focalizing the historical process that begins with the Roman transformation of an originative to a derivative metaphysical thinking and culminates in its globalization as technological or instrumentalist reason, chapter 3 retrieves the historical specificity of the Vietnam War that the triumphalist end-of-history discourse, aided and abetted by the culture industry and the collapse of the Soviet Union, has strategically forgotten. It suggests that this willed forgetting has had as its raison d'être the occlusion of the delegitimizing paradox precipitated by the United States's brutal conduct of the war: that "America" had to *destroy* Vietnam in order to "save" it. My intention is to retrieve a history in which the "benign" liberal democratic (onto)logic of exceptionalist America fulfills itself (comes to its end) in something like a genocidal violence against a recalcitrant Other, an Other that refused to be answerable to the "truth" of the Occident.

Chapter 4 then undertakes an *Auseinandersetzung* — an agonistic dialogue — with the dominant oppositional discourses, especially the neo-Marxism that identifies postmodernity with the logic of late capitalism, the New Historicism, and a certain postcolonialist discourse. It attributes the impasse of oppositional criticism in the aftermath of the Cold War — that is, in the context of the announcement of the *Pax Metaphysica* (the end of history) and the *Pax Americana* — to the fact that these postmodern/postcolonial discourses, in their abandonment of "theory" in favor of "practice," continue to resist in the very technological/instrumentalist language prescribed by the triumphant imperial culture.

Finally, chapter 5 returns, in the form of a "repetition," to the imperatives for thought disclosed by my solicitation of the dominant American culture's representation of Vietnam at the beginning of this introduction. It undertakes an interrogation of the recuperative neo-Hegelian end-of-history discourse not simply to expose the imperialist ideology informing its celebration of the global "triumph" of liberal capitalist democracy, but also to retrieve the Vietnam War that this discourse is compelled to obliterate in order to legitimize its claim that the triumph of liberal capitalist democracy in the Cold War constitutes the end of a universal historical process. By thus foregrounding the dominant culture's symptomatic compulsive will to forget the Vietnam War, it discloses this irrepressible event as a radical and delegitimizing contradiction in its logic that demands to be, but has not as yet been, thought. More specifically, it calls for a rethinking of the imperial thinking that, in fulfilling its positive possibilities, has exposed to view the "nothing" it finally cannot contain and thus always already haunts the regime of truth that would colonize and pacify "it." It calls for a rethinking that would, like the Vietnamese Other, refuse to be answerable to the triumphant technological/imperial discourse. In so doing, it points in a prologomenal way to the yet-to-be-thought solidarity of such a spectral thinking with a kind of incipient emancipatory political praxis inherent in the nomadic condition of the preterite, the pariah, the émigré, the exile, the unhomed that has been massively precipitated as the spectral contradiction that haunts the Occident's achieved imperial domination of the planet.

It will no doubt be objected by the adversarial critics with whom I am undertaking this *Auseinandersetzung,* especially by postcolonialists, that my "history" of Western philosophical and political imperialism is an ill-advised appropriation of Heidegger's *Seinsgeschichte* (history of Being) and thus constitutes another metanarrative that imposes a monolithic representation of the rhizoid complexities of the actual history of the West that undermines the very argument I am trying to make on behalf of difference/dissemination. Let me respond at the outset to this potential objection in such a way that might prove instructive to an opposition that would indiscriminately avoid such "totalizing" representations of Western imperial history. Though this objection is in one sense justifiable, it also entails a disabling blindness to the continuity of the European identity enabled by the representation of being in terms of the imperial metaphysical principle of presence. The historically specific practice appears to be more discontinuous than my Heideggerian interpretation will allow, but this apparent erraticness obscures the structural depth at which the West's metaphysical *representation* of being has worked to give directionality — and power — to the identity of the West and to Western thinking and practice. It is, I will claim, the marked tendency to succumb to the lure of this surface, the failure to plumb the ideological depths of the West's perennial power, that has disabled and continues to disable oppositional criticism of the polyvalent Western imperial project.

The objection I am anticipating has been recently — and instructively — leveled against Edward Said's inaugural *Orientalism* by his belated postcolonial critics, even though he deliberately eschews the ontological register of Heidegger's interrogation of the ontotheological tradition. As one of them puts it:

> Said's characteristically determinist vision of the operations of power in colonial relations leads him, in the first instance, to take

insufficient account of resistance or contradiction *within* imperial culture itself. At moments he suggests that even those who
were most critical of colonialism, like Marx, cannot escape the
determination of "latent" Orientalism so that "in the end it is
the Romantic Orientalist vision that wins out, as Marx's theoretical socio-economic views become submerged in [a] classically
standard image" of the East. At such points, moreover, *Orientalism* seems to reinscribe the very forms of cultural essentialism for
which Said condemns Orientalist discourse....

A further problem entailed by Said's failure to [think the hegemonic discourses of Orientalism historically] is that he does not
take account of the abundant evidence that Western discourse itself
registered the history which resisted its encroachments.[9]

Pressed to the extreme, as it is by most of these critics, the complaint
against Said's "homogenizing and totalizing" representation of Orientalism has resulted in a disabling irony. In overdetermining the historical
exceptions that resist Said's "metanarrative" (I put quotation marks
around the term to suggest that he, unlike his critics, understands his
representation as a forestructure), this argument reinscribes the liberal
humanist problematic, which assumes that the terms of the agon between the Occident and the Orient have the same weight and thus can be
"negotiated" in a parliamentary arena. Which is to say, they are dehis-
toricized, dislocated into a transcendental realm. Power in *this historical
world,* however, is always uneven, always, that is, a matter of injustice.
In the case of the provenance of Said's book, the Orient he would retrieve against the dominant Orientalist discourse was, patently, virtually
powerless to effect a radical change in the Occident's colonialist representation of the Orient, to say nothing of the imperial practices it
enables. In the case of my intervention, the idea of the West I am trying to put back into play — that its imperial origins lie in the Roman
reduction of an originative thinking (*a-letheia*) to a derivative and calculative (metaphysical) thinking that would facilitate its imperial project —
is also virtually powerless to displace the prevailing assumptions about
the origins of the identity of the West. To overdetermine the exceptions
to this rule, therefore, would be tantamount to accepting the pluralist
terms of the very truth discourse I am interrogating. This is not to say
that there are no exceptions or that the exceptions are irrelevant. It is
to say, rather, that it is first necessary to emphasize the strategic ten-
dentiousness of the dominant discourse's representational practices —
the inordinate degree to which its underlying ontological principle has
selected the historical evidence in order to legitimate itself — before

addressing these exceptions. Said's *Orientalism,* largely because of its "monolithically imposed" metanarrative, has instigated a massive, various, and *productive* field of study called "postcolonialism." I do not presume as much. But precisely by proffering the "monolithic" character of the Western representation of being as a forestructure to guide my inquiry, I think my study should, however modestly, contribute to a deeper, if not different, understanding of the anatomy of the global politics of the post–Cold War occasion than those oppositional discourses that overlook or consciously avoid its ontological ground in favor of more "practical" or "political" sites of interrogation. And, by way of attending to the exceptions that the Western imperial project has not been able to accommodate, it should also contribute something useful to the vexed problem of resisting its apparently irresistible power.

Chapter 1

The Ontological Origins of Occidental Imperialism

Thinking the *Meta* of Metaphysics

In the planetary imperialism of technologically organized man, the subjectivism of man attains its acme, from which point it will descend to the level of organized uniformity and there firmly establish itself. This uniformity becomes the surest instrument of total, i.e., technological, rule over the earth.   — MARTIN HEIDEGGER, "The Age of the World Picture"

The center is at the center of the totality, and yet, since the center does not belong to the totality (is not part of the totality), the totality *has its center elsewhere....* The concept of centered structure is in fact the concept of a play based on a fundamental ground, a play constituted on the basis of a fundamental immobility and a reassuring certitude, which itself is beyond the reach of play. And on the basis of this certitude anxiety can be mastered.   — JACQUES DERRIDA, "Structure, Sign, and Play
in the Discourse of the Human Sciences"

In the expansion of the great Western empires, profit and hope of further profit were obviously tremendously important.... But there is more than that to imperialism and colonialism. There was a commitment to them over and above profit, a commitment in constant circulation and recirculation, which, on the one hand, allowed decent men and women to accept the notion that distant territories and their native peoples *should* be subjugated, and, on the other, replenished metropolitan energies so that these decent people could think of the *imperium* as a protracted, almost metaphysical obligation to rule subordinate, inferior, or less advanced peoples.
— EDWARD W. SAID, *Culture and Imperialism*

Ontology, Imperialism,
and the "New World Order"

Traditional commentators on Western imperialism, whether imperialist or anti-imperialist in their sympathies, have invariably situated its historical origins in modernity, indeed, as concurrent with the emergence of

1

the Enlightenment. Until recently, these commentators have also tended to restrict the parameters of the imperialist project to economics or economics/politics. They have, as in the cases of Adam Smith, Ricardo, and the other classical capitalist economists, on the one hand, and Marx and Engels, on the other, privileged the economic site as a base to essentially epiphenomenal superstructural sites such as ontology, gender, religion, culture, and information. These commentators always refer to earlier European empires such as those of Alexander the Great and, above all, the Romans, but they invariably represent the imperialism of these empires as that which imperialism proper is not. These commentators refer to other sites besides the economic or economic/political, especially the cultural. But these sites are invariably represented as superstructural and thus, like Alexandrian Greece and imperial Rome, play no significant role in the elaboration of the genealogy, meaning, and administrative operations of modern imperialism.

More recently, by way of the implicit interrogation of the base/superstructure model by early "postcolonial" or "Third World" critics such as Frantz Fanon, C. L. R. James, and Albert Memmi, and of the explicit solicitation of this Ricardian/Marxist model by theoreticians such as Antonio Gramsci, Louis Althusser, Michel Foucault, and Raymond Williams, "postmodern" critics of imperialism — Edward W. Said, V. G. Kiernan, Homi Bhabha, Gayatri Spivak, Peter Hulme, Benedict Anderson, Mary Louise Pratt, and others — have begun to attend to the ways actual events undermine the structural relationship between the metropolitan center and the provincial periphery enabled by teleological interpretations of history. These thinkers, and the legion of "cultural critics" their work has instigated, have come to see what an earlier generation of commentators was blinded to by its base/superstructure interpretive model: the overdetermination of cultural or information production in the "postimperial" or "postcolonial" or "late capitalist" twentieth century. And that insight has enabled these critics to focus on the complicity of cultural production with the imperialist project.

This shift of attention from the economic or economic/political to the cultural site in the discourse about imperialism was inaugurated by Said's appropriation of Foucault's poststructuralist genealogy of the disciplinary society for his critique of Western knowledge production about the Orient. And it has contributed significantly to the understanding of modern imperialism and thus to the development of a discourse of resistance that could be adequate to the conditions of international power relations in late capitalism, the conditions that, by way of the "end" of the Cold War, have culminated in what I will call in this book the *Pax Americana*.

Despite original and telling insights, however, contemporary discourses of resistance have confronted an impasse in the face of the sudden collapse of actually existing communism and the representation of this event as the global triumph of liberal capitalist democracy in the late 1980s and 1990s. The very titles of books written from a Left perspective in the aftermath of the Cold War bear witness to this: *After the Fall; Whither Marxism? What's Left?*[1] If one does not accede to such representative triumphalist interpretations of the events of 1989–91 as that proffered by the intellectual deputies of the dominant cultural order, then one is compelled to ask what it is about the contemporary post–Cold War occasion that accounts for the inability of existing oppositional discourses to mount a convincing and effective critique of a global imperialism that represents its multiply situated brutalizing rapacity in the seductive image of an essentially benign agency of amelioration. This chapter will take a preliminary cut at this difficult question by undertaking a genealogy of modern Occidental imperialism — the *Pax Americana*. It will retrieve the *ontological* origin of this imperialism from the oblivion to which much postcolonial criticism has relegated it. Ironically, this obliteration of the ontological provenance of imperialism takes place even as the spirit of the latter's binary ontological categories (Identity and difference, Disciplinarity and amorphousness, Subject and object, Truth and error) and, above all, of the binary tropes — the "white mythology" — that this ontology *enables* (the Center and periphery, Light and dark, the Eye and the other senses, Culture and anarchy, Maturation and underdevelopment, Male and female, etc.) everywhere haunts this postcolonial discourse.

Such an undertaking does not presume to provide a completely adequate answer to the vexing question of imperialism. Nor, despite my reservations about their focus, is it intended to proffer an alternative to existing poststructural or postcolonial or post-Marxist or postfeminist discourses of resistance. It is, rather, meant to be an *Auseinandersetzung* — an antagonistic dialogue with them,[2] one that would disclose crucial aspects of actually existing imperialism that these allegedly more historical and more practical critical discourses are blind to. By retrieving the question of being (*die Seinsfrage*), in other words, I am not implying the recuperation of the *Summum Ens* (Being) that is endemic to the ontotheological tradition, the disciplinary category that has contributed fundamentally to the colonizing operations of its discourses and practices. My intention is to bring into focus the *indissoluble* lateral continuum that includes being as such, the subject, the ecos, gender, culture, race, economy, and the national and international *socius*. I mean, more specifically, the relay of sites that is always uneven because it always undergoes asymmetrical transformation in history.³ This is what is crucial. A particular historical conjuncture will overdetermine one or more "domains" of this relay over the others. Given the depth to which the arbitrary compartmentalization of being is inscribed in the Occidental consciousness — of even those who would resist its disciplinary/classificatory imperatives — the historically produced imbalance in the relay evokes the disabling illusion that the overdetermined site (or sites) is separate from and constitutes a universal and determining base to the other (epiphenomenal) superstructural sites. This seductive characteristic of the historical "destiny" of being, for example, explains Marx and Engels's tendency to represent the means of production as a foundational category in the middle of the nineteenth century, which bore witness to the rise and overdetermination of capital. It also, in a far more vulgar and misleading way, explains Fukuyama's representation of the underlying ontological principle of liberal capitalist democracy as a determining base at the end of the twentieth century.

In the years following the advent of "theory," the prevailing, praxis-oriented oppositional discourses have become indifferent or even hostile to the question of being. And this indifference or hostility is, admittedly, understandable, given the political impotence of the discourses of such "early" theorists as Heidegger, Derrida, and Lyotard, which have privileged ontological questions. Nevertheless, the abandonment of the question of being by recent oppositional discourses, I submit, has been disabling for criticism. In thinking the question of the imperial, I will therefore overdetermine the site of ontology. But this is not to imply that I am attributing this site with privileged ontological status. Rather, I want to compensatorily put back into play a crucial category of the imperial project. But it should be remembered, in keeping with what I have called the indissoluble continuum of being, that the ontological representation of being is polyvalent in essence. When, that is, I am referring to ontological categories such as Identity and difference, I am implicitly, however asymmetrically, referring to all the other sites on this continuous lateral relay.

The Imperialist Provenance of the Onto-theo-logical Tradition

Spatially central, the *ego cogito* constituted the periphery and asked itself, along with Fernandez de Oviedo, "Are the Amerindians human beings?" that is, Are they Europeans, and therefore rational animals?...We are still suffering from the practical response. The Amerindians were suited for forced labor; if not irrational, then at least they were brutish, wild, underdeveloped, uncultured — because they did not have the culture of the center.

That ontology did not come from nowhere. It arose from a previous experience of domination over other persons, of cultural oppression over other worlds. Before the *ego cogito* there is an *ego conquiro;* "I conquer" is the practical foundation of "I think." The center has imposed itself on the periphery for more than five centuries.

> — ENRIQUE DUSSEL, *The Philosophy of Liberation*

Did not Hegel hail Descartes as the Christopher Columbus of philosophical modernity?   — JACQUES DERRIDA, *Of Spirit*

Following Heidegger's destruction of the ontotheological tradition, my inquiry will be guided by the "presupposition" that the Occident has been *essentially* imperial since its origins in late Greek and especially Roman antiquity. In the name of a delineated, administered, and predictable social order emanating out of the Metropolis, Rome reduced the originative peripatetic thinking of the pre-Socratics and even the classical Greek philosophers to a derivative, calculative, and institutionalized mode of thought. Despite the obvious historically specific variations, the Occident has been essentially imperial ever since the Romans *colonized* and *pacified* an errant, polyvalent, and differential thinking that, *as such,* was not amenable to their polyvalent imperial project.

In appealing to Heidegger's representation of the Western philosophical tradition at large as an "ontotheological tradition" informed by an imperial will to power that is polyvalent in its practical historical manifestations, my argument will be confronted with a certain poststructuralist objection that it effaces the differential history of the West. It will be said that my argument overlooks Michel Foucault's powerful thesis (allegedly) that the Age of the Enlightenment — the age that, besides producing the panoptic/disciplinary society, also, as Edward Said's *Orientalism* suggests, bore witness to the formation of the Western imperial consciousness — constituted a decisive epistemic break in European history, a break that rendered what preceded incommensurate to what followed. Such an objection implies a questionable reading of Foucault's complex representation of this historical nexus. But even if explicit evidence for an alternative reading of Foucault cannot be found in his texts, this evidence is nevertheless everywhere articulated in his rhetoric — specifically, in what Foucault epitomizes as "the Roman reference."[4] It is a rhetoric that reinscribes the "mutated" Enlightenment into a disciplinary tradition that, precisely like Heidegger's genealogy of humanist modernity, has its origins in metropolitan Rome. This hypothetical objection of a certain strain of Foucauldians, then, can be seen to repeat what I will show to be the essential blindness of most postcolonial criticism, which has as its model Foucault's "discontinuous" history. It fails to think the imperial project back far enough in the process of employing in its critique the very language, especially the metaphysically grounded metaphors of empire, that originates in that inaugural historical occasion.

As for the objection that the Heideggerian representation of the history of Western philosophy as the ontotheological tradition reduces the historically specific differences of this tradition to a continuous monolithic discourse, it should be remembered that such a representation is referring not to Occidental history as such, but to the specific enabling Occidental *representations* of being in that history, a distinction that allows for the perception of an asymmetrical relationship between these two histories. However problematic this asymmetry is in Heidegger's discourse, I am offering this Heideggerian representation not as the absolute truth, but as a forestructure — a guiding contestatory fiction — in my *Auseinandersetzung* with a quite different dominant discourse that not only is oblivious to the possibility of such a representation, but asserts its own representation not as a risked presupposition, but as the self-evident truth.

Further, it has not been adequately remarked by his commentators that Heidegger, in the process of disclosing the genealogy of humanist modernity (what he identified as the "age of the world picture"), called this tradition "onto-theo-logical" to differentiate between three epochal *historical* phases of the history of Western philosophy. These are the inaugural onto-logical era (Greco-Roman, in which the *logos* as e-mergent *physis* becomes *ratio,* simultaneously imminent in and external to nature); the theo-logical (the medieval/Protestant, in which the *logos* as *ratio* becomes the visible and transcendental *Logos* or *Word* of God); and the anthropo-logical (the Enlightenment, in which the visible Word of God becomes the invisible *Logos* of Man). These epochal revolutions in the history of philosophy were epistemic in scope and depth. But the revolutionary character of these transformations should not obscure the recuperative representational impulse informing each phase of representation — not least the anthropological, the phase that is alleged by Foucauldians, and all-too-casually assumed by many cultural and postcolonial critics, to have constituted an epistemic break in the thought of the Occident. I mean the mimetological impulse that kept the *idea* of Europe intact even as it underwent massively historically specific transformations. What all three epochs have fundamentally in common, what "Europe" did not allow to pass away into historical oblivion, what it, in a virtually unthought way, carried over from the disintegration of the *episteme* of each phase, was the *logos*. Let me retrieve an inaugural postmodern theoretical insight into this stable differential/identical — logocentric — history that has by now become ineffectually sedimented in the posttheory occasion:

> [O]n the basis of what we call the center (and which, because it can be either inside or outside, can also indifferently be called the origin or end, *arche* or *telos*), repetitions, substitutions, transformations, and permutations are always *taken* from a history of meaning [*sens*] — that is, in a word, a history — whose origin may always be reawakened or whose end may always be anticipated in the form of presence....
>
> If this is so, the entire history of the concept of structure, before the rupture of which we are speaking, must be thought of as a series of substitutions of center for center, as a linked chain of determinations of the center. Successively, and in a regulated fashion, the center receives different forms or names. The history of metaphysics, like the history of the West, is the history of these metaphors and metonymies. Its matrix... is the determination of Being as presence in all senses of this word.[5]

By *logos,* I do not mean a particular historical entity: the Greek or Roman *logos,* the Christian *logos,* the humanist *logos.* I mean, rather, a historically constructed inaugural *metaphor* of presence or, to emphasize its spatial character, a *figure* or *diagram* that is both immanent in and outside of this history, which is to say provisionally, is polyvalent in its practical application. To appropriate Foucault's (contradictory) analysis of a historically specific manifestation of this figure, by *logos* I mean a "*diagram* of a mechanism of power reduced to its ideal form,"[6] a diagram, that is, that is applicable to *any* historically specific time and any historically specific condition involving a differential and "errant" multiplicity. The difference between a theological and an anthropological (Enlightenment) metaphysics, to put it provisionally, has to do with each epoch's representation of the difference that the diagram would reduce. The theological era, which was antagonistic toward worldly time — historicity — focused simply on the *spatiality* of the difference it would structuralize within its Providential History, whereas the Enlightenment, which had to acknowledge the claims of time (the prolific and mutable *thisness* of the world) focused on the *temporality* of the difference it would structuralize within its Universal History. In the anthropological epoch, that is to say, temporality assumed, as, for example, in Hegel (and to many of his post-Enlightenment critics), the more complex character of the dialectic or, rather, of the dialectical narrative, to overcome precisely the failure of the theological moment to adequately accommodate the claims of temporality. But in both phases, whatever the degree of complexity, it is the *logos* as polyvalent diagram of power that presides.

Thinking the *Meta* of Metaphysics

The nothing — what else can it be for science but an outrage and a phantasm? If science is right, then only one thing is sure: science wishes to know nothing of the nothing. Ultimately this is the scientifically rigorous conception of the nothing. We know it, the nothing, in that we wish to know nothing about it. — MARTIN HEIDEGGER, "What Is Metaphysics?"

When, on the basis of his destructive reading of its enabling thinkers (Aristotle, Plato, Descartes, Leibniz, Kant, Hegel, Nietzsche) and of its founding discourses (Latin and the Romance languages), Heidegger refers to the history of Western philosophy as the "ontotheological tradition," his intention is to counter a seductive ruse of the last (and present) phase of this tradition. I mean the anthropological phase, which would convey the impression of a progressive dialectical continuity, in which the contradictory negativities of the previous phases were decisively, however reverently, left behind because they had been taken up and overcome. Heidegger's intention is to thematize the *Presence* and thus the *metaphysics* that, despite its different historical manifestations, informs the thought of all three phases: the metaphysics, in other words, that is *visibly* at work (and thus vulnerable to resistance) in the earlier phases, but whose reductive operations remain *invisible* in the "objective" or "disinterested" knowledge-producing problematic of the present phase of this tradition.

What, then, we are compelled to ask by its historically privileged status, is metaphysics?[7] In attempting an answer to this question, I will not invoke the naturalized definition that is all too often the point of departure of even those who would expose and criticize the will to power that inheres in it. An investigation into the relation between Western ontology and imperialism would be better served by following Heidegger's relentless de-naturalization of the sedimented metaphors that constitute the veridical discourse of (Western) philosophy, that is, by disclosing its etymological origins. In a neglected passage of "What Is Metaphysics?" he writes:

Our inquiry concerning the nothing [*das Nichts*] should bring us face to face with metaphysics itself. The name "metaphysics" derives from the Greek *meta-ta-physika*. This peculiar title [which, for the Greeks meant the ontic-ontological or in-sistent/ek-sistent disposition of *Dasein,* the inquiring being] was *later* interpreted as characterizing the inquiry, the *meta* or *trans* extending out "over" beings as such.

And in a separate paragraph that signals the enabling importance of this later revision, he states: "Metaphysics is inquiry beyond or over beings which aims to recover them as such as a whole *for our grasp.*"[8]

Metaphysics, therefore, in its post-Greek, that is, Roman, form, is a way of thinking that perceives "beings" or "things-as-they-are" from a privileged vantage point "beyond" or "above" them, that is, from a distance — an "Archimedian point," to appropriate Hannah Arendt's apt phrase[9] — that enables the finite perceiver to "overcome" the ontologically prescribed limits of immediate vision or, to put it positively, to comprehend them in their totality. But incorporated implicitly in Heidegger's translation of the Greek prefix *meta* as "from above" is the idea of "from the end." For another meaning of the word *meta* is "after." These two meanings, it should be underscored, activate our awareness that the naturalization of the word "metaphysics" has congealed two metaphorical systems that are, nevertheless, absolutely integral with and necessary to each other: that which emanates from sight and that which emanates from the object it sees. But to disclose the indissoluble relationship of these metaphorical systems will require separating them out.

Holding in temporary abeyance the resonant specificity of the visual metaphorics of the "first" meaning in favor of thinking the second, we can say that the metaphysical interpretation of being involves the perception of "beings" or "things-as-they-are" (*physis*) from the *end,* not only in the sense of termination but also in the sense of the purpose or goal of a directional and totalizing temporal process, a process in which this end is present from the beginning. If we attend to the word *meta* as a category of time, we can be more specific about what "beings" actually refer to: it compels us to understand "them" as the radical *temporality* of being or, more precisely, the differences that temporality always already disseminates. To think meta-physically is thus to think backward. This means *retro-spectively* or *circularly,* for the purpose of accommodating difference to a preconceived end or of reducing the differential force of time to a self-identical, objectified, timeless presence, while preserving the *appearance* of the temporality of time.

To put this reduction in the terms precipitated by the implicit distinction between two kinds of time (one that is derivative and one that is original), to think metaphysically is to transform the spectral nothingness of being (*das Nichts*) into a comforting and/or productive totalized

Something, a *Summum Ens*. Behind and enabling Heidegger's statement is his monumental de-struction of the "hardened" Being of modernity in the appropriately titled *Being and Time:* his pro-ject to enable the claims of temporal difference, which the metaphysical tradition has perennially repressed by reifying them, to be heard.[10] Putting the circular structure of metaphysical perception in terms of the *reification* of a temporal force that is identifiable with the Nothing thus suggests the raison d'être of this destructive hermeneutics. In so doing, it points acutely to the foundations and structure of the logic of imperialism. Let me recall a fundamental moment in Heidegger's destruction of the truth discourse of the ontotheological tradition: his retrieval of the Nothing from "negation," which is to say, from the oblivion to which the reifying logic of modern science would relegate it. In this project of retrieval, Heidegger distinguishes between fear (*Furcht*), which is the response of one inhabiting a derivative (technologized) world, and the "fundamental mood of anxiety" (*Angst*):

> Anxiety [unlike fear, which has an object], is indeed anxiety in the face of . . . , but not in the face of this or that thing. Anxiety in the face of . . . is always anxiety for . . . , but not for this or that. The indeterminateness of that in the face of which and for which we become anxious is no mere lack of determination but rather the essential impossibility of determining it. In a familiar phrase this indeterminateness comes to the fore.
>
> In anxiety, we say, "one feels ill at ease [*es ist einen unheimlich*]." What is "it" that makes "one" feel ill at ease? We cannot say what it is before which one feels ill at ease. As a whole it is so for him. All things and we ourselves sink into indifference. This, however, not in the sense of mere disappearance. Rather in the very receding things turn towards us. The receding of beings as a whole that close in on us in anxiety oppresses us. We can get no hold on things. In the slipping away of beings only this "no hold on things" comes over us and remains.
>
> Anxiety reveals the nothing.[11]

Metaphysics is thus a circular mode of inquiry that, in beginning from the *end,* has as its end the (finally futile) total reification and determination of the essential anxiety-activating indeterminacy of the nothing, of temporality, of the differences that temporality disseminates: of a phantasmic alterity, as it were. To use the rhetoric in Heidegger's discourse that points to the essential imperialism of metaphysical ontology, it is an end-oriented mode of inquiry intended to *level* or *at-home* or *domesticate* or *pacify* — that is, to "civilize" — the "threatening" not-at-home (*die Unheimliche*) that being as such "is" for *Dasein*. The function of metaphysical thinking is not simply to annul the anxiety — the dislocating uncanniness (*die Unheimlichkeit*) — precipitated by being-in-the-not-at-home. By an easy extension inhering in Heidegger's ironic invocation of the metaphor of "grasping" — one of the essential and determining white metaphors of the truth discourse of the Occident, to which I will return when I take up the spatial metaphorics informing the word "metaphysics" — it can be said that the function of this "after" in the logical economy of metaphysics is also to transform the indeterminate realm of the uncanny to a condition that enables its *management*. The function of metaphysical thinking, in short, is "ideological." It serves to reduce the ineffable be-*ing* of being to what Heidegger will later call exploitable "standing reserve" (*Bestand*) and Foucault, "docile and useful body."

It is not, however, simply the Other of metaphysics — the nothing, the temporal, the accidental, the contradictory, the differential, or, to evoke the connotation of the ontological Other I want to underscore, the spectral — that metaphysical objectification and naming would domesticate and pacify. As the metaphorics released by the solicitation of the sedimented and innocuous (indeed, benign) names referring to the domestication (at-homing) of being suggest, it is also — and in a determined way — the "unknown," the "primitive," the "wild" or "savage," the an-archic, the dis-orderly, in their ecological and human (subjective, sexual, racial, ethnic, and sociopolitical) manifestations. It is, in short, the entire relay of being that haunts or threatens the authority of the received (hegemonic) discourse of the dominant, that is, Western, order.

This systematic metaphorization of being constitutes the origin of (and is obscured by) the naturalized and enabling principle of the logic — the truth discourse — of Occidental metaphysics: that *Identity is the condition for the possibility of difference.* And it is to the specificity of this constructed polyvalent metaphorical ("white") system that we must, above all, turn if we are to plumb the historical past of modern Western imperialism and, more important, the depth of its inscription as ideology in the modern Western subject and its language. But before undertaking that task of denaturalization directly, we need to elaborate the economy of the logic enabled by this principle of metaphysical principles.

As its binarism suggests, the foundational privileging of Identity over difference in metaphysical thinking means operationally that it enables the inquirer to read the temporal process as a *system* of evanescent or always changing signatures, fragments, enigmas, shadows, phantasms, and so on. It enables him/her to address the differential dynamics of time as a spectral subaltern surface (an adulterated or "fallen," and thus worthless, but always threatening Other) that obscures — or, rather, reveals as in a glass darkly — a prior informing luminous presence (an abiding or universal or permanent meaning) that a willed penetration will reveal. Plato, for example, in the *Phaedrus,* called the partial temporal body into which the soul had fallen a "polluted...walking sepulchre" that only the recollection (*anamnesis*) of a prior "pure" and "whole" state vaguely shadowed in this corrupt and partial body could redeem.[12] However that "otherly" surface is represented, whether as shadow (as in Plato) or as signature (as in St. Augustine and the Church Fathers) or as negation (as in Hegel) or as fragment (as in modern empirical science), the metaphysical mode of inquiry *assumes* that the difference the inquirer encounters is not an irresolvable contradiction or contingency, but a problem that can and must be solved in the name of the truth. It assumes the Other to be a *mere appearance:* a recalcitrant agency of concealment and instability that must yield what it conceals to the stabilizing truth of Identity, of the One, of the End, of Presence. In short, metaphysical inquiry represents that which is Other than its truth not simply as a negative term (specter or spirit), but, as such, as that which corroborates its Identity (Spirit) and endows its Truth with power. Thus perceiving *meta-ta-physika* produces and validates the essential logic of the ontotheological tradition. This is, of course, the hierarchized binary logic that enables the first, "major" term — the term representing a self-present and plenary object — to demonize the second, "minor" or "subaltern," term: the term representing an entity that is not present to itself. This binary logic, in other words, empowers the privileged term to represent the Other as nonbeing (spectral), as some kind of arbitrary threat to Being — the benign total order to which the first term is committed — and thus to subdue and appropriate this Other to the latter's essential truth. It is in this sense that one can say that Western metaphysical thinking is *essentially* a colonialism. By this, I do not simply mean, as does much postcolonial discourse that acknowledges in some degree the polyvalency of the imperial project, a *metaphor* appropriated to the thought of being (or of any site on the continuum of being other than the economic or political) from another "more practical and fundamental" — "real" — domain of reference.[13] In identifying Western metaphysical thought with colonialism, I am positing a literal and precise definition of the process of metaphysical inquiry.

The binary logic endemic to the very idea of the West had its origins, according to Heidegger, in late antiquity with the Romans' colonization of Greek (the vestiges of pre-Socratic) thinking, with, that is, their reduction of the originative thinking of the latter to a derivative (constructed) understanding of truth. More specifically, the provenance of this logic lies in the imperial Romans' politically strategic translation of *a-letheia* to *veritas,* truth as always already un-concealment to truth as *adaequatio intellectus et rei,* the correspondence of mind and thing.[14] This epochal reduction of an originative to a re-presentational mode of thinking — a thinking that places the *force* of being before one as a *thing* to be looked at — was calculatively determined by a relatively conceptualized understanding of the operations of metaphysical perception. In decisively establishing the binary opposition between the true and the false as the ground of thinking, this reduction also decisively established the ground for the eventual assimilation of an infinite relay of different but analogous oppositions into the totalized epistemic binary logic of the Western tradition. Under the aegis of the doctrine of the *adaequatio,* it was not only the binary opposition between Truth and falsehood that empowered the *correction* or *appropriation* or *reformation* or *disciplining* or *accommodation* or *civilizing,* which is to say, the *colonization,* of the "errant" or "deformed" or "wasteful" or "excessive" or "immature" (uncultivated) or "barbarous" or "feminine" force named in the second, demonized term. As the very metaphors used to characterize the "false" suggest, that opposition was simply one — no doubt the most fundamental — of a whole series of binary oppositions inhering, however asymmetrically developed, in History, in, that is, the founding Occidental representation of temporal being-as-a-whole by way of perceiving "it" *meta-ta-physika:* Being and time, Identity and difference, the Word and words, Being and nonbeing, Subject and object, Sanity and madness, Culture and anarchy, Civilization and barbarism, Man and woman, the White race and the colored races, the West and the east, the North and the south, and so on. What this emphatically suggests is that an oppositional criticism that would be adequate to the task of resisting imperialism must cease to think the imperial project in the disciplinary terms endemic to and mandated by the Occident's compartmentalization of being and knowledge.

The "White" Metaphorics of Metaphysics: Vision and Reification

> In the altogether unsettling experience of this hovering [in anxiety] where there is nothing to hold onto, pure Da-sein is all that is still there.
> — MARTIN HEIDEGGER, "What Is Metaphysics?"

Having shown how "thinking after" the-things-themselves enables a hierarchized binary logic that renders metaphysics complicitous with the repression of alterity in general, I want to return to the systemic metaphorics inscribed in the word "metaphysics" in order to think the complicity of the truth of metaphysics with this generalized repression more concretely. I want, that is, to retrieve Heidegger's translation of *meta* that I bracketed earlier in favor of the translation "after" or "from the end": "extending out 'over.' " "Metaphysics," we will recall, "is inquiry *beyond* or *over* beings which aims to recover them as such and as a whole for our grasp [*für das Begreifen*]." Though these meanings of *meta* are integrally related, it is this latter trope that most clearly figures — makes visible — the reductive operation vis-à-vis the Other that renders metaphysical inquiry an essentially imperial practice. I am referring to the (implicit) representation of the mind in the image of the transcendental divine/solar eye (and its light). This is the mediating sense that the late Greeks privileged over all the other more immediate senses in the pursuit of knowledge. It is also the sense that, by way of increasingly saturating the language of the philosophy of the ontotheological tradition with its tributary metaphorical systems, has, despite disruptions, invisibly determined the West's representation of being (the Other of the same) and its imperial sociopolitical practices throughout its various history.[15] By "tributary metaphorical systems" of the solar eye I mean, above all, *the centered circle* and *the seed* (planting/cultivating, which includes phallic insemination).

The implicit eye in the passage from Heidegger's "What Is Metaphysics?" quoted above articulates three, still general, affiliated metaphorical systems that both define and enact the power relations between metaphysical thinking and being, the "object" of its inquiry. These are what I have been referring to as *reification* or *objectification* (as in the objectification of [the] nothing); *spatialization* (as in the spatialization of time, the transformation of temporality into a totalized and enclosed visual figure); and, more indirectly, *cultivation* (as in the cultivation of the fruitful potential of a natural wilderness or the phallic domestication of the errant female). In what follows I will focus primarily on the first two systems, because they inhere immediately in the etymology and practice of metaphysics. I will elaborate the third system in the next chapter, which is entirely devoted to the genealogical origins and practical operations of the indissoluble relationship between culture and colonization: planting and cultivating seeds and planting settlements beyond the periphery. Since these apparently different metaphorical systems radiate out of the foundational trope of the commanding solar/patriarchal eye, they are indissolubly related. Indeed they are different aspects of each other and thus should not be understood as distinct categories. But in order to locate their origin in the metaphorics of the transcendental eye, to demonstrate the integral relationship of their differences, and to articulate their coercive function in the imperial economy of metaphysics, it will be necessary to treat them separately.

In comparison with the explanatory potential of the metaphorics of space vis-à-vis the imperial project, the metaphorics of reification is more generalized, but, as such, it is more foundational. It is this latter metaphorics that Heidegger (like Marxists such as Lukács and Jameson, not incidentally) insistently emphasizes over its other (spatial) allotrope, both in the above definition of metaphysics from "What Is Metaphysics?" and in his monumental attempt in *Being and Time* to retrieve the temporality of time from the oblivion to which Western philosophy has relegated it by representing being metaphysically. I will, therefore, begin by thinking the implications of this metaphorics of reification for the imperial disposition of the Other.

In addressing inquiry into being from after or above or beyond *physis* (against the received and reductive Roman translation, *natura,* I will define this Greek word "differential temporality"), metaphysical perception at large, from late Greek through Enlightenment modernity, has had as its essential end the annulment of the anxiety that has no *thing* as it object. Faced *in immediacy* with the phantasmic appearance of a temporal/spatial multiplicity that resists the taxonomic categories of the available language of reason, this metaphysical perception assumes that the anxiety-provoking indeterminacy is the consequence of *partial* perception (in all senses of the word). Thus it also assumes that a *mediated* perspective — the taking of a certain distance from this dislocating "chaos" — enables a fuller (literally "im-partial") view that will reveal the informing Presence and thus the meaning to which the immediate perspective is blinded by its partial vision. In the sedimented everyday language of Occidental knowledge production this distanced or mediated or impartial perspective enables *comprehension* of the unknown.

This interrogation of the essential movement of Occidental thought thus discloses not simply the metaphoricity of the Occidental tradition's idea of truth, but also the integral relationship between the metaphorics of vision and reification in its production. For the movement of distancing and mediation in the process of inquiry eventuates in the sundering of *Dasein* from being and the reduction of each to a singular, clear, and self-present status. This operation is usually referred to as the transformation of being-in-the-world into a subject-object binary. But to estrange the sedimented meaning of this verbal counter — and to draw attention to its relevance to the imperial project proper — I think it preferable as well as more accurate to refer to this splitting of *Dasein* from being as one in which the encompassing (Apollonian) eye and its seminal light are separated from and privileged over the other more immediate and truant senses in the pursuit of knowledge about being. This privileging of vision entails the representation of being metaphorically as a tenebrous *Unheimliche Welt* — a domain of disorienting and dislocating confusion, of obscurity and darkness. As such, it also brings to focus the indissolubility of the metaphorics of reification and that of the phallic seed, of amorphous and fallow femininity, and the inquiring mind/eye as a (masculine) agency of lighting up its dark heart: of *enlightenment*. Education, as far back as the Roman interpretation of Plato's allegory of the cave,[16] involves *ex ducere,* to lead [some *thing*] out of [the darkness] into the light of day (to be seized). But this apotheosis of vision, as the bracketed terms suggest, also entails the re-*presentation* of the recalcitrant spectral obscurity and indeterminateness of being into which the perceiver (as *subject*) is inquiring: the transformation of be-ing into an *object* of mastery by the hand. To *comprehend* (French, *comprendre;* Italian, *capistare*), in the discourse of the Western philosophical tradition, is not simply, as its sedimented meaning would have it, "to understand." It is an understanding that is also, as the Latin etymology suggests (*com+prehendere*), a total taking hold of, grasping, seizing. (The German equivalent of the English "comprehend" is *begreifen* [noun, *Begriff:* "understand," "comprehend," "conceive," "grasp," "touch," "feel," "handle"].) The separation and distancing, in short, that renders the knowledge of an intrinsically unnameable and unsayable force a matter of *looking at* (it) justifies and enables the reduction of the differential being of being to the calculable, measurable object. To highlight the complicity of the Western mind's hand with the literal hand (or its prosthetic extensions), this separation enables the *management* (from the Latin *manus:* "hand") and exploitation of the differential being it encounters.

It is this imperial violence enabled by privileging vision in thinking to which Heidegger is referring, no doubt with the inordinate, indeed, foundational, importance of the word "comprehension" (*Begreifen*) in the philosophical vocabulary of Hegel's dialectic of the Absolute Spirit in mind, when, in his evocation of its etymology, he says that "Metaphysics is inquiry beyond beings which aims to recover them as such and as a whole *for our grasp.*" It is also Heidegger's enabling thematization of this imperial Eurocentric violence against the alterity of being that explains his retrieval *for thought* of the *nothing* (the radically Other *of* Being) and of the dislocating or decentering anxiety of being-in-the-world. This is the anxiety, we recall, in which the "receding of beings as a whole" is accompanied by their paradoxical — and resonantly productive — return in the spectral form of a "world" in which "we can get no hold on things" (*Es bleibt kein Halt*), of a world where "there is nothing to hold on to" (*darin es sich an nichts halten kann*). Where, we might say provisionally, the see-er becomes the seen and the seen the see-er; where the sayer becomes the said, and the said, the sayer.

In thus invoking a technical term that pervades the language of Western philosophy increasingly from beginning to "end," I do not want to restrict the scope of this disclosure to the discourse of philosophy as such.[17] For the violence implicit in "comprehension," precisely because it is ontological, manifests itself as well in the obligatory narrative — the comprehensive end-oriented (or promise/fulfillment) structure — of canonical literary and literary critical production. Insofar as these latter reflect the "structures of feeling" of a people,[18] they suggest even more clearly than philosophy the degree to which the visually enabled will to power informing metaphysical thinking informs Western culture in general, though especially its latest, post-Enlightenment allotrope. I will amplify on this indissoluble relationship between Western philosophy and literature in the next chapter by way of interrogating certain representative passages from two canonical Western literary figures of the modern period whose poetry and criticism have had an enormous cultural influence, especially in England and North America, namely, Matthew Arnold and T. S. Eliot. Here it will suffice to say that both, like Hegel, invoke the idea of "comprehensive vision" in knowledge production in the name of "intellectual deliverance" (Arnold), but their articulation of its meaning clearly suggests that its real end is the willful spatialization and pacification of time and the difference it disseminates under the aegis of the imperial eye.

But even the extension of this disclosure of the epistemological violence inhering in the reifying visualism of the philosophical discourse of the West to include literary production, indeed, language itself, is not adequate as a measure of the depth and scope of its imperial sway. What needs to be made explicit is, if I may appropriate the term that Hannah Arendt invoked to articulate the essence of a limit case of this Occidental comportment toward being, its utter banality.[19] The metaphorical elements that manifest themselves in violence, that is, saturate the vocabularies and structures of the different languages of the Occident (especially, not incidentally, the Romance languages and those, like English, that have been profoundly influenced by Latin). Like the affiliated binary "white metaphorics" of White/black and Male/female, they constitute the very lifeblood, right down to its capillary circuits, of the cultural identity of the Occident.

I am not qualified to offer a justification of this assertion about the mimetological essence of Occidental languages by way of a technical analysis of their vocabularies and syntaxes. But even a layman's attentiveness to the sublimated and interiorized metaphorics that circulate within and reflect, indeed, determine, the periodic *shape of* the expressive structures of the everyday discourse of knowledge/culture production will amply testify to the pervasiveness of the bond that exists between visualization and reification and between enlightenment and colonization in the act of knowledge production. Let me thus retrieve a few representative instances of everyday locutions pertaining to learning *as re-presentation and/or mirroring or ideation* (the reduction of a temporal process to reified image [*eidos*]).[20] In the context I have established, they will bear witness to the binary metaphorics of the imperial Apollonian/manly eye and its light (but only to obscure its reifying function vis-à-vis the Other) and its correlatives, the hand and its prosthetic technological extensions. One speaks, for example, of "*seeing* what another means"; of "a *perspective* on a problem"; of "a *retrospective* understanding"; of "*inspecting* a body of knowledge"; of "a future *prospect*"; of "the *scope* of a study"; of "*speculative* inquiry"; of "*reflecting* on a difficulty"; of "making an *observation* about a question"; of "*envisioning* a solution"; of "*depicting* [or *portraying*] a person's life"; of "*foreseeing* the result of a process"; of "*evidence* in favor of an argument"; of "the truth *dawning* on one"; of "the *clarification* of a problem"; of "*revealing* a *feature* [or *trait* or *lineament*] of the truth"; of "an argument that *gives shape to* a mystery"; of a "meaning that is *transparent*"; of "*observations* about a question that are *revealing* [or *illuminating*]"; of "*exposing* the essence of a difficulty *to view*"; of a "*demonstration* that confirms the validity of an argument"; of an "*insight* that *sheds light* on what was hitherto *obscure*." Or, conversely, one speaks of "*being in the dark* about a certain matter"; of "*being blind* to the essence of events"; of "a *benighted* [or *myopic*] opinion"; of "an interpretation of events that is *shortsighted*"; of "a reading that does not *clarify* [or *make plain* or *clear-cut*] the *obscurity* [or *opacity*] of a text"; of "an *explanation* that remains *vague* [or *indistinct* or *indefinite* or *without focus* or *lacking in outline or form*]."[21] In all these typical locutions of the English language referring to the quest for truth, the temporal/differential "what" that provokes the assertion has undergone a silently violent reduction to a visible, self-present, and docile object in space set before the eye of the subject to be mastered and managed.[22]

The same ideological agenda becomes manifest by placing in this thematic context some representative everyday locutions pertaining to knowledge production that emphasize the other, more obviously harsh face of the symbiotic affiliation between the metaphorics of vision and reification: that which circulates around the philosophical abstractions referring to *objectivity, comprehension,* and *conception* (which derives from the Latin *capere,* "to take"). One speaks, for example, of *"taking, grasping, comprehending, mastering, capturing* [also, like 'concept,' deriving from the Latin *capere*], or *getting a grip on* the elusive truth"; of "pursuing truth with *tenacity*"; of *"maintaining* a thesis" (Latin: *tenere,* "to hold"); of *"getting to the bottom* of a mystery"; of "forcing an evanescent truth to *stand still*"; of *"hitting the mark."* All these locutions of everyday life involve the objectification — the bringing to presence, to light (before one's eyes) — of the undecidable nothing (the Other) and the foundational and enabling achievement thereby of *certainty* in the face of anxiety or, we might say, of crisis. (The word "certainty" derives ultimately from the Latin *certus,* "settled," which in turn tellingly "derives" from the Greek *krinein,* "crisis"!) Nor should it be overlooked that in almost every instance of both verbal categories, the temporal/differential "what" that is subjected to the objectifying violence of the eye is figured as the feminine.

This grave will to certainty in the face of alterity that informs the language of conceptualization explains the inordinate degree to which the discourse of simplification — of clarity, of cogency, of economy (and manliness) — is privileged in the discourses, the institutions of learning, and the information media of the Occident. Conversely, it also explains the utter contempt for the complex, nuanced, and generative ambiguities of the originative thinking of a Heidegger or a Derrida[23] or an Adorno, for example, the thinking — represented by the dominant "realistic" culture as obscurity, errancy, exorbitance, obesity, and, not least, waste[24] — that would respect the differential dynamics of being.

The reductive ontological drive to settle or fix by simplifying what in essence is unsettlable, unfixable, and irreducible is, of course, the metaphysical prerequisite to transform that which defies naming into *manageable* and exploitable objects. It is, as Heidegger puts the end of modern technological thinking, to reduce the recalcitrant and threatening Other to "standing [disposable] reserve" (*Bestand*), or, as Foucault represents the effects of the great disciplinary technology of the Enlightenment, to transform the force of alterity to "useful and docile body."[25] This reduction and assignment of the Other to its "proper place" — within the identical whole — this colonization of *physis,* in other words, could be said to be "its" "destiny" under the regime of metaphysical truth. This complicity between knowledge and power has its provenance far earlier than the period of the Enlightenment, where Foucault's or, rather, his followers' genealogy locates it: namely, in late Greek (Hellenistic) and, above all, imperial Roman antiquity.

White Metaphorics: Vision and Spatialization

> Knowing, as research, calls whatever is to account with regard to the way in which and the extent to which it lets itself be put at the disposal of representation. Research has disposal over anything that is when it can either calculate it in its future course in advance or verify a calculation about it as past. Nature, in being calculated in advance, and history, in being historiographically verified as past, become, as it were, "set in place" [*gestellt*]. Nature and history become the objects of a representing that explains.... Only that which becomes object in this way *is* — is considered in being. We first arrive at science as research when the Being of whatever is, is sought in such objectiveness.
> — MARTIN HEIDEGGER, "The Age of the World Picture"

The thematization of the sublimated and naturalized metaphorics of reification informing the truth discourse of the Occident points to the complicity of knowledge production (truth) and power over the Other. But its generality admittedly is not easily conducive to the articulation of the developed historically specific structures and operations of Occidental imperialism and to their paradigmatic status. It has been, perhaps, their tendency to delimit analysis of Occidental logocentrism to this generalistic metaphorical nexus that has rendered Heidegger's, Derrida's, and Levinas's powerful and resonant disclosure of the identity of ontology and imperialism[26] more or less invisible in the context of the "postcolonial" occasion. Which is to say, more or less irrelevant to the self-styled "praxis-oriented" discourses — especially the New Historicism, the various neo-Marxisms, and the neonationalisms — that the postcolonial occasion has privileged. It is necessary, therefore, to repeat the de-struction or, to anticipate, the de-colonization of metaphysics, this time focusing on and thinking the imperial implications of what I have called the spatialization of time, the allotrope of the metaphorics of reification that the etymology discloses.[27]

To perceive *physis* from *meta,* understood as "above," is not simply to privilege a transcendent eye that, therefore, must *represent* what it encounters in experience as an object. It is not, to invoke Jean-Paul Sartre (who, we should recall in a context that has forgotten it, was, with Bergson, one of the first "postmodern" thinkers to give prominence to the reifying effect of *le regard*), a Medusan gaze that turns the existent it looks at into stone.[28] From this "above" (*meta*) enabled by separating itself from the other "lowly" or "base" bodily senses, the privileged Apollonian or solar or patriarchal eye achieves a *retro-spective* or *re-presentational* standpoint positively capable of overcoming the dis-*abling* visual limits of its prior immediacy.[29] What, from the condition of being-in-the-world, the *inter esse,*[30] appeared hauntingly partial — darkly illegible, hopelessly indeterminate, uncanny, spectral, and thus anxiety-provoking, that is, paralyzing — now, from this disengaged vertical distance, takes on substantial and intelligible *shape*. The (mind's) eye is en-*abled,* in other words, to transitively *survey* (comprehend) time in its totality and thus to *see* — indeed, *foresee* — the lineaments of the pattern, the figure, the *structure* that is obscured by proximity, that hides behind the appearance of radically temporal difference. To introduce provisionally the third, related, metaphorical system circulating capillarily within the discourse and practice of imperialism, the distanced perspective enables the solar eye to see historicity as an *organic* (meta)narrative and thus to reduce and accommodate their differential force to a beginning-middle-end structure in which the plenary *telos* is *seminally* present and determinative, however, wastefully, from the inaugural moment.[31]

To put this empowerment in terms of a metaphorics that has been — and, in a naturalized form, continues to be — fundamental and indispensable to the Occidental imperial project since Roman antiquity, the perception of being *meta-ta-physica* authorizes the poet/thinker as *Vates* or *see(e)r* and the *prophecy/fulfillment* structure as its official narrative model. It is no accident, as I will show more fully in chapter 3, that the Occidental epic (the genre par excellence of nation and empire building — indeed, of the canonical narrative structure of Western literature at large) had its origins in what T. S. Eliot, by way of contrasting it with blind Homer's errant art, calls Virgil's "comprehensive" and "mature" "vision." It is no accident, to be more specific, that Virgil's "correction" of the "immature" deviations of the *Odyssey* took the form of the prophecy/fulfillment structure of the *Aeneid,* which, we should recall, was intended to justify the *imperium sine fine* of Augustus,[32] and that, as Richard Waswo has shown, became "the founding legend of Western civilization."[33] In its disposition of language in the future/anterior mode, a mode oriented toward a totalized and final (aesthetic) peace, Virgil's founding end-oriented narrative structure ruthlessly obliterates or accommodates every thing but the "peak points" of "history" — not least the differential Asian "seductress," Dido,[34] and the Greek Turnus. And in so doing, it precisely enacts the narrative structure of the racial destiny of the Roman people — the "seed" of Aeneas — and of their imperial disposition of the peripheral peoples of the world: the colonization of the extraterritorial Others in the benign name of the "at-homing" peace of the *Pax Romana.*

Nor is it an accident that the European narrative of the "New World" has its origin, as Tzvetan Todorov has shown, in Christopher Columbus's insistent "finalist" representation of his immediate experience in the New World in terms of the promissory structure of Christian providential history. Despite the resistances of actuality,

> the interpretation of nature's signs as practiced by Columbus is determined by the result that must be arrived at. His very exploit, the discovery of America, proceeds from the same behavior: he does not discover it, he finds it where he "knew" it would be (where he thought the eastern coast of Asia was to be found).... Columbus himself, after the fact, attributes his discovery of this a priori knowledge, which he identifies with the divine will and prophecies (actually quite slanted by him in this direction): "I have already said that for the execution of the enterprise of the Indies, reason, mathematics, and the map of the world were of no utility to me. It was a matter rather of the fulfillment of what Isaiah had predicted" (preface to the *Book of Prophecies*, 1500).[35]

This story of Europe's destined conquest of America, it should be remarked, achieves its fullest and perhaps most influential ideological affirmation in the American Puritans' divinely ordained epic "errand in the wilderness," the formal articulation of which is epitomized by Cotton Mather's *Magnalia Christi Americana* (1702).[36] I am referring to that deep "exceptionalist" structure of the American national identity, the theological ground of which metamorphoses into the secular ideology of Manifest Destiny in the westward expansionist nineteenth century[37] and into the global truth discourse of America in the aftermath of World War II.

Nor, finally, is it an accident that this imperial prophecy/fulfillment epic structure, in which, we may say with Jean-Paul Sartre, the imperial policing eye will allow no thing or no event to remain superfluous (*de trop*), continues, despite its naturalization, to inform the official literary forms of the modern bourgeois capitalist disciplinary society/empire. I am referring to the modern realist novel, whose inexorable linear/circular structural economy finds its banal fulfillment (and end) in the "retrospective" of the classic detective story:

> Things happen one way and we tell about them in the opposite sense. You *seem* to start at the beginning: "It was a fine autumn evening in 1922. I was a notary's clerk in Marommes." And in reality you have started at the end. It was there, invisible and present, it is the one which gives to words the pomp and value of a beginning.... The sentence, taken simply for what it is, means that the man was absorbed, morose, a hundred leagues from an adventure, exactly in the mood to let things happen without notic-

ing them. But the end is there, transforming everything. For us, the man is already the hero of the story. His moroseness, his money troubles are much more precious than ours, they are all gilded by the light of future passions. And the story goes on in the reverse: instants...are snapped up by the end of the story which draws them and each one of them in turn, draws out the preceding instant: "It was night, the street was deserted." The phrase is cast out negligently, *it seems superfluous;* but we do not let ourselves be caught *and we put it aside:* this is a piece of information whose value we shall subsequently appreciate. And we feel that the hero has *lived all the details of the night like annunciations, promises, or even that he lived only those that were promises,* blind and deaf to all that did not herald adventure.[38]

What, therefore, needs to be emphasized, in a postcolonial theoretical and critical context in which reference to the question of imperialism overlooks the Heideggerian de-struction and the Derridean deconstruction, or, more precisely, that has forgotten their essential provenance, is that this later and "advanced" perception and reading of being *meta-ta-physika* spatializes time in the sense of willfully reducing its differential temporal dynamics to an *objectified structure.* It reduces its disseminations to a miniaturized totality or microcosmic space that, unlike the object in the metaphorics of reification, *seems,* in its seductive emphasis on their unique play, to give temporality and the differences it disseminates their due. In fact, however, the spatializing perspective, like Hegel's philosophy of history, surreptitiously *accommodates* them, by way of the dialectic, to its identical self. As Derrida puts this ruse of a developed logocentrism, "The concept of centered structure is in fact the concept of a play based on a fundamental ground, a play constituted on the basis of a fundamental immobility and a reassuring certitude, which itself is beyond the reach of play. And on the basis of this certitude anxiety can be mastered."[39]

To recall the tradition extending from the late Greeks and Romans, through Descartes and Hegel (and the Marx*ists,* for that matter), to the post–Cold War purveyors of the end-of-history thesis, the structure precipitated by metaphysical perception constitutes an image of the arrival of time to its destined "end," which is to say, to its inclusive *closure.* Understood as such a desired and forced totalized closure of time on itself, beginning with end, this structure does not overtly annihilate temporal and spatial differences. Rather, it assigns every thing and every time to its *proper place* in the always unrealized but nevertheless real, total, self-identical, or self-present space of the whole under the aegis of the all-encompassing (policing/imperial) metaphysical eye, which is "elsewhere."

Let us think the *structure* of this prophecy/fulfillment structure produced by the invisible metaphysical eye more carefully, bringing back into play in the process the affiliated metaphorics of the center Derrida foregrounds in his brief history of logocentrism in "Structure, Sign, and Play," which I earlier bracketed. As the figure of the principle of Presence or Identity or Wholeness or the All or the Totality or Permanence, this metaphysical eye is represented not simply in terms of its vertical distance from the "field" or "domain" of its gaze. It is also figured as fixed: a *central* eye that sur-veys time past and time future — in all its minute particularity — pyramidally or more precisely conically.[40] The depth of the inscription of this image in the collective Western psyche will be suggested by recalling, while postponing discussion of its different historical modalities, its pervasive figural reiteration in the history of Western cultural production, especially in art and literature. One finds this figure in its most elemental (i.e., theo-logical) and visible form, for example, in the popular Renaissance emblem of God's relation to the fallen Adam, in which an eye, inscribed by the Latin legend *UBI ES,* looks down on and, with visible rays emanating conically from it, encompasses a naked fallen Adam cowering behind a sheltering tree. Appended to this emblem is the sententious rhyme:

> Behinde a figtree, him selfe did ADAM hide:
> And thought from God hee there might lurke, & should not bee
>   espide.
> Oh foole, no corners seeke, thoughe thou a sinner bee;
> For none but God can thee forgive, who all they waies doth see.[41]

This ubiquitous figure also informs the margins of the famous lines from Shakespeare's *Hamlet,* where Hamlet expresses his stoic indifference to the future duel with Laertes by saying that "there's a special providence in the fall of a sparrow."

However remote it may seem, this ancient cultural archetype — this "theoptics," as it were, of the smallest detail in being — is continuous with the modern imperial project. It informs and presides over those celebrated textual tableaux "depict[ing] [the author's] deepest moment of crisis" that Mary Louise Pratt invokes to distinguish the affiliated "anti-conquest" (private/sentimental) travel literature of the European Enlightenment such as that of Mungo Park from the scientific narratives of state- or public-sponsored European travelers like Anders Sparrman and John Barrow. Thus, for example, in narrating his experience in his search for the source of the Niger River, specifically, the climactic moment when, having been pillaged by bandits, he is left "naked and alone, surrounded by savage animals, and men still more savage," Parks writes:

> At this moment, painful as my reflections were, the extraordinary beauty of a small moss, in fructification, irresistibly caught my eye. I mention this to show from what trifling circumstances the mind will sometimes derive consolation; for though the whole plant was not larger than the top of one of my fingers, I could not contemplate the delicate conformation of its roots, leaves, and capsula, without admiration. *Can that Being (thought I) who planted, watered, and brought to perfection, in this obscure part of the world, a thing which appears of so small importance, look with unconcern upon the situation and sufferings of creatures formed after his own image? — surely not!*[42]

On a more resonantly political register, one also finds this central and concentering panoptic eye figured in the Great Seal of the United States, which also appears on the American one-dollar bill: a pyramid enclosed by a circle, at the apex of which is an all-seeing and all-encompassing eye (and its bright rays) and at the base of which, the Roman numerals MDCCLXXVI (the entire temporal history of the Christian world over which its providentially ordained commanding gaze presides). This resonant image bears the Virgilian mottoes *ANNUIT COEPTIS* (God has favored our beginnings) at the top and, especially pertinent for the purposes of this study, *NOVUS ORDO SECLORUM* (New World Order) at the bottom.[43] Most tellingly, as I will suggest more fully, it also informs Jeremy Bentham's Panopticon, the circular "inspection house" that enabled the super-vision and re-formation of the amorphous multiplicity of "deviants" — beggars, idlers, criminals, madmen, school children, and so on — that haunted the bourgeois Norm. This was, of course, the "diagram of power," according to Foucault, that became the structural model of the modern disciplinary society.

But the historical evidence of the ubiquity of this figure of the supervisory gaze is not restricted to the literature of the post-Renaissance occasion. The reiteration of this pervasive ocularcentric image reflects precisely the perennial European *figure* that presides not simply in metaphysical thinking, but also in metaphysical imagining from the beginning of European history, especially as that origin is focalized in and by imperial Rome. One finds it, for example, in the Roman architect Vitruvius's projections of the circular city in *Ten Books of Architecture* (first century B.C.); in the architecture and decorative art of the Byzantine and Romanesque basilica, in which the mosaic or painting in the central cupola represents the *visible* and sternly ubiquitous eye of the

"Pantocrator," scripture (of time) in hand, overlooking the hierarchical microcosm that is the basilica; and in the prefigurative paintings of El Greco, in which, as in *Christ on the Mount of Olives,* past and future history in the form of present emblematic figures is circumscribed by the Christic gaze.

Nor is this essential Occidental cultural image limited to the ontological or the theological occasions of European history. Though it descends from the heavens, it also presides, indeed, in a far more internal and efficient way, as the *invisible* eye of the "earth bound" artist in Renaissance architecture and painting, the securalized panoptic eye that had "newly discovered" the principle of per*spective:*

> The convention of perspective, which is unique to European art and which was first established in the early Renaissance, centres everything on the eye of the beholder. It is like a beam from a lighthouse — only instead of light travelling outwards, appearances travel in. The conventions call those appearances *reality.* Perspective makes the single eye the centre of the visible world. Everything converges on to the eye as to the vanishing point of infinity. The visible world is arranged for the spectator as the universe was once thought to be arranged for God.[44]

Thus, for example, the pervasive obsession, both in theory and practice, in eighteenth-century England (in Sir Joshua Reynolds, Henry Fuseli, James Harris, Alexander Pope, and many others) for the panoramic view of a landscape painting that privileged the distanced — ideal and "public" — eye. As Reynolds puts it against the depiction of nature by the sensual — "private" (ignorant, vulgar, and servile) — eye that, in the midst, saw partially and thus randomly: this was the eye that could "get above all singular forms, local customs, particularities, and detail of every kind." The polyvalent theory informing this politically productive panoramic landscape painting is resonantly epitomized by the British rhetorician George Campbell. In identifying the emergent Linnaean natural science with the surmounted landscape, he points proleptically to this eye's affiliation, not simply with the panoptics that Jeremy Bentham was about to apply to penology, but, as I will suggest later, with the systematic classification of the flora and fauna of the "new worlds" that inaugurated the imperial project proper:

> In all sciences, we rise from the individual to the species, from the species to the genus, and thence to the most extensive orders and classes [and] arrive ... at the knowledge of general truths. ... In this progress we are like people, who, from a low and confined bottom,

where the view is confined to a few acres, gradually ascend to a lofty peak or promontory. The prospect is perpetually enlarging at every moment, and when we reach the summit, the boundless horizon, comprehending all their variety of sea and land, hill and valley, town and country, arable and desert, lies under the eye at once.[45]

Far more immediately related to the imperial project, this same ideological impulse also lies behind the invisible, all-encompassing, all-arranging, mathematical eye of the maps projected by post-Renaissance cartographers on the basis of the miniaturizing perspectival grid imposed on the world by Mercator and in behalf of "exploring," which is to say, "inventing" and colonizing other worlds.[46]

The manifestations of this imaginative projection of the metaphysically enabled image of the gaze extend beyond the visual and plastic arts to which Martin Jay appears to have restricted them in his encyclopedic account of its prevalence in European culture. It is equally pervasive, though far more indirectly — and thus effectively — articulated, in the history of Occidental literature since the Romans' "correction" of the errancy of classical Greek narrative. One finds the gaze, for example, imbedded in Horace's *Ars Poetica,* specifically in his perennially imitated formulation of the relationship between poetry and painting (which itself derives from his reduction of Aristotle's meditation on dramatic time in *The Poetics* to the visualizable unity of time, place, and action) as *Ut pictura poesis* (The poem is a speaking picture).[47] In a more ideologically manifest way, it presides in the inaugural structure of Virgil's *Aeneid,* which enacts the vision of Jupiter's immutable eye (in book 1) concerning the destined history of Aeneas and his people. It informs Dante's *Divine Comedy,* in which Dante's Virgil-inspired terminal "view from God's eye" puts the errant Dante of the beginning, who finds himself lost in a dark wood, into a totalized perspective, that is, accommodates the latter's partial vision *in mezzo carmin* to the former's accomplished whole vision. It hovers over Shakespeare's *Troilus and Cressida* in the form of Ulysses' famous speech, which reflects what E. M. W. Tillyard has called the "Elizabethan world picture":

> The heavens themselves, the planets, and this centre
> Observe degree priority and place
> Insisture course proportion season form
> Office and custom, in all line of order;
> And therefore is the glorious planet Sol
> In noble eminence enthron'd and spher'd
> Amidst the other, whose med'cinable eye

Corrects the ill aspects of planets evil
And posts like the commandment of a king,
Sans check, to good and bad.[48]

Not least, this image of the gaze also determines the "prospect poem," the literary allotrope of the prospective landscape painting so prominent in the period of the Enlightenment. I am referring to the poetic genre that extends from Milton's *Paradise Lost* —

It was a Hill
Of Paradise the highest, from whose top
The Hemisphere of Earth in clearest Ken
Stretcht out to amplest reach of prospect lay.
Not higher that Hill nor wider looking round,
Whereon for different cause the Tempter set
Our second *Adam* in the Wilderness,
To shew him all Earths Kingdomes and their Glory.
His Eye might there command wherever stood
City of old or modern Frame, the Seat
Of mightiest Empires, from the destined Walls
Of *Cambalu,* seat of *Cathaian Can....*[49]

— through Thomas Gray's "Ode on a Distant Prospect of Eton College," to W. H. Auden's "Paysage Moralisé" and Yeats's "Sailing to Byzantium." In a related way, but one that brings into sharper focus the complicity of this hegemonized Occidental cultural archetype with the imperial project proper, the prospectival gaze also informs and presides over the promise/fulfillment structure of Daniel Defoe's *Robinson Crusoe,* in which Defoe's cunning protagonist is empowered by his Protestant/capitalist obsession with his "prospects" to achieve dominion over the island to which providence has brought him. In this proto-colonialist novel, Crusoe's calculations about his "prospects" are always articulated in the necessary visual terms of the Protestant pro-*vid*-ential design. (I use the word "calculations" to emphasize the distanced derivativeness — the visualism — of Crusoe's thinking about the "primordial" being he encounters on "his" island.) And these calculations invariably take the Puritan/capitalist form of self-examination: the table or ledger that differentiates only to dedifferentiate the minute and recalcitrantly "other" details of Crusoe's situation (which finally includes Friday).

This visual form of recollective "taking stock" recalls the prospectival cartographic projections of the Mercutorial eye and the perspectival vistas of the post-Renaissance painterly eye. And it was one of the precursors of the "prospectus" of such fundamental eighteenth-century projects of totalizing knowledge production as the *Encyclopédie* of the French *philosophes*[50] and, not least, as I will show later, of the related classificatory (disciplinary) tables of bourgeois Enlightenment science. I mean the spatializing economy by which, like the new Mercutorial maps, Crusoe is enabled not only to put every differential thing and event in its proper place, but, as in the case of Mungo Park's sentimentalized theoptics a century later, to render the unknown Other utterly predictable:

> I had a dismal prospect of my condition. . . . I had great Reason to consider it as a Determination of Heaven, that in this desolate place, and in this desolate Manner I should end my Life. . . . [A]nd sometimes I would expostulate with my self, Why Providence should thus compleatly ruine its Creatures, and render them so absolutely miserable, so without Help abandon'd, so entirely depress'd, that it could hardly be rational to be thankful for such a Life.
>
> But something always return'd swift upon me to check these Thoughts, and to reprove me, and particularly one Day walking with my Gun in my Hand by the Sea-side, I was very pensive upon the Subject of my present Condition, when Reason as it were expostulated with me t'other Way, thus: Well, you are in a desolate Condition 'tis true, but pray remember, Where are the rest of you? . . . . Why were not they sav'd and you lost? Why were you singled out? Is it better to be here or there, and then I pointed to the Sea? All Evils are to be consider'd with the Good that is in them, and with what worse attends them.
>
> Then it occurr'd to me again, how well I was furnish'd for my Subsistence, and what would have been my Case if it had not happen'd, *Which was an Hundred Thousand to one,* that the Ship floated from the Place where she first struck and was driven so near to the Shore that I had time to get all these Things out of her? . . . so that I had a tollerable View of subsisting without any Want as long as I liv'd, for I consider'd from the beginning how I would provide for Accidents that might happen, and for the time that was to come.[51]

Immediately following this retrospective meditation on his prospects, Crusoe invents a calendar, sorts out the surviving technological tools that would "keep things very exact," begins a journal, and, not least,

> [draws] up the State of my Affairs in Writing, not so much to leave them to any that were to come after me . . . as to deliver my

Thoughts from daily poring upon them, and afflicting my Mind; and as my Reason began now to master my Despondency I began to comfort my self as well as I could, and to set the good against the Evil, that I might have something to distinguish my Case from worse, and I stated it very impartially, like Debtor and Creditor, the Comforts I enjoy'd, against the Miseries I suffered, Thus . . . [52]

The distance from this primitive colonialist literary invocation of one's prospects under the aegis of a providential view of history capable of "mastering" anxiety to the appropriation of its calculative logic for the imperial project as such is not great. Indeed, the (disciplinary) promise/fulfillment structure of this literary perspective will become the model of the structure of the developed (administrative) colonial consciousness. Analyzing the travel writing of *An Account of Travels into the Interior of Southern Africa in the Years 1797 and 1798* (1801) by John Barrows — personal secretary of Lord George McCartney, the colonial governor of the Cape Colony, which was taken over by the British from the Dutch East India Company in 1795 — Mary Louise Pratt notes the essential relationship between the "prospects" understood in Crusoe's sense and the imperial project:

In Barrow's account, more so than in those of his predecessors, the eye scanning prospects in the spatial sense knows itself to be looking at prospects in the temporal sense — possibilities of a Eurocolonial future coded as resources to be developed, surpluses to be traded, towns to be built. Such prospects are what make information relevant in a description. They make a plain "fine" or make it noteworthy that a peak is "granitic" or a valley "well-wooded." The visual descriptions presuppose — naturalize — a transformative project embodied in the Europeans.[53]

Most tellingly, perhaps, the imperial gaze determines the representation of the "observer" of the hitherto secluded life of the denizens of the amorphous underworld in modern realistic or naturalistic fiction — the novels of Balzac, Zola, and Henry James, for example — and, in a way that makes the policing operations of the invisible imperial eye of the former explicit, in the classical detective novel of a Conan Doyle or an Agatha Christie. This is the testimony of Michel Foucault, the first critic of modernity to perceive the rise of the realistic novel as an instance of cultural production that was complicitous with the formation of the modern disciplinary society:

Since the seventeenth century, the West has witnessed the birth of a whole "fable" of the obscure life from which the fabulous found itself proscribed.... An art of language is born whose task is no longer to sing of the improbable, but to make what doesn't appear... appear: ...A kind of injunction to flush out the most nocturnal and the most everyday aspect of existence... acts to draw what is the line of literature's tendency since the seventeenth century, since it commenced to be literature in the modern sense of the word.... Fiction has from that time onward replaced the fabulous, the novel [*le roman*] throws off the yoke of the romanesque. ...Therefore literature forms that part of that great [disciplinary] system of constraint by which the West compelled the everyday to bring itself into discourse; but it occupies a special place there: bent on seeking everyday life beneath itself, on crossing over the limits, on brutally or insidiously disclosing the secrets, on ousting the rules and the codes, on causing the unavowable to be said.[54]

The most pertinent literary example of the pervasive figure of the panoptic eye's conical gaze for this study is the one singled out by Edward Said in *Orientalism* and amplified by Mary Louise Pratt in *Imperial Eyes*. I am referring to the figure, imbedded in and determining the discourse of eighteenth- and nineteenth-century travel writing, that represents the traveler as "the monarch of all I survey."[55] But, as I have tried to suggest by tracing its structural logic back to the metaphysical origins of the idea of the West, to locate the genealogical provenance of this visual metaphorics in the Enlightenment, as Said and especially Pratt do, is finally to restrict the critique of imperialism to a level that leaves the imperial perspective *in its essence* completely intact. Though its most visible and complex manifestation is indeed locatable in the late eighteenth and nineteenth centuries, imperialism is not an invention of a late historically specific moment of European history. It is an invention that is simultaneous with the invention of "Europe" itself.

White Metaphorics: The Centered Circle

There is no center, but always decenterings, series that register the halting passage from presence to absence, from excess to deficiency. The circle must be abandoned as a faulty principle of return; we must abandon our tendency to organize everything into a sphere.
— MICHEL FOUCAULT, "Theatrum Philosophicum"

Having demonstrated its ubiquity in the discourse, art, and literature of the Occident at large, I want to return to the structural analysis of the figure of the pyramidally or conically perceiving metaphysical eye — but now in terms of the resonant metaphorics informing the passage from Derrida's "Structure, Sign, and Play" quoted earlier. I am referring to the metaphorics of the *centered circle,* the allotrope of the trope of vision, which, according to Derrida, informed and in an increasingly invisible way determined the history of Western thought until the epistemic rupture reflected in Nietzsche's "critique of metaphysics," Freud's critique of "self-presence," and, above all, Heidegger's destruction of the "determination of Being as presence" forced it into visibility and called it into question.[56] In spatializing time, in willfully compelling the differential temporal process to turn back on itself, to return in the end, like the *ourobouros,* to its beginning, the metaphysical eye articulates *the figure* of the circle. This is the case whether this metaphysical eye is empirical or idealist, whether the narrative structure it articulates is "linear" or, as in the case of modernist literature, "spatial."

In the "contradictorily coherent" veridical and imaginative discourses of the ontotheological tradition, we will recall, presence manifests itself not simply in the figure of the all-seeing eye (and its light), but also as the affiliated center of an all-encompassing circle. Like the eye's gaze, which extends vertically from a fixed transcendent position to the things/events below that it circumscribes as a totality, the center is both inside and outside its circumference. That is to say, it is, like the metaphysical eye, "a center elsewhere" that is "beyond the reach of [free] play." As such, it is positively capable of accommodating (colonizing) the play of the contradictory differences to its immobile self and thus, in a locution that recalls an essential motif of Heidegger's destruction of metaphysical thinking, of "mastering" the spectral anxiety that has no thing as its object: "The concept of centered structure is in fact the concept of a play based on a fundamental ground, a play constituted on the basis of a fundamental immobility and a reassuring certitude, which itself is beyond the reach of play. And on the basis of this certitude anxiety can be mastered."

I will return to this double figure of the transcendent eye/"center elsewhere" in a later context, when I repeat the analysis of the structure of the circle precipitated by the metaphysical eye in terms of the historical specifics of its "interior" space. Here I want to pause over the general symbolic significance that the figure of the circle has had in the Western tradition at large. Like the eye and its light, the centered circle has, from the beginning of this tradition, been accorded by the West a privileged, indeed, a determining, status in its veridical and imaginative discourses about its collective identity and about the multiple Others that it, in all its manifestations, represents itself as not. More specifically, the centered circle has been the essential — and polyvalent — trope of the Beautiful, the Total, and the Perfect. This, as I have been suggesting, is because it is the trope of the plenary *telos* of metaphysics — of re-presentation —

itself: of, that is, the triumph of "illuminative" reason or imagination —
whether by suppression or accommodation — over the corrosive finitude
of differential time.[57]

As in the case of the metaphorics of the eye and its light, we
bear witness to the foundational and administered pervasiveness of this
meaning of the centered circle throughout the history of the discourse
and practice of the Occident. We find it, for example, in the philo-
sophical/aesthetic tradition that has addressed the "sublime." I mean the
tradition extending from Longinus's derivative (post-Greek, i.e. Roman)
codification, containment, and domestication of the experience of the
sublime through Immanuel Kant's, Edmund Burke's, and a host of Romantic writers' accommodation of the sublime to the beautiful and,
especially in the nineteenth-century American poets, to the imperial
project,[58] to Jean-François Lyotard's postmodern (de-centered) interrogation of this logocentric tradition in behalf of the liberation of the
sublime from the restricted economy of the beautiful.

More pertinently, we find this meaning of the circle in the same everyday language and structures of thought and imagination — grammar
in rhetoric, narrative in literature, and perspective in painting and the
plastic arts, for example — the interrogation of which disclosed the
pervasiveness of the metaphorics of the eye and its light. This is most
economically suggested by Leonardo da Vinci's celebrated emblematic
humanist figure — which itself constitutes a modification of the Roman
Vitruvius's image — representing the body of a man whose extended
members are circumscribed by a circle, the center of which is the ompha-
los.[59] It is the totality explicitly or implicitly visualized in this image of
the circle, in which the temporal/spatial parts are *integrally* subordinated
to the circumferential and self-present whole — in *perfect* relationship —
that the Western tradition, especially after the Renaissance, has identified as the "work of beauty/perfection" in both the literature and the
plastic arts at large.

Analogous with the idea of the poem as microcosm, which has been
one of the fundamental and abiding ideals of Occidental *poesis* — and
pointing to the indissoluble relationship between beauty and power —
we also bear witness to the valorization of the image of the centered
circle as figure of beauty/perfection in the architectural tradition of the
circular city. This is the tradition that extends back from the mod-
ernized Second Empire Paris of Emperor Louis Bonaparte and Baron
Georges-Eugène Haussmann[60] through Claude-Nicholas Ledoux (*Architecture Considered in Relation to Art, Manners, and Legislation,* 1804),
Vauban (*Essays on Fortification,* 1689), and many other eighteenth-
century city planners to the Renaissance humanists, both theoreticians

such as Campanella (*City of the Sun,* 1623) and Alberti (*The Ten Books of Architecture,* 1452), and practicing architects such as Filarete (*Treatise on Architecture,* ca. 1411), and finally to St. Augustine (*The City of God,* fifth century), Vitruvius (*The Ten Books of Architecture,* first century B.C.), and Plato (*The Laws,* fourth century B.C.).[61] As the historian Rudolph Wittkower has observed, "the geometry of the circle had an almost magical power over" all of these artists and theoreticians of the Western *polis.*[62]

But this extension of the testimony that identifies the figure of the centered circle with beauty and perfection in the self-defining discourse of the Occident to include the testimony of a space conventionally represented as a site of praxis is to anticipate. What needs to be thematized at this point is that which this self-affirming cultural discourse at large has perennially occluded in its benign, conclusive "white" rhetoric. Understood in the context opened up by the destruction of metaphysics, the privileged centered circle represented as the trope of the beautiful, the true, and the perfect — what Matthew Arnold called a "mighty agent of deliverance" — comes simultaneously to be seen as the trope of *domination,* of the will to power over the Other. For the resolution of conflict — the "peace," as it were — that constitutes the "end" of the metaphysical will to achieve the beauty/perfection of the inclusive circle is "won" by the conquest and forced reorientation of differently oriented energies: what we can now call the *periphery.* In the Western tradition at large, the circle of *Beauty* and the circle of *Domination* are the same.

The Reconfiguration of the Circle in the Age of the Enlightenment

> A whole history remains to be written of *spaces* — which would at the same time be the history of *powers* — from the great strategies of geopolitics to the little tactics of the habitat.
> — MICHEL FOUCAULT, "The Eye of Power"

What I want to emphasize by thus thematizing the will to power informing the interrelated metaphorics of the Gaze/other and the Circle/periphery that have been increasingly inscribed and naturalized in the discourse of truth and beauty in the West since its inception is precisely its defining *figurality:* its status as the *essential* structure of the West's cultural identity. As such a (constructed) structure, its "imperial" operation is not restricted to the particular site of ontology; it is *polyvalent* in its application. Understood in the context opened up by its destruction, the ontotheological tradition comes to be seen not simply as a philosophical or literary tradition, in which Being in its various historical guises and by way of the metaphorics of the eye/circle has always colonized difference understood as a category of thought or of imagination. It also comes to be seen as an economic, ecological, social, sexual, racial, and political tradition, in which this precise, if still all-too-generally described, colonizing process enabled by the metaphorics of the gaze/center operates simultaneously, however unevenly, at multiple sites.

In the early phases of this tradition it was knowledge production as such that was overdetermined (though, as I will suggest in chapter 2, the relative consciousness of the relationship between ontological imperialism and its more practical forms, especially educational and geopolitical imperialism, in the era of the Roman Empire complicates this generalization). Later, however, especially in the period of the Enlightenment (the anthropo-logical phase), the polyvalent imperial potential — and the subtle technologies of power — inhering in this truth/beauty discourse became increasingly clear to the dominant culture. The tentative, discontinuous, and unevenly developed intuition of the relationship between the imperial metaphysical gaze/center and educational institutions, gender relations, cultural production, economics, sociopolitics, and geopolitics that characterized the Western tradition from its beginnings coalesced in the *episteme* variously called the Enlightenment, the Age of Reason, and bourgeois capitalism. This was the *episteme,* according to Michel Foucault, that, in the wake of the American and especially French Revolutions, constituted the subject (the individual) in order to facilitate the achievement of a stable sociopolitical consensus (identity). Put alternatively, this "progress" involved the eventual recognition of the integral relationship between the perennially and increasingly privileged figure of the circle (understood as having its center elsewhere) as the image of beauty and perfection and the circle as the ideal instrument of a totalized sociopolitical domination that seemed like freedom to those on whom it was practiced.

The post-Renaissance humanists intuited a certain politically efficient and economical power (over the Other) inherent in, but not understood by, the older metaphysical epistemology: the latter's ability to *see* or re-*present* the differential force of temporality as *integral* and inclusive *picture* (structure, blueprint, design, table) or, negatively, to lose *sight* of and forget difference, in the pursuit of a certain inclusive philosophical order. As a result of this intuition into the "benign" power inhering in thinking from the end or from above the phenomena, the dominant (bourgeois) culture of modernity transformed the *over*sight of the earlier metaphysical perspective into a pervasive methodological or disciplinary instrument of *super*vision for the discreet coercion of difference into identity all through the field of forces that being comprises, from the ontological and epistemological sites through language and culture (*paideia*) to economics and sociopolitics (gender, family, state). More accurately, the intuition of the discreet power inhering in visualization enabled the dominant culture to appropriate by subordinating difference (the individual entity) to the purposes of normalization and utility.[63]

This new disciplinary instrument of invisible coercions, this modern allotrope of the gaze/centered circle, which, not incidentally, had as one of its primary enabling models the disciplinary Roman military camp, was the Panopticon, the circular penal building designed by the English Utilitarian thinker Jeremy Bentham to house social deviants of various kinds who could be supervised from a central tower. This epochal architectural model has, of course, been brilliantly analyzed by Michel Foucault. But with a few partial exceptions,[64] its origins, its spatial economy, its scope, and the hold it has had on the modern Occidental mind have not been adequately thought by those oppositional cultural, political, and postcolonial critics who, ostensibly, would resist the colonizing project of the imperial gaze, whatever its terrain:

> The Panopticon...must be understood as a generalizable model of functioning; a way of defining power relations in terms of the everyday life of men. No doubt Bentham presents it as a particular institution, closed in upon itself....But [it] must not be understood as a dream building: *it is the diagram of a mechanism of power reduced to its ideal form; its functioning, abstracted from any obstacle, resistance or friction, must be represented as a pure architectural and optical system: it is in fact a figure of political technology that may and must be detached from any specific use.*
>
> It is polyvalent in its applications; it serves to reform prisoners, but also to treat patients, to instruct schoolchildren, to confine the insane, to supervise workers, to put beggars and idlers to work.[65]

Though Foucault does not refer to it, we may infer from the exemplary nature of the practices he does — the reformation of prisoners, the treatment of patients, the instruction of school children, the confinement of the insane, the supervision of workers, the putting of beggars and idlers to work — that the panoptic diagram serves as well to "civilize" the "deviant" peoples of other "savage" or "primitive" or "undeveloped" worlds (peoples, it should be emphasized, represented by this gendered discourse as errant, incontinent, and seductive female). The binary logic inhering in this figure, in other words, includes the Metropolis and periphery.

I will return to the Roman origin of this architectural model in chapter 2. Here, I want to think more closely the imperial potential of the structure of the circle articulated by the metaphysical eye enabled by Foucault's situating this privileged figure as an instance of the complicity of knowledge with power within the historically specific occasion of the Enlightenment. It must not be forgotten that this is the period in which European imperialism inaugurates the process of becoming colonialist, that is, a self-conscious and highly articulated and administered discursive practice intended to render domination in the image of an act of benign concern for and intervention in behalf of the well-being of the Other. What occurs in this anthropological phase of the ontotheological tradition is not a mutation of the pre-Enlightenment structure of the centered circle, but a significant complication of its interior space. It is a complication that gradually transforms an earlier, economically and politically wasteful, European colonialist initiative into a more efficient process that renders the results of colonization more materially productive and politically economical. It is a complication, in other words, that establishes the imperial project proper.

I am referring to the reformation of a hitherto highly generalized and undefined space in which whatever it originally contained was represented by the early colonial eye as literally and figuratively devoid of being — as a "virgin land" — and thus justifiably open to conquest and subjection by the privileged *visible* "center elsewhere." As Enrique Dussel puts this older European opposition, "*The center is; the periphery is not.* Where Being reigns, there reign and control the armies of Caesar, the emperor. *Being is; beings are what are seen and controlled.*"[66] Such a representation of the space of the Other as nonbeing eventually enabled its re-formation in such a way as to render it more amenable to productive appropriation and subjection by the colonizing eye. Its representation as "nonbeing," in fact, was tantamount to a call to the Western *logos*/seed-bearer on the part of the nonexistent existences that inhabited this "empty" or "virgin" land to undertake a process that would transform it into a highly differentiated, articulated, and productive internal colonial "plantation." In short, it enabled the metamorphosis of this space into a table or grid or blueprint or map, in which every differential thing in it — flora, fauna, minerals, humans — is renamed, deprived of its original taxonomy, by the Enlightenment Adam. The ultimate purpose of this metamorphosis was to harness this space's otherwise amorphous and wasteful (female) energy to the ideological purposes of the larger identical whole presided over by the *invisible* center elsewhere.

To recapitulate, then, we can say that the Occidental tradition, in privileging metaphysical inquiry as access to the truth of being, has been, from its beginning in the Roman reduction of Greek *a-letheia* to *veritas* (the correspondence of mind and thing) to its end in the planetary "triumph" of technological thinking, a tradition that has represented the being of being — its nothingness, its temporality, the differences it disseminates — as a reduced totalized *space understood as an abstract category.* In the process, however, this abstract space became increasingly specified. Most tellingly, insofar as these tropes are endemic to the imperial project, it came to be *seen* as a *field* or *area* or *arena* or *region* or *province* or *domain* or *territory* to be mastered or conquered.

This historical process, in which the metaphysical representation of time as space is increasingly concretized, coalesces in the Roman-inspired Enlightenment to become the essential cultural agency of the European imperial project proper. This is precisely what Foucault belatedly discovers in his meditation on the complicity of Occidental knowledge production with the imperial will to power over the being of being. In his response to the critics who, continuing to think truth as external to power, have reproached him for his "spatial obsessions," Foucault says:

> But I think through them I did come to what I had basically been looking for: the relations that are possible between power and knowledge. Once knowledge can be analyzed in terms of region, domain, implantation, displacement, transposition, one is able to capture the process by which knowledge functions as a form of power and disseminates the effects of power. There is an administration of knowledge, a politics of knowledge, relations of power which pass via knowledge and which, if one tries to transcribe them, lead one to consider forms of domination designated by such notions as field, region and territory. And the politico-strategic term is an indication of how the military and the administrative actually come to inscribe themselves both on the material soil and cultural forms of discourse.... Endeavoring ... to decipher discourse through the use of spatial, strategic metaphors enables one to grasp precisely the points at which discourses are transformed in, through and on the basis of relations of power.[67]

What needs to be added provisionally to Foucault's enabling insight into the complicity of knowledge production and power is that this reduction of the truth of being to a space — a terrain — to be won, occupied, and dominated had its provenance, as Heidegger has insisted, in imperial Rome. It followed, that is, in the wake of the imperial Roman legions' conquest of the other worlds beyond the circle of the metropolis. "Region [of knowledge]," for example, derives from the Latin *regere:* (to command); "province," from *vincere* (to conquer); "domain," from *dominus* (master, lord); "arena," from *arena* (place of conflict); "territory," from *territorium* ("land of settlement as realm of command").[68]

It is the Enlightenment's extraordinary complication of the internal economy of the spatialization of the temporal being of being (the circle and its periphery) that distinguishes its representation of knowledge production as exploitable space from earlier representations of this imperial nexus. The emergence of empirical science, instrumental reason, the disciplines, and the disciplinary technological apparatuses, most notably the table, enabled not simply the far more economically and politically efficient domination of the body politic that constitutes the parameters of Foucault's reading of the Enlightenment. This epistemological development also enabled the far more economically and politically efficient colonization of the geographical and cultural spaces beyond the Occident's periphery. And it is to this extension in the period of the Enlightenment of the Occident's appropriation of the metaphysical spatialization of being to the imperial project proper that we must now turn.

The Circle as Disciplinary Table

There is a whole history to be written about such stone-cutting — a history of the utilitarian rationalization of detail in moral accountability and political control. The classical age did not initiate it; rather it accelerated it, changed its scale, gave it precise instruments, and perhaps found some echoes for it in the calculation of the infinitely small or in the description of the most detailed characteristics of natural beings. In any case, "detail" had long been a category of theology and asceticism: every detail is important, in the sight of God, no immensity is greater than a detail, nor is anything so small that it was not willed by one of his individual wishes.... For the disciplined man, as for the true believer, no detail is unimportant, but not so much for the meaning that it conceals within it as for the hold it provides for the power that wished to seize it.
— MICHEL FOUCAULT, *Discipline and Punish*

The space of the circle projected by the metaphysical eye before the Enlightenment was an empty or uninhabited space. Those who filled it were "seen" as nomadic — separated, in their mobility, from the land — and insofar as this nomadic existence precluded *cultivating* and *inhabiting* it, errantly nonhuman. I will return in the last chapter to think positively this negative representation of the "savage" or "barbarian" Other beyond the circumference of the metropolitan circle. My purpose here is simply to make the ideological implications of this representation explicit. Despite the obvious evidence that would belie such a projection, this is the pervasive testimony of European travelers and colonists in North and South America and in Africa, as many historians of colonial encounters have shown.[69] As Peter Hulme puts this calculatively blind representation of the indigenous people of the "New World" by their European "visitors":

> The strategies of colonial discourse were directed in the first place at demonstrating a separation between the desired land and its native inhabitants. Baffled at the complex but effective native system of food production, the English seem to have latched on to the one (minor) facet of behaviour that they thought they recognized — mobility, and argued on that basis an absence of *proper* connection between the land and its first inhabitants.[70]

Drawing from Francis Jennings's *The Invasion of America,* Hulme goes on to give examples of this early ideological representation of the space within the colonial circle, suggesting the degree to which it justified the overt use of violence by the colonizers:

In 1612 the Jesuit missionary Pierre Biard, describing Canadian Amerindians, wrote:

> Thus four thousand Indians at most roam through, rather than occupy, these vast stretches of inland territory and sea-shore. For they are a nomadic people, living in the forests and scattered over wide spaces as is natural for those who live by hunting and fishing only;

"roam rather than occupy" being a translation of Biard's *"non tenentur, sed percurruntur."* In 1625 Samuel Purchas wrote of the Virginia Algonquian:

> so bad people, having little of Humanitie but shape, ignorant of Civilitie, of Arts, of Religion; more brutish then the beasts they hunt, more wild and unmanly then that unmanned wild Countrey which they range rather then inhabite.

And in 1629 in New England John Winthrop assimilated Purchas's point to the legal argument of *vacuum domicilium* by which the Indian had "natural" but not "civil" rights over the land because they had not "subdued" it.[71]

What, however, the panoptic Eurocentric eye of the Enlightenment comes to see in the space within this reconfigured trope of the circle is no longer — or at least not exclusively — a vast "uninhabited" emptiness, in which the natives do not count as human beings. Rather, it comes primarily to see an un*informed terra incognita*. As the texts of early European travel writers (and social historians) invariably characterize this amorphous and ahistorical "new world," the European panoptic gaze falls on an *"unimproved"* space. As the privative prefix emphatically suggests, it is a space-time in which everything in it — flora, fauna, minerals, animals, and, later, human beings — is seen and encoded not so much as threatening, though that meaning is clearly there as well, as wasteful or uneconomical and thus as an untended fallow (female) terrain *calling futurally for* the beneficial ministrations of the (adult, male) center.[72] The predestinarian metaphorics of the circle precipitates a whole rhetoric of moral necessity. The "wilderness" as "underdeveloped" or "unimproved" or "uncultivated" (i.e., "unfulfilled" or "uncircular") space *must,* as the privative prefixes demand, be developed, improved, cultivated (i.e., fulfilled or circularized). Indeed, it is the wilderness's *destiny.* From this representation of the colonial Others as mired in and by their own chaotic primordial condition, one of the most debilitating of which is unproductive perpetual war, it is an easy step to representing them, as American writers and historians did the Indian race in the nineteenth century, as either *self*-doomed[73] or *appealing* to the European to save them from themselves by way of imposing his *peace* on their multiply wasteful strife.[74]

Referring to John Barrow's representative (enlightened) "anti-conquest" narrative about his travels as an agent of the British colonial governor in the interior of the Cape Colony at the end of the eighteenth century, Mary Louise Pratt writes:

> The visual descriptions presuppose — naturalize — a transformative project embodied in the Europeans. Often the project surfaces explicitly in Barrow's text, in visions of "improvement" whose value is often expressed as aesthetic....
>
> It is the task of the advanced scouts for capitalist "improvement" to encode what they encounter as "unimproved" and, in keeping with the terms of the anti-conquest, as *disponible,* available for improvement. European aspirations must be represented as uncontested. Here the textual apartheid that separates landscapes from people, accounts of inhabitants from accounts of their habitats, fulfills its logic. The European improving eye produces subsistence habitats as "empty" landscapes, meaningful only in terms of a capitalist future and of their potential for producing a marketable surplus. From the point of view of their inhabitants,

of course, these same spaces are lived as intensely humanized, saturated with local history and meaning, where plants, creatures, and geographical formations have names, uses, symbolic functions, histories, places in indigenous knowledge formations.[75]

This is an acute observation about the "anti-conquest" imperialist discourse of Enlightenment travel writing. But it is limited by its characteristic restriction of the word "improvement" to the historical context of modern capitalism (though the aside referring to the expression of the vision of improvement in aesthetic terms is suggestive). Like so much "postcolonial" criticism, its historicist problematic is blind to the genealogy of this modern "anti-conquest" concept. It fails to see that the rhetoric of "improvement" is a capitalist extension of a much older system of imperial tropes, one that, in naturalizing the latter, obscures the will to power over the Other that is visible in its earlier form. This word, that is, not only looks forward to "underdeveloped," the sedimented counterword that constitutes the base of the neocolonialist discourse of late capitalism, as Pratt seems to be suggesting. It also harks back to what Enrique Dussel calls the "developmental fallacy" informing Enlightenment philosophy of history from Adam Smith and John Locke through Hegel and a certain Marx to Habermas. Tracing the genealogy of Habermas's Eurocentric representation of modernity back to Hegel, Dussel writes:

> In the *Vorlesungen über die Philosophie der Weltgeschichte,* Hegel portrays world history (*Weltgeschichte*) as the self-realization of God, as a theodicy of reason and of liberty (*Freiheit*), and as a process of Enlightenment (*Aufklärung*)....
>
> In Hegelian ontology, the concept of development (*Entwicklung*) plays a central role. This concept determines the movement of the concept (*Begriff*) until it culminates in the idea — that is, as it moves from indeterminate being to the absolute knowledge in the *Logic.* Development...unfolds according to a linear dialectic; although originally an ontological category, today it is primarily considered as a sociological one with implications for world history. Furthermore, this development has a direction:
>
> > Universal history goes from East to West. Europe is absolutely the *end of universal history.* Asia is the beginning.
>
> But this alleged East-West movement clearly precludes Latin America and Africa from world history and characterizes Asia as essentially confined to a state of immaturity and childhood (*Kindheit*)....

> The immaturity (*Umreife*) marking America is total and physical; even the vegetables and the animals are more primitive, brutal, monstrous, or simply more weak or degenerate.[76]

Even more fundamentally, Pratt's "unimproved" has its origins in the more deeply inscribed metaphorics of the seed and its cultivation, as Dussel's recurrent invocation of the rhetoric of "immaturity" that informs the Hegelian discourse suggests. This is the trope (which is also an aesthetics) that, along with the gaze and the centered circle, informs the very etymology of "metaphysics" and that is encoded and naturalized in the truth discourse of the Occident. That is to say, the genealogy of the word "improvement" in the discourse of post-Enlightenment travel literature is traceable to the origins of Occidental history. (The metaphor of the "virgin land," which, as I have intimated, is equally pervasive in the discourse of early colonialism, constitutes a particularly telling gendered allotrope of this metaphorical system circulating around the seed. It focalizes the identification of the panoptic gaze that perceives this "unimproved" circular space with the brutal phallic will.)[77] A retrieval of the equally inaugural visual metaphorics with which it is affiliated will bring into visibility the ideological agenda hidden in the benign connotations of the metaphor of "improvement." In the positivist Enlightenment, the "unimproved" space of the "wilderness" is understood as a darkness, in the sense not so much of savage or barbarous (though, again, that meaning resonates in the word as well), as of a potentially knowable and usable unknown. What its eye beholds primarily is a terrain that, as the European cliché about the "inscrutability" of the Orient has it, compels *knowing* and *naming* precisely because its darkly unimproved state resists scrutiny and domestication. For the French natural scientist Michel Adanson, for example, the world of nature was

> a confused mingling of beings that seem to have been brought together by chance: here, gold is mixed with another metal, with stone, with earth; there, the violet grows side by side with an oak. Among these plants, too, wander the quadruped, the reptile, and the insect; the fishes are confused, one might say, with the aqueous element in which they swim, and with the plants grow in the depth of the waters. . . . This mixture is indeed so general and so multifarious that it appears to be one of nature's laws.[78]

In thematizing this knowledge-producing naming — this Linnaean classificatory motif — I do not, despite its decisive contribution to the imperial project proper, want to limit its origins to the Enlightenment. As the natural affiliation of seed with light (the spatialization of differential temporal phenomena) suggests, its ultimate origin lies in the Occident's appropriation of the biblical narrative of Adam, armed with the *Logos,* naming the beasts. In combinations with the classical apotheosis of the sun/seed, this narrative has played a decisive role of persuasion throughout the history of Christian European imperial conquest, not least in that history of genocidal American expansionism inaugurated by the Adamic Puritans' pacification of the American wilderness.[79]

To put it generally, then, this historically developed Enlightenment version of the imperial circle is understood not simply as an ever-expanding boundary or *frontier* tethered to the luminous center, but simultaneously as an unending process of enlightening and internalizing the outside darkness, or, what is the same thing, of bringing its (female) fallowness to fruition. This understanding of the relation between center and periphery is, of course, what Enlightenment Europe called its *mission civilisatrice.* And, it should not be overlooked, its ultimate origin is the Roman imperial model: the relation between a (manly) civilized Rome, the Metropolis — the City *as measure* — and the uncivilized periphery, the amorphous, unknown, and unnamed (obscure) or "unimproved" (uncultivated) provinces that were not yet incorporated into the *orbis terrarum,* that is, were not yet individuated into cities or integrated parts of the Metropolitan City.

But to speak of the circular space perceived by the Eurocentric eye of the Enlightenment as an unknown, unnamed, and unimproved space that "demands" to be known, named, and improved is to realize that the civilizing or enlightening mission of the Enlightenment also requires specification both of the articulation of that space and of the effects of that spatial economy on knowledge and power. To put it generally, the Eurocentric solar or panoptic eye of the Enlightenment turned the earlier "emptiness" of the circle of its vision into a *measurable space.*

Whereas the imperial eye of the pre-Enlightenment — the early Spanish conquistadores, for example — tended to (over)see the circle it projected as a generalized amorphous and thus immediately plunderable space, the Enlightenment eye came to oversee the (always expanding) circle it projected as a *mappable organic space,* a vital differential world in which the comparative *knowledge* of its details enhances the power of the encompassing eye of the beholder over its organic "branching." As his presiding analogy between the domain of knowledge and the geographical world clearly suggests, what the French *philosophe* D'Alembert says in 1751 about the domain of knowledge before and after the emergence of the mapping eye in his *Preliminary Discourse to the Encyclopedia of Diderot* applies as well to the relationship between the Enlightenment Metropolis and the provinces. Indeed, it applies right

down to the roles that "travelers'" narratives and the ensuing opening of lines of communication to the Metropolis play in the process of
mastering the labyrinthine Other:

> The execution ["of a genealogical or encyclopedic tree which will
> gather the various branches of knowledge together under a single
> point of view"] is not without difficulty.... The general system of
> the sciences and the arts is a sort of labyrinth, a torturous road
> which the intellect enters without quite knowing what direction
> to take.... The discontinuity of these operations is a necessary
> effect of the very generation of ideas. However philosophic this
> disorder may be on the part of the soul, an encyclopedic tree
> which attempted to portray it would be disfigured, indeed utterly
> destroyed....
>
> It is not the same with the encyclopedic arrangement of our
> knowledge. This consists of collecting knowledge into the small-
> est area possible and of placing the philosopher at a vantage point,
> so to speak, high above the vast labyrinth, whence he can perceive
> the principal sciences and the arts simultaneously. From there he
> can see at a glance the objects of their speculations and the op-
> erations which can be made on these objects; he can discern the
> general branches of human knowledge, the points that separate or
> unite them; and sometimes he can even glimpse the secrets that
> related them to one another. It is a kind of world map which is
> to show the principal countries, their position and their mutual
> dependence, the road that leads directly from one to another. This
> road is often cut by a thousand obstacles, which are known in each
> country only to the inhabitants or to travelers, and which cannot
> be represented except in individual, highly detailed maps. These
> individual maps will be the different articles of the *Encyclopedia*
> and the Tree or Systematic Chart will be its world map.[80]

The difference between the two historical moments, in other words,
is the difference between a mapped space understood, as in the case of
the early European explorers, as a *periplum* ("not as land seen on a
map/but sea bord seen by men sailing"),[81] and a mapped space conceived, as Foucault has shown, as a self-consciously mediative mode
of knowledge/power production analogous in its structure to, if not
entirely dependent on, the "tables" based on the *ontologically, invariably racially, grounded* systems of classification that emerged in the
Enlightenment. These were the polyvalent taxonomic tables — best exemplified by the *Systema Naturae* (1735), *Philosophia Botanica* (1751),
and *Species Plantarum* (1753) of Linnaeus, the *Histoire naturelle* (1749)

of Buffon, the *Nosologie methodique* (1772) of Boissier de Sauvages ("the Linnaeus of diseases"),[82] and the *Familles des plantes* (1763) of Michel Adanson[83] — that differentiated, named, graded, and accommodated an amorphous organic multiplicity within an inclusive structure that miniaturizes and renders visible a larger, otherwise invisible, and "ungraspable" totality. As such, they became the disciplinary model for the classroom, the mass production factory, the penal institution, the medical clinic, the psychiatric hospital, the capitalist system of economic exchange, and the practice of military warfare in the "disciplinary society":

> The first of the great operations of discipline is . . . the constitution of *"tableaux vivants,"* which transform the confused, useless or dangerous multitudes into ordered multiplicities. The drawing up of "tables" was one of the great problems of the scientific, political and economic technology of the eighteenth century: how one was to arrange botanical and zoological gardens, and construct at the same time rational classifications of living beings; how one was to observe, supervise, regularize the circulation of commodities and money and thus build up an economic table that might serve as the principle of the increase of wealth; how one was to inspect men, observe their presence and absence and constitute a general and permanent register of the armed forces; how one was to distribute patients, separate them from one another, divide up the hospital space and make a systematic classification of diseases: these were all twin operations in which the two elements — distribution and analysis, supervision and intelligibility — are inextricably bound up. In the eighteenth century the table was both a technique of power and a procedure of knowledge. It was a question of organizing the multiple, of providing oneself with an instrument to cover it and to master it; it was a question of imposing upon it an "order."[84]

To these differentiated dedifferentiated (accommodational) "imperial" structures produced by the miniaturization and spatialization of time should be added the reduction and hierarchized structuration of languages, of gender and race relations, and, not least, of the discourse and practice — the visualization or *re-presentation* and administration of — the nation-state and the colonial empire.

Foucault does not explicitly elaborate these imperial structures in his discussion of the spatialization of knowledge and of the table as the model of an affiliated comprehensive relay of strategic disciplinary social practices. But his very overdetermination of the table *as* polyvalent model implies them. Thus, to focus on the latter category of this series of discursive practices, which we should remember contains the others, it is no accident that Foucault concludes the chapter in *Discipline and Punish* from which the above resonant passage is drawn with a reference to the decisive role that the table plays in the advent of the Napoleonic Empire. In this particular case, the form the table takes is that of a "politics... conceived as a continuation, if not exactly and directly of war, at least of the military model as a fundamental means of preventing civil disorder":

> "Discipline must be made national," said Guibert. "The state that I depict will have a simple, reliable, easily controlled administration. It will resemble those huge machines, which by quite uncomplicated means produce great effects; the strength of this state will spring from its own strength, its prosperity from its own prosperity. Time, which destroys all, will increase its power. It will disprove that vulgar prejudice by which we are made to imagine that empires are subjected to an imperious law of decline and ruin...." The Napoleonic régime was not far off and with it the form of state that was to survive it and, we must not forget, the foundations of which were laid not only by jurists, but also by soldiers, not only councillors of state, but also junior officers, not only the men of the courts, but also the men of the camps. The Roman reference that accompanied this formation certainly bears with it this double index: citizens and legionnaires, law and manoeuvres.[85]

Edward Said has complained that Foucault did not elaborate the connection between the supervisory gaze that projects its circumscribed object in the spatial figure of the classificatory table and the patriarchal/racial colonial project. Nevertheless, this extension, both in its general and specific imperatives vis-à-vis knowledge and power, is inherent in the very structure of its visual projection.[86] As Said has shown in *Orientalism*, his (dis)seminal appropriation of Foucault's analysis of the panoptic gaze, Napoleon's conquest of Egypt was not, as in earlier imperial campaigns, simply a military project.[87] In accordance with the general imperatives of the mode of metaphysical thinking embodied in the tables (what Said calls the "textual/schematic" attitude), it was, rather, a military project that was simultaneously and integrally a project of knowledge production: a project, that is, intended to render "totally accessible to European scrutiny" "a land of obscurity and a part of the Orient hitherto known at second hand through the exploits of earlier travelers, scholars and conquerors."[88]

More specifically, it was no accident, to recall Foucault's analysis of the gaze-produced table, that Napoleon's Egyptian expedition included not only an army of soldiers but an army of scholars, whose purpose was to produce a body of differentiated knowledge that would "win the hearts and minds" of the Egyptians to the French idea of "Europe" and that could be utilized for purposes of establishing a more materially and politically productive dominion over the colonized. Referring to "that great collective appropriation of one country by another," the twenty-three-volume *Description de l'Égypte* compiled by the scholars of the French Institut, "the learned division of Napoleon's army," Said writes:

> To restore a region from its present barbarism to its former classical greatness; to instruct (for its own benefit) the Orient in the ways of the modern West; to subordinate or underplay military power in order to aggrandize the project of glorious knowledge acquired in the process of political domination of the Orient; to formulate the Orient, to give it shape, identity, definition with full recognition of its place in memory, its importance to imperial strategy, and its "natural" role as an appendage to Europe; to dignify all the knowledge collected during colonial occupation with the title "contribution to modern learning" when the natives had neither been consulted nor treated as anything except as pretexts for a text whose usefulness was not to the natives; to feel oneself as a European in command, almost at will, of Oriental history, time, and geography; to institute new areas of specialization; to establish new disciplines; to divide, deploy, schematize, tabulate, index, and record everything in sight (and out of sight); to make out of every observable detail a generalization and out of every generalization an immutable law about the Oriental nature, temperament, mentality, custom, or type; and, above all, to transmute living reality into the stuff of texts, to possess (or think one possesses) actuality mainly because nothing in the Orient seems to resist one's powers: these are the features of Orientalist projection entirely realized in the *Description de l'Égypte,* itself enabled and reinforced by Napoleon's wholly Orientalist engulfment of Egypt by the instruments of Western knowledge and power.[89]

Nor, finally, is it an accident that the emergent Linnaean system of classification — of identifying, naming, and classifying the flora and fauna of nature — inaugurated the global taxonomic projects, most notably that of his student Anders Sparrman,[90] that became the essential

European means of producing a modern or neoimperialist discourse, a discourse that, in the name of the truth of empirical science, invents or constructs the Other in the image of the First World. I am referring to what Mary Louise Pratt, in her Foucauldian study of the relationship between scientific travel writing and colonialism in South Africa and Latin America, has called the "anti-conquest narrative." This is the narrative "in which the naturalist naturalizes the bourgeois European's own global presence and authority" to differentiate its "benign" truth-producing motive from an earlier, overtly violent imperial narrative. In a way that recalls Foucault's and Said's differentiation of the visible and "inefficient" deployment of power in the *ancien régime* from the more invisible and materially and politically economical version of the Enlightenment, Pratt observes:

> Natural history asserted an urban, lettered, male authority over the whole of the planet; it elaborated a rationalizing, extractive, dissociative understanding which overlaid functional, experiential relations among people, plants, and animals. In these respects, it figures a certain kind of global hegemony, notably one based on possession of land and resources rather than control over routes. At the same time, in and of itself, the system of nature as a descriptive paradigm was an utterly benign and abstract appropriation of the planet. Claiming no transformative potential whatsoever, it differed sharply from overly imperial articulations of conquest, conversion, territorial appropriation, and enslavement. The system created...a utopian, innocent vision of European global authority, which I refer to as an *anti-conquest*. The term is intended to emphasize the *relational* meaning of natural history, the extent to which it became meaningful specifically in contrast with an earlier imperial, and prebourgeois, European expansionist presence.[91]

The difference between an earlier, pre-Enlightenment, and a later, post-Enlightenment, configuration of the internal space of the imperial circle is, of course, crucial to any understanding of the essence of imperial practice. But my purpose in thus invoking Foucault's analysis of the complicity of the classificatory table of the Enlightenment with the domination of the Other in the disciplinary society, and Said's and Pratt's extension of Foucault's genealogical insight to include the modern European imperial project, is not to bring a story about the development of the technology of European colonialism to its fulfillment and narrative closure, one that renders prior technologies of power anachronistic. It is, rather, to *retrieve* a fundamental dimension of this story that has been obliterated from memory even as it resonates unthought in the very contemporary language these postcolonial critics use to indict the truth discourse of the West as "imperial." I want to suggest that the classificatory table, as microcosm of a larger spatial totality and as the model for wider "imperial" practices (the mass production process, the panoptic penal system, the medical and psychiatric hospital, the family, the classroom, the nation-state, the colonial administration, and so on), is grounded in and enabled by the metaphysical principle of principles or, as Enrique Dussel puts it, "the ideology of ideologies":[92] that *Identity is the condition for the possibility of difference and not the other way around.*

Unlike its predecessor in the *ancien régime,* metaphysical inquiry at this advanced Enlightenment stage does not obliterate the contradictory, amorphous, unimproved, and "ahistorical" Other from the vantage point of a *visible* "center elsewhere." It "acknowledges" this Other's claims as contributive to (the knowledge of) the larger self-identical Whole. In other words, it "classifies" the amorphous Others from the vantage point of an *invisible* "center elsewhere." It differentiates these Others into discrete phenomena — attributes distinguishing identities to them — within and in behalf of a prior encompassing self-present total Identity. This individuation of the amorphous Other conveys a sense of the sovereign integrity of the differentiated entities, but it obscures the fact that their uniqueness is entirely *dependent* on a dominant synchronic Totality, the always present and determining center of which is always out of sight. To acquire validity the differentiated entity must *accommodate* its differential partiality to the prior Totality, must, that is, *objectify* and *subordinate itself* to — take its *proper* place within — the gridded structure of the dominant Identity. To become a subject it must heed the call — the hailing — of the *Subject.* As his invocation of the ontological metaphorics of the center and the circle should suggest, what the Lacanian Marxist Louis Althusser says about "the interpellation of the individual as subject" — the (subjected) subject invented by the bourgeois capitalist Enlightenment — applies by extension to the spatial economy of the (neo)imperial project as such:

> The Absolute Subject occupies the unique place of the Centre, and interpellates around it the infinity of individuals into subjects in a double mirror-connexion such that it *subjects* the subjects to the Subject, while giving them in the Subject in which each subject can contemplate its own image (present and future) the *guarantee* that this really concerns them and Him....
>
> The duplicate mirror-structure of ideology ensures simultaneously:

1. the interpellation of 'individuals' as subjects;

2. their subjection to the Subject;

3. the mutual recognition of subjects and Subject, the subjects' recognition of each other, and finally the subject's recognition of himself;

4. the absolute guarantee that everything really is so, and that on condition that the subjects recognize what they are and behave accordingly, everything will be all right: Amen— *"So be it."*

Result: caught in this quadruple system of interpellation as subjects, of subjection to the Subject, of universal recognition and of absolute guarantee, the subjects "work," they "work by themselves" in the vast majority of cases, with the exception of the "bad subjects" who on occasion provoke the intervention of one of the detachments of the (repressive) State apparatus. But the vast majority of (good) subjects work all right "all by themselves," i.e. by ideology (whose concrete forms are realized in the Ideological State Apparatuses).[93]

The fulfillment of this promissory accommodational project is called variously "beauty," "perfection," or, most tellingly, "peace" *(pax)*. In this reconstellated context the differential entity becomes, indeed, *productive,* but what it produces is a product of exchange value that benefits the economy and increases the authority of the dominant structure projected by the "supervisory gaze" or, alternatively, the invisible imperial "Subject" or "center elsewhere."

This political economy, in the sociopolitical domain, is what Foucault calls "the repressive hypothesis." Derived in part from its recognition of the *ancien régime*'s economically and politically wasteful economy of power, this is the seductive ruse of the emergent capitalist bourgeoisie that strategically represents knowledge (of the Other) as external to and the essential agent of deliverance from the constraints of power. It is the ruse that conceals the complicity between (Western) truth and power:

We must cease once and for all to describe the effects of power in negative terms: it "excludes," it "represses," it "censors," it "abstracts," it "masks," it "conceals." In fact, power produces; it produces reality; it produces domains of objects and rituals of truth. The individual and the knowledge that may be gained of him belong to this production.[94]

Recapitulation: The Historical Imperative to Think Ontological Representation in the Post–Cold War Occasion

> We must ask what remains unthought in the call "to the matter itself."
> Questioning this way, we can become aware that something that is no
> longer the matter of philosophy to think conceals itself precisely where
> philosophy has brought its matter to absolute knowledge and to ultimate
> evidence.   — MARTIN HEIDEGGER, "The End of Philosophy
> and the Task of Thinking"

To put the classificatory table — the spatial structuration of being that
became the model of a new, post-Enlightenment form of imperialism —
in terms of the metaphysical basis of the "repressive hypothesis" is
thus to precipitate a repetition (*Wiederholung*) of the provenance of the
"West" that will allow us to know what we know about modern imperialism for the first time. For this reconstellation of the origins of the
table — this "step back," at it were — will disclose the historical and
ideological depth to which the putatively modern imperial impulse is
inscribed in the Occidental consciousness.

More specifically, to understand the table in terms of the repressive
hypothesis prompts us not only to retrieve Heidegger's definition of
Western metaphysics as the perception of being from after or above
its temporal disseminations, as, that is, an over-seeing from a center
elsewhere that structures being in advance for the purpose of "compre-
hending/grasping" it. It also enables us to retrieve and put back into
play Heidegger's extension of this ontological disclosure to the site of
Western political practice as such in the neglected *Parmenides* text. Even
more suggestive than disclosing the historical depth to which the imperial project is backgrounded in Occidental history, it is an extension
that, while locating its genealogical origins at the beginning of Western
history, that is, in imperial Rome, points proleptically toward Foucault's
and Said's disclosure of the indirect and polyvalent (neo)imperial practice enabled by the harnessing of "truth" to power in the Enlightenment,
by, that is, its reduction of being to the figure of the classificatory table.

I will elaborate Heidegger's admittedly controversial genealogy of the
West in the next chapter. Here it will suffice for the purpose of recapitu-
lating my argument simply to recall the three indissolubly related phases
of Heidegger's effort to think the relationship between metaphysics and
imperialism. They not only constitute an exposition of the affiliation
between the Western structure of consciousness and imperial practice.
They also anticipate and provide a corrective to the postcolonial critique
of imperialism that focuses on its indirection or mediating strategy. De-

spite its resonant pertinence for the present, post–Cold War, occasion, it is an extension that has been utterly repressed by those who would identify Heidegger's thought with totalitarianism and overlooked by those postcolonial critics who assume that his "ontological" thought has been superseded by more worldly oppositional discourses such as the New Historicism, cultural discourse analysis, and postcolonial criticism.

Heidegger's analysis of this relationship between knowledge production and (imperial) power in the *Parmenides* has its point of departure in the "truth" predicated by metaphysical ontology. I am referring to the prevailing (Roman) concept of truth as *veritas:* as the adequation of mind and thing (correctness). This, we recall, is the reduced truth that, in the name of certainty, was precipitated by the splitting and hierarchizing of an earlier (Greek) understanding of truth (*a-letheia:* unconcealment), in which the negative (*pseudos:* dissembling) was understood, not, like the Roman *falsum,* as an antithetical negative, but as *belonging* "positively" with the "positive": "The essence of negativity is nothing negative, but neither is it only something 'positive.' The distinction between the positive and the negative does not suffice to grasp what is essential, to which the non-essence belongs. The essence of the false is not something 'false.' "[95] Whereas in Heidegger's earlier texts it is the "truth" of metaphysics (*veritas*) he solicits, in the *Parmenides* it is the "false" (Latin, *falsum*), the reduced counterterm of "truth" understood as the correspondence of mind and thing. But the purpose is the same: the disclosure of the violence that informs this privileged binary opposition.

In the first phase of his inquiry into the relationship between metaphysical perception and imperialism, Heidegger traces the Roman *falsum* back to the Greek *sfallo* — "to overthrow, bring to a downfall, fell, make totter" — which, according to the directive inhering in the stem following the privative prefix, was *not* for the Greeks the counteressence of *a-letheia.* By way of demonstrating that the Romans represented the ontological site as a domain or territory to be mastered, Heidegger suggests that their bypassing of the Greek *pseudos,* which is affiliated with *lathos* (concealment), was intended to put the truth (of being) — and its binary opposite, the false — at the service not simply of certainty but of the *imperium*:

> The realm of essence decisive for the development of the Latin *falsum* is the one of the *imperium* and the "imperial." We will take these words in their strict sense.... On its way through the French language, "commend" ["entrust to protection and sheltering cover"] became *commandieren,* i.e., more precisely, the Latin

> *imperare, im-parare* = to arrange, to take measures, i.e., *prae-cipere,* to occupy in advance, and so to take possession of the occupied territory and to rule it. *Imperium* is the territory [*Gebiet*] founded on commandments [*Gebot*], in which the others are obedient [*botmäsig*]. *Imperium* is the command in the sense of commandment. Command, thus understood, is the basis of the essence of domination, not the consequence of it and certainly not just a way of exercising domination.... In the essential realm of the "command" belongs the Roman "law," *ius.* This word is connected with *jubeo:* to enjoin [*heissen*] by injunction [*Geheiss*], to let something be done by bidding and to determine it through this doing and letting. The command is the essential ground of domination and of *iustum,* as understood in Latin, "to-be-in-the-right" and "to have a right." Accordingly, *iustitia* has a wholly different ground of essence than that of *dike,* which arises from *aletheia.* (P, 40)[96]

In this remarkably resonant passage Heidegger points to the affiliation between the word *prae-cipere,* which possesses the same stem as those words cited above that reveal the epistemological act as a grasping or mastering — and "metaphysics," the perception of being from the end or from above. It is an affiliation that transforms being into a spatial totality, a *territory* to be "occupied in advance." In keeping with this insight, the second phase of Heidegger's analysis invokes the visual metaphorics informing metaphysical inquiry to demonstrate that the false, as a fundamental dimension of commanding, is related to *over*-seeing, or, to suggest the continuity between Heidegger's and Foucault's thought, *sur*-veillance:

> To commanding as the essential ground of domination belongs "being on high" [or "above," *Obensein*]. That is only possible through constant surmounting of others [*Überhohung*], which are thus the inferiors [*Unteren*].
>
> In this surmounting, in turn, there resides the constant ability to oversee [super-vise and dominate, *Übersehen-können*]. We say "to oversee something," which means "to dominate it" [*beherrschen*]. (P, 40)

This oversight of an Absolute Subject, understood in Derrida's terms as a "Transcendental Signifier" or "center elsewhere" that is "beyond the reach of free play," is not, as it is understood in ordinary discourse, a matter of the failure of attention. It is the proper form of vision. Seeing, as it is understood in the ontotheological tradition, is not passive reception of that which the eye perceives. It is an *action,* a praxis: "To this commanding view, which includes surmounting, belongs a constant being-on-the-lookout [*Auf-der-Lauer-liegen*]. That is the form of all action that oversees [dominates from the gaze], but that holds to itself: in Roman, the *actio* of the *actus.*" And it is this reifying oversight, which, in *putting* everything/time it sees in its "*proper*" *place,* is an action, that identifies it essentially with the imperialist project:

> The commanding overseeing is the dominating vision which is expressed in the often cited phrase of Caesar: *veni, vidi, vici* — I came, I *oversaw* [*übersah*], I conquered [Heidegger's emphasis]. Victory is only the effect of the Caesarian gaze that dominates [*Übersehens*] and the seeing whose proper character is *actio.* The essence of the *imperium* resides in the *actus* of constant "action." The imperial *actio* of the constant surmounting of others includes the sense that the others, should they rise to the same or even comparable level of command, will be brought down — in Roman: *fallere* [participle: *falsum*]. This bringing-to-fall [*das Zu-Fall-bringen:* "the occasioning of an ac-cident" (from the Latin, *cadere,* "to fall or perish")] belongs necessarily to the domain of the imperial. (*P,* 40)

Having thus established the literal identity of metaphysical ontology, over-seeing or sur-veillance, and imperial domination of the Other(s), Heidegger goes on in the last and most resonantly contemporary phase of his meditation on the provenance of the Western idea of the false to distinguish a primitive and implicitly uneconomical and inefficient (resistible) imperial practice from a fully articulated ("proper") and highly economical, efficient, and virtually invulnerable imperial practice. It should not be overlooked that this developed form of imperial practice is informed not only by the metaphorics of vision but by the affiliated figure of the circle as well:

> The "bringing-to-fall" can be accomplished in a "direct" assault [*Ansturm*] and an overthrowing [*Niederwerfen:* literally, "throwing down"]. But the other can also be brought down by being outflanked [*durch die Um-gehung*] and "tripped up" from behind. The "bringing-to-fall" is now the way of deceptive circumvention [*Hinter-gehen*].... Considered from the outside, going behind the back is the roundabout and therefore mediate "bringing-to-fall" as opposed to immediate overthrowing [*Niederwerfen*]. Thereby, those who are brought to fall are not annihilated, but are in a certain way raised up again — within the boundaries [*in den Grenzen*] which are staked out by the dominators. (*P,* 40)

In thematizing this imperial practice's textualization (mediation) of power — its appropriation of truth for the purpose of domination — the distinction Heidegger locates in Roman imperialism cannot but recall Foucault's and Said's differentiation between power relations in the *ancien régime* and in the Enlightenment. More specifically, it points proleptically to their disclosure of the complicity of the microcosmic table — the structural model of knowledge production — with the colonization and pacification of the Other:

> This staking out [*Abstecken*] is called in Roman *pango,* whence the word *pax* — peace. This is, imperially thought, the fixed situation of those who have been brought to fall. In truth, the "bringing-to-fall" in the sense of deception [*Hintergehens*] and roundabout action [*Umgehens*] is not the mediate and derived imperial *actio,* but the imperial *actio* proper. It is not in war, but in the *fallere* of deceptive circumvention [*hintergehenden Umgehens*] and its appropriation to the service of domination that the proper and "great" trait of the imperial reveals itself. The battles against the Italian cities and tribes, by means of which Rome secured its territory and expansion, make manifest the unmistakable procedure of roundabout action and encirclement through treaties with tribes lying further out. In the Roman *fallere,* "to bring-to-fall," as a going around, there resides deceiving [*Täuschen*]; the *falsum* is the insidiously deceptive: "the false."
>
> What happens when the Greek *pseudos* is thought in the sense of the Roman *falsum?* The Greek *pseudos* as what dissimulates and thereby also deceives is now no longer experienced and interpreted in terms of concealment [*Verbergen*], but from the basis of deception. The Greek *pseudos*...is *trans*ported [*übergesetzt*] into the imperial Roman domain of the *bringing-to-fall.* (P, 41)

The end of the pursuit of knowledge, according to this developed — postcolonial — form of imperial practice, is to produce *peace,* but this peace will be achieved only by the total colonization and pacification of the Other. Theory (understood as a mode of inquiry that privileges seeing, *theoria*) and practice are coterminous. The *Pax Metaphysica is* the *Pax Romana.*

My intention in invoking Heidegger's ontological genealogy of imperialism has not been to offer an alternative to that of Foucault, Said, and most postcolonial critics who would interrogate imperialism as an economic and/or political practice or as economico-political practice to which cultural texts contribute in a fundamental way. As Heidegger's entanglement with the German National Socialist project testifies, his restricted ontological focus is hardly adequate to the complex actualities of modern imperial practice. My purpose, rather, has been to demonstrate that the contemporary — postcolonial — critique of imperialism is disabled by a significant lack or, perhaps more accurately, by a resonant unthought in its discourse. What I have tried to make explicit by reconstellating Heidegger's de-struction of the metaphysical thinking of the ontotheological tradition (and by thematizing the affiliative system of sedimented tropes inscribed in it) into the context of more "practical" postcolonial critiques of imperialism is that these oppositional discourses, whether Foucauldian or New Historicist or Marxist or nationalist, tend to be blind to (or refuse to take seriously) the enabling degree to which Western imperialism is not simply a practice as such, but a deeply inscribed ideological state of mind produced by a "truth" endemic to a metaphysical ontology. More specifically, they overlook the fact that the modern imperial project is informed by a re-presentational or a "visual" problematic that has its constructed origins in the origins of the very idea of the West. These oppositional discourses, in short, are blinded by their overdetermination of "practice" to the reality that the idea of the West and imperialism are synonymous. To wring a turn on Enrique Dussel's resonant insight into Descartes's "I think; therefore I am," the identity of the collective Western subject is epitomized by the statement: "I think; therefore I conquer."

In other words, my invocation of Heidegger's meditation on the genealogy of the Occidental concept of the true and the false suggests that the contemporary genealogies of imperialism, which have turned to history against the prior hegemony of "theory" in order to undertake their critique, *have not been historical enough*. The disabling consequences of this failure are manifold, but the most serious has to do with the relationship between the West as a state of mind that sees/grasps the truth of being and as a relay of imperial practices this state of mind compels. The preceding interrogation of the ontotheological tradition has shown that the metaphysical orientation it privileges at the outset involves the re-presentation of being. That is to say, it metaphorizes (i.e., reifies) the mutable be-ing of being. More specifically, it reduces being to the microcosmic *figure* of the centered circle supervised by the panoptic (solar) eye, a figure that becomes increasingly complex, especially in the period of the so-called Enlightenment, in its internal structure and its relation to the exterior Other (the periphery). This means that the Western consciousness at large comports itself before "reality," no matter what its site, in such a way that it transforms "it" into a region or territory or domain that it can survey at a glance. As such an optical technology, it perceives and orders — renders intelligible, brings "peace" to — every differential thing and every differential event it encounters according to the taxonomic imperatives of its measuring center. The West represents the end of this ocularcentric operation as the truth that brings the peace of fulfillment, of a completed development. But the destruction of the ontology of the ontotheological tradition discloses that this intelligibility and this peace of the Western dispensation — this *Pax Metaphysica* — are the consequences of a blindness to or a coercion or accommodation of any thing or event that is external to its circumference: is the result, that is, of its colonization of the "false."

As such a transcendental diagramming or structuring machine that renders being intelligible by accommodating "it" to its luminous measuring center, then, the Western consciousness is an imperial consciousness not simply in relation to ontological alterity. It is also an imperial consciousness in relation to what the dominant culture represents as all the "more practical" differential sites that constitute the continuum of a territorialized being: from the individual subject (and the educational institutions that reproduce it) through gender and race relations all the way across to the collective "Third World" subject. To reconstellate Foucault's commentary on Bentham's Panopticon quoted earlier into this more deeply backgrounded historical context, the imperial Western consciousness itself, from its beginning, is "the diagram of a mechanism of power reduced to its ideal form; its functioning, abstracted from any obstacle, resistance or friction, must be represented as a pure architectural and optical system: it is in fact a figure of political technology that may and must be detached from any specific use." As I have shown, this figure is the (gridded) centered circle that is the symbol of Beauty and/or Perfection — and of Domination.

In the modern (post-Enlightenment) era, the *actio* of this polyvalent diagram of knowledge/power takes the form of indirection. Its *actio* is strategically intended not simply to hide the totalizing imperial will to power operative in it, but to encode that power in the semblance of a benign project in behalf of the "improvement" (cultivation, development, maturation) of the "unimproved" (uncultivated, underdeveloped, adolescent) Other. It represents the act of violence as a mediating and disinterested project intended to bring peace to warring factions. The circumference's "center elsewhere," which was always visible and thus vulnerable in its prior historical allotropes, becomes naturalized and invisible in its latest guise. In so doing, it also becomes a far more efficient and irresistible instrument of imperial power, since power in this "enlightened" dispensation is internalized as knowledge in the Other on which it is practiced.

But this change, as I have argued, should not be interpreted, as Foucault inadvertently suggests and, especially, those postcolonial critics who read Foucault literally assume, as a mutation that occurs in the period of the Enlightenment. It should be read, rather, as a historical development of this founding ontological figure of the identity of the West into what Heidegger calls the "imperial *actio* proper." However more complicated, all the enabling aspects of this original figure that I have thematized — the relay of tropes informing it, its structure, its operational dynamics, and so on — are operative in this developed modern allotrope. To read this foundational figure as a mutation, then, is to be blinded to what is essential, however occluded by the new preference for "practice" over "theory," to the poststructuralist de-centering of the panoptic gaze. Such an interpretation precludes perceiving that the privileged figure of knowledge/power — the centered circle — is not the symbol exclusively of a particular practice or group of practices in a historically specific period of this history of the Occident, but that it is the polyvalent "truth" of the Occident at large. Indeed, to interpret this Benthamite figure as the result of a historical break is not simply to succumb to the ruse of disciplinarity, the ruse that the dominant liberal democratic/capitalist culture of the Enlightenment invented to deflect attention away from the indissoluble relay of imperialisms that is enabled by a "truth" that derives from thinking being *meta-ta-physika*. It is also to blind criticism to the essence of the dominant culture's representation of the contemporary, "postcolonial," occasion.

To understand the advent of the panoptic figure as the symptom of a historical break is to occlude the otherwise obvious fact that the dominant culture's representation of the post–Cold War as the "end of history" and the "advent of the New World Order" is also a pronouncement of the fulfillment of the promissory narrative of Occidental history: of the "practical" establishment of the *Pax Metaphysica,* the global "peace" that has been the perennially (self-)promised dream of Occidental philosophy. It is also to occlude our awareness that this pronouncement at the end of the Cold War is precisely the pronouncement of the planetary triumph of Western technological thinking that Heidegger insistently announced as an admonition a generation before its arrival:

> The end of philosophy proves to be the triumph of the manipulable arrangement of a scientific-technological world and the social order proper to this world. The end of philosophy means the beginning of the world civilization based upon Western European thinking.[97]

I am referring to the spatialized, timeless time that Heidegger appropriately called the "age of the world picture" (*die Zeit des Weltbildes*),[98] that global "enframement" (*Ge-stell*) and banalization of being within whose encompassing circumference everything, every person, and every event has been named, differentiated, graded, and reduced to standing and disposable reserve (*Bestand*).[99]

Let me recall at this point the "Hegelian" version of this triumphalist representation of the end of the Cold War as the end of history, focusing on its "qualifying" terms. I am referring to its obligatory "admission" that it is not so much the actually existing political system but the *idea* of liberal capitalist democracy itself that has triumphed globally, that, in other words, Universal History has precipitated as the end of its dialectic process. As Francis Fukuyama, the most prominent proponent of this representation, puts it:

> [T]he fact that there will be setbacks and disappointments in the process of democratization, or that not every market economy will prosper, should not distract us from the larger pattern that is emerging in world history. . . .
>
> What is emerging victorious, in other words, is not so much liberal practice, as the liberal *idea*. That is to say, for a very large part of the world, there is now no ideology with pretensions to universality that is in a position to challenge liberal democracy, and no universal principle of legitimacy other than the sovereignty of the people. . . . *Even non-democrats will have to speak the language of democracy in order to justify their deviation from the single universal standard.*[100]

The "qualification" might be interpreted as disabling this neo-Hegelian argument, but it would be a mistake to do so precipitously. For to read it too hastily as a logical flaw is to minimize the centrality of its content. It would deflect attention from its overdetermination of a (Euro-Americocentric) *way of thinking* that has achieved planetary authority on the basis of the alleged universality of its truth — even its critics will have to use its logic — to the peripheral actual political practices. This displacement, which is precisely dependent on, indeed, determined by, the very globally triumphant truth discourse that Fukuyama is celebrating, is, in fact, what Richard Haass's influential revision of the end-of-history thesis in *The Reluctant Sheriff: The United States after the Cold War* is tacitly intended to achieve by way of accommodating the apparently contradictory post–Gulf War events to the discourse of the New World Order.[101] Indeed, this deflection of attention away from the imperial implications of the announcement of the global hegemony of liberal/democratic/capitalist thinking is precisely what the Clinton administration has achieved in justifying NATO's (i.e., the United States's) practical intervention in Serbia as a humanitarian war against a fascist dictator.

If the genealogy of the triumphalist imperial thinking I have undertaken in this chapter teaches us anything at all, it is to take this telling "qualification" of the end-of-history discourse seriously. Doing so puts one in a position to perceive not only the inordinately persuasive power of this kind of contradiction-defying "technological" thinking, but also its weakness, a weakness that up to now has been obscured by oppositional discourses that contradictorily think resistance in the logic prescribed by the dominant thought of the Enlightenment, the very thought they would oppose. If, indeed, the highly prized Western consciousness as such is a technological optical machine of conquest, if the Western will to know is simultaneously a will to total power, if the Western subject in fact defines itself as "I think; therefore I conquer," and if it is this imperial ocularcentric Western mode of thinking that has gained complete discursive dominion over the planet, then surely in this interregnum the time has come for those who would effectively resist the practical fulfillment of the *Pax Metaphysica* as the *Pax Americana* to return to the site of ontology *as point of departure*. I mean the site of Heidegger's de-struction and of the deconstruction of those like Derrida, Levinas, Lyotard, Lacoue-Labarthe, Nancy, and others whose thought — even their critique of Heidegger's — Heidegger's catalyzed. In thus calling for such a "step back," I am not positing the ontological in *opposition* to the other more "political" sites that, admittedly, these thinkers originally neglected or rarefied. I am suggesting, rather, that the "triumphant" liberal/capitalist democratic culture's overdetermination of the "truth" (the correspondence of mind and thing) in justifying its "triumph" has rendered a rigorous analysis of the ontological ground of this imperial truth an imperative of political resistance against the New World Order, the *Pax Americana*, that would follow this *Pax Metaphysica*. I mean an analysis such as that inaugurated in the post-Vietnam decade by these "postmetaphysical" thinkers, but this time reconstellated into the context of the global imperial politics enabled by metaphysical thinking in its fulfilled technological/instrumental phase.

Far from being identifiable as totalitarian in tendency or simply obsolete, as so many New Historicist, neo-Marxist, cultural, and postcolonial critics have all-too-hastily concluded, these postmetaphysical or postlogocentric or postocularcentric discourses imply recognition not only of the global triumph of the imperialist thought they would oppose. Equally important, they constitute inaugural efforts, precipitated by the very planetary technologization — that is, colonization — of thought, to think thinking *differently* or, rather, *differentially*. They are, that is, *symptomatic* manifestations of the contradictions — the subverting or decolonizing Other — that the "fulfillment" and global "triumph" of metaphysical thought, like the end of philosophy, according to Heidegger's quite different reading of modernity, necessarily precipitate at its limits. They are, to put it in Heidegger's terms, symptomatic gestures of the *Abgeschiedene,* the "ghostly" wandering stranger, who, aware of the global colonization of originative thinking by the total instrumentalization and banalization of "enlightening" thought, has parted from the solar "at-homeland," but whose very spectral nonbeing haunts the "victorious" culture of the "age of the world picture."[102]

As such, these postmetaphysical (or postocularcentric) efforts to think differentially are, not accidentally, analogous to, indeed — however asymmetrically — indissolubly continuous with, the potentially subversive or decolonizing political resistance to the polyvalent Occidental (neo)colonialism inherent in the various constituencies of the human community that have been unhomed by the planetary fulfillment of the "promise" of the original, metaphysically justified imperial project. I am not only referring to the potential resistance of those highly civilized "barbarian" beings on the dark periphery who, according to Dussel, are invisible to and thus deprived of being by the enlightened metaphysical eye of the Apollonian Occident and, as such, have indeed become the menacing spectral "threat" it named them in order to justify its colonization and exploitation of their being:

> Against the classic ontology of the center, from Hegel to Marcuse — to name the most brilliant from Europe and North America — a philosophy of liberation is rising from the periphery, from the oppressed, from the shadow that the light of Being has not been able to illumine. Our thought sets out from non-being, nothingness, otherness, exteriority, the mystery of no-sense. It is, then, a "barbarian" philosophy.[103]

I am also, and above all, referring to the subversive potential inhering in that massive and various population of displaced persons who, in a resonant irony that needs to be marked, have been compelled by the global depredations of Western colonialism to revert — but in a relatively knowing way — to that "barbarian" nomadic condition that "justified" the West's appropriation of their land and its civilizing project. For, like the symptomatic thinking of the antimetaphysical thinkers I have invoked, these de-territorialized postcolonial *others-of-the-Occident,* precisely because of their compelled apartness — their mobile and un*assimilated* status — have no reason to be answerable to the truth and practice of imperialism and thus exist in their "nonbeing" as specters that symptomatically haunt the hegemony of the imperial culture.

It will be the purpose of the final chapter of this book to reconstellate the postmodern antimetaphysical initiative into the context of the politics of the postcolonial occasion. More specifically, it will attempt to think in a prologomenal way the positive possibilities for resistance inhering in the relationship between the spectral ontological contradiction precipitated by the fulfillment (the coming to its end) of the logical economy of Western metaphysics in the age of the world picture and the spectral political contradiction (the postcolonial other-of-the-Occident) precipitated by the fulfillment of the Western imperial project in the "New World Order." This, I will claim, is the final imperative of thinking the *meta* of Western metaphysics.

Chapter 2

Culture and Colonization

The Imperial Imperatives of the Centered Circle

> We need to reflect more thoughtfully on this Roman transformation of Greece. That the Occident still today...thinks the Greek world in a Roman way...is an event touching the most inner center of our historical existence. The political, which as *politikon* arose formerly out of the essence of the Greek *polis,* has come to be understood in the Roman way. Since the time of the *Imperium,* the Greek word "political" has meant something Roman. What is Greek about it is only its sound.
> — MARTIN HEIDEGGER, *Parmenides*

Edward Said's rethinking of colonialism sets out with a deep recognition of the ambivalence of humanist culture's Eurocentrism:

> For the first time in modern history, the whole imposing edifice of humanistic knowledge resting on the classics of European letters, and with it the scholarly discipline inculcated formally into students in Western universities through the forms familiar to us all, represents only a fraction of the real human relationships and interactions now taking place in the world.... New cultures, new societies, and emerging visions of social, political, and aesthetic orders now lay claim to the humanist's attention, with an insistence that cannot long be denied.
>
> But for perfectly understandable reasons they are denied. When our students are taught such things as "the humanities" they are almost always taught that these classic texts embody, express, represent what is best in our, that is, the only, tradition. Moreover they are taught that such fields as the humanities and such subfields as "literature" exist in a relatively neutral political element, that they are to be appreciated and venerated, that they define the limits of what is acceptable, appropriate, and legitimate so far as culture is concerned. In other words, the affiliative order so presented surreptitiously duplicates the closed and tightly knit family structure [filiation] that secures generational hierarchical relationships to one another. Affiliation then becomes in effect a

64

literal form of *re-presentation,* by which what is ours is good, and therefore deserves incorporation and inclusion in our programs of humanistic study, and what is not ours in this ultimately provincial sense is simply left out.[1]

In thus showing that the alleged universality of humanist cultural production is historically specific and, paradoxically, its global reach, provincial, Said achieves an estrangement effect that has given his project of demystification a persuasive force. The numerous books and essays in postcolonial criticism his insight has instigated are testimony to this. In overdetermining Western humanist scholarship and cultural production, however, Said overlooks and renders practically invisible the inextricably related question of the relationship of the specifically colonized Others *all along the continuum of being* from ontological to geopolitical imperialism. It is an oversight that continues to disable the postcolonial criticism indebted to his work. Said implicitly refers to the ontological basis of humanist cultural production (the teaching of the humanities and of literature in particular as if they "exist in a relatively neutral political element") and to the metaphorics of this ontological basis (Center/"periphery"; "incorporation and inclusion"/exclusion; absenting/"*re-presenting*" [darkness and light, visibility and invisibility]; the developed ["affiliative"] and undeveloped seed). But insofar as he does not think this basis, Said characteristically minimizes, if he does not entirely efface, the role that the *anthropologos* and its centering and accommodational power plays in the ideological relay he is intent on thematizing and interrogating. What I want to suggest in thus putting ontological representation back into play in the chain of oppositions that has determined the very identity of the Western (onto-theo-logical) tradition is that the third — the anthropological or humanist — phase, significantly named "the Enlightenment," does not constitute a mutation in this tradition, but is continuous with it. It is the moment of this tradition that bore witness to the emergence of a Eurocentric colonialism whose origin lies in Roman imperialism and that represents itself (as in the case of Hegel) as a civilizing project grounded in the "truth" of being or as a project of "winning the hearts and minds" of extraterritorial Others to the essential principles informing its "way of life."

If, therefore, there is any validity to Said's claim that humanist culture is complicitous with imperialism, it behooves the genealogist of modern imperialism to look deeper into the historical and ideological origins of humanist culture than Said and other postcolonial critics have done in making this claim.[2] A genealogy of imperialism must confront not simply modern liberal humanist culture, but human*ism* as such. More specifically, it must view with suspicion the assumption of virtually all modern theoreticians and practitioners of liberal humanism that its privileged discourse derives from the originative — "disinterested and free" — inquiry of classical Greece. For such a genealogy will show that this sedimented assumption is a construction, in keeping with what Foucault has called the invention of "the repressive hypothesis," inaugurated by the Enlightenment; that it is the result, in Nietzsche's term, of a "monumental history" finally intended to obscure the imperial will to power informing the "free" discursive practices of modern humanism. It will show that this assumption is the result of a long cultural process of "remembering" the West's past that has culminated in the obliteration of its actual origins in imperial Rome: the modern West at large sees its Greek origins through imperial Roman eyes. Such a genealogy must not be understood as an antiquarian project. Nor should it be seen as one remote from the question of imperialism as it is largely debated at the present, "postcolonial," historical conjuncture. It should be understood, rather, as an urgent imperative of the contemporary occasion.[3]

Veritas, Humanism, and Their Imperial Legacy: Toward a Genealogy of Liberal Democracy

According to Heidegger's account of the relationship between Greek and Roman culture — and here he is extending Nietzsche's genealogy of European modernity — Greek thinking was not grounded in the modern ideal of Truth as correspondence between mind and thing; it was instigated by a notion of truth understood as un-concealment (*a-letheia*). The hardening process that eventually rendered being a Total Thing (*Summum Ens*) and rendered thinking a reified and free-floating "philosophy of presence" begins with the Romans' translation of *a-letheia* to *veritas* as *adaequatio intellectus et rei*, a concept of truth that, whether it is understood as "the correspondence of the matter to knowledge" or "the correspondence of knowledge to the matter," has "continually in view a conforming to ... and hence think[s] truth as *correctness* [*Richtigeit*]."[4] It begins, that is, when the Romans began to think the force of temporality on the *basis* or *ground* achieved by originative Greek thinking: "The translation of Greek names into Latin," Heidegger writes, "was in no way the innocent process it is considered to this day. Beneath the seeming and thus faithful translation there is concealed, rather, a *trans*lation of Greek experience into a different way of thinking. *Roman thought* emphatically and insistently *takes over Greek words without a corresponding, equally original experience of what they* *say, without the Greek word. The rootlessness of Western thought be-gins with this translation.*"[5] Henceforth, and increasingly, "the ontology that thus arises is ensnared by the tradition, which allows it to sink to the level of the obvious and becomes mere material for reworking (as it was for Hegel). Greek ontology thus uprooted became a fixed body of doctrine."[6] In other words, the humanist representation of classical Greek inquiry results in a thinking that ab-stracts, as the etymology sug-gests, an essence from material *events* for intellectual manipulation. Put alternatively, it conceptualizes a lived and transitive (phenomenological) experience of *thinking,* a thinking that emerges from being-in-the-world. It becomes a mode of thought informed by a structural model grounded in a fixed Idea of (European) Man — an Anthropology, as it were — and is thus self-confirming: a thinking process legitimized tautologically by an unwittingly tendentious selection of particulars from the prolific and contradictory (differential) disclosures of original Greek thinking. In Althusser's still-to-be-understood term, humanistic representation is in-formed by a "problematic" of "oversight"[7] that both substantiates the preconceived End and makes the Norm and Method of inquiry, educa-tional practice, and cultural production a Measure, a Standard, a Rule that renders invisible — *nonexistent* — anything that would contradict its logic.[8] It is a mode of thought that alienates the truth of being in the process of willfully willing its errant and differential motion to stand (around its center). As such this "Greek" humanistic ideal privileges — canonizes — those cultural products ("monuments") that verify its cir-cular and circularizing interpretive procedure. According to Heidegger's interrogation of the ontotheological tradition, this derivative/calculative mode of thought has become normative since the Enlightenment (also called the Augustan Age or the Neoclassical Age, not incidentally). In his tenacious search for certitude and mastery of the prolific earth, Man at this conjuncture of European history finally reduces (reifies) the tem-porality of being into the *Summum Ens* (Being), the *logos* as *legein* (words) into the *Logos* as *Ratio* (the Word of Reason), and *a-letheia* (un-concealment) into *veritas* (*Adaequatio Intellectus et Rei*). In short, the destruction of the discourse of modern liberal humanist culture dis-closes that the metaphor of the centered circle informing its disinterested or objective mode of inquiry — the metaphor privileged by the humanist tradition as the figure of Beauty and Perfection — is simultaneously the figure of power and domination.

As the Latinate rhetoric that takes over the discourse of truth from the Greek suggests, the "classical" *paideia* of modern humanists since Johann J. Winckelmann is not Greek at all (or is at most late Greek, i.e., Hellenistic). Rather, as Heidegger, following a lead in Nietzsche's quite different representation of classical Greece in *The Birth of Tragedy,*[9] says of the humanist tradition in general, this *paideia* is ultimately Roman insofar as it valorizes a derivative — circular — mode of thinking as primary, a "virtuous" or "manly" model to be imitated against the apparent ("female," as ontology reminds us) "disorder" of lived experience.[10] Heidegger's revision of the received interpretation of this history affects our understanding of modern humanist culture and its relationship to European imperialism in a deep and wide-ranging way. Since his revolutionary revision of Western cultural history has been inexplicably neglected by modern classical scholars and perhaps strategically circumvented by postmodern theorists such as Levinas, Derrida, Lyotard, and Lacoue-Labarthe, the representative passage from "Letter on Humanism" (1947) to which I am referring deserves extended quotation. It is a passage, not incidentally, that extends Heidegger's interrogation of metaphysics in *Being and Time* and "What Is Metaphysics?" and, not least, his enabling distinction between *a-letheia* as unconcealing and *veritas* to include the question of the historical origins of Western culture:

> *Humanitas,* explicitly so called, was first considered and striven for in the age of the Roman Republic. *Homo humanus* was opposed to *homo barbarus. Homo humanus* here means the Romans, who exalted and honored Roman *virtus* through the "embodiment" of the *paideia* [education/culture] taken over from the Greeks. These were the Greeks of the Hellenistic age, whose culture was acquired in the schools of philosophy. It was concerned with *eruditio et institutio in bonas artes* [scholarship and training in good conduct]. *Paideia* thus understood was translated as *humanitas.* The genuine *romanitas* of *homo romanus* consisted in such *humanitas.* We encounter the first humanism in Rome: it therefore remains in essence a specifically Roman phenomenon, which emerges from the encounter of Roman civilization with the culture of late Greek civilization. The so-called Renaissance of the fourteenth and fifteenth centuries in Italy is a *renascentia romanitatis.* Because *romanitas* is what matters, it is concerned with *humanitas* and therefore with Greek *paideia.* But Greek civilization is always seen in its later form and this itself is seen from a Roman point of view.[11]

Heidegger's distinction between the Greek and the Roman *paideia* is, admittedly, highly generalized. But that it demands the attention that modern scholars have not given it is warranted by the ubiquity of the indissoluble relationship between Roman education and empire in Roman texts. The speech given by the *rhetor* Eumenes in the spring of 298 A.D. at the Forum of Autun in France, for example, provides a striking specific instance. It bears historical witness to the way the Republican and imperial Romans appropriated visual education — in this case, knowledge deriving from the recording of geography in the form of a map of the world colonized by the Romans — to *eruditio et institutio in bonas artes* and to the aggrandizement of the empire. In this speech, which constitutes a remarkable parallel with the uses to which Agrippa's famous map of the world in the reign of Emperor Augustus was put by Augustus himself, Eumenes thanks "the Tetrachs... for their benefactions," devotes "the peroration to the restoration of the town's schools," and closes with "the famous description of the map found in their *porticus*":

> And, furthermore, may the youth of our city look under these porticoes, and daily consider all the lands and all the seas, all the towns restored by their goodness, the peoples conquered by their bravery, the nations paralyzed by the terror which they inspire. For there, since you too have seen it, I suppose, while teaching the young people and making them learn more clearly by their eyes those concepts which the ear has some difficulty in apprehending, there is represented the position of all the countries with their names, their extent, the distance which separates them, as well as all the rivers of the world with their sources and their mouths, the points where the coasts curve in to form gulfs and those where the Ocean surrounds and embraces the earth or where his heedless waves make incursions.... And may this map, because it indicates opposing regions, permit them to review the magnificent deeds of our valiant *principes,* making them see, when couriers arrive continuously, covered with sweat and proclaiming victory, the twin rivers of Persia, the parched plains of Libya, the curve of the Rhine's branches, the manifold mouths of the Nile, and inviting them to contemplate each of these countries, whether it be Egypt, recalled from its madness and claimed under your mild rule, Diocletian Augustus, or whether it be at you, invincible Maximian, hurling thunder against the now-cursed Moors, or whether, thanks to your mighty armies, Emperor Constantius, Batavia and Brittany raising their soiled heads above rivers and forests, or at you, Maximian Caesar [Galerius], trampling underfoot the bows and quivers of the Persians. Now indeed we have true pleasure in studying the map of the world, now at last we see that no country is foreign.[12]

What needs to be kept in mind is that the origin of the calculative spatially oriented educational tradition to which Eumenes is appealing is concurrent with the emergence of the idea of the Roman Empire, not with the classical Greeks, for whom map-making was in essence temporally oriented — a matter of "itinerary," rather than global in perspective. As Claude Nicolet observes:

> Graphics and writing are closely linked and often undistinguishable in [Greek] antiquity: an itinerary is sometimes merely a list, a text.... Inversely, if the texts of the [Greek] geographers ... up to and including Strabo and Pliny ... sometimes spread out from the global vision of the *oikoumene* and of the "parts" of the world ..., they often amazingly resembled itineraries. They enumerated the names of areas and of towns often in a topographical order (for example, along coasts or a route).... Their vocabulary itself appears sometimes borrowed from the *periplus,* in its concrete and visual character: "we find," "we reach," "beyond," etc.[13]

Indifferent to Heidegger's genealogy (which tacitly takes over the original meaning of *barbarus:* "one who does not speak Greek"), traditional Western historiography locates the provenance of the distinction between the civilized man and the *barbarus* in classical Greece, deriving its interpretation primarily from Aristotle's identification of the barbarian with the slave — and women — in the *Politics:*

> Among the barbarians [contrary to the Greeks] ... the female and the slave occupy the same position — the reason being that no naturally ruling element exists among them.... This is why our poets have said,
>
>> Meet it is that barbarous peoples should be governed by
>>   the Greeks
>
> — the assumption being that barbarian and slave are by nature one and the same.[14]

But this deeply inscribed assumption about the origins of this cultural distinction needs to be interrogated. For Aristotle's identification of the barbarians, slaves, and women as a relay in a binary opposition to the privileged, civilized "Greeks" reflects a *late* Greek comportment toward these constituencies of "classical" Greek society. The *Politics* betrays an emergent anxiety about the fate of the Greek city-state system in the face of the crisis of the older, looser structure of the *polis,* a crisis precipitated by the Peloponnesian War, by the simultaneous redistribution of the demographics within the city-states (by Aristotle's time slaves constituted an ominous 50 percent of the population of Athens),[15] and by the consequent exposure of Greece to the "threat" of "foreign" invasion. The unequivocal ethnocentrism (and patriarchy) of this passage in Aristotle's *Politics,* in other words, is ideologically motivated by the sociopolitical circumstances of his late Greek historical occasion. As such, his representation is contestable. It cannot be taken, as it has been by traditional literary historians, cultural critics, and political scientists and continues to be by contemporary postcolonial critics, as a definitive representation of the collective or national attitude of the classical Greeks toward these constituencies of Others. For the classical Greeks, the status of barbarians, slaves, and not least women was a profoundly compelling *question.* This, despite its occlusion by traditional classical criticism, is everywhere borne witness to by their writing, not least the tragedies. It therefore bears heavily on the question of the relationship between Greek and Roman culture with which I am concerned.

That the Greeks were in fact deeply conflicted over this relay of others can be suggested by reconstellating Aristotle's free-floating invocation of "our poets" to justify Greek imperialism into the dramatic context from which it derives. The famous passage he quotes is not, as his locution implies it is, an assertion of the generalized poet. They are the words of a character, indeed — and this should make one pause — a *woman,* in a play the meaning of which, as the contested history of its interpretation makes clear, is fraught with ambiguities. They occur in the climactic speech of Iphigenia to her mother, Clytemnestra, in Euripides' *Iphigenia in Aulis* (produced in 405 B.C.). In this speech, which comes shortly after Iphigenia's moving plea that her father, Agamemnon, withdraw his decree that she be sacrificed in behalf of the Greek cause against Troy, she abruptly accedes to her death:

> All Greece turns
> Her eyes to me, to me only, Great Greece
> In her might — for through me is the sailing
> Of the fleet, through me the sack and overthrow
> Of Troy. Because of me, never more will
> Barbarians wrong and ravish Greek women,
> Drag them from happiness and their homes
> In Hellas. The penalty will be paid
> Fully for the shame and seizure of Helen....
> To Greece I give this body of mine.
> Slay it in sacrifice and conquer Troy.
> These things coming to pass, Mother, will be
> A remembrance for you. They will be

> my children, my marriage; through the years
> My good name and my glory. It is
> A right thing that Greeks rule barbarians,
> Not barbarians Greeks.[16]

Throughout this surprising peripeteia, Iphigenia identifies Helen not simply as the innocent victim of Paris's lust and her "abduction" by the Trojan as the potential dark fate of Greek womanhood at large. She also represents Helen's abduction by Paris as symbolic of the future fate of Greece itself at the hands of the "barbaric" Trojan hordes. But prior to this strange turn, the play has rendered Helen not as a victim, but as the willing participant in her removal to Troy. This latter motif presides, for example, in Clytemnestra's agonized confrontation with Agamemnon, after she discovers that it is not the marriage with Achilles but the sacrifice of Iphigenia that has brought the mother and daughter to Aulis. In this confrontation, Clytemnestra attributes Agamemnon's sacrifice of their daughter to his calculative indifference to Helen's infidelity to Menelaus. It is an indifference underscored by her pitting the point of view of the private sphere (the *oikos,* the space allotted by the male *polis* to women) against that of the privileged public sphere, the sphere of manly action — reduced to the marketplace — from which Agamemnon speaks:

> If any man should ask you why, why
> Do you kill your daughter? What answer will
> You make? Or must your words come from my mouth?
> I kill her, you must answer, that Menelaus
> May win Helen back. And so our child,
> In her beauty, you pay as price for a woman
> Of evil. So you buy with our best beloved
> a creature most loathed and hated. (*IA,* 277)

Tellingly, Agamemnon does not respond to Clytemnestra's powerful verbalization of his manly motive, suggesting that her interpretation, in opening up to view and problematizing the binary between the *oikos* and public sphere, has a certain persuasive force. And Clytemnestra's denunciation of Helen is reiterated by the Chorus of women, who, after Iphigenia's appeal to her father to be spared, exclaims:

> O wicked Helen, through you, and through your
> Marriage, this terrible ordeal has come
> To the sons of Atreus and to the child. (*IA,* 281)

Furthermore, Euripides portrays Agamemnon (and Menelaus and the Greek army, as well) in a way that falls far short of instilling confidence in his audience that the Greek cause against the "barbarian" Trojans is a just one. Although he depicts him as a father who truly loves his daughter, he also shows him to be proud, hungry for glory, and politically ambitious. In keeping with these characteristics, the dramatist portrays him, above all, as driven by political expedience. Consonant with Clytemnestra's representation, which she extends in exposing the hold the army has over his thinking (*IA*, 278), Agamemnon is totally committed to maintaining his power in the face of the Achaeans' — the *polis's* — expectation that he will do the goddess Artemis's bidding. Despite his genuine love for his daughter and the pain he expresses over his dilemma, he is inexorably driven by his will to power to think and act calculatively, as one who is fixed beforehand in his purpose and thus who must read the events that precede, however contradictory, in its centralizing light.

This fundamental aspect of Agamemnon's character manifests itself from the beginning (especially in his dialogue with Menelaus) to the end, but it is most tellingly revealed late in the play, after Iphigenia, in her speech of supplication, draws her father's attention to the injustice of his manly decision: the incommensurability between her death and the "marriage" (*gamon*) of Helen and Paris — "Oh, oh — the marriage of Paris and Helen — Why must it touch / My life? Why must Paris be my ruin?" (*IA*, 280).[17] Iphigenia's softened judgment of Helen's adultery, which, in its characteristic generosity, shifts the emphasis of the blame for her impending death from Helen to Paris, is reversed immediately following her speech by the Chorus's unambiguous attribution of the "terrible ordeal" that has befallen "the sons of Atreus and...the child" to Helen's adultery. It is not, however, the Chorus's indictment of Helen to which Agamemnon responds. It is to Iphigenia's moderated version of the circumstances that have precipitated the Greek enterprise, thus resonantly disclosing what his will to power compels him to conceal. It is at this point, as if Iphigenia's formulation of her question has provided him with the opportunity, that Agamemnon for the first time identifies the necessity of his daughter's sacrifice with the national Greek cause:

> O child, a mighty passion seizes
> The Greek soldiers and maddens them to sail
> With utmost speed to that barbarian place
> That they may halt the plunder of marriage beds
> And the rape and seizure of Greek women....
>   Nor am I here
> At Menelaus' will, but Greece lays upon me

> This sacrifice of you beyond all will
> Of mine. We are weak and of no account
> Before this fated thing.
>   O child,
> Greece turns to you, to me, and now,
> As much as in us lies she must be free. (*IA,* 281–82)

By his calculated appropriation of Iphigenia's refocusing of the cause of her impending death to emphasize Paris's brutal abduction over Helen's promiscuity and certain of the Greek army's bigotries vis-à-vis the Trojans, Agamemnon is thus enabled to reduce the multiple ambiguities of this occasion into the certain, polyvalent, and imperial logic of binary oppositions, the "Us" and "them," the "Same" and the "other." It is not simply that he turns what the play has shown to be essentially a calculative egotistical adventure into a self-sacrificial national cause against a race of predators, an imperial aggressor into a free people fighting for their survival against a barbarian horde. Oblivious to the irony that it is a Greek woman whom he is about to slaughter in behalf of saving Greek womanhood from and Greek freedom against the predations of the Trojan barbarians, he also confirms — and highlights — the complicity of this imperialist logic with a patriarchal logic that assumes the indissoluble relationship between the barbarian and the feminine Other.

If at this point in the unfolding of the drama such a reading is only a suggestion, what follows dispels any doubt. I am referring to Iphigenia's otherwise inexplicable peripeteia, previously quoted, in which she repeats Agamemnon's binarist justification for the expedition virtually word for word in the speech from which Aristotle appropriates the line in behalf of his ethnocentric and patriarchal argument: "Because of me, never more will / Barbarians wrong and ravish Greek women, / drag them from happiness and their homes / In Hellas."

This is not to suggest that Iphigenia's sudden peripeteia implies her mindless acknowledgment of the justice (*dike*) of Agamemnon's ethnocentric justification. On the contrary, her reversal suggests that she has intuited Agamemnon's justification all too well. Iphigenia is without a language capable of countering the polyvalent imperial public language Agamemnon and the Greek army speak.[18] She is, in Heidegger's resonant term, the *die Abgeschiedene,* the one who has parted from the homeland, or, in a more current vocabulary, the émigré, the exile, the nomad, precipitated *as* a contradiction by the fulfillment of the imperial logic of the (male) *polis.* As the silenced Other of the patriarchal *polis,* therefore, she must die. But in choosing to die *on her own terms* — to be a "free citizen" — she reverses the center/periphery binary and, by this displacement, decisively delegitimizes the very patriarchal/ethnocentric public discourse that condemns her to death.

This Greek woman, whom the dominant militarist/imperial culture, in its binarist logic, represents as another peripheral Other — the equivalent of the slave and the barbarian — rises up from the shadowy margins, like a specter, to haunt the very light of the "civilized" logic of the center, which is to say, to disclose its slavish barbarism. This, finally, is what she means when, in Agamemnon's language, she "says" that it is right that the "free" should "rule" the barbarians because the latter are "bondsmen and slaves." Her appropriation of her father's words is a disappropriation of their ideological content. In repeating them, she does not endorse the Greek invasion of Troy; she undermines the logic of its justification. Her act, in other words, is a classic example of what Heidegger calls "repetition" (*Wiederholung*): the "circular" mode of inquiry that ends not, as in the metaphysical logic of calculation, in the confirmation of the Same it begins with, but in the difference that haunts that imperial logic. And this reading is enforced by the deus ex machina that Euripides "appends" apparently inexplicably to a dramatic action that has ostensibly arrived at tragic closure.[19] For in saving Iphigenia from the finalizing knife, the goddess Artemis's intervention deconstructs the (political) "peace" that would ensue from the accommodation of Iphigenia to the *logos* of the Greek *polis*. It is as if Euripides were saying that even the goddess herself was persuaded by the justice (*dike*) of Iphigenia's free act.[20]

Far from confirming Aristotle, the essential momentum of the *Iphigenia,* in other words, calls his appropriation of Iphigenia's lines into question. In foregrounding the incommensurability of the Greek *polis*'s representation of the private (female) sphere and the public (male) sphere, Euripides' play, like his *Medea*,[21] is finally intended to interrogate the very imperial binary logic that Aristotle uses the play to affirm. And yet it is Aristotle's strictly binarist interpretation of the relationship between the Greeks and the *barbaroi* that has prevailed in the West. And it continues to hold sway in the "postcolonial" discourses that would expose the Eurocentrism informing the Western discourse of freedom and challenge its planetary hegemony. It even enables postcolonial critics like V. Y. Mudimbe and David Spurr, who, unlike most of them, are aware that Western colonialism has deeper roots in Western history than the obligatory Enlightenment, to overlook the Roman Empire as the determining moment of its origin. In an otherwise compelling analysis of the hegemonic discourse of the West, Spurr writes, for example:

We know that for the ancient Greeks the *barbaros,* or barbarian, was literally one who babbled, who did not speak the language of civilized humanity. The incoherence of barbarians was linked to their lawlessness and homelessness, their incapacity to master the instincts and passions of the body. Finding the lack of this "naturally ruling element" in barbarians, Aristotle in the *Politics* compares them to slaves, and adds, "This is why the poets say 'it is fitting for Greeks to rule barbarians,' the assumption being that barbarian and slave are by nature the same thing." In this early example of colonial discourse, the negation of civilized language as a faculty of the Other leads, through a series of related negations, to a conclusion which upholds the justice of colonial rule.[22]

Heidegger's genealogy of Occidental culture constitutes a radical revision of this traditional interpretation that assumes that the Greeks thought their relationship to the *barbaroi* in terms of the paradigm of the commanding center and the periphery. He is no doubt aware of Aristotle's "colonialist" representation of the barbarian, but it should be remembered that, for him, Greek culture means primarily the period between the pre-Socratics and Plato and Aristotle. Though these post-Socratics may have established the ground for the late Hellenistic and Roman reification of Being's truth as *a-letheia* in behalf of imperial conquest, they were, nevertheless, *engaged by the question of being and did not intend their meditations to be understood as final and essential truths,* which means that the figure of the center and periphery was a contested paradigm.[23]

Contrary to the received interpretation of their attitude toward foreigners, most preclassical Greek poets (Homer and Hesiod, for example) and even later "geographers" up to the Roman colonization of Greece — Herodotus, Hecataeus of Miletus, Dicaearchus, Eudoxos, Patrocles, Eratosthenes, Scylax, Ctesias, and so on — do not, as Aristotle and his poets here do, represent the barbarians in their geographical commentaries ethnocentrically: in such a way as to "uphold the justice of colonial rule."[24] Referring to a certain geometricist Greek representation of the *oikoumene* (the known world; Latin, *orbis terrarum*) as round with Greece at its center and, in turn, Delphi at the center of Greece, Herodotus, for example, says mockingly, "I cannot help laughing at the absurdity of all the map-makers — there are plenty of them — who show Ocean running like a river round a perfectly circular earth [as if it had been done by a compass], with Asia and Europe of the same size."[25]

Herodotus and most of the early Greek "travel writers" were peri-

patetics, not, like the Roman and Romanized historians/geographers —
Pliny, Strabo, and Polybius, for example — sedentary scholars who
imposed in advance their culturally inscribed ethnocentric imperial ideology on the geographical spaces and peoples they were representing.
On this crucial question about Herodotus's representation of the various
peoples within and beyond the *oikoumene,* the postmodern American
poet Charles Olson is more reliable, I submit, than most tradition classical scholars. In "Letter 23" of *The Maximus Poems,* he says, "I would
be a historian as Herodotus was, looking / for oneself for the evidence
of / what is said," an anti-Hegelian passage he glosses elsewhere in the
following way:

> Herodotus may have been conscious of a difference he was making
> when he did add the word "history" [to the synonyms for "what is
> said": *logos* and *muthos*]. The first word of his book — *oi logoi* —
> are "those skilled in the logoi" — not "historians," *'istorin* in him
> appears to mean "finding out for oneself," instead of depending
> on hearsay. The word had already been used by philosophers. But
> while they were looking for truth, Herodotus is looking for the
> evidence.[26]

As such a conscious peripatetic, who mocked preestablished and tele-
ologically oriented representations of the Others of Greece, Herodotus
was enabled to perceive and sympathetically articulate the different cultures — the Egyptian, Scythian, and, in some degree, even the Persian
enemies of Greece, for example — he encountered on the way. That
this "multiculturalism" was indeed the case is borne witness to by the
degree to which Herodotus's sympathetic representations of the "barbarians" were vilified in the period after the Roman colonization of
Greece. As Martin Bernal has shown, Plutarch, in the second century
A.D., condemned Herodotus as being "philobarbarous."[27]

Indeed, Herodotus's and the early Greek geographer's sympathetic
disposition toward those other cultures within the *oikoumene* carried
over in some degree to those beyond it, whether the Ethiopians, Hyper-
boreans, Scythians, Arimaspasians, or *kunocephaloi.* As James Romm
has argued, their comportment toward these cultures was fundamentally ambiguous and dialogic, oscillating between "ethnocentrism and
its inverse," a comportment that went as far as "privileg[ing] the edge
of the earth over the center," thus rendering Greece a periphery to the
"barbarian" center by such an inversion:

> This inverse or negative ethnocentric scheme envisions foreigners
> growing not less but more virtuous in proportion to their distance

from the Greek center, which is here [in Strabo] depicted as the most morally degenerate spot on earth.

In such negative schemes...it is the peoples of the *eschatiai,* in this case the Nomad Scythians, who become most prominent as ethical *paradeigmata* for the Greeks, since they are assumed to differ most widely from the rest of humankind. In other words, just as the Greeks tended to correlate historic time with geographic space,...thereby locating the earliest stratum of cosmic evolution beyond the edges of the earth, so they also envisioned rings of progressively more primitive social development surrounding a Mediterranean hearth; in the furthest ring, at the banks of Ocean, social primitivism becomes absolute. Moreover, whether these outermost tribes...were imagined in terms of "soft" or "hard" versions of primitive life, their extreme distance seemed to the Greeks to confer on them a unique ethical prerogative, licensing them to mock, preach to, or simply ignore the peoples of the interior. In their eyes "normal" human values, as defined by those who imagine themselves at the privileged center, can appear arbitrary and even laughably absurd.[28]

Romm's too schematic representation of this Greek comportment toward the Other beyond the *oikoumene* in terms of the trope of the center/periphery is misleading. It can be interpreted as simply a reversal of the kind that rendered the Native American a "noble savage" to eighteenth- and early nineteenth-century European and American writers such as Chateaubriand and James Fenimore Cooper, thus reinscribing the colonial attitude in a more complex form. However, as Romm goes on to suggest by way of invoking Herodotus's account of the humiliating defeat of the Persian Cambyses at the hands of the Macrobian Ethiopians ("a people whom [he] explicitly locates at the borders of the earth [*es ta eschata ges* (book 3)]), Herodotus's criticism of Persians' culture was based precisely on their adherence to a kind of ethnocentrism that "sees a central position in the world as the basis of cultural superiority": " 'They [the Persians] honor most the peoples nearest to themselves, next the people next to those, and others in proportion to their remoteness, and those dwelling furthest from them they hold in the least honor (book 1).' "[29] In short, Herodotus's (and the early Greek geographers') representation of these people beyond the *oikoumene* is not based on a geometrically figured spatial trope systematically oriented toward knowledge and conquest. It is, rather, fundamentally ambiguous and dialogic or, at least, like the classical Greek representation of women and slaves, a contested paradigm.

   Against the conventional assumption that derives in large part from
Aristotle's interpretation of Euripides in the *Politics,* I want to claim
that the cultural transformation that appropriated the geography of
the *oikoumene* (and its figure of the center and periphery) to the European ethnocentric/imperial project was inaugurated when Augustus,
in his calculated effort to legitimize the principate, *strategically* thematized and *put into administrative practice* the hitherto assumed but
unthought idea that Rome was the center of the world. Given its de-
liberate metropolitan perspective, it was inevitable that this Augustan
imperial initiative should take the form of territorialization: the *systematic* mapping of the known world, the organization of geographical
space, the classification and census-taking of the indigenes, the administration of colonial territories, all in behalf of "Romanizing" the subject
peoples.[30] Not accidentally, as Claude Nicolet has shown, it was in
the work of Vitruvius, the Augustan architect, "completely engaged
in the aedilician program of the new *princeps,* that we find between
24 and 20 B.C., but now linked to the imperial destiny of Rome, the
concept that this [geographic] excellence puts Rome and Italy in the
center of the world that they must dominate." As Vitruvius puts this
ontological/geographical/imperial project:

> Such being nature's arrangement of the universe and all these
> nations being allotted temperaments which are lacking in due
> moderation, the truly perfect territory, situated under the middle of
> the heaven, and having on each side the entire extent of the world
> and its countries, is that which is occupied by the Roman people.
> ... Italy presents grounds of praise for its temperate and unsur-
> passed (climate).... Thus the divine mind has allotted to the city
> of the Roman people an excellent and temperate region in order to
> rule the world.[31]

It was this Vitruvius, tellingly, who became the source of the European architectural ideal of the circular city, whose disciplinary history
extends from his visual projections through St. Augustine in the early
stages of the Christian era, Filarete, Campanella, and Alberti in the
Renaissance, and Vauban in the Neoclassical Age, to the Rousseauan
Claude-Nicholas Ledoux in the Enlightenment and Baron Georges-
Eugène Haussmann in the period of the empire of Napoleon III. I am
referring to the circular city that, according to Michel Foucault, is the
precursor of Jeremy Bentham's Panopticon and the panopticism of the
modern disciplinary society.[32]

   This cultural transformation was accomplished, as Heidegger sur-
mises, with the Roman colonization of Greek thinking. It is not the

peripatetic Herodotus (and his fellow Greek geographers), but a Roman, Pliny the Elder, who represented the Others beyond the *oikoumene* as monstrous in the moral, cultural, and political as well as physical sense. It was, specifically, Pliny's academic *Natural History* that not only established once and for all the representation of the Other beyond the *orbis terrarum* of the ancient Roman-Greco world as the "monstrous" "Plinian Races." As its ideologically compelled identification of Aristotle's biological taxonomic project with Alexander the Great's imperial project (book 8) suggests, it was Pliny's text that also rendered these outlandish races the object of imperial colonization. This Romanization of the erratic Greek representation of the Others beyond the *oikoumene* is precisely the point Romm makes, *if* his concluding reference to "the light of Greek rationalism" is understood as the "light" of Greek thought (*a-letheia*) *mediated* by the imperial Roman eye. In fact, Pliny's emphasis on the "maturation" of Indian studies during the hegemony of Rome, specifically the imperial reign of Augustus, compels such a reading:

> [Pliny's] account of Alexander's sponsorship of Aristotle's biology — for which, it must be said, there is not a shred of historical evidence — marks an important moment in the development of the Indian wonders [*Indika*].... Strabo and others had attempted to clean up the Indographic record using the new, more accurate data collected during Alexander's march. But what Strabo had tried to do by linking Alexander with Patrocles ["a Macedonian general, who served in India under Alexander's successors, Antiochus and Seleucus," and whose record of Alexander's Indian discoveries, now lost, Strabo found trustworthy], Pliny ... accomplishes even more effectively by attaching Alexander to a collaborator of unimpeachable authority: Aristotle himself. In this way he gives new substance to the vision of Alexander's conquest of the East as a scientific crusade, aimed at dispelling the cloud of fable and half-truth [disseminated by the earlier, erratic Greek geographers] which had so long obscured that region. By way of this imagined partnership of the omnipotent commander and omniscient philosopher, a cognitive dominion is established over the East, allowing the light of Greek rationalism to be shone under every rock and into every thicket.[33]

If we recall the imperial uses to which the European Enlightenment put the Linnaean classificatory tables from its colonialist beginnings to Napoleon's Egyptian expedition, we cannot but be struck by the proleptic nature of the Plinian project: the establishment of "a cognitive dominion" over the Orient.

Heidegger's genealogical disclosure of the origins of the humanistic *paideia* in Rome is, as always, determined by his ontological orientation toward the Western philosophical tradition at large. However, his emphasis on the ontological question in his genealogy of modern Western humanism does not preclude implicating the sociopolitical order of modernity in the imperialism of the truth, the pedagogy, and the culture of Roman *humanitas*. Indeed, it might be said that this Roman ontological reduction of be-*ing* of the Greeks to Being — their colonization of the ontological difference, as it were — constitutes the origin and something like the base of the modern sociopolitical superstructure we call imperialism.

Heidegger makes this complicity between knowledge production and Roman imperialism proper remarkably clear in his lectures on the *Parmenides* (winter semester 1942/43). What is assumed, and is thus only implicit in the distinction he draws between Greek *a-letheia* and Roman *veritas* in "Letter on Humanism," becomes explicit in these lectures, however problematic it is rendered by their historically specific context.[34] In the "Letter," Heidegger's destruction of the ontological discourse of modern humanism discloses the complicity of the humanist "center elsewhere" with a super-visory *paideia* designed to inculcate a (manly) Roman *virtus:* to reduce those on whom it is practiced to dependable — docile and useful — citizens of an imperial metropolis. In the *Parmenides,* he extends this genealogical disclosure of the complicity of ontological representation and pedagogy to include the site of the sociopolitical *imperium* proper. In so doing, he anticipates in a remarkable way Michel Foucault's insistent, but overlooked, emphasis on the enabling role played by the Roman (not Greek) model in the production of culture and sociopolitical formations in the Age of the Enlightenment. This was the period, according to Foucault's genealogy of humanist modernity, that bore witness to the transformation in Europe of the figure of the circle as ontological principle of Beauty/Domination into the polyvalent panoptic diagram that gave rise to the practices of the disciplinary society, not least to the production of the interpellated or (subjected) subject: like the "commanding oversight" that enables the imperial *actio* proper,[35] "the Panopticon must not be understood as a dream building: it is the *diagram* of a mechanism of power reduced to *its ideal form.* . . . It is polyvalent in its applications."[36] Foucault subordinates the site of empire on the chain of dominating practices — the reformation of prisoners, the treatment of patients, the instruction of schoolchildren, the confinement of the insane, the supervision of workers, the putting of

beggars and idlers to work — enabled by the polyvalent circular diagram of power. But this does not warrant Edward Said's attribution
to Foucault of a Eurocentrism that blinds him to the role that culture
plays in the domination of the extra-European Other.[37] That Foucault
is aware of the applicability of this diagram to the (Western) imperial
project is suggested by his emphasis on what he calls "the Roman reference" — his insistent thematization of the self-representation of the
Enlightenment, especially its version of knowledge production, in the
image of Rome:

> One should not forget that...the Roman model, at the Enlight-
> enment, played a dual role: in its republican aspect, it was the
> very embodiment of liberty; in its military aspect, it was the ideal
> schema of discipline. The Rome of the eighteenth century and of
> the Revolution was the Rome of the Senate, but it was also that
> of the legion; it was the Rome of the Forum, but it was also that
> of the camps. Up to the [Napoleonic] empire, the Roman reference
> transmitted...the judicial ideal of citizenship and the technique
> of disciplinary methods....In the eighteenth century, 'rank' [under
> the aegis of the Roman model] begins to define the great form of
> distribution of individuals in the educational order.[38]

More specifically, the applicability of Foucault's analysis of the disciplinary discursive practices of modernity to the imperial project is
suggested by his genealogical location of the Enlightenment diagram
of power and its panoptic gaze between the structure of the camps
of the imperial Roman legions and the citizen/legionnaire ideal of the
Napoleonic Empire. Commenting on Guibert's call in 1772 ("*Discours
préliminaire,*" *Essai général de tactique,* 1:xxiii–xxiv) for the nation-
alization of discipline on the model of the Roman legions and his
prediction that the state thus produced "will disprove that vulgar preju-
dice by which we are made to imagine that empires are subjected to an
imperious law of decline and ruin," Foucault observes,

> The Napoleonic regime was not far off and with it the form of
> state that was to survive it and, we must not forget, the founda-
> tions of which were laid not only by jurists, but also by soldiers.
> ...The Roman reference that accompanied this formation cer-
> tainly bears with it this double index: citizens and legionnaires,
> law and manoeuvres.[39]

Heidegger's genealogy of the discourse of modern humanism is not
restricted to his disclosure of the origins of its representation of the

true and the false in Rome and its complicity with imperial power in general. This genealogy also provides an ontological basis for distinguishing between the classical imperial project of the Enlightenment and the imperial project of twentieth-century capitalism. I am referring to the difference between an imperialism whose ontology of truth (as in the case of its appropriation of the Linnaean classificatory system) is subordinated to the overt use of force (military conquest) and a *neo*imperialism whose use of overt force is strategically subordinated to the ontology of truth: is held in reserve, that is, until the imperial truth discourse of hegemony undergoes a crisis of belief, as Gramsci observes about power relations in the modern capitalist state.[40]

Heidegger's genealogy of the modern humanist concept of the false in the *Parmenides,* which locates its provenance in the Roman reification of the originative Greek *pseudos* to the derivative *falsum,* in other words, not only sheds a backward light on the Roman imperialism enabled by the "Plinian" geographic project referred to above. More important, it also prefigures and affords a deeper insight into Foucault's related genealogy of the "repressive hypothesis" of Enlightenment modernity (as well as into Althusser's genealogy of the "interpellated subject" of late capitalism). It is a prefiguration that extends the operational scope of the repressive hypothesis beyond the domestic sociopolitical site, which Foucault more or less overdetermined, to include international space. I am referring to the ruse, fundamental to the representation of power relations in modernity, that, in Foucault's account, was developed in and by the Enlightenment to legitimize its disciplinary project against the *ancien régime*'s overt (visible) — and thus economically wasteful and politically vulnerable — use of power. It is the ruse that represents the relationship between truth and power not as the relay it actually is, but as incommensurable and adversarial practices.

Reconstellated into the context of the ontological distinction Heidegger's genealogy of imperialism discovers in the *Parmenides* lectures, Foucault's "repressive hypothesis" undergoes a resonant sea change. What for Foucault's commentators is essentially a characteristic of the modern political state comes to be seen both as endemic to the metaphysical ontology — and the inscribed panoptics — of the West at large and as applicable to the neoimperialist practices of modern liberal democratic capitalism. It comes to be seen, in other words, as the seductive and powerfully enabling strategy that has transformed the brutally aggressive colonialism of eighteenth- and nineteenth-century Western imperial states — Britain, France, Germany, and the United States — into the "benign" *neo*colonialism of twentieth-century liberal capitalism. To recall Heidegger's distinction between the two forms of imperialism latent in the Roman translation of the Greek *pseudos:*

> The "bringing-to-fall" can be accomplished in a "direct" assault [*Ansturm*] and an overthrowing [*Niederwerfen:* literally, "throwing down"]. But the other can also be brought down by being outflanked [*durch die Um-gehung*] and "tripped up" from behind. The "bringing-to-fall" is now the way of deceptive circumvention [*Hinter-gehen*].... Considered from the outside, going behind the back is a roundabout and therefore mediate "bringing-to-fall" as opposed to immediate overthrowing [*Niederwerfen*]. Thereby, those who are brought to fall are not annihilated, but in a certain way raised up again — within the boundaries [*in den Grenzen*] which are staked out by the dominators. This "staking out" is called in Roman: *pango*, whence the word *pax* — peace.... In truth, the "bringing-to-fall" in the sense of deception [*Hinter-gehens*] and roundabout action [*Umgehens*] is not the mediate and derived imperial *actio,* but the imperial *actio* proper.[41]

It will most likely be objected that Heidegger's genealogy of the imperial *actio* proper — the winning of the "hearts and minds," as it were, of the colonized Other by circumvention — is simply speculative. To counter this objection let me cite two exemplary passages from imperial Roman texts that constitute remarkable practical examples of Heidegger's theoretical analysis of the accommodational strategy of the (neo)imperial project. They are passages the naturalized calculatedness of which — especially their consumerist appeal to the trappings of "civilized" luxury that deflect attention from its real purpose — is repeated throughout the Roman discourse on empire, whether of Romans such as Cicero and Tacitus or colonized Greeks such as Polybius, Strabo, and Diodorus Siculus. The first is from Tacitus's biography of Agricola (the appropriately named Roman governor of Britain, A.D. 77–84) and regards the Roman peace:

> By repressing these evils at once in his first year [Agricola] cast a halo over such days of peace as the carelessness or arrogance of previous governors had made not less dreadful than war.... [By] his clemency, after he had overawed [the Britons] sufficiently, he paraded before them the attractions of peace. By these means many states which up to that time had been independent were induced to give hostages and abandon their hostility: they were then so carefully and skillfully surrounded with Roman garrisons and forts that no newly acquired district ever before passed over to Rome without interference from the neighbors.

The winter which followed was spent in the prosecution of sound measures. In order that a population scattered and uncivilized, and proportionately ready for war, might be habituated by comfort to peace and quiet, he would exhort individuals, assist communities, to erect temples, market-places, houses: he praised the energetic, rebuked the indolent, and the rivalry for his compliments took the place of coercion. Moreover he began to train the sons of the chieftains in a liberal education, and to give preference to the native talents of the Briton as against the trained abilities of the Gaul. As a result, the nation which used to reject the Latin language began to aspire to rhetoric: further, the wearing of our dress became a distinction, and the toga came into fashion, and little by little the Britons went astray into alluring vices: to the promenade, the bath, the well-appointed dinner table. The simple natives gave the name of "culture" to this factor of their slavery. [*Idque apud imperitos humanitas vocabatur, cum pars servitutis esset.*][42]

The second passage is from the *Geography* of the "Greek" Strabo, who, as we have seen, was ideologically committed to Augustus's imperial project. As in Tacitus, it is this Roman consumerist strategy of containment by accommodation (interpellation) that underlies its commentary on the domesticating power of the Roman discourse of hegemony in the westernmost reaches of Iberia:

The qualities of both gentleness and civility [*to imeron ke to politikon*] have come to the Turditanians; and to the Celtic peoples, too, on account of their being neighbors to the Turditanians, as Polybius has said. ... The Turditanians, however, and particularly those that live about the Baetia, have completely changed over to the Roman mode of life, not even remembering their own language any more. And most of them have become Latins, and they have received Romans as colonists, so that they are not far from being all Romans. ... Moreover, all those Iberians ... are called "Togati" [wearers of the toga]. And among these are the Celtiberians, who were once regarded the most brutish [*theriodestatoi*] of all.[43]

The contemporary Western media's characteristic representation of the East German public's response to the spectacle of West German affluence after the dismantling of the Berlin Wall bears exemplary witness to the abiding currency of this "Roman" accommodational strategy: the seductive lure of "civilized" luxury.

Heidegger's dependence on the ontological base for the disclosure of the complicity between the discourse of truth, the practice of education, the production of knowledge (and culture), and the (neo)imperial project of modernity results in a highly rarefied representation that blurs the crucial historical specificity of this relay at the time he gives his *Parmenides* lectures. An adequate genealogical account of the *studium humanitatis* would, therefore, have to modify Heidegger's highly generalized but direct ontological identification of modern liberal humanism with the derivative Roman *paideia*. It would have to understand this Heideggerian nexus in terms of Foucault's historically specific, but indirect, identification of liberal post-Enlightenment cultural production with the disciplinary machinery of the military camp of the Roman (and Napoleonic) imperial legions. My immediate purpose, however, is to demonstrate that the appeal to the "classical" ideal by the founders of modern European and Anglo-American humanist culture, from Winckelmann, Goethe, Schiller, and the Schlegels through the American founding fathers, Emerson, Bancroft, and Parkman to Sainte-Beuve, Arnold, Babbitt, Richards, Leavis, and Trilling, in their respective calls for the formation and reformation of culture, is finally an appeal to the Roman, not Greek, literary model. This "Roman" problematic also determines the visibilities and invisibilities of the cultural discourses of those post–Cold War humanists — conservatives such as William Bennett, Walter Jackson Bate, Lynne Cheney, Allan Bloom, Dinesh D'Souza, Roger Kimball, Francis Fukuyama, and James Ceaser as well as liberals such as E. D. Hirsch, M. H. Abrams, and Gerald Graff, and, in France, Luc Ferry and Alain Renaut — who would recuperate the authority of the humanist *paideia*. It is, therefore, Heidegger's text that, as it were, *brings home* to the imperial center the spectral implications of "postcolonial" criticism.

The *paideia* that modern humanists since Wincklemann would recuperate in the face of recurrent knowledge explosions ("disseminations") that precipitated crises in modern "European" culture is not the errant but originative thinking of the Greeks that was always willing to risk its prejudices in dialogic engagement (*Auseinandersetzung*) with a recalcitrant time and history. It is not the e-ducation (as *a-letheia*) or the e-mergence (*physis*) of a Heraclitus or Parmenides or Anaximander or even of a Plato or Aristotle.[44] Far from reflecting the agonistic élan of Greek dialogic thinking as it claims, the *paideia* — the education and culture — espoused by the modern humanist tradition beginning with Winckelmann represents, rather, a domesticated, Roman, *paideia* (mediated through the eyes of the Romanized Enlightenment). As decorous imitation of a model — "the blueprint" or "organizational chart" (I. A. Richards) or "the core curriculum" (William Bennett) — designed to inculcate *virtus*, "the best self" (Matthew Arnold), "the centripetal measure" (Irving Babbitt), "essential being" (Allan Bloom), this humanist *paideia* is one based on an authorized and authoritative abstraction from and inclusive miniaturization of the original (errant) Greek experience of time/space (being). It is a "structuralist" reduction or "mapping" of temporality that is designed not only to annul the dread (*Angst*) its differential force instigates, but also, by comprehending its errancy, to render it docile and useful. What I am suggesting here about the humanist model — its structuralizing structure, its enabling visual metaphorics, and its polyvalent Eurocentric imperial operation — is perfectly exemplified by Claude Lévi-Strauss's structuralist — one is tempted to say "Roman" — account of the hermeneutic process:

> What is the virtue of reduction either of scale or in the number of properties? It seems to result from a sort of reversal in the process of understanding. To understand a real object in its totality we always tend to work from its parts. The resistance it offers us is overcome by dividing it. Reduction in scale reverses this situation. Being smaller, the object as a whole seems less formidable. By being quantitatively diminished, it seems to us qualitatively simplified. More exactly, this quantitative transposition extends and diversifies our power over a homologue of the thing, and by means of it the latter can be grasped, assessed and apprehended at a glance. A child's doll is no longer an enemy, a rival or even an interlocutor. In it and through it a person is made into a subject. In the case of miniatures, in contrast to what happens when we try to understand an object as a living creature of real dimensions, knowledge of the whole precedes knowledge of the parts. And even if this is an illusion, the point of the procedure is to create or sustain the illusion, which gratifies the intelligence and gives rise to a sense of pleasure which can already be called aesthetic on these grounds alone.[45]

This formulation of the *paideia* envisaged by the modern humanist tradition beginning with the German classicists, it should be noted, also constitutes a remarkably appropriate example of what Heidegger, in the *Parmenides* lectures, calls the "imperial *actio* proper" inaugurated by the Romans. By interpreting the differences time disseminates negatively, this seminal or re-presentational *paideia* thus justifies and instrumentally enables their *circumscription, cultivation,* and *colonization.* I will return later to this resonant relay that adds the (patriarchal) seed to the metaphorics of the panoptic eye and the centered circle informing metaphysical perception. Here, it will suffice to say that, in thus enabling this relay of practices, the representational Roman *paideia* is designed to guide the immature wayward and (potentially "effeminate") ephebe out of the dark wood of adolescent "desire" into the enlightened maturity (and high seriousness) of "civilized" (correct) and "sublimated" conduct and filial duty to a higher (patriarchal) authority, from feminine weakness into manly power (*virtus*), from *homo barbarus* into *homo romanus:* in short, into a productive ethnocentric nationalist. "[I]n the effort to turn his son against Greek culture," we recall from Plutarch's *Lives,* "[Cato the Elder] allowed himself an utterance which was absurdly rash for an old man: he pronounced with all the solemnity of a prophet that if ever the Romans became infected with the literature of Greece, they would lose their empire."[46]

As *eruditio et institutio in bonas artes,* the end envisioned by the modern liberal humanist *paedeia,* like that of the Romans, has been the reproduction of a responsible and reliable citizenry in and for the hegemonic empire.

To put this reciprocal relationship between mature (Roman) citizen and empire in a way that recalls an essential tenet of the cultural discourse of any number of modern humanist theoreticians from Matthew Arnold to T. S. Eliot and Allan Bloom, the self-present and disciplined — manly — subject as citizen thus produced becomes the structural model of the human *polis.* The self-present humanistic *anthropologos* justifies the domestication by cultivation and colonization (making docile and productive) of the peripheral — differential, errant, and female — energies of immature youth (or other undeveloped or unimproved enclaves of the nation). So, too, the self-present Metropolis or Capital justifies the cultivation and colonization — the incorporation, enlightenment, and improvement — of the darkly feminine and barbarous energies of those extraterritorial or peripheral peoples whose unimproved and thus errant state threatens its civilized and fruitful space.

In short, the *paideia* that would reduce the errant ephebe to predictable "Roman" patriot would also transform him into a metropolitan vis-à-vis the provinces. *Eruditio et institutio in bonas artes* would enable him to see the "worldless" world beyond the periphery not simply as a threatening heart of darkness to be enlightened, that is, planted and cultivated, but also as a virginal or concupiscent feminine space to be impregnated by the male seed in anticipation of bringing forth its mature fruit "in the fullness of time," or to be subdued and domesticated by the phallic male will.

The Roman educational imperative implied in the high seriousness of Cato's representative Roman anxiety about his errant son's attraction to Greek literature is indissolubly related to, if not the very ground of, the narrative of the epochally decisive Battle of Actium pictorially inscribed on Aeneas's shield in the *Aeneid* (9.675–928). There, Virgil represents Augustus, the matured Roman progeny of the providentially ordained errand of the seed-bearing Trojan Aeneas, whose destiny was to found Rome in the fullness of time, as the symbol of the West. In resonant binary opposition, he represents the volatile and promiscuous Cleopatra, who has, in unmanning Antony, threatened Rome's divinely ordained mission to establish the Roman peace, as the symbol of the black East. Virgil underscores his ideological motive by willfully imposing Egyptian identity on a Greek woman, thus rendering her the historical counterpart of the Dido of his story. As David Quint has shown, this patriarchal/racist ideology is fundamental not simply to Virgil's enabling epic, but to the Occidental epic tradition it inaugurated:

> If Antony has Cleopatra for his consort, Augustus is accompanied by his *two* fathers: by Apollo and by the star of Caesar; *he* is the true Julian heir. The Western empire is an all-male business, a patriarchy that is marked by the use of "patribus" to describe the senators and thus by the repetition "patribus/patrium" in verses 679–81. Woman is subordinated or, as is generally the case in the *Aeneid,* excluded from power and the process of empire building. This exclusion is evident in the poem's fiction where Creusa disappears and Dido is abandoned, as well as in the historical circumstances that made Augustus the adopted son of Julius Caesar. Woman's place or displacement is therefore in the East, and epic features a series of Oriental heroines whose seductions are potentially more perilous than Eastern arms: Medea, Dido, Angelica, Armida, and Milton's Eve.
>
> The danger for the West is to repeat the fate of Antony, to become Easternized and womanish. Such a fate implies castration and the loss of the sign of fatherhood that shines so brightly above Augustus's head. Woman cannot possess an independent identity, and there is more than a mere convention of Augustan political propaganda in the suppression of Cleopatra's name in this episode. The loss of identity is illustrated by Cleopatra's and Antony's absorption into the lap of the Nile, leaving no trace behind.[47]

It is to this Roman gendering of the space beyond the periphery, this appropriation of the phallic allotrope of the seed, that one must return in order to locate the genealogical origins of that modern Occidental everyday language of empire that, in the name of culture, of improvement, or development, represents the Other's space as virgin, whore, or dangerously unmanning seductress.[48]

It is precisely this "Roman" relay between a (manly) citizenry and (patriarchal/imperial) *polis* grounded in the ontological principle of Identity that, for example, George Orwell, despite a certain characteristic reticence to pursue its implications (especially those pertaining to gender) too far, thematizes in his novel *Burmese Days* (1934), which bitterly denounces British imperialism in Southeast Asia. In this novel, Orwell's protagonist, Flores, the anti-imperialist timber merchant, is warned by his self-deprecating, because "backward," Anglophile Indian friend, Dr. Veraswami, of the danger posed by the cunning libel of a duplicitous native magistrate. In response, Flores self-mockingly reassures his friend of his invulnerability by invoking his imperial credentials:

> "There is another thing of which I would warn you, though you will laugh, I fear. It iss that you yourself should beware of U Po Kyin. Beware of the crocodile! For sure he will strike at you when he knows that you are befriending me."
>
> "All right, doctor, I'll beware of the crocodile. I don't fancy he can do me much harm, though."
>
> "At least he will try. I know him. It will be hiss policy to detach my friends from me. Possibly he would even dare to spread hiss libels about you also."
>
> "About me? Good gracious, no one would believe anything against *me. Civis Romanus sum.* I'm an Englishman — quite above suspicion."[49]

In thus invoking this resonant Latin sentence as sign of his metropolitan identity, Flores is not simply alluding to the myth of the Trojan/Roman origins of imperial Britain, most notably recorded by Geoffrey of Monmouth in the twelfth century.[50] More specifically, he is also retrieving and parodying its more recent invocation in modern British history — one that had decisively inscribed itself in the Victorian consciousness — by Foreign Secretary Lord Palmerston in his famous defense of his gunboat diplomacy against the recalcitrant Greek government in the so-called Don Pacifico affair in 1850, a defense that is as revealing about Victorian British ethnocentrism as Macaulay's famous "Minute" of 1835 on Indian Education. In invoking the panoptic eye that is strategically attentive to the smallest detail, Palmerston's speech constitutes a remarkable witness to the relay between the ocular metaphorics I thematized in chapter 1 as endemic to metaphysical inquiry and the imperial project (not to say, the continuity between imperial Rome and imperial Britain):

> I contend that we have not in our foreign policy done anything to forfeit the confidence of the country.... I therefore fearlessly chal-

lenged the verdict which this House, as representing a political, a commercial, a constitutional country, is to give on the question now brought before it; whether the principles on which the foreign policy of Her Majesty's Government has been conducted, and the sense of duty which has led us to think ourselves bound to afford protection to our fellow subjects abroad, are proper and fitting guides for England; and whether, as the Roman, in days of old, held himself free from indignity, when he could say *Civis Romanus sum;* so also a British subject, in whatever land he may be, shall feel confident that the watchful eye and the strong arm of England will protect him against injustice and wrong.[51]

Earlier in the same conversation between Flores and the ventriloquized Indian doctor, the latter had praised the British Raj and "the great administrators who have made British India what it is: consider Clive, Warren Hastings, Dalhousie, Curzon," and in doing so had invoked their "public school spirit" (*BD*, 38). In carnivalizing Palmerston's famous impersonation of the imperial Roman — in "push[ing] the masquerade to its limit"[52] — Flores is not simply condemning the complicity of the "classical" education of the English public schools with British imperialism. As an earlier parodic reference to the *Pax Britannica* suggests, he is also disclosing the Roman genealogy of the public school system and, above all, "the (British) white man's burden" it inculcates in the future administrators of the British colonies. I am referring to the "benign" narrative in the name of whose truth and by means of its tremendous power to persuade, the Britain Empire, through its Civil Service, was enabled to represent itself as a metropolitan center and thus to pacify and exploit the human and material resources of a much larger and radically different — "underdeveloped," "teeming," and "feminine" — world thousands of miles away from the British Metropolis:

> "My friend, my friend, you are forgetting the Oriental character. How iss it possible to have developed us, with our apathy and superstition? At least you have brought to us law and order. The unswerving British Justice and the Pax Britannica."
> "Pox Britannica, doctor, Pox Britannica is its proper name. And in any case, whom is it pax for?" (*BD*, 41)[53]

Understood in the forgotten or repressed context of this Roman origin, in short, the ontologically grounded principle of disinterested inquiry prized by the modern "liberal" humanist problematic betrays its essential dependence on an *anthropo-logos,* which is simultaneously a center (elsewhere), a panoptic eye, and a seminal seed, and which enables and empowers a relay of circumscription, cultivation, and colonization. This relay is not simply political or even cultural/political, but rather, one that saturates the historical continuum of being extending from the representation of the ecos, through the subject and the subject of culture, to gender and race relations, civil society, political society, and, not least, international society.

This is, in fact, the testimony to which Edward Said bears witness in his brilliant and powerful, but not quite disempowering, readings of the great canonical texts of Western culture. I say "not quite" because Said's resistance to theory precludes his saying it in a way that is entirely adequate to the present post–Cold War occasion. This limitation is epitomized at a crucial conjuncture of his reading of *Heart of Darkness,* where he attempts to discriminate between an older and a newer form of imperialism. In his reading of this seminal text, Said overlooks the Roman reference, which saturates the British discourse of culture throughout the age of imperialism. Instead, he takes Conrad at his word concerning the genealogy of British imperialism, a representation intended to dissociate the "benignly" efficient British imperial project in Africa from the rapacity of Belgium's:

> Recall that Marlow contrasts Roman colonizers with their modern counterparts in an oddly perceptive way, illuminating the special mix of power, ideological energy, and practical attitude characterizing European imperialism. The ancient Romans, he says, were "no colonists; their administration was merely a squeeze and nothing more." Such people conquered and did little else. By contrast, "what saves us is efficiency — the devotion to efficiency," unlike the Romans, who relied on brute force, which is scarcely more than "an accident arising from the weakness of others." ... In his account of his great river journey, Marlow extends the point to mark a distinction between Belgian rapacity and (by implication) British rationality in the conduct of imperialism.
>
> Salvation in this context is an interesting notion. It sets "us" off from the damned, despised Romans and Belgians, whose greed radiates no benefits onto either their consciences or the lands and bodies of their subjects. "We" are saved because first of all we needn't look directly at the results of what we do; we are ringed by and ring ourselves with the practice of efficiency, by which land and people are put to use completely; the territory and its inhabitants are totally incorporated by our rule, which in turn totally incorporates us as we respond efficiently to its exigencies.[54]

Said's formulation of the relationship between culture and imperialism in this passage is decisive. Indeed, its force derives from the
resonant homology with the distinction, on the one hand, between
the truth/power relations of the *ancien régime* and of the Enlightenment (epitomized by the "repressive hypothesis") and, on the other,
between the truth/power relations of the arbitrary, irrational, and inefficient imperialism of Belgium and the disinterested, rational, and efficient
imperialism of Great Britain. Said, that is, recognizes that the imperialism represented by Conrad and Great Britain is not a political/economic
practice separated from and irrelevant to culture (the lived "truth"
of a people), but, rather, an imperialism in which political/economic
practices and culture are integrally and indissolubly related. These, in
Said's words, constitute a "far from accidental convergence" (*CI,* 70).
What, then, is inadequate about Said's otherwise persuasive assessment
of Conrad's cultural/imperial project? It has to do, I suggest, with his
representation of Conrad's salvational and redemptive "idea": the "idea
at the back of [imperial Britain's conquest of the earth], not a sentimental pretense but an idea; and an unselfish belief in the idea — something
you can set up, and bow down before, and offer a sacrifice."[55] Said,
like Foucault, identifies this saving idea with (reformist) rationality and
efficiency, the utilitarian value system that was the legacy in Great Britain of the Enlightenment. And, like Foucault, he is justified in making
this claim. But, unlike Foucault, Said does not quite perceive, or is un-
willing to admit, even as his rhetoric circulates around it, that Conrad's
"idea," like that of British imperial culture at large, is a *meta-physically*
grounded belief system whose truth, however unsentimental (like theology in the nineteenth century), compels an assent that includes devotion
and sacrifice: "Redemption is found in the self-justifying practice of an
idea or mission over time, in a structure that completely encircles and is
revered by you, even though you set up the structure in the first place,
ironically enough, and no longer study it closely because you take it for
granted" (CI, 70).

Said fails to acknowledge that Conrad's idea is an *ontological* category whose genealogy extends back to the origins of the British national
identity, indeed, of the very idea of Europe, in Rome: that this idea
is a historically authorized European anthropo-logy, in which a transcendental "center elsewhere" enables the re-presentation of being as a
universally applicable circle. I mean the polyvalent *figure* invented by
Rome to justify its humanist "truth" (*veritas:* the adequation of mind
and thing); its hierarchized binary logic (*homo romanus* and *homo barbarus,* Civilization and savagery); its humanist "culture" or *paedeia* (the
eruditio et institutio in bonas artes) and the self-confirming humanist

prophecy/fulfillment — or "developmental" — (meta)narrative structure of its literature and historiography; and, as Virgil puts it in the *Aeneid,* his great inaugural and polyvalent European imperial text, its *imperium sine fini.*[56]

This imperial relay — which in Conrad's novels (as well as in the fiction of other major modern British novelists such as Rudyard Kipling, Robert Louis Stevenson, H. Rider Haggard, Evelyn Waugh, Joyce Cary, and even E. M. Forster) extends from the representation of being through language and culture to sociopolitical relations in terms of the naturalized tropes of the center and periphery, light and dark, planted and unplanted earth — pervades the discursive practices of the Rome of the Republic and of the empire. This is suggested by the passage from Tacitus's *Agricola* quoted above. But it is put most succinctly, perhaps, by Strabo (63 B.C.–ca. A.D. 18) in his *Geography.* Though Greek, he was, like Polybius, Diodorus Siculus, and other prominent Greek geographers and historians in the period of Roman hegemony, clearly a colonized Greek who wrote precisely at the moment that precipitated the empire. About the Lusitanian mountain people at the farthest Western reaches of Iberia, for example, Strabo writes:

> The quality of intractability and wildness in these people has not resulted solely from their engaging in warfare, but also from their remoteness; for the trip to their country, whether by sea or by land, is long, and since they are difficult to communicate with, they have lost the instinct of sociability and humanity. They have this feeling of intractability and wildness to a less extent now, however, because of the peace and of the sojourns of the Romans among them. But wherever such sojourns are rarer the people are harder to deal with and more brutish; and if some are so disagreeable merely as the result of the remoteness of their regions, it is likely that those who live in the mountains are still more outlandish.[57]

Rome, as the exemplary nostalgic meditations on its empire of Sir Philip Sidney, Edward Gibbon, Henry James, Henry Adams, Sainte-Beuve, Theodor Haecker, and T. S. Eliot among many other modern "European" intellectuals make clear, was not just another moment in European history that time has obliterated, its "brute force," as Said, quoting Conrad, puts it, scarcely more than "an accident arising from the weakness of others." It was, as Heidegger has persuasively suggested, the founding moment of European history, that is, of its self-representation. Rome, in other words, is not, as both Conrad and Said, his critic, imply, incommensurably opposed to modern British (or European, including American) civilization. It is the "organic" source and end — the *(anthropo)logos* — of the Occident's representation of being/truth and of its essential (imperial) identity. In other words, the modern Occident's use of "brute force" to subdue and incorporate the people of the periphery to the Metropolis is, as it was to the Romans, *intrinsic* to its "humane" logic, to its "unselfish belief in the idea [at the back of its imperial project]." Overt force, according to this "Roman" logic, is always held in reserve. It is only used, as Gramsci and Althusser observed about the internal operations of truth and power in capitalist modernity, when the about-to-be-colonized or the colonized Others refuse their spontaneous consent to the (hegemonic) truth discourse of the colonizer: to the alleged *Pax Romana,* as it were.

Said summarizes his critical commentary on Conrad's distinction between Roman (and Belgian) and British imperialism in the following resonant way:

> Conrad encapsulates two quite different but intimately related aspects of imperialism: the idea that is based on the power to take over territory, an idea utterly clear in its force and unmistakable consequences; and the practice that essentially disguises or obscures this by developing a justificatory regime of self-aggrandizing, self-originating authority interposed between the victim of imperialism and its perpetrator.
>
> We would completely miss the tremendous power of this argument if we were merely to lift it out of *Heart of Darkness,* like a message out of a bottle. Conrad's argument is inscribed right in the very form of narrative as he inherited it and as he practiced it. Without empire, I would go so far as saying, there is no European novel as we know it, and indeed if we study the impulses giving rise to it, we shall see the far from accidental convergence between the patterns of narrative authority constitutive of the novel on the one hand, and, on the other, a complex ideological configuration underlying the tendency to imperialism. (*CI*, 69–70)[58]

Said's recognition of the intimate relatedness of empire and cultural production (the "European novel"), of an imperialism "based on the power to take over territory" (*Niederwerfen,* overthrowing, in Heidegger's term) and an imperialism that interposes "a justificatory regime" of representation between "the victim of imperialism and its perpetrator" (*hintergehenden Umgehens,* deceptive outflanking), is what is most valuable about his genealogical project in its critical phase. But it is partial. It leaves unsaid the (onto)logic that explains the intimate relatedness of these "two quite different" modes of imperialism: the *form,* as it were, of the form of cultural narrative that is essentially complicitous with empire. In so doing, it occludes, as well, the deep, polyvalent ideological structure that identifies the very idea of Europe with imperialism. Without empire, I would add to Said's powerful parabolic conclusion, there is not simply "no European novel as we know it"; there is no "Europe."

The practice of modern imperialism is not limited to the conquest of extraterritorial peoples and their space, nor to the sites of culture as such and geopolitics, as the title of Said's book, if not its rhetoric, implies. The imperial *actio* proper, rather, is, as the unthought anticolonialist tropics of a large and varied number of contemporary disciplinary discourses suggest, a meta-physically or panoptically enabled act of circumscription, cultivation, and colonization, that, however unevenly in any historically specific occasion since the Roman Empire, has traversed the indissoluble lateral continuum of being, from the language of being as such, through the "facts" and discourses of ecos, subject, gender, and culture, to national and international economico-sociopolitics. This is why, despite the now doctrinaire implication by the Right and the Left of Heidegger's thought with Nazi practice virtually accomplished by the "anti-antihumanists" enabled by Victor Farias's *Heidegger et le nazisme,* it is necessary to retrieve his momentous but neglected historical genealogy of modern Occidental civilization and its representation of the ideal of peace.

In thus identifying the history of Europe, especially in its post-Enlightenment phase, as essentially the history of *homo romanus,* I by no means want to suggest that the kind of historically specific distinction Said is making is unnecessary. It is to say, rather, that it is equally important — especially in the present historical conjuncture, when the American imperial project is being represented as the "end of [universal] history" — to thematize the representation of being that has always constituted the condition of possibility for these differential imperialisms.

We see this correlation between theory and practice more clearly in juxtaposing the relay between the figure of the centered circle, culture, and colonization with Conrad's assertion in *Heart of Darkness* that the ancient Romans "were no colonists. . . . They were conquerors, and for that you want only brute force. . . . They grabbed what they could get for the sake of what was to be got."[59] It is no accident of history, I submit, that the words "culture," "cultivate," "acculturation," and so on — the privileged Latinate names that have expressed the ideal end of education for modern humanists from Friedrich Schiller to E. D. Hirsch — are cognates of *colonize* (from the Latin *colonus,* "tiller," "cultivator," "planter," "settler": the French settlers in Algeria were called *colons*) and *colere* ("cultivate," "plant": colonies, for example, were called "plantations" by the English settlers in the New World). Nor is it an accident that the temporal process idealized by both humanist education and the Western colonizing project is informed by a phallic/genetic metaphorics that is indissolubly affiliated with the metaphysically enabled imperial metaphorics of vision (light/darkness) and of the circle (center/periphery). I am referring to the trope that represents the temporal process as the *maturation* of the potential of a planted seed: "improvement" of the "unimproved," "development" of the "un-" or "under-developed." Nor finally is it a historical accident that the receiving or passive object and end — the *agros* (field), as in "agriculture" — of this (phallic) action of the *colon* or *agricola* (farmer) derives from the Greek *agrios* (wild, monstrous, savage), which the Romans, in keeping with their gendered reification of being and their consequent aggressive relationship to the peripheral Other, seem to have substituted for the more original and originative Greek words for these: *georgia* (*gea+ourgos:* earth-working) and *georgos* (one who works the earth).[60]

"Culture," "cultivate," "colony," "colonization": all these enabling names or, in Raymond Williams's phrase, "key words" of Western cultural discourse have their origin not in ancient Greek words referring to such agents and acts of domination, but in the historically epochal Roman appropriation of the Greek word *kyklos* (cycle) or *kirkos* (ring, circle), the spatial image symbolizing "Beauty" and "Perfection." This reductive codification of the "errancy" of originative Greek thinking and the dialogical *paedeia* to which it gave rise (*Auseinandersetzung,* as Heidegger more accurately puts it in his genealogy of "Europe") constitutes the origins of humanism and its cultural and political institutions. It was this circumscription, cultivation, and colonization of the truth understood by the Greeks as always already *a-letheia* that produced *homo humanus* as *homo romanus* and the Roman educational project devoted to *eruditio et institutio in bonas artes* (the *studia humanitatis,* the *litterae humaniores*); legitimated the Roman will to power over the "barbarians" or *agrioi*; and, in some fundamental sense, enabled the idea of the Roman *imperium sine fini* and its *pax*. As the prominence of the (phallic) plow, the circle, and the *Orbis Terrarum* in his discourse suggests, it is this foundational and epochal relay to which Plutarch, the ideologically ambivalent Greek intellectual, is referring in the following passage describing the official representation of the sacred origin of Rome, the imperial Metropolis of the Roman Empire, from his "Life of Romulus":

> Romulus, having buried his brother Remus, together with his two foster-fathers on the Mount Remona, set to building his city; and sent for men of Tuscany, who directed him by sacred usages and written rules in all ceremonies to be observed, as in a religious

rite. First they dug a round trench about that which is now the
Comitium or Court of Assembly, and into it solemnly threw first-
fruits of all things either good by custom or necessary by nature;
lastly, every man taking a small piece of earth of the country from
whence he came, they all threw them promiscuously together. This
trench they called, as they do the heavens, *Mundus:* making which
their centre, they described the city in a circle round it. Then the
founder fitted to a plough a brazen ploughshare, and, yoking together a bull and a cow, drove himself a deep line of furrow round
the bounds; while the business of those that followed after was to
see that whatever earth was thrown up should be turned all inward toward the city; and not to let any clod lie outside. With this
line they described the wall, and called it, by a contraction, Po-
moerium, that is, *postmurum,* after or beside the wall; and where
they designed to make a gate, there they took out the share, carried
the plough over, and left a space, for which reason they consider
the whole wall as holy, except where the gates are, for had they
adjudged them also sacred, they could not, without offense to religion, have given free ingress and egress for the necessaries of
human life, some of which in themselves are unclean.[61]

That Plutarch's verbal description of the mythical founding of Rome
in terms of the polyvalent symbolism of the spatializing eye, the incorporating center and periphery, and the cultivating plowshare is not
simply anecdotal but foundational is borne witness to by its pictorial
repetition in the ubiquitous Roman coins that memorialize this double
"agri-cultural" founding event.

The imperial theory and practice enabled by the Romans' ontologi-
cal/cultural reduction of the originative agonistic thinking of the Greeks
(*a-letheia*) to the discourse of "correctness" (*veritas*) did not expire
with the "fall of Rome." As the ubiquitous and massively enabling,
but relatively unnoticed, "Roman reference" — especially its embodiment in Virgil's story of Aeneas's founding of Rome — in the cultural
discourse of the Occident at large suggests, this polyvalent Roman logic
and its inscribed system of metaphors have informed the great imperial
projects of the historical Occident at large, including modern America,
as a deep structure ever since Roman antiquity.[62] More specifically, the
Roman *translatio imperii et studii* provided the structural model — at
first overtly, but increasingly in a naturalized way — for the various
historical manifestations of the idea of Europe, both religious and secular: the Holy Roman Empire (from Charlemagne in the ninth century
to Napoleon and after); the imperial projects of Portugal, Spain, Eng-

land, France, and the Netherlands in the age of exploration; and those
of France and Great Britain in the nineteenth century and even of Fascist Italy and Nazi Germany in the twentieth.[63] And, more discreetly
and indirectly, but no less fundamentally, this Roman logic, as a certain
reading of Sacvan Bercovitch's ground-breaking *American Jeremiad* will
suggest, has also informed the theory and practice of American colonialism from the Puritans' "errand in the wilderness" (which, like Aeneas's
band, was undertaken from the perspective of a "saving remnant"),
through the founding of the Republic and its westward expansionism
into a "virgin land" in the name of Manifest Destiny, to the invasion
of Vietnam in the name of "the New Frontier," and (after the revision
of its history) to the announcement of the end of history and the New
World Order in the aftermath of the Cold War. However sublimated, it
is this destinarian Roman logic, announced in Virgil's *Aeneid* against a
certain Homeric errancy, that continues to inform the American imperialist project that goes by the name of the *Pax Americana* and is Edward
Said's immediate concern.[64]

Said's unquestioning replication of Conrad's distinction between
Roman rapacity and the "redeeming" British idea suggests, in short,
that his historical discourse on imperialism is finally, like most postcolonial criticism of Western imperialism, not historical enough. This
is the case despite his quite justified effort to reclaim the historical
specificity of history neglected by contemporary theory.

Homo Humanus/Homo Romanus:
The "Roman Reference" in the Discourse
of Modern Humanist Culture

The essential Hellenic stamp is veracity: — Eastern nations drew their
heroes with eight legs, but the Greeks drew them with two; — Egyptians
drew their deities with cats' heads, but the Greeks drew them with men's;
and out of all fallacy, disproportion, and indefiniteness, they were, day by
day, resolvedly withdrawing and exalting themselves into restricted and
demonstrable truth.   — JOHN RUSKIN, *Aratra Pentelici*

Lest this Apollonian tendency freeze all form into Egyptian rigidity, and
in attempting to prescribe its orbit to each particular wave inhibit the
movement of the lake, the Dionysian floodtide periodically destroys all
the circles in which the Appollonian will would confine Hellenism.
                    — FRIEDRICH NIETZSCHE, *The Birth of Tragedy*

Humanists, whether liberal or conservative, will surely object that the
ontological genealogy of the modern *paideia* I have retrieved is remote
from and incommensurable to the texts modern Western scholars have

invariably invoked since the Enlightenment to establish this lineage. In opposition to the Roman source, they would point to the overwhelming privilege that leading Anglo-American and European, especially German, historicist intellectuals have accorded to the "classical" Greek literary canon, often in opposition to the Roman tradition. Against the claim that Rome constituted humanism and the *studia humanitatis* they would invoke Homer's art as the obvious origin of the Western literary tradition and its formal élan as the spirit that has, despite periods of deviation such as the Neoclassical or Augustan, guided its *poiesis* up until the recent past, when the nihilistic "postmodern" impulse usurped its natural authority. It is true, of course, that modern Anglo-American literary humanists (as opposed to French intellectuals like Saint-Beuve) have apotheosized Homer's *Odyssey* as the origin of that tradition. This has been the case especially since the reevaluation of Greek literature in the late decades of the eighteenth and early decades of the nineteenth centuries. I am referring to the tradition of "classical" scholarship and criticism inaugurated in Germany by Winckelmann, Hegel, the Schlegels, Schiller, Goethe, and so on, the tradition that was essentially taken over by the English Romantics and then by the Victorians in the high imperialist period (Matthew Arnold, Thomas Carlyle, John Ruskin, William Ewart Gladstone, Richard Jebb, Benjamin Jowett, and Gilbert Murray, for example), and by antebellum Americans in the expansionist period informed by the principle of Manifest Destiny (writers such as William Cullen Bryant, Ralph Waldo Emerson, Nathaniel Hawthorne, and Walt Whitman and, above all, historians such as George Bancroft and Francis Parkman). Despite the protestation of those who continue to adhere to this post-Enlightenment representation (and that of a certain contemporary strain of cultural "Hebraic" thought that includes Erich Auerbach, Theodor Adorno, Emmanuel Levinas, and Jacques Derrida),[65] it is not Homer's Odysseus who stands at the determining head of this European literary/cultural tradition. Whatever the differing emphases, it is, rather, as it was for Nennius (*Historia Brittonum*), Geoffrey of Monmouth (*History of the Kings of Britain*), and Dante in the Middle Ages and, despite the secularization of the Christian *logos,* for Luíz de Camoëns (*The Lusiad*), Edmund Spencer (*The Faerie Queene,* book 2), Sir Philip Sidney (*Defence of Poetry*), indeed, of virtually all the humanists of the Renaissance, Virgil's dependable and obedient Aeneas, the founding "culture-bringer."[66]

In his *Defence* (ca. 1579), for example, Sidney not only conflates the Greeks and the Romans throughout his text, but also represents them from a disciplinary point of view that is distinctly Roman in its reduction of Greek errancy to abstract instructional value:

Tully taketh much pains, and many times not without poetical helps, to make us know the force love of our country hath in us. Let us but hear old Anchises speaking in the midst of Troy's flames, or see Ulysses in the fullness of all Calypso's delights bewail his absence from barren and beggarly Ithaca.... See whether wisdom and temperance in Ulysses and Diomedes, valour in Achilles, friendship in Nisus and Euryalus [in the *Aeneid*], even to an ignorant man carry not an apparent shining; and, contrarily, the remorse of conscience in Oedipus, the soon repenting pride of Agamemnon, the self-devouring cruelty in his father Atreus, the violence of ambition in the two Theban brothers [Eteocles and Polynices], the sour-sweetness of revenge in Medea:... all virtues, vices, and passions so in their own natural seats laid to the view, that we seem not to hear of them, but clearly to see through them.[67]

Indeed, what Sidney insistently privileges in his defense of poetry, whether Greek or Roman or English, is heroic Roman virtue understood, as Heidegger observes of the German Enlightenment humanists, as a manly model for imitation. And no example of this disciplinary end of poetry in the *Defence* is more visible than Virgil's Aeneas:

But if anything be already said in the defence of sweet poetry, all concurreth to the maintaining the heroical, which is not only a kind, but the best and most accomplished kind of poetry. For as the image of each action stirreth and instructeth the mind, so the lofty image of such worthies most inflameth the mind with desire to be worthy, and informs with counsel how to be worthy. Only let Aeneas be worn in the tablet of your memory, how he governeth himself in the ruin of his country; in the preserving his old father, and carrying away his religious ceremonies [religious relics]; in obeying God's commandment to leave Dido, though not only all passionate kindness, but even the human consideration of virtuous gratefulness, would have craved other of him; how in storms, how in sports, how in war, how in peace, how a fugitive, how victorious, how besieged, how besieging, how to strangers, how to allies, how to enemies, how to his own; lastly, how in his inward self, and how in his outward government — and I think, in a mind not prejudiced with a prejudicating humour, he will be found in excellency fruitful; yea, even as Horace saith, "melius Chrisippo et Crantore" [Better than Chrysippus and Cranto].[68]

The *Aeneid*, for Sidney, as it was for Geoffrey of Monmouth in the twelfth century, is the enabling narrative of the relic- or seed-bearer of the shattered City — the paragon of responsibility (*pietas*) to the "higher" cause, to the logocentric "center elsewhere," as it were. And it is this Roman text, whatever it is named, that modern humanists, in the guise of a saving remnant that would replant the City, have affirmed and continue to privilege as the standard, the model, and the measure for Western Man and for the (imperial) itinerary of narrative construction, personal, cultural, and sociopolitical. To be more accurate, it is the *Odyssey* — and Greek literature in general — *mediated through the corrective eye of Virgil* (and the Patristic and American Puritan biblical exegetes), who, like Strabo and Pliny the Elder in relation to the peripatetic geography of Herodotus, reduced Homer's errant art to a disciplined and rigorously structured Art of Truth in behalf of the legitimation of imperial power.[69]

Let us recall Matthew Arnold's exemplary and inordinately influential appeal to the Greek classics in his effort to promote a "disinterested" pedagogy capable of forming a British culture characterized by Hellenic "sweetness and light" against a recalcitrantly moral individualist Hebraism and, not least, the threat of anarchy posed by the emergence of a working-class consciousness in capitalist Britain in the turbulent last half of the nineteenth century. In his inaugural lecture as professor of poetry at Oxford University, for example, Arnold calls for the reclamation of the legacy of "Classical Greek Literature" — that "mighty agent of deliverance" — from the oblivion to which a rampant Hebraism would relegate it. More specifically, he deliberately displaces Sainte-Beuve's representation of Virgil as the *classic* poet of the Western tradition in favor of what, following the late eighteenth- and early nineteenth-century German classical scholarship on which Arnold everywhere relies, he misleadingly calls the "seriously cheerful" poets of Periclean Athens, especially Sophocles.[70] But his displacement does not reject or even modify the pride of place normally given to the prophecy/fulfillment (teleological) narrative structure of Virgil's *Aeneid*. Nor does it displace — as Nietzsche's retrieval of Dionysus was to do fifteen years later in *The Birth of Tragedy* — the German idealist representation of the classic as the organic embodiment of a "comprehensive," "mature," and "adequate" *vision* that "sees life steadily and sees it whole." Arnold's substitution of Sophocles for Virgil did not displace the idea of the classic as a figure of super-vision capable of making a complex "expansive" age — an age threatened by intellectual and sociopolitical anarchy — intelligible, graspable, and appropriatable.

These inclusivist characteristics are precisely the ones that make Greek literature (and "the small remnant" professing it)[71] the necessary measure for those committed to the "deliverance" (the *pax* of modernity) from the disruptive "incompleteness," that is, partiality, of peripheral or "provincial" perspectives. They are the characteristics that Sainte-Beuve,[72] Theodor Haecker, and T. S. Eliot after him singled out as the defining terms of Virgil's redemptive art: an art, in Eliot's words from another but related context, that could give a "shape and significance to the immense panorama of futility and anarchy which is contemporary history."[73] In this effort to contain the proliferation of novel knowledges within the comprehensive circumference of his vision, Arnold, in fact, repeats the concentering strategy of the anxious imperial Roman geographers in the expansive Age of Augustus who, like their contemporary, Virgil, bore witness to the emergence consciousness of "other" worlds and cultures beyond the *Orbis Terrarum* and the need to centripetalize their centrifugal force. "On the Modern Element in Modern Literature" not simply demonstrates how deeply the ideology of the supervisory center elsewhere is inscribed in Arnold's "disinterested" cultural criticism. It also shows how Virgilian it is in its self-dramatization as "saving remnant" and in its "comprehensive" and civilized resonance: how much, that is, his exemplary humanist truth discourse, despite its nominal appeal to Periclean Greece, is written by the imperial Roman code:

> I propose, in this my first occasion of speaking here [at Oxford], to attempt . . . a general survey of ancient classical literature and history as may afford us the conviction . . . that . . . the literature of ancient Greece is, even for modern times, a mighty agent of intellectual deliverance. . . . The demand [for intellectual deliverance in "such an age as the present"] arises, because our present age has around it a copious and complex past; it arises, because the present age exhibits to the individual man who contemplates it the spectacle of a vast multitude of facts awaiting and inviting his comprehension. The deliverance consists in man's comprehension of this present and past. It begins when our mind begins to enter into possession of the general ideas which are the law of this vast multitude of facts. It is perfect when we have acquired that harmonious *acquiescence of mind which we feel in contemplating a grand spectacle that is intelligible to us; when we have lost that impatient irritation of mind which we feel in presence of an immense, moving, confused, spectacle* which, while it perpetually excites our curiosity, perpetually baffles our comprehension.
>
> This, then, is what distinguished certain epochs in the history of the human race [especially the age of Pericles]: on the one hand, the presence of a significant spectacle to contemplate; on the other hand, the desire to find the true point of view from which to

contemplate this spectacle. He who has found that point of view, he who *adequately comprehends* this spectacle, *has risen to the comprehension of his age.*[74]

Arnold's displacement of Sainte-Beuve's Virgil, like John Ruskin's and that of virtually all the classical scholars of that high humanist (and imperial) period, does not abandon the Jovean "comprehensive" panoptic/imperial eye — "the true point of view from which to contemplate this spectacle" — that oversees Virgil's providential and globally perceived world. Nor, to invoke its artistic and sociopolitical allotropes, does it reject the abiding "center" or "capital" and its "peace." It simply relocates the ontological, cultural, and sociopolitical center/capital from Rome to (a Victorian British version of) Athens. As such a "metropolis," the Arnoldian "classic" retains the authority and power that enable it to annul by cultivating and domesticating the periphery. I mean by this last the "provincialism" or the differential — the "immature" and "barbarous" — "doing as one likes" that, as for Sainte-Beuve (as well as the proponents of the British Empire), constitutes the most ominous contemporary threat to the law and order (the "peace") of literature, literary history, the *studium humanitatis,* culture, and the (imperial) State.[75]

For all Matthew Arnold's appeal to the "sweetness and light" of the "seriously cheerful" and "adequate" Greeks he admired, his Greeks, like the Greeks of the German idealists from whose representation he is borrowing, are not Greek at all.[76] The "culture" that "sees life steadily and sees it whole" and the "academy" — the custodian of the Cultural Memory — that preserves and transmits its monuments had their origins less in the agonistic dialogics of the Greek Sophocles' profoundly ambivalent *Antigone* than in the certainties of the Roman Cicero's *De Officiis*[77] or Horace's "Dulce et decorum est."[78] And, as Arnold's valorization of the *Pax Metaphysica,* that "harmonious acquiescence of mind which we feel in contemplating a grand spectacle that is intelligible to us," suggests, the pedagogical and cultural end of culture and the academy was finally to inscribe a blind ethnocentric code that, like the imaginary of the English public school system, reduced the energies of youth to the sacrificial — and brutal — service of the State's global imperial project: its *Pax Britannica.* This, at the domestic site, is the genealogical testimony of the victims — English and non-English alike — of such a classical culture, those who were living and dying in the great war that brought the epistemic economy driving the imperial Victorian era to its contradictory and cataclysmic end. It is the testimony, for example, of Wilfred Owen's "Dulce et Decorum Est," his great poem from the trenches of France bitterly protesting a hegemonic discourse that would render young Englishmen *Civiti Romani* (and English women their maiden spurs). It should not be overlooked, as it always has been, that Owen addresses this poem, filled not with "sweetness and light," but with bitterness and gall, to the contemporary institutional custodians of the "classical" legacy bequeathed to them by Dr. Thomas Arnold, the "Roman" headmaster of Rugby and founder of the English public school system, and his school-inspector son. I mean those cultivated and mature subjects who, like Arnold's "Greeks," had found "the true point of view from which to contemplate" and "adequately comprehend" "this ['significant'] spectacle" and, in so doing, had "risen to the comprehension of [their] age":

> If in some smothering dreams you too could pace
> Behind the wagon that we flung him in,
> And watch the white eyes writhing in his face,
> His hanging face, like a devil's sick of sin;
> If you could hear, at every jolt, the blood
> Come gargling from the froth-corrupted lungs,
> Obscene as cancer, bitter as the cud
> Of vile, incurable sores on innocent tongues, —
> My friend, you would not tell with such high zest
> To children ardent for some desperate glory,
> The old Lie: Dulce et decorum est
> Pro patria mori.[79]

This contradiction in the logic of *homo humanus* is not simply the testimony of the internal victims of the imperial ("Roman") imaginary — the "truth" of "the white man's burden" — and the *Pax Britannica*. It is also, whatever the degree of consciousness, the emergent testimony of the advanced spokespersons of the Metropolis's extraterritorial victims, the "unimproved" peoples of the periphery, as it were. I am referring to all those consciously colonial and postcolonial voices — Frantz Fanon, C. L. R. James, Amilcar Cabral, George Antoninus, Ranajit Guha, S. H. Alatas, Salman Rushdie, Gabriel García Márquez, Ngugi wa Thiongo, Chinua Achebe, and so on — whom Edward Said invokes to implicate the structure of Western narrative with the violence of the Metropolis, and to articulate a theory of de-colonization that is also committed to liberation. This last is the theory of a postcolonialism dedicated to the imperatives that "the center (capital city, official culture, appointed leader) must be deconstructed and demystified" and that "a new system of *mobile* relationships must replace the hierarchies inherited from imperialism" (*CI*, 274–75; my emphasis). This insight into the ontologically grounded power of the imperial strategy of blaming the (immature) victim is articulated by Achebe, for example, near the end of his great novel ironically titled, after Yeats, *Things Fall Apart* (1959):

> "If we should try to drive out the white men in Umuofia we should find it easy. There are only two of them. But what of our own people who are following their way and have been given power? They would go to Umuru and bring the soldiers, and we would be like Abame." He paused for a long time and then said: "I told you on my last visit to Mbanta how they hanged Aneto."
>
> "What has happened to that piece of land in dispute?" asked Okonkwo.
>
> "The white man's court has decided that it should belong to Nnama's family, who had given much money to the white man's messengers and interpreter."
>
> "Does the white man understand our custom about land?"
>
> "How can he when he does not even speak our tongue? But he says that our customs are bad; and our own brothers who have taken up his religion also say that our customs are bad. How do you think we can fight when our own brothers have turned against us? The white man is very clever. He came quietly and peaceably with his religion. We were amused at his foolishness and allowed him to stay. Now he has won our brothers, and our clan can no longer act like one. He had put a knife on the things that held us together and we have fallen apart."[80]

Achebe's critical insight into the essential deviousness of the imperial project — what Heidegger characterizes as the "deceptive outflanking" (*hintergehenden Umgehens*) that constitutes the "imperial *actio* proper" — does not originate from the experience of overt imperial oppression. As Said emphatically remarks of the postcolonial intellectuals he distinguishes from those who reinscribe the very imperial ontology of identity that victimized them, it also derives from this colonized Nigerian's inextricable relationship to the colonizing Metropolis. It issues from his knowledge both of the source of the power of the discourse and practice of the Metropolis and of what in it is most vulnerable: its representation of the truth of being. In focusing on what he called this "voyage in" of the postcolonial writers with whom he identifies, Said writes: "No longer does the logos dwell exclusively, as it were, in London and Paris. No longer does history run unilaterally, as Hegel believed, from east to west, or from south to north, becoming more sophisticated and developed, less primitive and backward as it goes. Instead, the weapons of criticism have become part of the historical legacy of empire" (*CI*, 244–45). This is an accurate representation of the critical perspective that guides the "especially interesting hybrid work" of the postcolonial writers he singles out, including Achebe. I would simply add, in order to underline the ontological site that too often disappears in Said's discourse, that Hegel's synecdochic representation of History as moving inexorably from the East to the West — as a westering, as it were — is incorporated in the very name of the cultural space Hegel's ("developmental") History is intended to produce and legitimize ontologically: the "Occident" (from *occidere:* "to go down," "to set"; a correlate of *cadere:* "to fall," "to perish," "to die"; and *occasus:* "setting of the sun"). This Latin name had its origin in Rome's inaugural identification of its culture as different from and, insofar as it had subdued the body in the name of the mind and its truth, superior to the "Orient" (from *oriens,* participle of *oriri:* "rising," "rising sun," "east") in order to justify ontologically its conquest and exploitation of the other's space.

T. S. Eliot, the *Aeneid,* and the Idea of an "Imperial" Europe

> We are all, so far as we inherit the civilization of Europe, still citizens of the Roman Empire, and time has not yet proved Virgil wrong when he wrote *nec tempora pono: imperium sine fine dedi.*
> — T. S. ELIOT, "Virgil and the Christian World"

This Roman provenance of "Europe" and of the modern humanist representation of Greece is an integral aspect of what Martin Heidegger has called the forgetting of *die Seinsfrage* (the question of being, which engaged Greek thinking in an originative way) in the historical process of the Occident's fulfillment of its (onto)logic. Thus the "Roman" origin of the metaphorical chain (circle/culture/colony — its optic and agricultural allotropes) and of the relay of binary oppositions its logical economy enabled (Identity/difference, Citizen/deviant, Manliness/femininity, Civilization/barbarism [provincialism, immaturity, partiality, eccentricity, irrationality, and so on]) is, in varying degrees, only implicit in the "Greek" discourse of Winckelmann and the German classical scholars of the Romantic period. It is also only implicit in the "Hellenism" of Matthew Arnold (and the legion of Anglo-American humanists — I. A. Richards, F. R. Leavis, Lionel Trilling, for example — his cultural discourse has influenced). It is, however, openly thematized in the "mature" cultural criticism of T. S. Eliot, one clearly of this company, as his appropriation of the same enabling constellation of terms informing their cultural discourse suggests, however critical he was of the geographical, ideological, and temporal "provincialism" of their anthropological humanism.[81] He was, it should be recalled, the leading intellectual of the Anglo-American academy and beyond in the post–World War II period.

In pursuing the logical economy of this historically constituted humanist tradition, Eliot came to know all too well that it was not the culturally immature and erratic Greeks who could, once retrieved, redeem a disintegrating modern Europe by "giving a shape and a significance to the immense panorama of futility and anarchy which is contemporary history." Nor was it the Europeans of the Renaissance, whose Roman heritage had become Romance: a vulgarized and provincial Romanism or, to put it another way, a cultural discourse that had forgotten Virgil's figural significance by accommodating it to a secular and localized teleology and empire. It was, rather, *homo romanus* — the "classical" (Augustan) Roman — that would save Europe from dissolution. This Roman "world," as Eliot puts it, following the German critic Theodor Haecker,[82] was preferable to the "*world* of Homer" because it was "a more civilized world of dignity, reason and order" ("VCW," 124), because, to reinvoke the third category in the chain of metaphors privileged by the humanist discourse of culture, it was characterized by greater "maturity of mind":

> Maturity of mind: this needs history, and the consciousness of history. Consciousness of history cannot be fully awake, except where there is other history than the history of the poet's own people: we need this in order to see our own place in history. There must be the knowledge of the history of at least one other highly civilized people, and of a people whose civilization is sufficiently cognate to have influenced and entered into our own. This is the consciousness which the Romans had, and which the Greeks, however much more highly we may estimate their achievement, ... could not possess.[83]

According to the cultural logic of Eliot's (Christian) humanism, the model for such an adult world, then, was not the Greek Homer, but, as it was for Dante in the Middle Ages and Sidney in the Renaissance, the Roman Virgil. For Virgil possessed a (meta-physical) historical consciousness and thus a "maturity of mind" that (like Arnold's "adequate" Sophocles) enabled him to transcend the provincial, that is, ec-centric, immediacy of his itinerant Greek predecessor. More precisely, Virgil's "consciousness of history" made possible his perception of the presence of the *logos* informing the differences that temporality disseminates, which Homer, in his errant immediacy, only glimpsed through a glass darkly: prefiguratively, as it were. It enabled him to achieve a distanced "centrality," a centeredness elsewhere, beyond the reach of the free play of criticism ("WC," 69). Virgil's historical consciousness, that is, made it possible for him to *see* the historical continuity not simply between his regular Roman art and the irregularity of Homer's, but also between the stable Roman civilization his art represents and the volatile and erratic Greek civilization that Homer's represents (an oversight, not incidentally, that, despite Eliot's condescending — and aporetic — "praise," rendered the Greek's an imperfect art and world, and thus subject to correction [i.e., colonization]. Unlike his Greek precursor's uncultivated or "immature" or "provincial" historical sense, Virgil's mature and disciplined historical consciousness enabled a *"comprehensiveness"* ("WC," 67) of vision. It enabled him to see through the contingencies of historical existence into the *"universality"* of being ("WC," 67) — into the Presence that relates their differential tenor — and thus to properly locate the "accidents" of the historically specific occasion within the accommodational circumference of the comprehensive symbolic order. Thus informed, as the eccentric Homer was not, by the enabling specular (dialectic) principle of metaphysics — that Identity is the condition for the possibility of difference — Virgil's historical consciousness, in short, empowered him not simply "to see life steadily and see it whole," as in the case of Arnold's Sophocles, but to *foresee* and *comprehend,* indeed, to prophesy the future and end of art and (European) history:

> From the beginning, Virgil, like his contemporaries and immediate predecessors, was constantly adapting and using the discoveries, traditions and inventions of Greek poetry.... It is this development of one literature, or one civilization, in relation to another, which gives a peculiar significance to the subject of Virgil's epic. In Homer, the conflict between the Greeks and the Trojans is hardly larger in scope than a feud between one Greek city-state and a coalition of other city-states: behind the story of Aeneas is the consciousness of a more radical distinction, a distinction which is at the same time a statement of *relatedness* between two great cultures and finally, of their reconciliation under an all-embracing destiny. ("WC," 61–62)

Behind Eliot's version of Western literary history, in which Virgil is privileged over Homer, yet is continuous with him, lies a very old but still operative theoretical/exegetical apparatus, as Eliot's invocation of the Christian adventist representation of Virgil's fourth *Eclogue* in "Virgil and the Christian World" makes clear:

> The mystery of the poem does not seem to have attracted any particular attention until the Christian Fathers got hold of it. The

> Virgin, the Golden Age, the Great Year, the parallel with the
> prophecies of Isaiah; the child *cara deum suboles* — 'dear offspring
> of the gods, great scion of Jupiter' — could only be the Christ
> himself, whose coming was foreseen by Virgil in the year 40 B.C.
> Lactantius and St. Augustine believed this; so did the entire me-
> diaeval Church and Dante; and even perhaps, in his own fashion,
> Victor Hugo. . . .
>
> He looks both ways; he makes a liaison between the old world
> and the new, and of his peculiar position we may take the fourth
> *Eclogue* as a symbol. ("VCW," 122–23)

I am referring to the "imperial" typological method of interpretation
of the Patristic Fathers (modified by the great Victorian Anglican theologians behind whom lies the Hegelian dialectic). As Erich Auerbach
has definitively put it, this was the strategy of biblical exegesis that
understood history in terms of the promise/fulfillment structure: the
"real" events prior to the coming of the *theo-logos* into history (the
Incarnation) as a prefiguration of that (real) coming:

> Figural interpretation establishes a connection between two events
> or persons, the first of which signifies not only itself but also the
> second, while the second encompasses or fulfills the first. The two
> poles of the figure are separate in time, but both being real events
> or figures, are within time, within the stream of historical life.
> Only the understanding of the two persons or events is a spiritual
> act, but this spiritual act deals with concrete events whether past,
> present, or future and not with concepts or abstractions; these are
> quite secondary, since promise and fulfillment are real historical
> events, which have either happened in the incarnation of the Word,
> or will happen with the second coming.[84]

Eliot Christianizes the promise/fulfillment structure of Virgil's imperial art, an accommodation that overtly continues a fundamental
medieval Christian exegetical operation culminating in Dante's *Divine
Comedy*. But this should not obscure the continuity between Eliot's
providential understanding of the distinction between Homer's and Virgil's poetry, which is at the same time a "relatedness between two great
cultures," and Matthew Arnold's secular and less theoretical distinction
between his representation of the Homeric and the Periclean cultures,
which is also a relatedness:

> Aeschylus and Sophocles represent an age as interesting as them-
> selves; the names, indeed, in their dramas are the names of the
> old heroic world, from which they were far separated; but these

names are taken, because the use of them permits to the poet that free and ideal treatment of his characters which the highest tragedy demands; and into these figures of the old world is poured all the fullness of life and of thought which the new world has accumulated. This new world in its maturity of reason resembles our own; and the advantages over Homer in their greater significance for us, which Aeschylus and Sophocles gain by belonging to this new world, more than compensate for their poetic inferiority to him.[85]

Both Eliot's and Arnold's representations of their respective histories — and the ideas of culture they espouse — have their condition of possibility in the ontological priority of Identity over difference, the *principle,* to repeat, of metaphysical principles.

To put this ontological binary opposition in terms of the relay of tropes to which it gives rise and that subsumes Eliot's polyvalent genetic model, the paradigm of the cultivated adult world he prefers is not "blind Homer"; it is the *visionary* (panoptic) Virgil: the seer (*vates*) and his commanding gaze. For the prophecy/fulfillment structure in the *Aeneid* and the fourth *Eclogue* — and the global "comprehensiveness" and "maturity" ("WC," 55, 67) of the logocentric ontology enabling it — not only rectified Homer's "adolescent" (uncultivated, eccentric, provincial) errancy.[86] By apotheosizing the idea of historical destiny (*fatum*) in terms of the prefigurative model, its logical economy also justified the *Pax Romana,* which is to say, the inexorable dynastic claims of the Augustan Metropolis on the scattered, errant, and "unimproved" worlds beyond the periphery of *Orbis Terrarum.* There is no doubt that Eliot, like the legion of imperial-minded European predecessors going back to Geoffrey of Monmouth and beyond, is thinking of the following lines from the *Aeneid* when he refers to this multiply colonized world — and its "peace" — as the destined "*imperium romanum*" ("VCW," 126, 129):

Fear no more, Cytherea. Take comfort, for your people's
Destiny is unaltered; you shall behold the promised
City walls of Lavinium, and exalt great-hearted Aeneas
Even to the starry skies. I have not changed my mind.
I say now — for I know these cares constantly gnaw you —
And show you further into the secret book of fate:
Aeneas, mightily warring in Italy, shall crush
Proud tribes, to establish city walls and a way of life, . . .
Thus it is written. An age shall come, as the years glide by,
When the children of Troy shall enslave the children of
    Agamemnon,

Of Diomed and Achilles, and rule in conquered Argos.
From the fair seed of Troy there shall be born a Caesar—
Julius, his name derived from great Iulus—whose empire
Shall reach to the ocean's limits, whose fame shall end in the stars.
He shall hold the East in fee; one day, cares ended, you shall
Receive him into heaven; him also will mortals pray to.
Then shall the age of violence be mellowing into peace:
Venerable Faith, and then Home, with Romulus and Remus,
Shall make the laws; the grim, steel-welded gates of War
Be locked; and within, on a heap of armaments, a hundred
Brazen knots tying his hands behind him, shall sit
Growling and bloody-mouthed the godless spirit of Discord.
So Jupiter spoke, and sent Mercury down from on high
To see that the land and the new-built towers of Carthage offered
Asylum to the Trojans, for otherwise might queen Dido,
Blind to destiny, turn them away.[87]

By introducing the specifically Roman ontological idea of destiny—
the fulfilled promise of the Trojan seed — inscribed in the *"Sacred
Book"* of historical time ("the secret book of fate"), Virgil justified
the extension of ontological imperialism (the incorporative logic of the
"classical measure" ["WC," 69] to include sociopolitical imperial rule:
the right, indeed, the obligation, ordained by Destiny, of the Metropolis
to territorialize, to impose its civilized measure on, the immature extraterritorial provinces. He thus both accounted for the Greek past and
also prefigured the "future of the Western World" ("VCW," 128). Virgil's monumental text established the *imperium romanum* and its *Pax
Romana* as the type or, more accurately, *figura* of the historically actualized providential design of the Christian *Logos:* the Holy Roman Empire
and its fruit-bearing "peace" promised in "the fullness of time." To the
rhetorical question, "What then does this destiny which no Homeric
hero shares with Aeneas mean?" Eliot replies: "For Virgil's conscious
mind, and for his contemporary readers, it means the *imperium romanum.* This in itself, as Virgil saw it, was worthy justification of
history.... You must remember that the Roman Empire was transformed
into the Holy Roman Empire. What Virgil proposes to his contempo-
raries was the highest ideal even for an unholy Roman Empire, for any
merely temporal empire" ("VCW," 129). And in a reiteration of the
truth of Virgil's comprehensive and mature vision, Eliot adds: "We're
all, so far as we inherit the civilization of Europe, still citizens of the
Roman Empire, and time has not yet proved Virgil wrong when he
wrote *nec tempora pono: imperium sine fine dedi*" ("VCW," 129–30).

Despite the religious reference, this declaration cannot but recall Lord Palmerston's arrogant *"Civis Romanus sum,"* indeed, the British imperial tradition that goes all the way back to Geoffrey of Monmouth's founding myth of the Trojan Brut. It is not simply the Roman dominion over the *Orbis Terrarum* that Virgil's comprehensive and mature historical consciousness justified; it was also and even more fundamentally, the Roman dominion over temporal being itself.

In thus discovering or prefiguring the principle of Presence informing the history of Europe, Virgil's logocentric narrative, in other words, also acquired the "centrality of the unique classic," the status of "criterion," of "classical standard," of "classical measure" for Europe as a whole, especially "in its progressive mutilation and disfigurement [in the modern period], the organism out of which any greater world harmony must develop" ("WC," 69). The passage from Eliot to which I am referring warrants quoting at length not only for the precision and comprehensiveness of its testimony to my entire argument about the provenance of the idea of Europe and polyvalent imperial operations of the ontological center and the periphery in this history, but for its proleptic announcement, at the beginning, of the end of the Cold War and the "end of history":

> And of all the great poets of Greece and Rome, I think that it is to Virgil that we owe the most for our standard of the classic.... His comprehensiveness, his peculiar kind of comprehensiveness, is due to the unique position in our history of the Roman Empire and the Latin language: a position which may be said to conform to its *destiny.* This sense of destiny comes to consciousness in the *Aeneid.* Aeneas is himself, from first to last, a "man in fate," a man who is neither an adventurer nor a schemer, neither a vagabond nor a careerist [note the allusions to Homer's Odysseus that colonize his errancy], a man fulfilling his destiny, not under compulsion or arbitrary decree, and certainly from no stimulus to glory, but by surrendering his will to a higher power behind the gods who would thwart or direct him. He would have preferred to stop in Troy, but he becomes an exile, and something greater and more significant than any exile; he is exiled for a purpose greater than he can know, but which he recognizes; and he is not, in a human sense, a happy or successful man. But he is the symbol of Rome; and, as Aeneas is to Rome, so is ancient Rome to Europe. Thus Virgil acquires the centrality of the unique classic; he is at the centre of European civilization, in a position which no other poet can share or usurp. The Roman Empire and the Latin language were not any empire

and any language, but an empire and a language with a unique destiny in relation to ourselves; and the poet in whom that Empire and that language came to consciousness and expression is a poet of unique destiny. ("WC," 67–68)

As the figure of centeredness, Virgil becomes for Eliot what Sophocles was for Matthew Arnold and his German predecessors: the unsurpassable because definitive *model* — the principle of Identity — to be imitated by contemporary poets, transmitted by contemporary literary critics and teachers, and studied in the schools by contemporary students. For such a Virgilian paradigm is alone capable of enabling the future resolution of a prodigal, eccentric, and errant European narrative of literary, cultural, and, above all, political history gone increasingly astray since the abandonment of the Virgilian "imperial" measure in favor of provincial temporal standards. These are the errant standards that not only confound "the contingent with the essential, the ephemeral with the permanent," but also, in privileging the immediate and novel present over the past, make the world impious: "the property solely of the living, a property in which the dead hold no share" ("WC," 69).

To shift the horizonal focus to another site on the continuum of Eliot's imperial discourse, Virgil's Roman text, as classic, becomes the authoritative model for the recuperation of the "common heritage of thought and feeling" ("WC," 70) and of the historical peace shattered by the intellectual warfare precipitated by the "dissociation of sensibility" — and the proliferation of knowledges it occasioned — in the seventeenth century. Despite his disclaimer that "my concern here is only the corrective to provincialism in literature" ("WC," 69), what is ultimately at stake in Eliot's postwar effort to recuperate Virgil as "the centre of European civilization" is, as in the case of Arnold's effort to recuperate a Victorian version of the Sophoclean standard in the face of the emergence of a working-class consciousness, a global political agenda. Instigated in part by the precarious triumph of "European" culture over a resurgent pagan barbarism in World War II, Eliot, that is, envisioned a traditional Eurocentric and hierarchical world order (and a *Pax Europa*) that would be culturally strong enough to withstand the seductions of the alternative — planned and managed — world order proffered to both Western and postcolonial peoples by a Western Marxism attuned to Soviet communism in the struggle for hegemony of the world shattered by the war:

> So [on the analogy of Aeneas's destined itinerary] we may think of Roman literature: at first sight, a literature of limited scope, with a poor muster of great names, yet universal as no other literature

can be; a literature unconsciously sacrificing, in compliance to its destiny in Europe, the opulence and variety of later tongues, to produce, for us, the classic. It is sufficient that this standard should have been established once and for all; the task does not have to be done again. But the maintenance of the standard is the price of our freedom, the defence of freedom against chaos. We may remind ourselves of this obligation, by our annual observance of piety towards the great ghost who guided Dante's pilgrimage: who, as it was his function to lead Dante towards a vision he could never himself enjoy, led Europe towards the Christian culture which he could never himself know. ("VCW," 70)

The parallel with the humanist cultural project of Matthew Arnold (and of the German classicists who precede him, above all, Hegel, and the Anglo-American humanists who follow him) should now be quite obvious. The names — authors, artistic perspectives, texts, origins — are different, but the beginning, agency, and end are fundamentally the same: the *Logos* (or "Center Elsewhere" or "Seed"), Culture, and the Hegemony of Occidental Civilization (Colonization). To put this relay of tropes in terms of the discourse of the post-Enlightenment, they are the Comprehensive (Panoptic) Eye, the Disciplinary Circumscription of the Other, and the Containment, Pacification, and Utilization of its erratic force. The Occidental *paideia* — its representation of the truth of being, of culture, of human being's comportment toward the world — has been essentially and deeply complicitous with the imperial project ever since Rome colonized the Greeks' originative and errant way of thinking being. The European ideal of the *Pax Romana,* in short, is identical with the domination and pacification of the Other.

Modernism and the "Advent" of the "New World Order"

At this point, however, it might be legitimately asked: What, beyond a historicist interest, justifies invoking the modernist T. S. Eliot in a context ostensibly devoted to discovering the genealogy of a triumphant liberal democratic discourse that represents the contemporary post–Cold War occasion apocalyptically as the end of history or, what is the same thing, as a global peace? After all, it is likely to be claimed, especially by postcolonial critics, his project to recuperate "the still point in the turning world" has been decisively deposited as a monument in and of a now-questioned literary tradition, if not superseded by the postmodern cultural turn, the decentering of the European center and the emergence of the postcolonial condition. The answer to such a question becomes resonantly manifest if, as there is every reason to do, we recall and attend, with Derrida, to the synecdochic *adventist* rhetoric informing the triumphalist Western discourse precipitated by the end of the Cold War. I am referring, for example, to Francis Fukuyama's "Hegelian" announcement in the wake of the collapse of Soviet communism of the apocalyptic "good news" that a profound twentieth-century Western pessimism — exemplified by the paralyzing aporetic logic of contemporary destructive or deconstructive theory — has, by way of a *too shortsighted* view of world history, "distracted" us from seeing/hearing. This "distractive" history includes the massive slaughter of two world wars; the proliferation and use of high-technological fire power, including the atomic bomb, to obliterate indiscriminately entire populations; the violence bordering on genocide of the Vietnam War; a globalized market system that has impoverished the peoples of the Third World; and so on. In a feeble, if not dishonest, effort to disarm the objection that his reading of this terrible history of the modern world as "coherent," "intelligible," and "directional" is speculative in a Hegelian or Marxist sense, Fukuyama writes:

> We in the West have become thoroughly pessimistic with regard to the possibility of overall progress in democratic institutions. This profound pessimism is not accidental, but born of the truly terrible political events of the first half of the twentieth century.... Indeed, we have become so accustomed by now to expect that the future will contain bad news with respect to the health and security of decent, liberal, democratic political practices that we have problems recognizing good news when it comes.
>
> And yet, good new has come.... [L]iberal democracy remains the only coherent political aspiration that spans different regions and cultures around the globe. In addition, liberal principles in economics — the "free market" — have spread, and have succeeded in producing unprecedented levels of material prosperity, both in industrially developed countries and in countries that had been, at the close of World War II, part of the impoverished Third World.[88]

At the end of World War II, which bore witness to the defeat of a "pagan" totalitarianism by a coalition of traditional Christian/European nations (and, it had to be grudgingly acknowledged, a communist society), and the outset of the Cold War, T. S. Eliot, the leading man of letters in all of Europe and America, insistently reiterated his adventist Virgilian global vision of a future *Pax Europa* under the aegis of the Christian humanist *Logos* — his announcement of "gospel," as it were. In the name of an adventist view of history, he called for a coalition of the dominant "European" religious, cultural, economic, and political orders for the purpose of securing the *Pax Europa* against the "specter" of another totalitarianism of the Left.[89] Fifty years later, in the aftermath of the "revolutions" in Eastern and Central Europe and the collapse of the Soviet Union, Fukuyama, the student of Allan Bloom and Leo Strauss[90] and one of the intellectual deputies of the neoconservative coalition in American politics, following in the spirit of a certain Hegel, announces the end of the Cold War as the end of history and the advent of the New World Order presided over by liberal capitalist democracy — the *Pax Americana,* as it were. And, implicitly, he appeals to a coalition of "European" religious, cultural, and political orders to lend their combined force to the obliteration, once and for all, of the "specter" of a now-dead communism. This historical configuration — "Eliot" and his adventist rhetoric/"Fukuyama" and his evangelist rhetoric — is no accident. Despite the exaggerated claims of its protagonists, it is symptomatic and thus has explanatory value for a traditional economico-political opposition that has been disarmed by the triumphant hegemonic discourse of the post–Cold War West. It is not simply that this configuration of apocalyptic cultural voices bears witness to the continuity of a Cold War "cultural" discourse with a post–Cold War "political" discourse. In the explicitness of his correlation of the fulfilled imperial logic of metaphysics and its teleological/providential history with the advent of the Truth, of Universal Peace, and of a New World Order, Eliot's adventist "Virgilian" discourse exposes to view the imperial ideology and its "Roman" origin that are implicit in Fukuyama's analogous "Hegelian" (liberal democratic) discourse. It also makes manifest the resonantly telling "holy" nature of the alliance that the post–Cold War discourse would effect against any resurgence of that which it has pronounced dead. As Jacques Derrida has observed, however, this insistent call for such an alliance betrays the anxiety (of a ghostly "visitation") that lies behind the end-of-history discourse's inordinate protestation of the triumph of "Occidental" — Roman — civilization over the "specter" of Marxism.

Derrida's interrogation of this end-of-history discourse takes its point of departure precisely from Fukuyama's annunciation of "the teleo-eschatological good news."[91] In keeping with his strategic retrieval of the ontological site in his "political" critique of the "triumphant" liberal democratic capitalist alliance, Derrida identifies this "evangelistic figure" (*SM,* 57) with a certain "Hegelian neo-evangelism" that a "certain Marx" — the Marx, I would add, most closely affiliated with a "certain Heidegger"—went all out to expose and condemn. He invokes the first moments of *The Communist Manifesto* to show how this post–Cold War adventist discourse repeats that of the "Holy Alliance" of Old Europe—"Pope and Czar, Metternich and Guizot, French Radicals and German police spies"[92]—that converged at the "end of" the revolutionary period of 1848 to convoke in order to revoke (to "conjure away" [*SM*, 99], "to exorcise" [*SM*, 100]) the "specter of communism":

> Who could deny it? If an alliance is in the process of being formed against communism [in the post–Cold War era], an alliance of the old or the new Europe, it remains a holy alliance. The paternal figure of the Holy Father the Pope, who is then cited by Marx, still figures today in a prominent place in this alliance, in the person of a Polish bishop who boasts...that he was not for nothing in the collapse of communist totalitarianism in Europe and in the advent of a Europe that from now on will be what it should always have been according to him, a Christian Europe. As in the Holy Alliance of the nineteenth century, Russia could once again take part. That is why we insisted [earlier] on the neo-evangelism—the Hegelian neo-evangelism—of a rhetoric of the "Fukuyama" type. It was a Hegelian neo-evangelism that Marx denounced with great verve and vehemence in the Stirnian theory of ghosts. (*SM*, 100)

Derrida does not here cite the "Holy Alliance" against "the specter of communism" in the process of formation during and after World War II of which the adventist rhetoric of the T. S. Eliot type is representative. And though he refers to Marx's recognition in *The Eighteenth Brumaire* of the role that the Roman model played not only in the bourgeois French Revolution but also, however parodically, in the establishment of the empire of Louis Bonaparte, he does not think this reference in terms of the (end of) history he is confronting. Derrida's brilliant insight into the continuity between the Europe of 1848 and the West of 1991 is enabling. But he misses the opportunity afforded by his strategic ontological reading of the apocalyptic text of the New World Order to thematize the Roman origin of the new Holy Alliance as this origin is handed down in modernity from Hegel through Matthew Arnold to T. S. Eliot and his Anglo-American ephebes. In so doing, he also misses the chance to mark the essential imperialism of Fukuyama's Universal History and of the "peace" of the New World Order this history's fulfillment precipitates. Not least, he misses the opportunity to thematize the important role that the modernist Spirit plays in the formation of this conservative post–Cold War Holy Alliance.

This omission in Derrida's text, however, should not too hastily be read as a failure of insight (though Derrida has an ideological stake in repressing or discounting the "Roman reference," which is to say, in eliding Greece and Rome).[93] It should be understood, rather, as an unthought of a deconstructive logic that overdetermines the complicity of the end-of-history discourse with a nineteenth-century European "Hegelian neo-evangelism." The historical ideological nexus to which I am referring is, in fact, implicit in Derrida's affirmation of the viability, indeed, the absolute necessity, of "a certain Marx" in confronting the dominant discourse and practice of the post–Cold War era. This is resonantly, if marginally and incompletely, suggested by Fredric Jameson in his brilliant — and, given his long-standing suspicion of deconstruction, in many ways inaugural — commentary on Derrida's *Specters of Marx*. Recalling and emphasizing the topicality of Derrida's enabling and abiding ideological distinction between Spirit (*Geist*) and spirit (or specter) in the face of "the more defuse rehearsal of such polemics" in America, Jameson writes:

> Although Derrida fails to touch on the central figure in the Anglo-American reinvention of a politics of modernism qua spirituality — in the critical as well as the poetic work of T. S. Eliot — he does significantly single out Matthew Arnold [in *De l'esprit*]. Above all, however, he insistently returns to that French-language figure who was in so many ways the continental equivalent of T. S. Eliot (and whom the latter's cultural strategies, above all in his journal *The Criterion*, aimed at enveloping and as it were introjecting), namely Paul Valéry. Significantly a major portion of Derrida's polemic warning about the cultural politics of the new Europe — *Autre Cap* [1991] — is given over to Valéry's symptomatic thoughts about the menaced and vulnerable Europe of the period between the two Wars, for it is precisely this high-cultural European strategy, the Roman-Christian European tradition very precisely from Virgil to Valéry, that the current ideological operation of patching together a new pan-European cultural ideological synthesis around figures like Milan Kundera (in the place of T. S. Eliot) has imitated and reproduced as in Marx's famous prediction (the second time as farce!). One is tempted to characterize these very openly high-cultural moves as a replay of "*Encounter* culture" (as their most successful attempt to play off a NATO high culture, now led by the US, against an anti-cultural bolshevism), but one today possibly available for intervention in a hegemonic struggle *against* the US competitor.[94]

In disclosing the affiliation between the Eurocentric cultural discourses of Arnold, Eliot, and Valéry and their collective relationship
to the idea of "the Roman-Christian European tradition very precisely
from Virgil to Valéry," this augmentation of Derrida's history constitutes
a valuable contribution to the thematization of the constitutive parts
of the new Holy Alliance. But as the point of departure and the conclusion of his elaboration suggest, Jameson's "European" perspective,
in consonance with Derrida's, minimizes "America" in his analysis of
the formation of the New World Order that would forget Marx. However justified the judgment that American debates have trivialized the
issues Derrida thinks, we need to add, on the analogy of the *Pax Romana,* that the New World Order its intellectual deputies are celebrating
as the end of history is, in fact, the *Pax Americana.* It is an apocalyptic "peace" that is not simply a matter of global economic or political
or even cultural domination and pacification of the Other. It is also —
this needs to be underscored — a matter of the planetary "triumph" of
an "American" way of *thinking* whose origins go back to the Puritan
"errand in the wilderness" and, as Cotton Mather's *Magnalia Christi
Americana* suggests, its appropriation of Virgil's imperial story about
Aeneas's seed-bearing mission to plant the New Troy.

The new Holy Alliance Fukuyama speaks for in his anxious effort to
obliterate the specter of Marx, that is, includes not simply the "Polish
bishop" and the Europeans to whom he appeals, but, however contradictorily, the religious (fundamentalist) Right in America and all those secular
(neo)conservative and "liberal" democratic constituencies — the presidency, the Congress, the Supreme Court, the culture industry, the schools,
and so on — that have gone far to align themselves with its global ideological goals. This genealogy of the "peace" promised by the apocalyptic
annunciation of the "end of history" should not be overlooked, as it has
been, by those postcolonial critics who would resist the New World Order.

Recapitulation: Imperialism and
the "Repressive Hypothesis"

> We must cease once and for all to describe the effects of power in neg-
> ative terms: it "excludes," it "represses," it "censors," it "abstracts," it
> "masks," it "conceals." In fact, power produces; it produces reality; it
> produces domains of objects and rituals of truth. The individual and the
> knowledge that may be gained of him belong to this production.
> — MICHEL FOUCAULT, *Discipline and Punish*

In this chapter, I have shown that the origins of humanism (and liberal
democracy) lie in the Romans' reconstitution of the Greek understand-

ing of truth as *a-letheia* to *veritas* — an originative to a derivative (circular) mode of thought that reduces the play of difference to the hierarchical binary opposition between the True and the false. I have also shown that, through and simultaneous with this reconstitution, the agonistic Greek *paideia* was reduced to a "manly" *eruditio et institutio in bonas artes* designed to produce *cives Romani* for the sake of the Roman *imperium sine fini*. Seen in the demystified terms of this genealogy, the cultural ideal proffered by the discourse of humanism comes to be recognized as something quite different from its representation by the traditional humanist custodians of culture. Far from being a "mighty agency of deliverance," it comes to be understood as a powerful polyvalent instrument of "cultivation" that is intended to inscribe in the "young" a relay of colonialisms extending from the ecos, through consciousness, language, gender, and race, to civil, political, and international society. This genealogical insight into the Roman origins of imperialism and of the relation between culture or civilization and barbarism is what I would add to the conclusion Walter Benjamin (and so many other materialist or worldly critics of culture he has influenced) draws in "brushing [European] history against the grain," namely, that "there is no document of Civilization which is not at the same time a document of barbarism. And just as such a document is not free from barbarism, barbarism taints also the manner in which it was transmitted from one owner to another."[95]

What needs to be foregrounded in the context of Edward Said's representative invocation of Conrad's ideological distinction between a "Roman" and a "British" imperialism — an imperialism of "brute force" as opposed to an imperialism justified by the idea of productive efficiency — is that "Rome" and "Great Britain" are, however different, not historically and ideologically incommensurable. As the continuity I have remarked between Arnold's representative German/Greek and Eliot's Virgilian definition of "Culture" suggests, "Rome" and its *Pax Romana* informs "Great Britain" and its *Pax Britannica*. As Guibert, Napoleon, Palmerston, Haecker, Eliot, and Orwell observed, we Westerners are still, despite the cataclysmic "fall of the Roman Empire," citizens of Rome, *cives Romani*. Violence — and its efficient administration — against the Other is intrinsic to the "redeeming idea," to the (onto)logic of a "developed," benignly productive efficiency, which, according to Heidegger, is the "imperial *actio* proper." It is simply held strategically in reserve until a discursive explosion de-centers the hegemonic center/metropolis, that is to say, until the differential victims of the redemptive idea refuse their spontaneous consent to its (accommodational) truth. To put this strategy in terms of the unthought metaphorics that pervade the discourse of contemporary cultural criticism, violence is kept invisible by the liberal democratic State until the circle represented as the truth of being comes to be seen by a segment of those it would accommodate as the polyvalent (Occidental) figure of imperial domination. As I will show in the next chapter, we bear witness to this contradictory violence in the American government's reaction, both at home and abroad, to the discursive explosion precipitated by its imperial intervention in Vietnam.

Edward Said's magisterial demonstration of the complicity of culture with imperialism — and, not least, his critique of certain postcolonial discourses that reinscribe the very principle of identity that victimized the constituencies they represent — constitutes a major contribution to the contemporary oppositional cultural discourses committed to resisting the repressive power of the dominant liberal capitalism that masks its global imperial will to power in the benign image of freedom. Indeed, given the political impotence of the studied localism of the New Historicists and the odd parochialism — the blindness to the imperial reach of Occidental culture — of even some of our best cultural critics such as Raymond Williams, Said's globalization of cultural criticism is enabling. But insofar as the ontology informing the indissoluble relay between culture and imperialism is left unthought, his contribution remains symptomatic and thus finally inadequate to the conditions of global power relations precipitated by the end of the Cold War. Moreover, Said's failure or refusal to think the ontological ground that the dominant culture has overdetermined in its representation of the post–Cold War occasion — not least, its practically enabling metaphorics — rarefies his critique of the identity politics of the various colonial and postcolonial discourses with which he would identify his thought. Equally important, it renders his provocative positive recommendation for "an emergent non-coercive culture" (*CI*, 334) inadequate to the volatile demographics of the world precipitated by the ravages of imperialism. I am referring to his call for a "nomadic" or "migrant" discourse and practice that would refuse to answer to the imperative of answerability that sustains and aggrandizes the power of the imperial Metropolis.

In Said's conclusion to *Culture and Imperialism*, the biographical motif that accompanies his diagnosis and critique of European imperialism coalesces with the latter as the lyrical cry of a "damaged life":

> [It] is no exaggeration to say that liberation as an intellectual mission, born in the resistance and opposition to the confinements and ravages of imperialism, has now shifted from the

settled, established, and domesticated dynamics of culture to its unhoused, decentered, and exilic energies, energies whose incarnation today is the migrant, and whose consciousness is that of the intellectual and artist in exile, the political figure between domains, between forms, between homes, and between languages. From this perspective then all things are indeed counter, original, spare, strange. From this perspective also, one can see "the complete consort dancing together" contrapuntally [a quotation from T. S. Eliot's *Four Quartets*]. And while it would be the rankest Panglossian dishonesty to say that the bravura performances of the intellectual exile and the miseries of the displaced person or refugee are the same, it is possible...to regard the intellectual as first distilling then articulating the predicaments that disfigure modernity — mass deportation, imprisonment, population transfer, collective dispossession, and forced immigrations. (*CI*, 332–33)

This is a profound and moving insight not simply into the savage legacy of European civilization, but into the contradictions in the logical economy of the imperialist *actio* proper, which is to say, into its essential vulnerability. And I will return by way of reconstellating this suggestive insight in the last chapter of this book. Here I want to ask: Is it, as it stands, profound in the sense of soliciting the secret cause of imperialism's continuing ravages and moving in the sense of activating an authentically productive engagement with it? Doesn't the unthought invocation of a variation of T. S. Eliot's metaphysical "still point in the turning world" compel us to add that to precipitate a sea change in the mournful lyric cry, it is necessary to theorize — to *think* — this desperate, yet positively potential, condition? It is, at any rate, because of my uneasiness in the face of the first question that I have felt the need to retrieve the historical and ontological origins of European imperialism, to put Rome and the equation of *homo romanus* and *homo humanus* back into play in anti-imperialist discourse. For, in attempting to overcome the practical limitations of theory, this allegedly postmodern emancipatory discourse has gone far to reinscribe the very theoretical limitations of liberal practice that instigated it. I mean the limitations of a humanist discourse that, in its reconciliatory emphasis, comes perilously close to thinking the uneven balance of power characterizing the present "postcolonial" occasion as though it were a realm in which all opposing points of view are equal, that is, in which power is equally distributed and thus a matter of negotiation rather than of struggle.

To recognize that the origin of modern European (neo)imperialism lies in the Romans' epochal translation of *a-letheia* to *veritas* — and that this translation has achieved planetary status at the end of the anthropological phase of the Western tradition (what Heidegger has called "the age of the world picture") — is to realize that the imperative of an oppositional culture in the post–Cold War era, in the interregnum, as it were, is to rethink thinking itself. It is, in short, to think the shadow of the dominant discourse of light — the dark "barbarian" — positively.

This, in a wonderfully resonant way, is the implicit Nietzschean witness of one of the most civilized — and marginal — poets, neither Occidental nor Oriental nor both, of our century, the Alexandrian Greek Constantine Cavafy:

> — What are we waiting for gathered in the market-place?
>   The barbarians are supposed to arrive today.
> — Why so little activity in the Senate?
>   Why do the senators sit there without legislating?
>   Because the barbarians are arriving today.
>   Why should the Senators make laws any more?
>   The barbarians, when they come, will do the law-making.
> — Why has our emperor gotten up so early,
> and why does he sit at the city's largest gate
> on the throne, in state, wearing the crown?
>   Because the barbarians are arriving today.
>   And the emperor is waiting to receive
>   their leader. In fact, he's prepared
>   a parchment to give him. In it
>   he has inscribed many titles and names to him.
> — Why did our two consuls and our praetors go out
> today in their scarlet, their embroidered, togas;
> Why did they wear bracelets with so many amethysts,
> and rings with brilliant, sparkling emeralds;
> Why today should they take up precious staves
> inlaid splendidly with silver and gold?
>   Because the barbarians are arriving today:
>   and such things dazzle barbarians.
> — And why don't the worthy orators come as usual
> to deliver their speeches, to say their say?
>   Because the barbarians are arriving today:
>   and they are bored by eloquence and oratory.
> — Why this uneasiness all of a sudden
> and this confusion? (the faces, how sober they've become!)

Why are the streets and squares rapidly emptying,
and why is everyone going back home so lost in thought?
  Because night has fallen and the barbarians haven't come.
  And some have arrived from the frontiers
  and say there are not barbarians any longer.
—And now what will become of us without barbarians?
  Those people were a kind of solution.[96]

Chapter 3

Vietnam and the *Pax Americana*

A Genealogy of the "New World Order"

Swerve me? ye cannot swerve me, else ye swerve yourselves! man has ye there. Swerve me? The path to my fixed purpose is laid with iron rails, whereon my soul is grooved to run. Over unsounded gorges, through the rifled hearts of mountains, under torrents' beds, unerringly I rush! Naught's an obstacle, naught's an angle to the iron way!
— CAPTAIN AHAB, in Herman Melville, *Moby-Dick*

Robert "Blowtorch" Komer, chief of COORDS, spook anagram for Other War, pacification, another word for war. If William Blake had "reported" to him that he'd seen angels in the trees, Komer would have tried to talk him out of it. Failing there, he'd have ordered defoliation.
— MICHAEL HERR, *Dispatches*

"Kill Nam," said Lieutenant Calley. He pointed his weapon at the earth, burned twenty quick rounds. "Kill it," he said. He reloaded and shot the grass and a palm tree and then the earth again. "Grease the place," he said. "Kill it." — TIM O'BRIEN, *In the Lake of the Woods*

Introduction: The Question of the American Cultural Memory

All too many "progressive" academics are now affirming that the various emancipatory discursive practices precipitated by the Vietnam War have established a revisionary cultural momentum that promises to affect the sociopolitical site of American, indeed of global, being in a decisive way. This, it would seem, is suggested by the significant transformation of the canonical curriculum accomplished in the academy and other institutions of cultural production since 1968. It is also suggested by the increasingly vocal representation of this transformation by the cultural and political Right as a usurpation of power by a radical Left, one that has imposed a totalitarian discourse of political correctness — a new McCarthyism in reverse. Yet one cannot escape the feeling in 1999 that the emancipatory "postmodern" discursive practices precipitated during and by the occasion of the Vietnam decade to resist the evils of racism, patriarchy, and, especially, postcolonial colonialism have reached an impasse, if not an exhausted dead end. Despite the surface optimism in the academy, this feeling of exhaustion, in fact, pervades the intellectual climate of North America as a paralyzing virus. Its signs are discoverable everywhere. One finds it in the futile predictability — the indifference — of a differential "cultural critique" of the so-called postmodern agencies of knowledge transmission and in its loud muteness about the global cultural and sociopolitical conditions precipitated by the West's representation of the events of 1989–90 in China, and in Eastern and Central Europe and the Soviet Union, not simply as the "fall of communism," but even more triumphantly as the "end of history" and the "advent of the New World Order." This sense of exhaustion can even be discerned in the very "emancipatory" cultural and political practices — the so-called multicultural initiative at both the domestic and international sites — that these agents of countercultural production have in large part enabled. And this impasse, in turn, has instigated a disabling reorientation of critique on the part of many of the most vitally provocative Left critics writing in America today, more specifically, a refocusing that, on the basis of the "decline of the nation-state" and the emergence of transnational capitalism, would abandon the site of "America" as a determining planetary force in favor of a global perspective in which "America" as a national culture is represented maximally as an outmoded or minimally as a subordinate category.[1]

The rhetoric usually employed to articulate this feeling of impasse circulates around the terms "institutionalization" or "professionalization."[2] The original revolutionary impulse that would have undermined the American discourse of hegemony, it is claimed, has been co-opted and pacified by its success: its (self-)incorporation in the discourse of "America," by which I mean the liberal humanist discourse of a nation-state whose "truths" have become planetary. This thesis is superficially true. But in its theoretical abstraction, it is symptomatic of precisely what theory in its historical origins discovered to be one of the most powerful political strategies of the discourse of hegemony. It displaces historically specific conflict, *where imbalances of power — injustices — determine praxis,* to the rarefied and free-floating space of liberal debate, *where all positions are equal:* to a context that enables this kind of reformist thinking to accommodate resistant voices.

In this chapter, I want to retrieve the virtually forgotten historical origins of what has come to be called postmodern theory. This, not simply for its own sake, but also to suggest the one needful thing capable of breaking through the impasse into which the emancipatory discursive practices enabled by postmodern theory have become mired. I mean the retrieval of the Vietnam War *as event* from the oblivion to which the custodians of the American Cultural Memory have systematically relegated it and consequently the need to rethink the critical imperatives *this* historically specific war — it *cannot* be represented as simply any war — has disclosed about the post-Enlightenment American/Occidental *episteme.*

The very adversarial discourse the contradictions of this war in large part enabled has, however inadvertently, become complicitous with the dominant culture's amnesiac strategy. If a reconstellation of American criticism to the global scene is an imperative of the contemporary occasion, as, of course, it is, such a reconstellation must always keep in mind the determinative role that the idea of "America" — especially the myth of American exceptionalism — continues to play in the formulation and disposition of the cultural and sociopolitical issues of this expanded space: Kosovo, for example. The failure to do so, I submit, constitutes a disabling blindness to the essence of the globalization of the questions that confront postmodern men and women in the "post"–Cold War era. The impasse confronting emancipatory discursive practices in the aftermath of the "revolutions" in Eastern and Central Europe and the Soviet Union and the apparently decisive triumph over a despotic state in the Gulf War is not so much symptomatic of the anachronistic status to which these discursive practices have been relegated by their institutionalization. It is primarily the result of their insistent failure to think the radically critical imperatives spontaneously disclosed by the *self*-destruction of the exceptionalist discourse of "America" in the decade of the Vietnam War. I mean by this the hegemonic discourse that, since the Puritans' "errand in the wilderness," has increasingly — right up to the present — taken upon itself the "burden" of fulfilling the planetary promise ordained by the *Logos* of God or by History, the promise, of course, betrayed by a "decadent" Old World.

This blindness becomes tellingly ironic if, as its unrelenting force and massive scope demand, one reads the dominant culture's multifaceted effort to bury Vietnam as a subliminal recognition that its ghost continues to haunt the American Cultural Memory in the post–Cold War era.

The Forgetting of Vietnam and the Hegemony of the End-of-History Discourse in the Post–Cold War Era

What, after the revelatory event of Vietnam, should be astonishing to anyone living in the present historical conjuncture is the enormous power of the end–of–the–Cold War discourse. This, as I have reiterated, is the discourse, common to both cultural conservatives and liberals, that represents the successful "revolutions" against Stalinist communism first in the Eastern Bloc and then in the Soviet Union itself, the brutal suppression of the uprising in Tianamnen Square by the Old Guard communist regime, and the surgically executed military victory against Saddam Hussein in the Gulf War as the "fall of communism," that is, as the irreversible manifestation of the universal illegitimacy of the founding principles of socialism. Conversely, and more tellingly, it is the discourse that represents the global events of the late 1980s and early 1990s as a decisive manifestation of the *universal* legitimacy of the *idea* of American democracy. I am referring to the theory, most starkly exemplified by Francis Fukuyama's Hegelian interpretation of these events, that interprets the end of the Cold War as the culmination and fulfillment of a dialectical historical process that has precipitated liberal capitalist democracy as the "absolute" or planetary form of government and, in so doing, has brought the "developmental" dialectical economy of historical differentiation to its noncontradictory fulfillment and end in a totalized and identical self-present world order.[3] Despite a certain toning down of the triumphalist rhetoric compelled by the ongoing civil/racial strife in Bosnia, Kosovo, and other parts of the world and the reassessment of the "decisive" defeat of Saddam Hussein, this triumphalist American representation of the contemporary post–Cold War occasion continues to determine the content and parameters of cultural and sociopolitical discourse and practice not simply in the West but everywhere in the world. (It is a mistake to conclude, as too many on the Left have, that the continuing strife these post–Gulf War events reflect has effectively delegitimated the end-of-history discourse. The dominant culture's representation of America's global role has not abandoned this triumphalist vision. Rather, as in the case of Richard Haass's *The Reluctant Sheriff: The United States after the Cold War,* it has accommodated these events to America's perennial, historically ordained, exceptionalist mission.)[4] As such, this triumphalist representation has effectively obliterated or accommodated any differential event the contradictory force of which might legitimate a resistant impulse, not least the history of the Vietnam War. In so doing, it has also empowered itself to demonize any such resistant impulse as "political correctness." Symptomatic of the inordinate power of this global post–Cold War discourse (and of the inadequacy, if not obsolescence, of the traditional and even postmodern Left-oriented problematics) is the dearth of significant challenges to this representation of the end of the Cold War as the end of history. The principal spokespersons of the various oppositional discourses that have emerged in the academic marketplace as "victors" over deconstruction and other discourses focusing on the ontological question have not only largely ignored this epochal end-of-history thesis. They have also paid little attention to the practices it has enabled: the American invasion of Panama, the Gulf War, the "relief" of Somalia (Operation Hope), the intervention in Haiti, and, more recently, the interventions in Bosnia and Kosovo (though not, for example, in Rwanda) and, in the name of securing the world from the threat of "weapons of mass destruction," once again in Iraq. Most of these discourses (they include not only the New Historicism, critical genealogy, and the various neo-Marxisms that derive from the "critical theory" of the Frankfurt School and from the interpretation of postmodernism as the cultural logic of late capitalism, but also much of black criticism, feminist criticism, and even postcolonial criticism) practice their adversarial criticism as if this triumphalist end-of-history discourse did not exist or is too trivial to warrant serious attention. They seem to have forgotten their provenance *in* the Vietnam War, in the spectacle of an Occidental state practicing something like genocide (by means, in part, of an army largely conscripted from its oppressed minorities) in the name of *the fundamental principles* of liberal democracy (the "free world").

How, then, is one to account for the present cultural power of this triumphalist discourse of the New World Order? Why is it that an adversarial postmodernist discourse instigated in large part by the unequivocal exposure during the Vietnam War of the contradictory imperial violence inhering in the "benign" political discourse of Occidental "freedom" — what Foucault has called "the regime of truth" — has been reduced to virtual silence in the face of the reaffirmation of America's global errand in the aftermath of the Cold War? The Vietnam War bore witness to the decisive self-destruction of the logical economy propelling the American intervention in Vietnam, a self-destruction synecdochically enacted in the mad rationality of the American military officer who made history by declaring to his interlocutor that "we had to destroy Ben Tre in order to save it."[5] Why, then, do the adversarial discourses that emerged from the rubble of this self-destruction seem now without recourse to confront the dominant liberal capitalist culture's representation of the end of the Cold War as the advent of the New World Order, which is to say, as the *Pax Americana*? Why, on the twentieth anniversary of the fall of Saigon, does this oppositional discourse tacitly acknowledge the culture industry's decisive pronouncement that Robert McNamara's strategically timed memoirs as secretary of defense in the Kennedy and Johnson administrations constitute the definitive and final resolving act of the Vietnam War?

In this confessional book, after all, McNamara simply reiterates the long-standing "liberal" rationalization of the war: that he and his governmental colleagues made "an error not of [American] values and intention but of judgment and capabilities."[6] And by thus containing critique to such damage-control management he vindicates the idea of "America."[7] More important, the discourse he employs to confess his and his Pentagon colleagues' "mistakes" remains the same terribly banal "problem-solving" American discourse that destroyed Vietnam. Despite the fact that his very account of the failure to "win the hearts and minds" of the Vietnamese people to American values symptomatically exposes to view the life-destroying inhumanity of this banal instrumental reasoning, this "educated" McNamara is incapable of seeing it. In his recollection of General Westmoreland's and the Joint Chiefs' fateful argument for escalating the war in 1965, for example, he writes:

> Although I questioned [their] assumptions during my meetings with Westy and his staff, the discussions proved superficial. Looking back, I clearly erred by not forcing — then or later, in Saigon or Washington — a knock-down, drag-out debate over the loose assumptions, unasked questions, and thin analyses underlying our military strategy in Vietnam. I spent twenty years as a manager, identifying problems and forcing organizations — often against their will — to think deeply and realistically about alternative courses of action and their consequences. I doubt I will ever fully understand why I did not do so then.[8]

I am not presumptuous enough to assert that the questions I have asked above are amenable to easy answers, let alone to proffer them here. But I do believe that a beginning in this direction is possible on the basis of what I take to be a glaring — I am tempted to say "studied" — unthought in the various practice-oriented emancipatory discourses that are now subsumed under the term "postmodern." It is, I suggest, an unthought the thinking of which would go far to explain their inadequacy to the task of resistance, to say nothing about their contribution to a positive alternative to the dominant idea of the *polis*. But to inaugurate a thinking of this crucial unthought that haunts these adversarial discourses, a thinking, that is, which is adequate to the conditions of the present global occasion, will require a detour into the productive technology of forgetting endemic to the American Cultural Memory *as this amnesiac technology has worked itself out in the twenty years following the fall of Saigon.*

No war in American history, with the possible exception of the Civil War, has affected the collective American psyche so profoundly and for so long as the Vietnam War. Though World War I and especially

World War II were far wider in scope and larger in scale, brought far more of the American population directly in contact with war, and killed and wounded far more American youth, the Vietnam War has remained a national obsession. Some indefinable "thing" about the justification and conduct of the war — something having to do with the name "America" — instigated a national anxiety, a collective psychic trauma (from the Greek *trauma*: wound) that has become the spectral "measure" of the intelligibility of the domestic and international cultural and sociopolitical discourse and practice of the United States, regardless of the historically specific context, since the 1960s and especially the Tet Offensive of 1968. This is clearly suggested by the continuing outpour of histories, documentaries, biographies, autobiographical reminiscences, memoirs, films, fiction, videos, even comic books specifically about the war and by the repeated official and media-sponsored stagings of national rituals of "remembrance,"[9] most notably what Sacvan Bercovitch would call American jeremiads.[10] It is also — and more insidiously — suggested by the ever-extending capillary saturation of this obsession into adjacent and even remote spaces of cultural production. I am referring, for example, to the concerted and increasingly widespread and strident representation of the multicultural initiative in American colleges and universities by the National Association of Scholars and other conservative intellectuals as a "new McCarthyism of the Left"[11] and to the unrelenting effort of both conservative and liberal humanists alike to demonstrate the causal relation between Paul de Man's and Martin Heidegger's Nazi politics and the "antihumanism" of their "post-Enlightenment" philosophical thought.[12] Given the scope and depth of this national anxiety and the manifestly massive and multisituated need to allay by reifying its indeterminate "object" — its spectral presence, as Derrida might say of this *revenant* — it is quite clear that the American Cultural Memory has been intent since the end of the war on forgetting/repressing a momentous disclosure about its collective self. What precisely it was that thus showed itself and would be forgotten — what continues strangely to haunt the period-oriented American Cultural Memory, to *visit* its perennial *visitor,* as it were — will be a fundamental purpose of this chapter to think.

I could, of course, name this specter at the beginning, but to represent "it" as such an abstraction would attenuate the profoundly dislocating ontological, cultural, and sociopolitical implications of the United States's intervention and conduct of the war in Vietnam for its historical, including present, self-representation. I choose, therefore, to undertake a detour within this detour into the Vietnam War guided by the manifest anxiety afflicting the American Cultural Memory. Given the importance of discovering the repressed origin that nevertheless continues to haunt the present post–Cold War occasion, it seems to me preferable as a provisional imperative of such a genealogy to retrieve the historically specific symbolic forms in which this national obsession to forget Vietnam has manifested itself since the end of the Vietnam War. Attentive to this national anxiety as a forestructure, we must, in Heidegger's terms, first enter the hermeneutic circle in the spirit of "care" (*Sorge*): "primordially and wholly."

What we discover, in thus retrieving the history of the American culture industry's representation of the Vietnam War — and by "culture industry" I mean not simply the media, but also the institutions of knowledge production — is that this history has constituted a process of remembering that, in fact, has been a willful forgetting of the actualities of the war. And it takes broadly four different but increasingly assertive forms according to the chronological and psychological distance from the defeat of the United States, an assertiveness enforced by a series of historical events determined and/or represented in some fundamental ways by this recollective will to forget. It is, of course, impossible to do justice to the massive textual archive that, after a decade of silence, has been produced since the dedication of the Vietnam Veterans Memorial in 1982 for this purpose of forgetting Vietnam or, to anticipate the metaphorics associated with this recuperative project, of "healing the wound" in the American collective consciousness "inflicted by" the war. (In its ritualized memorial character, the Vietnam Veterans Memorial is itself a crucial instance, indeed, the inaugural act, of this sustained recuperative effort.)[13] That larger genealogy must wait for another time.[14] Here it will have to suffice to invoke a small number of synecdochic texts from an immense stock of cultural capital that have been decisive in the virtually undeviating effort of the American Culture Memory to renarrativize the recalcitrant event of the Vietnam War: to bring the contradictory history of this first postmodern war to its closure.[15]

The first phase of this recuperative national project, in fact, preceded the end of the war, but indirectly acknowledged imminent defeat. It was characterized by a belated but proleptic effort to rehabilitate the shattered image of the American military mission by placing the blame for its failure to achieve its announced goal on the alleged complicity between the media, which by 1968 had in some degree turned against the war, and the protest movement in the United States. This inaugural phase is epitomized by John Wayne's *Green Berets,* produced, with the support of the Lyndon Baines Johnson faltering presidency, in 1968, the year, we might say, of the apparition of the specter that was increasingly to haunt the discourse of "America" in the following years. This epochally imagined American jeremiad is fundamentally about represen- tation. At a briefing staged for journalists by the Green Berets, Colonel Kirby (Wayne), the pioneer-like commander of a detachment of Green Berets, who has been assigned to establish and hold a base camp in the heart of enemy territory in Vietnam, challenges a prestigious an- tiwar reporter for a powerful American newspaper, Beckworth (David Jansen), to reconsider his typically negative representations of the Amer- ican Mission in the Vietnam wilderness. He tells Beckworth that the antiwar sentiments he transmits to the American public are grounded in hearsay; that, like the liberal American press he represents, he is, in fact, the unwitting dupe of the ideological fictions of a dangerously ex- panding subversive element in the United States. And he concludes by telling the reporter that if he were there in Vietnam to *see and experience* the "real" war for himself, he would realize the damage his ideologically mediated antiwar writing was doing to the noble national cause of truth, freedom, and human dignity in the "free world's" struggle in behalf of the threatened Vietnamese people against a savage enemy who was him- self the puppet of the Soviet Union.[16] Beckworth is thus "compelled" by Kirby's "reasonable" appeal to this hegemonic discourse to accompany the colonel's Green Berets to Vietnam. Thus interpellated by Amer- ica's call, Beckworth experiences "immediately" both the cowardly and grotesque brutalities of the Asiatic hordes, especially against the inno- cent Montagnards (which include the raping of their children), and the pioneer-like self-reliance, the courage, and the selflessness of the Green Berets (and their South Vietnamese allies): their Alamo-like defense of the base camp and their winning of the hearts and minds of the Viet- namese Montagnards.[17] Beckworth thus undergoes a conversion to the "Truth." This "immediate" Truth is, of course, an ideological represen- tation intended to rehabilitate the shattered official image of America's allegedly benign mission in Southeast Asia. It simply superimposes the American culture industry's commodified narrative of America's rep- resentation of the American frontiersman's violence against the Other as a heroic struggle against a savage enemy, who diabolically impedes the providentially ordained mission to settle the "virgin land," on the complex and recalcitrantly differential reality of the people's war be- ing fought in Vietnam: "Fort Dodge," as the base camp is named in the film, on the Vietnamese "wilderness."[18] By way of this perennial American distrust of mediation, this commitment to "immediate" (em- pirical) experience, what was in reality a brutally aggressive act on the part of the United States is represented by the American culture industry as the enactment of the perennial and historically validated disinterested goodwill of America toward a distant people suffering under the yoke of oppression.

The second phase of this amnesiac representational history was characterized by a (very audible) national silence about the war that had just been lost, especially about the returning veterans. Unlike the triumphant veterans of World War II, the veterans of the Vietnam War were ignored by the American culture industry. In the resonant rhetoric Thomas Pynchon uses to trace the genealogy of Protestant/capitalist American modernity back to the Puritan errand in the wilderness, they were "preterited" or "passed over." But this preterition of the Vietnam veteran was in effect a symptomatic representation by the National Memory that rendered them scapegoats for the American defeat in Vietnam. As late as 1977, Philip Caputo recalls and laments the senselessly heroic death of a Marine comrade in arms in the bitterly ironic terms of Wilfred Owen's anti-Horatian (and -imperial) "Dulce et Decorum Est":

> You died for the man you tried to save, and you died *pro patria*. It was not altogether sweet and fitting, your death, but I'm sure you died believing it was *pro patria*. You were faithful. Your country is not. As I write this, eleven years after your death, the country for which you died wishes to forget the war in which you died. Its very name is a curse. There are no monuments to its heroes, no statues in small-town squares and city parks, no plaques, nor public wreaths, nor memorials. For plaques and wreaths and memorials are reminders, and they would make it harder for your country to sink into the amnesia for which it longs. It wished to forget and it has forgotten. But there are a few of us who remember because of the small things that made us love you.[19]

This second phase, which is historically represented by its non-representation, initiated a collective strategy of rationalization by the American Cultural Memory that became more clearly differentiated and increasingly forceful after the dedication of the Vietnam Veterans Memorial in 1982: in the third and especially the fourth, post–Cold War, phase. The silence of this second phase, that is, implicitly intimated the *betrayal* of the principles informing "America" by those conducting and fighting the war in Vietnam. In doing so, it foreclosed any question, despite persuasive marginal voices both in the United States and abroad, like those of Noam Chomsky, Martin Luther King, Jean-Paul Sartre, and Bertrand Russell, about the culpability of the very *principles* themselves.

The third and decisive phase was initiated during the Reagan administration and was concurrent with the massive initiative to regain a culturally and politically conservative — and militaristic — national consensus in behalf of its imperial interventions in Granada, El Salvador, Nicaragua, and the Middle East, in behalf, that is, of the Cold War against Soviet communism. In Reagan's rhetoric, this was the initiative that would "build the city on the hill" against the global threat of "the evil empire." Not incidentally, this third phase was also concurrent with the highly visible "reform" initiative in higher education inaugurated by Harvard University in 1978 with the publication of the "Harvard Core Curriculum Report" and promulgated by the Reagan administration under the direction of William J. Bennett, director of the National Endowment for the Humanities and later secretary of education. I am referring to the initiative that was intended to recuperate the core curriculum, which, according to the representation proffered by the Harvard faculty (and nationally mediatized by the American press), was "eroded" by the "promiscuous" demands of students, women, blacks, and ethnic minorities in the 1960s, but which, in effect, was intended to accommodate the gains made by the civil rights and women's movement to the hegemonic center. That is to say, it was in reality intended to forget the complicity of the American colleges and universities with the State's intervention and conduct of the war in Vietnam.[20]

Specifically, this third phase of the renarrativizing process was inaugurated when the preterited veterans began to demand recognition for the sacrificial services they had performed in behalf of their country's call, a momentum that culminated in the dedication of the Vietnam Veterans Memorial in Washington, D.C., in 1982. This national ceremony was accompanied by a deluge of retrospective cultural production — movies, fiction, video documentaries, histories, autobiographical accounts of veterans' experiences — that in a virtually monolithic way represented the post-Vietnam American occasion as a time for reconciliation, a sentiment expressed in terms of the pervasive and resonant (but never rigorously interpreted) metaphor of the national need to "heal the wound." What, in the historical context, this ubiquitous trope meant generally — at the conscious level — to the American public was the national imperative to rehabilitate the dignity and honor of the vilified and ostracized Vietnam veteran and to reintegrate him (*sic*) into American society. At a deeper ideological level this trope was a hegemonic (jeremiadic) call of the American public to itself to reconcile the sociopolitical divisions precipitated by the war in behalf of the recuperation of the national consensus. This meant, in effect, a call to free itself from the seductive discourse of a certain social constituency that, in its continuing contestation of the rationale and conduct of the war, exacerbated the festering laceration inflicted on the American body politic. More accurately, it meant a call to recuperate the health of the American psyche —

its traditional collective self-representation — that had been shattered by a defeat largely caused by this same vocal minority that had resisted the war, that is, had prevented America from winning it.

This third phase of the recuperative representational process can be broadly subdivided into two moments. The first includes the letters home (*Dear America: Letters from Vietnam* [1985]); the oral histories (*Everything We Had* [1981], *To Bear Any Burden* [1985], *Nam* [1981], and *Bloods* [1984]); the autobiographies (John Caputo's *A Rumor of War* [1977] and Ron Kovic's *Born on the Fourth of July* [1976]); and the spate of Hollywood films initiated by *The Deerhunter* (1978) and *Coming Home* (1978) but epitomized ideologically by the *Rambo* trilogy (1982, 1984, 1988) (and its multiple offshoots having their point of departure in the MIA issue).[21]

Rehearsing John Wayne's fraudulent distinction between a "false" (mediated) protestant representation of America's involvement in Vietnam and a "true" representation based on *being there,* the first moment of this third phase is epitomized by Al Santoli's best-selling oral history of the Vietnam War, *Everything We Had.* It takes the form of a prefatorial direct address to an implied American public that was perilously confused about its national identity and invokes an unmediated (objective) "reality" — seeing the Vietnam War "as it was": with the eyes of the "thirty-three [representative] soldiers who fought it" — against a "prevailing" mediated (and ideologically negative) representation that could only exacerbate the collective psychic "wound":

> In our book we hope you will see what we saw, do what we did, feel what we felt. Until the broader public fully comprehends the nameless soldier, once an image on your television screen, the nation's resolution of the experience called Vietnam will be less than adequate.
>
> The American people have never heard in depth from the *soldiers themselves* the complicated psychic and physical realities of what they went through in Vietnam.[22]

In implicitly positing the "individual's" eyewitness as more authentic than any mediated standpoint, the texts of this group, like John Wayne's *The Green Berets,* reduces *this* war — the Vietnam War — to war-in-general, and "the raw experiences" of the American soldier fighting in *this* war to the timeless and noble agony of the universal soldier. It thus displaces the disturbing current focus on the United States's historically specific cultural and sociopolitical conduct of the Vietnam War (and on the dislocating psychological consequence of its defeat by a Third World people) in favor of a represented focus that celebrates the heroism and dignity — the "triumph" — of the (American) human spirit in the face of the carnage of war, which, in this internalized discourse, is referred to as "the supreme test of manhood." Nor should it be overlooked that this triumph of the individual is precisely the characteristic that, according to a fundamental motif of this hegemonic discourse — one that is also exploited in *The Green Berets* — distinguishes the "American" (Occidental) self from the "Asiatic hordes." This, finally, is the ideological agenda of the numerous "letters home" and "oral histories" that would "heal the wound" by substituting the American soldier's immediate account of the war for representations that were "adulterated" by (Left) politics. As Santoli puts this ideologically compelled internalization and universalization of specific American political history in the last of the three epigraphs of *Everything We Had* — without consciousness of the contradiction of quoting an Oriental:

> Though it be broken —
> Broken again — still it's there,
> The moon on the water.
> — Chosu

The second subdivision of this third phase — epitomized by Sylvester Stallone's *Rambo* trilogy — repeats the representational imperative "to see what we saw, . . . feel what we felt" against the mediated representations of the ideologically radical Left. The difference between this representation and that of the earlier oral and epistolary histories (besides the fact that it constitutes a self-parody of the latter) is, however, that its recuperative narrative strategy is bolder. It is not accidental that this more assertive recuperative initiative was coincidental with the emergence of a strident reactionary cultural discourse, represented by Allan Bloom, Roger Kimball, David Lehman, Dinesh D'Souza, Hilton Kramer, and the members of the National Association of Scholars, that represented the institutions of higher learning in America — indeed, the cultural agencies of knowledge production and transmission at large — not simply as a process of randomizing the curriculum as the "Harvard Core Curriculum Report" had alleged in 1978, but as having been taken over by now "tenured radicals" of the 1960s (white postmodernists, feminists, and blacks) who resisted the Vietnam War. Unlike the universalist accounts projected by the earlier oral histories that individualized and universalized the war, this revisionary discourse represents the mediated accounts of the Vietnam War as the primary cause of the American defeat in Vietnam.

The subversive protest movement in America, according to this emboldened representation, succeeded in passing off its ideologically grounded representations of the Vietnam War as the truth of this history not only to determinative segments of the political and military leadership of America, but also to the American public at large. It thus established juridical, sociopolitical, and military constraints that made it impossible for the American soldiers to win the war. That is to say, it precluded the fulfillment of "America's" global mission to resist the insidious imperial machinations of the evil empire in the name of the free world.

The *Rambo* trilogy, for example, begins (*Rambo: First Blood*) with the return of a disillusioned Green Beret veteran to "the world" (in the form of a typical small American town in the Pacific Northwest). The film establishes the viewer's sympathy for this alienated and bitter Rambo at the outset by representing his return as a visit to the parents of his dead black comrade (a representation, not incidentally, that turns the black soldier into a symbol of the betrayed American ideal). What he discovers instead is that the world not only does not want his like in its midst, but, when he insists on his rights as an American citizen, treats him as if he were a psychopathic killer, spawned by the Vietnam War, who threatens the order and tranquillity of this typical American community. In the process of depicting Rambo's cunningly ferocious resistance against an America turned into a Vietnam in reverse, the film transforms the Green Beret (the American warrior of John F. Kennedy's "New Frontier") into a cross between a technologized Natty Bumppo and a Vietcong guerrilla. It thus draws the emergent revisionary conclusion that America lost the war not because its brutal conduct destroyed the credibility of its justification for intervening in Vietnam, but because John Rambo and his valiant and ultrapatriotic comrades in arms against the global aspirations of communism were not allowed by the misled, indeed, corrupted, deputies of the American body politic to win it.[23]

The trilogy then passes through a reductive melodramatic narrative, *Rambo: First Blood II*, reminiscent of the western captivity film, which represents the hero as the lone and silent American frontiersman who has learned his deadly craft from his savage enemy, a representation whose genealogy extends from dime westerns of the 1890s back through Francis Parkman's histories of the French and Indian Wars to Judge James Hall's "The Indian Hater" (1829) and Robert Montgomery Bird's *Nick of the Woods* (1837).[24] This film, playing on the question of the MIAs that the Reagan presidency inflated into a national political issue in the 1980s, depicts Rambo's single-handed (and ferociously single-minded) effort to rescue some American prisoners in Vietnam. In the process, it reiterates the perennial official — and calculatedly staged — Cold War representation of the Vietnamese insurgency as the narrative project of an underdeveloped and inferior race of puppets utterly controlled by strings emanating from Moscow. The trilogy, which from the outset assumes the "negatively interpellated" point of view of the saving remnant, ends with the reaffirmation of a national consensus in the struggle of a small minority in the United States against a massive domestic momentum that would betray "America" and against the "evil empire" (and its "domino" strategy) now waging war in Afghanistan(!) (*Rambo: First Blood III*).

This revisionist ideological initiative was not restricted to the simulacral productions of Hollywood. It was, in fact, the essential project of the culture industry at large. This is emphatically suggested by such immensely popular "documentaries" as Al Santoli's *To Bear Any Burden* (1985), which, in collecting the personal "testimony" about the "Vietnam War and its aftermath" of "Americans and Southeast Asians" "who remember,"[25] duplicates this melodramatically imagined transformation of a recuperative ideology of reconciliation (i.e., accommodation) to a more aggressive attack against the countermemory. "After the publication of *Everything We Had,*" Santoli writes in his preface, "I realized that the recognition given to it and to Vietnam veterans in general is only one step in our coming to terms with the Vietnam trauma. The larger story is more than one of combat by American soldiers in Vietnam, or one that ends with America's direct involvement there. It seemed necessary to take a look at the revolution that preceded America's involvement, as well as the effects of the Communist victory in Vietnam, Cambodia, and Laos" (*BAB,* xvi–xvii). The "truth" to which this "objective" (retrospective) look bears witness is suggested in a paragraph preceding this one: "I did not want to see the Communists succeed or the lives of my friends wasted. But with no mandate for victory, and a senseless obsession with body-counts, I felt that our lives and ideals meant nothing. We were just cold statistics in Washington's political computers. Everything I ever believed in was turned upside down" (*BAB,* xvi). Hidden behind Santoli's appeal to a cross-section of eyewitness accounts is a self-confirming future-anterior selective process ("the effects of the Communist victory in Vietnam") as recounted by "a larger community of veterans" (*BAB,* xvii) — not only Americans (soldiers, journalists, diplomats, relief workers), but Cambodian refugees and former Vietnamese insurgents themselves. It is, in other words, a process that, like the *Rambo* trilogy, articulates a narrative that would bring a war that refused to end to decisive closure by demonstrating the "negative" consequences for the Vietnamese and for adjacent Southeast Asian peoples of the United States's withdrawal from Vietnam. Santoli's book attributes this withdrawal, of course, to a neurotic protest movement that did not allow the American military to win the war. With this symbolic denouement, the "wound" suffered by "America" has been utterly, if not explicitly, healed. To invoke an analogous metaphor, the ghost that has haunted the collective American psyche is exorcised. The internal divisions within the American body politic have not only been reconciled; the reconciliation has rendered the *res publica* stronger and more dedicated to the principles of American democracy in its struggle against radicals and communist imperialism. But what, in the context of the emergence of the end–of–the–Cold War discourse, needs to be thematized is that the metaphor of *trauma* has undergone a telling metamorphosis: the metaphor of the wound, which implies healing, that is, ideological reconciliation, has become — or is at the threshold of being represented as — a collective psychological illness, a national "syndrome," which implies the imperative to blame a negative ideological cause.

The fourth and "final" phase of the American culture industry's re-narrativization of the Vietnam War was inaugurated on the concurrent occasion of the collapse of the Soviet Union and the United States's surgically executed "victory" against Saddam Hussein in the Gulf War. What is especially telling about the official representation of this historical conjuncture, especially by the television networks, is that, from beginning to end, it was this contrasting negative measure of Vietnam that utterly determined its narrative shape: the linear/circular structure of decisive victory. From the inaugural debates about the question of the legitimacy of America's intervention in the face of Iraq's invasion of Kuwait through the brief period of the war itself to its immediate aftermath, it was the specter of the Vietnam War — the "divisive" and "self-defeating" national anxiety precipitated by its radical indeterminacy — that the narrative structure of closure, enabled by a "victory" by the United States in the Cold War, was intended to decisively efface. This transformation of a national anxiety into a productive negative image was symptomatically reflected by President Bush's virtually unchallenged guarantee to the American public on the eve of the war that it would not be "another Vietnam"[26] and, more strategically, by the exclusive mediation of the events of the Gulf War by the American military information agencies in a way that the events of the Vietnam War had made unthinkable. And it was the long process of cultural forgetting, which had ostensibly (re)constituted the actual defeat of the United States into a drastically mistaken withdrawal from Vietnam, that had prepared the ground for this cultural transformation. In short, the representational forgetting of the actualities of the war systematically undertaken by the ideological state apparatuses had gradually arrived at a form of remembering it that attributed the defeat of America to the infectious impact of the multisituated protest movement in the United States on the American public and its intellectual deputies.

In this "final" phase, that is, the earlier public need to "heal the wound" — a recuperative and conciliatory gesture of forgetting — became, in the words of President George Bush and official Washington, a matter of "kicking the Vietnam syndrome."[27] Aided and abetted by the culture industry, this early gesture of forgetting metamorphosed at the time of the Gulf "crisis" into a virulently assured assumption that the resistance to America's intervention and conduct of the war in Vietnam in the 1960s was a symptom of a national neurosis. (This interpretation of the active resistance to the Vietnam War was not a sudden reactionary political initiative enabled by the circumstances of the Gulf War. Its origins can be traced back to the period of the Vietnam War itself, to the reaction against the protest movement by such influential conservative and liberal humanist intellectuals as George Kennan, Walter Jackson Bate, and Allan Bloom, among many others. The disruptions of the traditional white Anglo-American and male-dominated cultural value system in American colleges and universities — whether in the form of the common body of shared knowledge informing the general education program [the *litterae humaniores*] or the canon of great books — were undertaken in the name of relevance. In the name of high seriousness, these anxious traditionalists reduced this emancipatory initiative to an unhealthy or neurotic obsession with novelty and/or vulgarity and represented it — as Arnold had represented the rise of working-class consciousness in late Victorian Britain — as a symptom not simply of a "centrifugal" process precipitating a dangerous cultural "heterogeneity," but as a collective "death wish" [Bate] on the part of the American academy.)[28] Whatever its limitations, the protest movement in the Vietnam decade was, in fact, a symptomatic manifestation of a long-overdue and promising national self-doubt about the alleged legitimacy of America's representation of its internal constituencies (blacks, women, gays, ethnic minorities, the poor, the young, and so on) and about the alleged benignity of its historically ordained exceptionalist mission to transform the world (the barbarous Others) in its own image. In this last phase of the amnesiac process, this healthy and potentially productive self-examination of the American cultural identity came to be represented as a collective psychological sickness that, in its disintegrative momentum, threatened to undermine "America's" promised end.[29] By this I mean the end providentially promised to the original Puritans and later, after the secularization of the body politic, by History: the building of "the city on the hill" in the "New World," which is to say, the advent of the New World Order and the end of history.

In the wake of the Cold War, and especially the defeat of Saddam Hussein's army — and the consequent representation of the shattered American consensus occasioned by the Vietnam War as a recovery of a collective mental illness — there came in rapid and virtually un-challenged succession a floodtide of "reforms," reactionary in essence, intended to annul the multiply situated progressive legacy of the protest movement(s) of the Vietnam decade by overt abrogation or accom-modation. Undertaken in the name of the "promise" of "America," these reforms were intended to reestablish the ontological, cultural, and political authority of the enlightened, American "vital center" and its circumference and thus to recontain the dark force of the insurgent dif-ferential constituencies that had emerged at the margins in the wake of the disclosures of the Vietnam War. At the domestic site, these included the coalescence of capital (the Republican Party) and the religious and political Right into a powerful dominant neoconservative culture (a new "Holy Alliance," as it were) committed to an indissolubly linked mil-itantly racist, antifeminist, antigay, and anti-working-class agenda; the dominant liberal humanist culture's massive indictment of deconstruc-tive and destructive theory as complicitous with fascist totalitarianism; the nationwide legislative assault on the post-Vietnam public univer-sity by way of programs of economic retrenchment affiliated with the representation of its multicultural initiative as a political correct-ness of the Left;[30] the increasing subsumption of the various agencies of cultural production and dissemination (most significantly, the elec-tronic information highways) under fewer and fewer parent, mostly American, corporations; the dismantling of the welfare program; and, symptomatically, the rehabilitation of the criminal president, Richard Nixon. At the international site, this "reformist" initiative has mani-fested itself as the rehabilitation of the American errand in the world, a rehabilitation exemplified by the United States's virtually uncontested moral/military interventions in Panama, Somalia, Haiti, Bosnia, the Middle East, and Kosovo; its interference in the political processes of Russia by way of providing massive economic support for Boris Yeltsin's democratic/capitalist agenda against the communist opposition; its uni-lateral assumption of the lead in demanding economic/political reforms in Southeast Asian countries following the collapse of their economies in 1998; its internationalization of the "free market"; and, not least, its globalization of the instrumentalist version of the English language.

What needs to be foregrounded is that these global post–Cold War "reformist" initiatives are not discontinuous practices, a matter of his-torical accident. Largely enabled by the "forgetting" of Vietnam — and of the repression or accommodation or self-immolation of the emergent decentered modes of thinking the Vietnam War precipitated—they are, rather, indissolubly, however unevenly, related. Indeed, they are the multisituated practical consequences of the planetary triumph (the "end") of the logical economy of the imperial ontological discourse that has its origins in the founding of the idea of the Occident and its fulfilled end in the banal instrumental/technological reasoning in the discourse of "America." In thus totally colonizing thinking, that is, this imperial "Americanism" has come to determine the comportment toward being of human beings, in all their individual and collective differences, at large — even of those postcolonials who would resist its imperial order. This state of thinking, which has come to be called the New World Order (though to render its rise to ascendancy visible requires reconstellating the Vietnam War into this history), subsumes the representative, but by no means complete, list of post–Cold War practices to which I have referred above. And it is synecdochically represented by the massive mediatization of the amnesiac end-of-history discourse and the affiliated polyvalent rhetoric of the *Pax Americana*.

Understood in terms of this massive effort to endow hegemonic status to the transformation of the metaphorics of the "wound" to (neurotic) "syndrome," the *forgotten* of the systematic process of forgetting apparently accomplished by the renarrativization of history since the humiliatingly visible fall of Saigon in 1975 takes on a spectral resonance of epochal and planetary significance. As such, it calls on the differential community of oppositional intellectuals to undertake a genealogy of this end-of-history discourse that would retrieve (*wiederholen*) as precisely as possible the essence of *that which* the United States's intervention in Vietnam and its conduct of the war disclosed, *that which* the American Cultural Memory, in the form of a "new Holy Alliance," has feverishly attempted to bury in oblivion by way of its multisituated and long-term labor to hegemonize a demonic representation of this (self-)disclosure.

The Logical Economy of the American Intervention in Vietnam

The tradition of all the dead generations weighs like a nightmare on the brain of the living.
— KARL MARX, *The Eighteenth Brumaire of Louis Bonaparte*

In dread, as we say, "one feels something uncanny [*unheimlich*]." What is this "something" and this "one"? We are unable to say what gives "one" that "uncanny feeling." "One" just feels it generally. All things, and we with them, sink into a sort of indifference. But not in the sense that everything simply disappears; rather, in the very act of drawing away from us

everything turns towards us. This withdrawal of what-is-in-totality, which then crowds round us *in dread,* this is what oppresses us. *There is nothing to hold on to. The only thing that remains and overwhelms us whilst what-is slips away, is this "nothing."*
Nothing begets dread.
— MARTIN HEIDEGGER, "What Is Metaphysics?"

Ghost or *revenant,* sensuous-non-sensuous, visible-invisible, the specter first of all sees *us.* From the other side of the eye, *visor effect,* it looks at us even before we see *it* or even before we see period. We feel ourselves observed, sometimes under surveillance by it even before any apparition. Especially — and this is the event, for the specter is *of* the event — it sees us during a *visit.* It (re)pays us a visit. Visit upon visit, since it returns to see us and since *visitare,* frequentive of *visere* (to see, examine, contemplate), translates well the recurrence of returning, the frequency of a visitation.   — JACQUES DERRIDA, *Specters of Marx*

It is impossible in this limited space to undertake a fully articulated genealogy of the end-of-history discourse that now, albeit in a more nuanced form, saturates American cultural production and sociopolitical practice. But the increasingly abyssal gap between the logical economy of the representation of the Vietnam War by the dominant culture and the recalcitrant differential actualities of the war's history — what, adapting Derrida to my purposes, I having been calling its spectrality — enables us at least to suggest a persuasive provisional outline of such a genealogical project. For this all-too-visible spectral gap foregrounds a virulent imperial will to reduce an irreducible differential occasion to decidability. It reveals, as it were, that this will is tantamount to torturing the Other into a confession of a preestablished "truth."[31] As such, it repeats at the level of cultural discourse precisely the undeviating essentialist "logic" of the United States's conduct of the war against the Vietnamese Other: the "European" or "imperial" logic informing its expectation of the decisive battle that ended not in a conclusive victory, but in an inconclusive defeat. And it is precisely this spectral gap — or rather, this indissoluble relay of spectral gaps — that is at stake in the argument.

The American intervention in Vietnam was not determined solely by the Cold War scenario as such. It was not undertaken simply in the name of the capitalist economic/political "base." It was also, and indissolubly, undertaken in the name of the (superstructural) discourse of (Occidental/American) "Truth," that is, the ontological *principles* informing liberal/capitalist democracy. I mean the Enlightenment's representation of being that conferred legitimacy to "freedom and equality": those values insistently invoked by the end-of-history discourse to characterize the universal essence of the economic/political system that, it claims, has emerged triumphantly from the dialectical process of Universal History.[32] It is a seriously disabling mistake, in thinking the epochal event we call Vietnam, to subordinate, as all-too-much oppositional criticism has done, the ontological site — consciousness or theory — to the site of economics and/or politics, as if the latter were a base to the former's superstructurality; as if, that is, the essential — and essentialist — *principles* of liberal democracy were simply a matter of false consciousness.[33] And it is a mistake, not incidentally, that derives in large part from the "Marxists'" sundering and hierarchizing of Marx's de-centering of the "Hegelian" "consciousness" and yoking it by this violence to the "real life-process" of men and women. "Consciousness," Marx writes, "can never be anything else than *conscious existence*."[34] All too characteristic of Marxist or Left critique of the United States's intervention in Vietnam, the restriction of interrogation to the economistic/political terms of the Cold War problematic (the privileging of the imperialist/capitalist motive) renders the ontological representation of the United States's imperialist intervention in Vietnam epiphenomenal. Which is to say in effect, *unthinkable*. As such, this reduction of an indissoluble relay of lived experience to single and determinative base has predisposed criticism to be blind to the most crucial disclosure — certainly for the post–Cold War moment — of the Vietnam War: the disclosure that the hegemonic discourse of forgetting has occulted. Assuming provisionally that this blindness is the case, we are compelled to put the ontological principles informing the American intervention in Vietnam and its conduct of the war back into play, not as a base to economic, political, and military superstructures, but as a lateral site of representation indissolubly, if unevenly, related to these.

The "mission" of the American Mission in Saigon was from the beginning of the United States's involvement in Vietnam exceptionalist. Its self-ordained responsibility was to "win the hearts and minds" of the postcolonial Vietnamese to the self-evident truth principles of "the (always new) free world" in the face of their profound contempt for European — Old World — imperialism. This representation of the American Mission in terms of its original "errand in the wilderness," which set America off from the rapacious and decadent Old World, is clearly suggested by the pervasive New Frontier rhetoric that accompanied the inauguration of President Kennedy's administration — a rhetoric integrally related to Kennedy's establishment of the Special Forces, better known as the Green Berets. This was the cultural as well as military arm that was given the motto *De opresso liber* (To free the oppressed) and deployed in an advisory capacity in Vietnam with the intention of recalling and exemplifying to the world at large — both to the Soviet

Union and to a Europe recovering from the self-inflicted catastrophe of World War II — the perennial pioneer spirit of "America." The American Mission, that is, represented its illegal and aggressive intervention in the civil struggle following the decisive defeat of the French by the Viet Minh at Dien Bien Phu in 1954 not simply by contrasting its benignly disinterested motive to bring the principles of "freedom" to the Vietnamese people with the totalitarianism of Soviet and Chinese communism. The New Adamic American Puritans justified their colonization of the "New World" by contrasting their exceptionalist errand in the wilderness with the repressive and exploitative practices of a spiritually decadent Europe. Similarly, the American Mission in Vietnam attempted to legitimate its intervention by insistently differentiating its democratic ethos not only from communism but also from the decadent racist colonialism of France, the European imperial power that had ruled and exploited the Vietnamese people for a century before World War II and that, despite the war's activation of a global anticolonialism, would continue to do so after the war.

This deeply backgrounded and resonant cultural opposition was fundamental to the official and mediatic representation of the United States's involvement in Vietnam from the beginning of this involvement in the aftermath of the Geneva Convention. The testimony of the foreign policy of the Eisenhower administration and, not least, of such nationally popular Cold War and anti–Old World texts as Dr. Tom Dooley's memoirs *Deliver Us from Evil* (1956) and Eugene Burdick's and William Lederer's *The Ugly American* (1958) bears witness to this, the former, in apotheosizing by enacting the noble American frontier spirit in Vietnam, and the latter, in castigating the America mission in Southeast Asia for having abandoning it. But it was the English novelist Graham Greene who disclosed the (neo)imperial significance of this exceptionalist ideology in *The Quiet American* (1955), a novel that, predictably, was condemned in the United States as a reactionary affirmation of the anachronous Old World ethos, more specifically, as " 'an exercise in national projection' by a member of the British Empire history had passed by."[35] Graham Greene's development of the exceptionalist cultural motif is integrally related to his satiric critique of the murderously innocent intentions of Alden Pyle (Greene's fictionalized version of the legendary American counterinsurgency figure Colonel Edward Lansdale, whose task was to develop a native "Third Force" in Vietnam that was neither French colonialist nor communist). And it is epitomized by the following conversation between Greene's narrator, Fowler, the cynical and not entirely reliable English reporter, who, though he condemns French colonialism, prefers it to the colonialism that is practiced devastatingly in the name of anticolonialism by the United States, and "the quiet American," Alden Pyle, the unquestioning ephebe of the influential American Asian expert (we would now, in the wake of Edward Said's great book, call him an "Orientalist") York Harding, whose "objective" analysis of America's mission in the world, Greene implies, is utterly determined by the Cold War scenario. They have been caught in a tower manned by two young and frightened French Vietnamese soldiers at nightfall on their return to Saigon from a Caodaist festival at which Fowler accidentally learns that Pyle is secretly contacting a certain General The, the leader of this "Third Force," in behalf of the American Mission:

> "You and your like are trying to make a war with the help of people who just aren't interested."
> "They don't want Communism."
> "They want enough rice," I said. "They don't want to be shot at. They want one day to be much the same as another. They don't want our white skins around telling them what they want."
> "If Indo-China goes . . . "
> "I know the record. Siam goes, Malaya goes. Indonesia goes. What does 'go' mean? . . . "
> "They'll be forced to believe what they are told, they won't be allowed to think for themselves."
> "Thought's a luxury. Do you think the peasant sits and thinks of God and Democracy when he gets inside his mud hut at night?"
> "You talk as if the whole country were peasant. What about the educated? Are they going to be happy?"
> "Oh no," I said, "we've brought them up in *our* ideas. We've taught them dangerous games, and that's why we are sitting here, hoping we don't get our throats cut. We deserve to have them cut. I wish your friend York was here too. I wonder how he'd relish it."
> "York Harding's a very courageous man. Why, in Korea . . . "
> "He wasn't an enlisted man, was he? He had a return ticket. . . . These poor devils can't catch a plane home. Hi," I called to them, "what are your names?" . . . They didn't answer. . . . "They think we are French," I said.
> "That's just it," Pyle said. "You shouldn't be against York, you should be against the French. Their colonialism."[36]

If the ameliorative benignity of America's exceptionalist errand that differentiated it from the imperial rapacity of the Old World was self-evident to the American Mission, it was not to an Oriental people deeply rooted in another, radically different, culture. This indifference and/or resistance to the American Mission's effort to win the hearts and minds of the Vietnamese precipitated an American reaction that has been well documented, but the crucial significance of which has not adequately been understood *and* thematized by the historians of the Vietnam War. The refusal of their assent to these "self-evident" New World truths instigated an American practice that, however reluctantly, was characterized by the increasing visibility of the will to power informing the benign truth discourse of liberal democracy. To adapt Jacques Derrida's rhetoric to my purposes, it compelled the "center elsewhere" of the American Mission's freedom discourse, which is normally "beyond the reach of free play," down into the visible arena of the free play of criticism.[37] The "first" symptom of this "contradiction" was, of course, the American Mission's violent remapping of Vietnam — its representation of this single ancient culture as two distinct countries — and then the *imposition,* or, rather, the recurrent imposition, of a "legitimate" government in South Vietnam (the "Third Force," in the language of the Cold War scenario) that was represented as being "committed" to the "disinterested" discourse and practice of liberal democracy.

Indeed, it might be said that the successful military strategy of the National Liberation Front (NLF, misleadingly represented by the American Mission as the "Vietcong") and, later, the North Vietnamese Army (NVA) — their practice of the "nomadic" hit-and-run tactics of guerrilla warfare — against an infinitely more formidable army was in some fundamental way based on their awareness of this resonant contradiction in the logical economy of the discourse of Occidental liberal democracy. It is as if, having deciphered the imperial imperatives informing the ontological structure of the collective Occidental self during the long and painfully oppressive period of French colonial rule — the European perception of being in terms of the binary opposition between center and periphery and the linear/circular (decidable) narrative this binary enables — the Vietnamese Other discovered the Achilles' heel of America's (anthropo)logic and mounted their military resistance precisely in order to exploit this vulnerability. As Herman Rapaport observes in a brilliant Deleuzian reading of the "anticlimactic" art of war practiced by the NLF and the NVA:

Truong Son of the N.L.F. reports that the North Vietnamese took very much into account the American expectation that one ought to win "decisive battles" in Vietnam. "Though somewhat disheartened, the Americans, obdurate by nature and possessed of substantial forces, still clung to the hope for a military solution,

for decisive victories on the battlefield." Truong Son's comments
are based on the perception that an American view of an all-or-
nothing victory can easily be converted to a tactic by which the
"superior forces," anxious for quick victory, are by way of a certain fracturing, reduced to something less than victory. That is,
the North Vietnamese immediately realized that a moleculariza-
tion of its forces among those of the Southern resisters would
force the United States to spread its resources thin. Son's assessment of this American strategy is that "it did not specifically center
on anything" and that "the Americans and their puppets had no
definite way of utilizing their mobile and occupation forces.... "
For this reason, even when conflict was "head on," that conflict
would be articulated in terms of a certain passivity, since action did not necessarily lead to anything more than action itself.
Moreover, the communists saw to it that the "corps" would be
disarticulated along various mobile "fronts" all at the same time.
In doing so they insured that "action" would be reduced to random or marginalized events which even if successfully won by the
Americans would not mean victory.[38]

Put negatively, the Vietnamese Other refused to resist the American
military machine in the binary narrative terms prescribed by the logocentric discourse of the Occident. Rather, this Eastern Other countered
the Occidental discourse and practice of structuration by de-structuring
its (anthropo)logic: by a devious practice that drew the will to power
informing its "disinterestedness" out *as* a futile, however destructive,
contradiction glaringly visible to the world. Specifically, the NLF and
NVA chose a strategy of absence (of invisibility, of silence) in the face of
a massive and formidable military force that, whatever its exceptionalist claims, was utterly and pervasively inscribed by a European cultural
narrative of presence. I mean the "Roman" narrative of decidability, the
(meta-physical) logical economy of which articulates, at the site of military practice, a distanced and totalized field of directional references and
coordinates that facilitates an end (or objective) understood as the decisive battle. The strategy of the Vietnamese Other, on the other hand, was
analogous to that of the Eastern martial arts (most notably those deriving from the Tao), which, grounded on a comportment toward being
that acknowledges the harmonious belongingness of being and nothing, privilege a "passivity" that allows the aggressor to defeat himself.[39]
Based on the predictability of the American reaction, this "feminine"
Vietnamese strategy of resistance fragmented and disarticulated a totalized military structure inscribed by a logocentric ontology and its

privileged panoptic vision and oriented futurally toward a preconceived and decisive end: victory.[40]

This ironic exploitation of the Occidental dread of Nothing and its imperially logocentric imperative to reify or spatialize (make visible and graspable) its temporal differentiations[41] is borne witness to by virtually all the American soldiers who fought in Vietnam, as the insistently visible negatives in their symptomatically anguished reminiscences overwhelmingly testify. It is, for example, the reiterated witness of Philip Caputo in his autobiographical confession, *A Rumor of War*:

> Forming a column, my platoon started toward its first objective, a knoll on the far side of the milky-brown stream. It was an objective only in the geographical sense of the word; it had no military significance. In the vacuum of that jungle, we could have gone in as many directions as there are points on a compass, and any direction was as likely to lead us to the VC, or away from them, as any other. The guerrillas were everywhere, which is another way of saying nowhere. The knoll merely gave us a point of reference. It was a place to go, and getting there provided us with the illusion we were accomplishing something.[42]

It is also the testimony of Tim O'Brien in his novel *Going after Cacciato*:

> They [the American soldiers] did not know even the simple things: a sense of victory, or satisfaction, or necessary sacrifice. They did not know the feeling of taking a place and keeping it, securing a village and then raising the flag and calling it victory. No sense of order or momentum. No front, no rear, no trenches laid out in neat parallels. No Patton rushing from the Rhine, no beachheads to storm and win and hold for the duration. They did not have targets. They did not have a cause. They did not know if it was a war of ideology or economics or hegemony or spite. On a given day, they did not know where they were in Quang Ngai, or how being there might influence larger outcomes. They did not know the names of most villages. They did not know which villages were critical. They did not know strategies. They did not know the terms of the war, its architecture, the rules of fair play. When they took prisoners, which was rare, they did not know the questions to ask, whether to release a suspect or beat on him. They did not know how to feel.[43]

The American Mission systematically divided the ineffable and volatile Vietnamese land into four clearly defined and manageable units — I Corps, II Corps, III Corps, IV Corps — and within these large units

imposed and reimposed smaller tables providing reference points to facilitate communication and directionality to the war effort. Despite this
panoptic cartographic and classificatory strategy, which, as I suggested
earlier in this book, constitutes the essential technology of the developed (post-Enlightenment) imperial project, Vietnam, like no other land
mass on which the United States army has fought in modern times,
refused to be reduced to this spatialized, classificatory, manageable —
and banalized — abstraction. As virtually everyone who was "in country" bears witness, it remained for such technologically inscribed eyes a
dread-provoking and malevolent labyrinth with no exit.[44]

Indeed, the related invisibility of the insurgents within the dislocating Vietnamese landscape was so baffling to the American soldier
that it precipitated a common and — given their deeply inscribed pos-
itivistic ("American") frame of reference — an ontologically resonant
rhetoric of spectrality. Commensurate with the rhetoric of invisibility
that determines the meaning of Caputo's and O'Brien's representative testimony about the Vietnamese "enemy," the autobiographical
literature of the Vietnam War is saturated with a *culturally induced*
language that can do nothing other than identify the invisible Vietnamese insurgents with a dread-provoking substantial insubstantiality,
with "spirits," "phantoms," "wraiths," or "spooks" that "haunt" the
American hunter:

> We called the enemy ghosts. "Bad night," we'd say, "the ghosts
> are out." To get spooked, in the lingo, meant not only to get
> scared but to get killed. "Don't get spooked," we'd say. "Stay cool,
> stay alive." Or we'd say: "Careful, man, don't give up the ghost."
> The countryside itself seemed spooky — shadows and tunnels and
> incense burning in the dark. The land was haunted. We were fight-
> ing forces that did not obey the laws of twentieth-century science.
> Late at night, on guard, it seemed that all of Vietnam was alive
> and shimmering — odd shapes swaying in the paddies, boogie-men
> in sandals, spirits dancing in old pagodas. It was ghost country,
> and Charlie Cong was the main ghost. The way he came out at
> night. How you never really saw him, just thought you did. Al-
> most magical — appearing, disappearing. He could blend with the
> land, changing form, becoming trees and grass. He could levitate.
> He could fly. He could pass through barbed wire and melt away
> like ice and creep up on you without sound or footsteps. He was
> scary. In the daylight, maybe, you didn't believe in that stuff. You
> laughed it off. You made jokes. But at night you turned into a
> believer: no skeptics in foxholes.[45]

The patrol that morning had the nightmare quality which characterized most small-unit operations in the war. The trail looped and twisted and led nowhere. The company seemed to be marching into a vacuum, haunted by a presence intangible yet real, a sense of being surrounded by something we could not see. It was the inability to see that vexed us most. In that lies the jungle's power to cause fear: it blinds. It arouses the same instinct that makes us apprehensive of places like attics and dark alleys. (*RW,* 80)[46]

Oh, that terrain! The bloody, maddening uncanniness of it! When the hideous Battle of Dak To ended at the top of Hill 875, we announced that 4,000 of them were killed; it had been the purest slaughter, our losses were bad, but clearly it was another American victory. But when the top of the hill was reached, the number of NVA found was four. Four...Spooky. Everything up there was spooky, and it would have been that way even if there had been no war. You were there in a place where you didn't belong, where things were glimpsed for which you would have to pay and where things went unglimpsed for which you would have to pay, a place where they didn't play the mystery but killed you straight off for trespassing. The towns had names that laid a quick, chilly touch on your bones.[47]

The valley floor was even more eerie than the mounds. The rain continued. It was nearly impossible for Alpha to establish their precise position. Surrounded by fog and high grass they could not sight landmarks. The flat valley revealed no clues....

Cherry sat where he had been standing....For extended hours they all humped without speaking. For hours he marched seeing only the one man before him and at times not even seeing him. Cherry longed for a CP meeting. He looked to his rear....An uneasy feeling came upon Cherry. He looked left then right. Somebody was watching. He looked over his shoulder again at McCarthy. The mist was so thick it blurred his image. Cherry could feel eyes on the back of his neck. He glanced around anxiously. He could see nothing but dense walls of elephant grass. Maybe it's better not to look, he thought. He tried to ignore it. His stomach tightened. He felt as if something was about to reach out and grab him.[48]

Crazy Earl holds his bottle by the neck and smashes it across a fallen statue of a fat, smiling, bald-headed gook [a Buddha]. "This ain't a war, it's a series of overlapping riots. We blow them away.

They come up behind us before we're out of sight and shoot us in the ass. I know a guy in One-One that shot a gook and then tied a block of C-4 to him and blew him into little invisible pieces because shooting gooks is a waste of time — they come back to life. But these gooks piss you off so bad that you got to shoot *some* thing, *any* thing. Man, half the confirmed kills I got are civilians and the other half is water boes.[49]

The last of these representative passages bearing witness to the bafflement of the American soldier in the face of the invisible enemy is perhaps the most telling. This is not only because the bafflement precipitated by the Other's invisibility most starkly discloses the utter inefficiency and wastefulness of the rigorous and efficient logic of decidability to which it is necessarily (culturally) restricted: its inability to name and contain the mysterious Other. It is also because, in its deployment of this restricted narrative logic, it self-destructs. To anticipate, it makes explicit the symbiotic relationship between the discursive practices of instrumental reason and spectrality: the seer/hunter becomes the seen/hunted.

In thus overdetermining the spectrality of the invisible "enemy," this baffled writing, which would come to terms with the event of Vietnam, betrays what a purely political or economic analysis of this war, in its reliance on the disciplinary imperatives of positive "science," is precluded from attending to. It does not simply disclose the blindness to alterity — to the Other, the lack, the difference, the trace, that is, the Nothing — *of* the imperial "truth" discourse informing this writing. As the grotesquely rigorous reasoning of the last passage makes chillingly clear, it also discloses the unthought violence that informs the logical economy of its narrative.[50]

The response of the American Mission to the "de-structive" strategy of the elusive Vietnamese Other was not to readjust its "European" military tactics of decidability to a kind of warfare in which the spectral enemy was always hauntingly invisible and unknowable, in which, in other words, the differential Other refused to *obey* the Western rules of warfare. The American Mission, that is to say — and it is important to emphasize this — did not reorient its Western logocentric concept of war in the face of an enemy that refused *to answer to* the fundamental epistemic imperatives of the European Enlightenment: those emanating from the grounding principle of differentiation (within a larger identical structure). I mean by this last, the knowledge-producing disciplinary table (uniforms, insignia, rank, and so on) that would distinguish soldiers from civilians (and women and children) and its linear/circular imperial tactical geometries that would render the enemy's moves locatable, predictable, and masterable. On the contrary, the American response to these unexpected and psychologically and practically baffling conditions precipitated by the enemy's refusal to adhere to the structural imperatives of the hitherto self-evident liberal democratic narrative was — *predictably* — reactive. As is well known (despite the official effort to repress this knowledge), the Pentagon managers and the American Mission in Saigon simply substituted one European form of warfare for another, the frontal assault that would end in the decisive battle for a war of attrition. The "body count," it was hoped, would eventually deplete the spectral numbers of the Vietnamese Other's army to — in a telling locution — the point of no return. True to this unrelenting American will to convert the spectral to verifiable numbers (tabulation), this technologization (and routinizing) of death — Caputo refers to his soul-destroying duties as "Regimental Casualty Reporting Officer" as keeping "Wheeler's [his commanding officer's] scoreboard" (*RW*, 159)[51] — the American Mission retaliated by unleashing a technological firepower against the recalcitrantly invisible and undifferentiated Other unprecedented in (nonatomic) military history:

> We took space back quickly, expensively, with total panic and close to maximum brutality. Our machine was devastating. And versatile. It could do everything but stop. As one American major said, in a successful attempt at attaining history, "We had to destroy Ben Tre in order to save it."[52]

It was, if we recall the testimony of the Bertrand Russell International War Crimes Tribunal of 1968 in Stockholm, a firepower that, in the scope, violence, and, above all, the necessary *indiscriminateness* of its application, bordered on genocide.[53]

When this indiscriminate violence against the Vietnamese people and their earth at large became inescapably visible to the American public, a significant — and still to be adequately questioned — transformation of the representation of America's involvement in Vietnam began to manifest itself in the hegemonic discourse of the culture industry and in that of many government officials and intellectuals who had hitherto supported or had acquiesced to it, a transformation that eventually aligned itself with that of the prominent antiwar spokespersons. The brutal conduct of the war came increasingly to be represented as a political *betrayal* of the principles of liberal democracy. As I have been suggesting in demonstrating the impossibility of differentiating the ontological representation and the military practice of America in Vietnam, it is of crucial importance to remark about this turn that the genocidal — leveling — assault on the Vietnamese people was not simply a military violence aimed at achieving an economic/political objective. It was also and indissolubly a violence at the sites of ontology and culture, not to say of race and gender. The ugly justification by General Mark Clark, one of the great American commanders of World War II, for the obliterative B-52 bombings of North Vietnam in 1968 was no accident: "I don't think it's necessary to have an invasion of North Vietnam. And it would be just exactly what the enemy wants. He'd like us to put down 100,000 men in the field. He'd put down 100,000. They're willing to lose half of theirs, and ours is a precious commodity. And I wouldn't trade one dead American for 50 dead Chinamen."[54] (It is beyond the scope of this chapter to apply Clark's racist logic to the demographics of death within the American military body. Given the obvious fact that proportionately far more blacks than whites were fighting "Chinamen" in Vietnam, one is compelled to ask whether the dominant culture that Clark represents believed that the black man was, in the general's typically "American" rhetoric, as precious a commodity as his white counterpart.)

This indissoluble relay of quantified violence mounted by the United States against the spectral Other (the Military Mission called this indiscriminate violently reductive process "pacification") is clearly suggested by Frances FitzGerald in *Fire in the Lake* (1972). It is a book that remains one of the most profound meditations on the Vietnam War and one that, despite its predating of the posthumanist occasion, deserves to be carefully considered in any rethinking of the Vietnam decade in the post–Cold War period, especially that aspect of the war pertaining to the question of the relationship between cultural representation (narrative) and practice:

> At the Guam conference [April 1967] President Johnson took the long-awaited step of putting all civilian operations under the command of General Westmoreland. His move signified that Washington no longer gave even symbolic importance to the notion of a "political" war waged by the Vietnamese government. The reign of the U.S. military had begun, and with it the strategy of quantity in civilian as well as military affairs.
>
> As an assistant to Westmoreland, Robert Komer had something of the general's notion of scale. After all the history of failed aid programs, he believed that the only hope for success lay in saturation.... The U.S. government had no choice but to force its supplies upon the Vietnamese people: thousands of tons of bulgar wheat, thousands of gallons of cooking oil, tons of pharmaceuticals, enough seed to plant New Jersey with miracle rice, enough fertilizer for the same, light bulbs, garbage trucks, an atomic re-

actor, enough concrete to pave a province, enough corrugated tin to roof it, enough barbed wire to circle it seventeen times, dentists' drills, soybean seedlings, sewing kits, mortars, machine tools, toothbrushes, plumbing, and land mines.

In part, of course, this aid was absolutely necessary, for the U.S. military was at the same time bombing, defoliating, and moving villages at such a rate that all the aid the United States could ship would not have been excessive as refugee relief.[55]

In other words, this *Logos*-enabled totalizing and reifying will to narrative decidability manifests itself at this juncture of America's involvement in Vietnam in a promissory instrumental logical economy gone mad — a mono-mania, as it were. Like Wallace Stevens's jar in Tennessee, as Michael Herr puts the synecdochic instance of the "Battle" of Khe Sanh, it "took dominion everywhere":

> All that was certain was that Khe Sanh had become a passion, the false love object in the heart of the Command.... In its outlines, the promise was delicious: Victory! A vision of as many as 40,000 of them out there in the open, fighting it out on our terms, fighting for once like men, fighting to no avail. There would be a battle, a set-piece battle where he could be killed by the numbers, killed wholesale, and if we killed enough of him, maybe he would go away. In the face of such a promise, the question of defeat could not even be considered, no more than the question of whether, after Tet, Khe Sanh might have become militarily unwise and even absurd. Once it was all locked in place, Khe Sanh became like the planted jar in Wallace Stevens' poem. It took dominion everywhere.[56]

In *Ariel and the Police,* Frank Lentricchia brilliantly appropriates Herr's historically resonant insight into the affiliation between planting a promissory discourse and its taking dominion everywhere (the affiliated imperial metaphorics of the center and the periphery should not be overlooked) for his "New Americanist" project. In the process, he suggests how deeply backgrounded in the American national self this nexus between knowledge production (the quantification/technologization of the spectral nothing) and imperial power is. He invokes the critiques of its imperial operations by such otherwise unlikely representative figures from quite various sites of American cultural production and times of American history as Stevens, William James, and Herr:

> Had Wallace Stevens lived through our Vietnam period he might have had the right answer to the question posed by Norman Mailer in 1967: *Why Are We in Vietnam?* Had he forgotten

what he knew, long before our military intervention in Southeast Asia, he would have been (had he lived so long) reminded by Michael Herr who at the end of his book *Dispatches* (1970) wrote: "Vietnam Vietnam Vietnam, we've all been there." Herr maybe in part knew what he knew because he had read Stevens, who taught him about where we've all been, all along: "Once it was all locked in place, Khe Sanh became like the planted jar in Wallace Stevens' poem. It took dominion everywhere." Herr's perversely perfect mixed metaphor of the "planted jar," if it might have struck Stevens as an incisive reading of his poem, might also have awakened in him an obscure memory of one of the powerful philosophical presences of his Harvard days, William James, writing out of the bitterness of his political awakening, writing on 1 March 1899 in the *Boston Evening Transcript* against our first imperial incursion in the Orient: "We are destroying down to the root every germ of a healthy national life in these unfortunate people.... We must sow our ideals, plant our order, impose our God." James might have ended his letter: "The Philippines the Philippines the Philippines, we've all been there."[57]

But Herr's resonant genealogical insight should not be restricted to the site of (geo)politics alone, as Lentricchia tends to do. This providentially justified promissory planting that took dominion everywhere was not — and has never been — confined simply to geopolitical space. It was, from the beginning (when the Puritans — the "saving remnant" or "seed-bearers" — planted the Massachusetts Bay Colony), carried out by America all along the indissoluble continuum of being, from the ontological (which is to say, the site of thinking as such) through the cultural, sexual, and racial to the sociopolitical sites. Indeed, as Herr's quite revealing focus on representation (the futural power of the promise informing the metaphorical planting) suggests, it is even arguable that America overdetermined the central ontological site, rendered it, that is, the basis of it polyvalent conduct of the Vietnam War. It did not simply serve as the ultimate justification for, but also as the enabling *principle* of, the indiscriminate genocidal military practice of attrition.

What I am suggesting in thus demonstrating the complicity between the principles informing the American project of "winning the hearts and minds" of the Vietnamese people and the genocidal devastation of Vietnam — indeed, the priority of these principles over the (superstructural) latter — is that the savagely civilized execution of the war disclosed a terrible but essential contradiction in the discourse of "America." It is a contradiction that, if it did not decisively delegitimize its claims to universal truth at that time, has haunted them ever since. The pursuit of the end of its instrumentalist logical economy by the United States — of its "objective," as the affiliated rhetoric of military tactics would put it — ended in the self-de-struction of that logic. The "America" that intervened in Vietnam as early as the end of World War II represented itself as that exceptionalist collective cultural identity that had its origins in the Puritans' New Adamic errand in the wilderness (a wilderness haunted by the native "salvages," who appeared to the Puritans as Satanic "spirits"). It was thus an "America" that represented its intervention in Vietnam as a benign New World mission intended to plant the Word (the universal principle of freedom) that Europe, in the form of a decadent French colonialism, had forgotten in its selfish materialist pursuit of power. In the process of fulfilling what it represented as its historically ordained mission, "America" (like Aeneas vis-à-vis Turnus at the end of the *Aeneid*) showed itself to be informed by a murderous (onto)logic, a logic of over-sight that, at a certain critical point in the encounter, justifies and compels the practical obliteration of any differential and resistant force that would undermine its claim to universal truth and thus to its universal authority.

Indeed, the self-destruction of America's cultural identity showed that this informing essentialist and imperial onto-logic rendered the process of obliteration productively possible by its reifying specular or panoptic imperatives. I mean the inherent power of this metaphysical logic to reduce difference (*physis*) to identity from above (*meta*), to name the nothing and the spectral differences it disseminates and thus to "comprehend" them: to make them *totally graspable (com+prehendere)*, an "it" that thus becomes "practically assailable," as it were. Thus, like Oedipus in Sophocles' de-struction of the emergent positivist discourse of seeing in classical Greece (or Darius in Herodotus's analogous reversal of the hunter/hunted relationship in his paradigmatic account of the Scythians' defeat of the invading Persians) and the detective of the postmodern anti–detective story,[58] the self-certain American detective in this antinarrative turns out to be the criminal; the judge turns out to be the judged; the man of reason turns out to be the madman. In short, to invoke the metaphorics that saturates the literature of witness emanating from the Vietnam War — and which I have said is intrinsic to the imperial project — the *see*-er turns out to be the *seen*.

"Search and destroy": this ubiquitous phrase in the discourse of the Vietnam War — by now reduced to a cliché emptied out of the horrible content it acquired with the exposure of such atrocities as the My Lai massacre — is, in fact, a codification of the indiscriminate violence *mandated* by the reactive military strategy developed by the relay of commands constituting Military Assistance Command Vietnam (MACV) to defeat the uncannily invisible and elusive enemy in Vietnam. In thus putting ontological representation (and its origins in Roman imperialism) back into play in this genealogical retrieval of the event called "Vietnam" that would contribute to the writing of the history of the present global occasion, I want to suggest that this sedimented locution must be understood in more than simply military terms. It must also be read as the fulfillment in practice — as the material *end* — of the benign logical economy of the "disinterested" pursuit of truth. It must, that is, be understood as the violent process of reification, inaugurated by imperialist Rome, privileged and developed by Enlightenment Europe, and appropriated by an "exceptionalist" America in modernity, that reduces the differential and elusive nothingness of being — its "spectrality" — to an identical *something* in order to bring "it" to light under the commanding and encompassing gaze of the concentering imperial eye.

This delegitimizing contradiction in the logic of "America" — this complicity between the representation of being and power, seeing and domination, that is, searching out and destroying — manifested itself a quarter of a century ago in the epochal decade of the Vietnam War. But this chronology should not be allowed to justify the politically conservative interpretation of this disclosure that views it as an irrelevant aberration within American history (Francis Fukuyama and James Ceaser, for example). Nor should it be allowed to justify the politically liberal interpretation, which views it as an "error of judgment" (Arthur Schlesinger, Robert McNamara, and Richard Rorty, for example). It should not, that is, occlude the perception of the indissoluble continuity between the America of the Vietnam War and the America of the historical "revolutionary" past and of the post–Cold War present. As the rhetoric I have underscored to foreground its essence suggests, this resonant contradiction in the discourse and practice of "America" was, for example, the proleptic testimony of Herman Melville, whose epochal witness, especially in *Moby-Dick,* has been consensually obliterated by the custodians of the American Cultural Memory, not only by the enraged "Americanists" of his generation, but by the idolatrous founders of American literary studies — F. O. Matthiessen, Lionel Trilling, Richard Chase, R. W. B. Lewis, Quentin Anderson, and so on — at the outset of the Cold War.[59] For in that anticanonical, indeed, subversive, novel, Melville recognized that Captain Ahab's deadly *mono*mania was the fulfillment and end of the (onto)logic the "first" European settlers of America: the Puritans' New Adamic representation of being and its providentially ordained historical errand in the wilderness. He recognized, in other words, that Ahab's unrelenting and

unerring pursuit of the elusive white whale was precisely an American
search and destroy mission against a spectral enemy that, like the American Mission's in Vietnam, was informed, legitimized, and enabled by
the (American) Word. Reconstellating Melville's witness into the context
of the Vietnam War, one can no longer read the following "canonical"
passage from *Moby-Dick* without visualizing the systematic torching of
Vietnamese villages, the defoliation of the Vietnamese landscape, the
chemical poisoning of the rice paddies, the relentless B-52 bombings —
all undertaken in the name of "saving Vietnam" for the free world:

> The White Whale swam before him as the monomaniac incarna-
> tion of all those malicious agencies which some deep men feel
> eating in them, till they are left living on with half a heart and
> half a lung. That intangible malignity which has been from the
> beginning; to whose dominion even the modern Christians ascribe
> one-half of the worlds; which the ancient Ophites of the east rever-
> enced in their statue devil; — Ahab did not fall down and worship
> it like them; but deliriously transferring its idea to the abhorred
> white whale, he pitted himself, all mutilated, against it. All that
> most maddens and torments; all that stirs up the lees of things;
> all truth with malice in it; all that cracks the sinews and cakes
> the brain; all the subtle demonisms of life and thought; all evil, to
> crazy Ahab, were visibly personified, and made practically assail-
> able in Moby Dick. He piled upon the whale's white hump the sum
> of all the general rage and hate felt by his whole race from Adam
> down; and then, as if his chest had been a mortar, he burst his hot
> heart's shell upon it.[60]

This complicity between an ontology of presence and a concentering violence is also and fundamentally the symptomatic testimony of
virtually all the American soldiers — not simply of Lieutenant William
Calley's notoriously visible account of the My Lai massacre — who
have written about their "experiences" in Vietnam, even as they try
desperately to transform the brutal *thisness* — the historical specificity
of America's brutal conduct — of the Vietnam War into war in general. Philip Caputo's *A Rumor of War,* for example, is a retrospective
meditation on the always and increasingly dislocating evanescence of
the enemy — and the consequent "irresistible compulsion to do something." It culminates in a recollection of his fateful decision to order the
cold-blooded execution of two young Vietnamese boys suspected of being Vietcong, who, along with the girl who was beaten in the process,
turned out to be civilians. In his agonized effort to render his act of

murder intelligible, Caputo has recourse to a rhetoric that is remarkably similar to Melville's representation of Captain Ahab's state of mind:

> My thoughts and feelings over the next few hours are irretrievably jumbled now, but at some point in the early evening, I was seized by an irresistible compulsion to do something. "Something's got to be done" was about the clearest thought that passed through my brain. I was fixated on the company's intolerable predicament. We could now muster only half of our original strength, and half of our effectives had been wounded at least once. If we suffered as many casualties in the next month as we had in the past, we would be down to fifty or sixty men, little more than a reinforced platoon. It was madness for us to go on walking down those trails and tripping booby traps without any chance to retaliate. *Retaliate.* The word rang in my head. *I will retaliate.* It was then that my chaotic thoughts began to focus on the two men whom Le Dung, Crowe's informant, had identified as Viet Cong. My mind did more than focus on them; it fixed on them like a heat-seeking missile fixing on the tailpipe of a jet. They became an obsession. I would get them. I would get them before they got any more of us; before they got me. I'm going to get those bastards, I said to myself, suddenly feeling giddy. (*RW*, 298–99)[61]

Caputo symptomatically resists the reductive charge of murder leveled by the Marine Command in its characteristically cynical effort to exonerate itself (and "America") of culpability. But like virtually all of the testimony of those "eye witnesses" who fought the war, he fails to conceptualize adequately the necessarily analogical relation between the logic informing his private act and that intrinsic to the United States's public practice. Instead, he attributes his temporary aberration to the dehumanizing effects of "the war," whereas his text at large points to the absolute complicity between his *American* (anthropo)logic and the culminating act of violence. In a way that Melville does not, Caputo fails to perceive or resists acknowledging that the logic that drove him to this act of murder is the logic of the culture he represents. He cannot see or resists admitting that this reifying logic is one that finally and inexorably manifests itself in an obsessed "focus" and "fixing," a "monomaniacal" reification, as it were, of the omnipresent uncanny force of the spectral Other intended, as Melville says of Ahab's objectification of the white whale into Moby Dick, to render "it" "practically assailable," that, in other words, it constitutes the necessary replication *in miniature* of the identifying logic of the collective totality of which he is an inscribed individual part. I do not simply mean the instrumental logic pursued by the military court that is trying Caputo's "case," the logic of *closure* that obliterates the Vietnam War (including the political motives of the United States) in the blank — spectral — space of the trial's formal detective-story scenario. I also, and above all, mean the founding New Adamic/frontier logic and practice of "America" at large in Vietnam. This is what Caputo does not quite say in his agonized climactic effort against his inscribed grain to read the "conspicuously blank" square on the official form containing — and predisposing once and for all — the "truth" of the history of his "case":

> There was a lot of other stuff — statements by witnesses, inquiry reports, and so forth — but one square on form DD457 was conspicuously blank. It was the square labeled EXPLANATORY OR EXTENUATING CIRCUMSTANCES ARE SUBMITTED HEREWITH. Early in the investigation, I wondered why the investigating officer had not submitted any explanatory or extenuating circumstances. Later, after I had time to think things over, I drew my own conclusion: the explanatory circumstance was the war. The killings had occurred in war. They had occurred, moreover, in a war whose sole aim was to kill Viet Cong, a war in which those ordered to do the killing often could not distinguish the Viet Cong from the civilians, a war in which civilians in "free-fire zones" were killed every day by weapons far more horrible than pistols and shotguns. The deaths of Le Dung and Le Du could not be divorced from the nature and conduct of the war. They were an inevitable product of the war. As I had come to see it, America could not intervene in a people's war without killing some of the people. But to raise those points in explanation or extenuation would be to raise a host of ambiguous moral questions. It could even raise the question of the morality of American intervention in Vietnam; or, as one officer told me, "It would open up a real can of worms." Therefore, the five men in the patrol and I were to be tried as common criminals, much as if we had murdered two people in the course of a bank robbery during peacetime. If we were found guilty, the Marine Corps' institutional conscience would be clear. Six criminals, who, of course, did not represent the majority of America's fine fighting sons, had been brought to justice. Case closed. If we were found innocent, the Marine Corps could say, "Justice has taken its course, and in a court-martial conducted according to the facts and the rules of evidence, no crime was found to have been committed." Case closed. Either way, the military institution won. (*RW,* 305–6)[62]

If Caputo's witness against America is distorted by his vestigial inscription by "America," specifically by the postwar therapeutic discourse of universalism, Michael Herr's is not in the aftermath of the Tet Offensive in 1968. The tragic horror in Melville's antebellum text becomes the ludic horror of carnival in Herr's own postmodern testimony, as the intonations recalling the Hollywood frontiersman voice of John Wayne in the last sentence of the inaugural passage of his great book suggest. But, like Caputo's symptomatic testimony, Herr's text bears witness not only to the specter that haunts both the American grunt and the collective totality of which he is a member, but also to the complicity of their monomaniacal — indiscriminately violent — search and destroy logic:

> *At the end of my first week in-country I met an information officer*
> *in the headquarters of the 25th Division at Cu Chi who showed*
> *me on his map and then from his chopper what they'd done to*
> *the Ho Bo Woods, the vanished Ho Bo Woods, taken off by giant*
> *Rome plows and chemicals and long, slow fire, wasting hundreds*
> *of acres of cultivated plantation and wild forest alike, "denying the*
> *enemy valuable resources and cover."*
>
> *It had been part of his job for nearly a year now to tell people*
> *about that operation; correspondents, touring congressmen, movie*
> *stars, corporation presidents, staff officers from half of the armies*
> *in the world, and he still couldn't get over it. It seemed to be keep-*
> *ing him young, his enthusiasm made you feel that even the letters*
> *he wrote home to his wife were full of it, it really showed what you*
> *could do if you had the know-how and the hardware. And if in*
> *the months following that operation incidences of enemy activity*
> *in the large area of War Zone C had increased "significantly," and*
> *American losses had doubled and then doubled again, none of it*
> *was happening in any damn Ho Bo Wood, you'd better believe it.*[63]

Thinking the Specter of Vietnam

The Question of the nothing puts us, the questioners, in question.
— Martin Heidegger, "What Is Metaphysics?"

Pyle said, "It's awful." He looked at the wet on his shoes and said in a sick voice, "What's that?"
    "Blood," I said. "Haven't you ever seen it before?"
    He said, "I must get them cleaned before I see the Minister."
— Graham Greene, *The Quiet American*

We are now, after this lengthy detour, prepared to address the question posed earlier about the unabated persistence of the national obsession over Vietnam long after the end of the war, indeed, after the official announcement of the end of its end in the wake of the United States's victory over the Iraqi army in 1991. I mean the question about the unrelenting and unassuagable anxiety that continues to afflict the American national self: What, precisely, has the post-Vietnam American cultural agenda of forgetting been trying obsessively to forget? What, as it were, is the specter that has haunted "America" since its intervention a half-century ago in a people's war in a Third World country in Southeast Asia? The foregoing retrieval of the historical specificity of the Vietnam War suggests that the answer to this question lies precisely in the American Cultural Memory's systematic (if not conspiratorial) occlusion of its historicity by metaphorizing the actual cultural and sociopolitical effects of the war, first in the therapeutic terms of "healing a wound" and later, in the context of the end of the Cold War, of "kicking" a national neurosis (the Vietnam syndrome). The retrieval of the *thisness* of the Vietnam War from its generalization, in other words, suggests that what is at stake in the obsessive national effort to allay this ghost is far more ideologically important than the belated rehabilitation of the American veteran. Indeed, the ideological stakes are far more important than the recuperation of the national (good)will (as it has been iteratively claimed by those consensus builders who are calculatively aware of this amnesiac process) or, for that matter, than America's loss of its first war (as it is claimed by those adversarial intellectuals who would resist this amnesiac process). The retrieved historical context suggests, rather, that this would-be forgotten is nothing less than the symptomatic recognition of the abyssal aporetic space opened up in the logic of liberal democracy by the disclosure of the necessary complicity between the ontologically derived principles of American democracy not simply with imperialism, but also with the violent practice of genocidal power. It is a complicity that, in keeping with the Enlightenment's "repressive hypothesis," had heretofore been occluded by the alleged incommensurability between the principles and the violence. The retrieval of the *thisness* of the Vietnam War suggests, in short, that this would-be forgotten — this spectral trace, as it were — is the dreadfully intolerable because culturally and politically disabling awareness of an epistemic break. I mean a break that has rendered the truth of the *idea* of "America" vulnerable to radical interrogation at a moment when it is loudly representing itself as the plenary "end" — the noncontradictory truth — of History.

By thus remembering the spectral reality that the American Cultural Memory would forget and "naming it" an "epistemic break," I am not restricting my critique to a constituency of the dominant culture that would employ power overtly in the name of the self-evidently benign principle of "America." I am also, and above all, pointing to the delegitimation of an "alternative" — liberal/recuperative — but finally continuous critique that represents this resonantly spectral contradiction as an *accident* of American history: as the consequent, that is, either of a "mistake" of individual and/or national judgment (Robert McNamara, for example) or of a political "betrayal" of the positive principles of liberal American democracy (Senator William Fulbright, Arthur Schlesinger Jr., and Richard Rorty, for example). By "epistemic break" I mean, rather, like Foucault, the decisive and irreversible disintegration and delegitimation of the indissoluble relay of representational discourses — ontological, epistemological, cultural, sociopolitical — that collectively, however unevenly, constitute what a period at large assumes and represents to be the self-evident universal truth. I mean specifically the (self-)exposure of the latent obliterating violence against being — we are entitled now to call it "the Ahabism" — informing the logical economy of the principles of freedom and equality professed by exceptionalist "America": "America," that is, understood in terms of the secularization of the Puritan errand in the wilderness in the period of the Enlightenment (the American Revolution and the making of the American Constitution) and its expansionist practice in the nineteenth century in the name of Manifest Destiny.[64] To appropriate Antonio Gramsci's historically specific terms, I mean the self-de-struction of the hegemonic discourse of the American cultural identity and its radical and decisive delegitimation. Henceforth, "America" will no longer be able to repress the Other or accommodate it within its imperial structure; the Other will always already manifest itself as a specter that haunts the "truth" of "America." This decisive appearance of the spectral gaze is what I have taken and continue to take the "postmodern condition" to mean — if it is recognized that America's global mission is the consequence not of its self-professed exceptionalist status, but of its self-proclaimed assumption of the burden of fulfilling the *mission civilisatrice* that Europe (the Old World) betrayed in its decadence.

Let me recall at this critical conjuncture the post–Cold War Hegelian theorization of the dominant culture's general representation of the end of the Cold War as the planetary triumph of liberal capitalist democracy and the end of history. Reconstellated into the historical context I have retrieved — the context that this neo-Hegelian problematic would, because of its "historical superfluity," obliterate as a "distraction" from "the larger [completed] pattern" of History[65] — this post–Cold War representation of contemporary history comes to seem remarkably hollow. It takes on the lineaments of a kind of desperate rewriting — or "airbrushing"[66] — of history that liberal democratic Cold Warriors always

and relentlessly accused communist Cold War historians of perpetrat-
ing. As its deletion of this epochally transformative hot moment of the
Cold War suggests, in other words, this "objective" representation of
the post–Cold War global scene becomes itself, like the monomaniacal
logic that propels Captain Ahab's inexorable pursuit of the white whale,
the self-confirming imperial end of the *all*-inclusive and ruthlessly repressive Cold War narrative inaugurated at the end of World War II to
contain any thought or action — both within and beyond America's borders — resembling Marxist communism. Or, rather, this end-of-history
discourse becomes the decisive resolution *in theory* of that recuperative
phase of the relentlessly undemocratic democratic Cold War narrative
undertaken to pacify the threat to the national consensus posed by the
withdrawal of spontaneous consent to the "truth" of "America" by a
large constituency of American society in response to the self-disclosure
of the terrible contradictions — the genocidal violence — informing the
benign logic of America's intervention in the Vietnam "wilderness" and
its conduct of the war. That is to say, this end-of-history discourse can
be seen as the fulfillment of the postwar cultural imperative "to heal the
wound."

But the implications of this retrieval of the terrible specificity of the
Vietnam War are not limited to the exposure of the historical occlusions
thematized by the amnesiac end-of-history discourse. In foregrounding
the inordinately important role played by ontological representation in
the renarrativization of the Cold War after the decisive self-destruction
of the discourse of "America" during the decade of the Vietnam War,
this retrieval also suggests why the presently privileged oppositional discourses are inadequate to the task of resisting the dominant culture's
representation of the global post–Cold War occasion as the end of history (the *Pax Metaphysica*) and the advent of the New World Order
presided over by the United States: the *Pax Americana*. I am referring
specifically to the neo-Marxist discourse deriving from Fredric Jameson's
identification of postmodernism with the cultural logic of late capitalism, to the New Historicism, to the cultural and postcolonial criticisms
that in large part derive from the former, and to that postnational discourse, exemplified by Bill Reading's, that, in attempting to overcome
the ineffectuality of these, would assume a global perspective focused
on transnational capital that represents "America" as obsolete.

It will be the purpose of the remaining chapters of this book to an-
alyze the inadequacies of these "postmodern" discourses to the task
of resisting the discourse of the *Pax Americana* and to proffer prolo-
gomemally an alternative on the basis of this critical analysis. Here, it
will suffice to suggest that these oppositional discourses are, each in its

own particular way, blinded by their insights not only to precisely what, in the present historical conjuncture, is strongest in the discourse of the dominant liberal/capitalist culture of the post–Cold War period: its justification of global power on the *basis* of an ontological representation of temporal history (being) that ends in the triumph of the cultural, social, political, and especially economic formations that are constructed on its foundation. In failing to perceive what is strongest in the "triumphant" imperial discourse of liberal/capitalist democracy, each of these oppositional discourses, in turn, is also blinded to what is weakest and most vulnerable in it. I mean, to repeat, the ontological contradiction — what I have been calling the specter — at the enabling center of its "benign" global discourse: the violent genocidal will to power that was the "end" of the (onto)logical economy that justified America's intervention in Vietnam and its indiscriminately murderous conduct of the war.

All of which is to say, finally, that an adversarial discourse that would be adequate to the task of resisting the New World Order — that, in Noam Chomsky's aptly ironic phrase, would be capable of "deterring democracy"[67] — would do well not simply to reconstellate and rethink "Vietnam" in the context of the annunciation of the end of history, but, in doing so, to take its directives precisely from the *spectral contradictions* (the radical differences) precipitated by the "fulfillment" of the imperial logic of the American *anthropologos* in the Vietnam War. In other words, the retrieval of the repressed history of the Vietnam War points to an adversarial strategy that would refuse to engage its infinitely more formidable antagonist according to the terms prescribed by the latter's imperial problematic, would not, that is, be answerable to the "truth" of its visibly invisible metanarrative. It calls for the adoption of a strategy that exploits its adversary's essential weakness: the powerful will to closure that hides behind its tolerance of difference, its alleged pluralism. It calls, that is, for an adversarial strategy that, like the strategy of the Vietnamese Other in the face of the utterly predictable narrativity of the American invaders' metaphysically structured discourse and practice, takes the form of an itinerant spectrality. I mean a nomadic phantasmagoric absence, a mobile nonpresent presence, a haunting invisibility, that reverses the panoptic gaze of the dominant culture in transforming itself as seen into absent see-er. In short, the retrieval of the repressed history of the Vietnam War calls for a de-structive strategy that, like the Vietnamese Other vis-à-vis "America," resists identification and thus frustrates the will to closure of the triumphant culture and in so doing dis-integrates its discourse of decidability and arrival, which is to say, disempowers and delegitimizes its imperial power and legitimacy.

   Commenting on the representation of the Vietnam War by the American Mission and the legion of American correspondents based in Saigon who got their truths from it, Michael Herr writes decisively:

> [I]n back of every column of print you read about Vietnam there was a dripping, laughing death-face; it hid there in the newspapers and magazines and held to your television screen for hours after the set was turned off for the night, an after-image that simply wanted to tell you at last what somehow had not been told.[68]

It is not simply the story — the "secret history"[69] — that had somehow not been told by the American media that now, in the post–Cold War occasion, calls for retrieval. What the collective will to forget this story demands beyond that imperative is that we *think* the laughing death-face — the polysemous specter of Vietnam — that remained to haunt our information-filled American living room long after we turned our television set off. For in that haunting apparition there resides a "reality," a "saying," that, precisely because of its "unreality" and its unsayableness, can have no proper place in the tables of the New World Order. To say that this "reality" — this "saying" — can have no proper place in the tables of the New World Order is to say, of course, that "it" constitutes a mortal threat to the "triumphant" technological "age of the world picture."

Chapter 4

"Theory" and the End of History
Rethinking Postmodernity

What is decisive is that the Latinization [of Greek thinking] occurs as a *transformation of the essence of truth and Being* within the essence of the Greco-Roman domain of history. . . . This transformation of the essence of truth and Being is the genuine event of history. . . . [We] still think the Greek *polis* and the "political" in a totally un-Greek fashion. We think the "political" as Romans, i.e. imperially.
— MARTIN HEIDEGGER, *Parmenides*

The Vietnam War, as I have suggested, was the epochal moment in contemporary history that bore witness to the "end" of the discourse of ("American") Man. It did not simply disclose the violent contradictions, including its continuity with Europe, inhering in the benign exceptionalist logic of liberal American democracy. This disclosive moment also instigated the e-mergence of a multiplicity of historical subject positions (contradictory Others) hitherto repressed or marginalized by a larger and dominant cultural identity: "America."[1] But because this multi-situated emergence remained intransigently symptomatic throughout the Vietnam decade, it failed to accomplish the potential social revolution that the decentering of the anthropological center — the postmodern occasion — promised. In the wake of this failure, and partly because of the protest movement's resistance to theory, the late 1960s also precipitated a variety of (often overlapping) adversarial theoretical discourses — deconstruction, post-Freudian psychoanalysis, neo-Marxism, genealogy, semiology, feminism, gay criticism, black criticism, postcolonial criticism, and so on — each committed to thinking the multiple possibilities vis-à-vis the subject, gender, sexual identity, race, culture, or socio-politics that this decentering/inaugural event disclosed. These theoretical initiatives went far to confirm the essential illegitimacy of the dominant discourse and to suggest viable alternatives. Despite their relatedness, however, they have remained vestigially disciplinary — each more or less a base to the superstructurality of the (epiphenomenal) others. As a consequence, the history of "postmodern" theory since the Vietnam War

170

has been characterized by an internecine struggle of theoretical identities for institutional ascendancy. The failure to think the decentering of the subject beyond itself to its transdisciplinary imperatives also precluded the possibility of thinking a new, truly postmodern, polity against the anthropologism of the dominant culture: a coalitional solidarity of *identityless identities,* identities based not on ontologically essentialist grounds, but on the historically specific and fluid imbalances of power relations in post-Enlightenment modernity.[2]

Initially, in the years immediately following the Vietnam War, it was deconstruction that determined the meaning of postmodernism and gained dominance as the representative of opposition in North America. But it was not long before the easy institutionalization of deconstructive theory foregrounded its essential limitations, especially in the eyes of the practitioners of more "worldly" adversarial discourses. Its textualization of the ontological difference — the radical temporality of being — precipitated by the decentering of the *anthropologos* rendered the *différance* of its discourse in-different. It became, especially in the work of the American followers of Derrida, a formalist — ahistorical — textual practice that reduced the historical specificity of the texts it addressed to a free-floating and entropic Same.[3] As a result of this failure to harness its antimetaphysical and decolonizing ontology to sociopolitical critique, deconstruction lost its authority to represent the postmodernity of the "postmodern age" for an adversarial culture. And its positive and enabling contribution — its disclosure of the imperial "center elsewhere" informing the discourse of Enlightenment humanism — was rendered suspect in the eyes of the more "worldly discourses" that superseded it.

Two of these have achieved a degree of transdisciplinary inclusiveness. One is that representation of the postmodern occasion deriving from neo-Marxist theorists such as Guy Debord, Fredric Jameson, and Jean Baudrillard. This is the discourse that represents the postmodern as *symptomatic* — the cultural dominant — of the age, the discourse, in other words, that identifies postmodernism not with a radical subversive initiative in cultural/critical production, but with the (simulacral) cultural logic of late capitalism. The other is the New Historicism, which has been appropriated by what is generally and vaguely called "cultural critique" and that includes certain forms of feminist, homosexual, black, ethnic, and postcolonial criticism. Often (mistakenly) identified with Michel Foucault's critical genealogy, this New Historicism assumes the postmodern moment to be a historical mutation *without* roots in the past, a radical break in a continuous (Occidental) tradition of ontological representation that has its narrative origin in the Roman appropriation of Greek thinking in behalf of the *imperium sine fini.*

These two representations of postmodernism have by now established their hegemony over Left criticism in North America (though their failure to affect the world has instigated a growing reactionary momentum from the Left that would recuperate the Marx of the Enlightenment in behalf of completing the "unfinished project of modernity").[4] But in privileging historical specificity against the indifferent ahistoricality of the textualized *différance,* these versions of postmodernism simply reverse the binary opposition that limits deconstruction. They ignore, eschew, or circumvent, that is, resist thinking, the site of ontological representation — the site that deconstruction overdetermined. However preferable to this early version of deconstruction, these privileged representations of postmodernism, that is, manifest paradoxically the *forgetting* of the decisive and critically enabling contradictions inhering in the humanist discourse of American modernity (not least its representation of history) disclosed by its self-destruction in the decade of the Vietnam War.

In order to establish the context of my critique of these prevailing neo-Marxist and New Historicist discourses, I want again to retrieve and underscore what to them is, if not entirely invisible, a matter of relative indifference. I am referring to the rehabilitated "Hegelian" metaphysics informing the dominant culture's triumphalist — hegemonic — representation of the post–Cold War historical conjuncture as the end of history presided over by liberal/capitalist democracy. Only Jacques Derrida has recognized this triumphalist discourse to be the exemplary expression of a recuperated reactionary planetary hegemony, of an ominous cultural dominant, sponsored by a renewed "Holy Alliance" that is imperial in essence, against "the specter of communism."[5] And this is no accident. For Derrida's belated but very suggestive effort to reconcile deconstruction — that is to say, an anti-onto-logical ontology — with a "certain spirit of Marx" (one of several)[6] constitutes not simply a tacit recognition of the inadequacy of deconstruction *as such* to the present historical task of deterring liberal/capitalist democracy, the *Pax Americana.* Equally, if not more importantly, Derrida's reconciliatory gesture is informed by an acute awareness of the inadequacy of the prevailing New Historicist and neo-Marxist representations of postmodernism to this task. For, he implies, in representing deconstruction (the "founding" discourse of postmodernism) as obsolete or even complicitous with the dominant culture, these "emancipatory" discourses have, in the name of history, ironically blinded themselves to the historical imperatives — the polyvalent (neo)imperialism — enabled by the logocentrism that continues to constitute the ground of the recuperated and triumphant discourse of liberal/capitalist democracy.

"Jamesonian" Postmodernism and the Elusive Center

I think first of all that the Western theoretical establishment should take a moratorium on producing a global solution.... Try to behave as if you are part of the margin, try to unlearn your privilege. This, I think, would be a lesson that one could draw, in a very crude way, from the post-structuralist enterprise.   — GAYATRI CHAKRAVORTY SPIVAK,
"The Post-modern Condition: The End of Politics?"

Let me consider the "Jamesonian" representation of postmodernity, which identifies it with the "logic of late capitalism," that is to say, with the triumphant emergence of global consumerism.[7] According to this neo-Marxist interpretation, postmodernism (or postcolonialism, its allotrope),[8] operates in terms of a radically new "spatial logic of the simulacrum," a deontologized view of being as, in Baudrillard's term, "hyperspace." In this postmodern hyperspace, historical depth (including that informing modernism)[9] — and the affect intrinsic to it — is annulled by way of the reduction of historicity to a self-referential surface of multitudinous fragments or simulacra: "a field of stylistic and discursive heterogeneity without norms," in which the "past as 'referent' finds itself gradually bracketed, and then effaced altogether, leaving us with nothing but texts."[10] Thus cultural production at large — which, not incidentally, includes the discourse of poststructuralism[11] — in this globalized version of postmodernism serves what Jameson, following Guy Debord, calls the capitalist *société de la spectacle.*[12] Even those cultural products that are intended to be critical of late capitalism become "pastiche" and thus implicated in late capitalist hegemony. This, for example, is the fate of Derrida's deconstructive discourse (Heidegger's destruction, like Vincent Van Gogh's and Edvard Munch's destructive paintings, is apparently excepted or "saved" from this fate by its relegation to high modernism) or, say, E. L. Doctorow's historical fiction (*Ragtime,* for example) or Andy Warhol's *Diamond Dust Shoes,* or Frank Gehry's Santa Monica house or the Clash's punk rock.

Under Jameson's retrospective gaze, in other words, the critical edge of these "postmodern" works is reduced to "blank parody": "a neutral practice of [parodic] mimicry, without any of parody's ulterior motives, amputated of the satiric impulse, devoid of laughter and of any conviction that alongside the abnormal tongue you have momentarily borrowed, some healthy linguistic normality still exists."[13] In thus reducing the parodic to a binary opposition between a decentered practice that is complicitous with the logic of late capitalism and a centered one that has historically served to protect the dominant culture from the deviant other in its midst or at its periphery, Jameson precludes the possibility of reading (some of) the postmodern texts he identifies with late capitalist commodification as parodic in a third sense: as postmodern parodies that are both decentered yet negatively capable of retaining their critical/projective edge.

Jameson's definition of postmodern parody, that is, should be seen in the context of Mikhail Bakhtin's and Michel Foucault's quite different (Nietzschean) understanding of both traditional and nontraditional parody. Unlike Jameson's, both of these versions, but especially Foucault's, refuse to answer to the imperial binarist terms established and insisted on by the discourse, especially the "monumental" history, of the ontotheological tradition. Though Jameson would probably identify them as symptomatic of the cultural logic of late capitalism, Bakhtinian and Foucauldian parody are both decentered or nonidentical *and* politically emancipatory in their project to "unrealize" the "reality" produced by the monologic fictions of Enlightenment identity. As Foucault puts this mode of parody in his version of Nietzsche's threefold genealogical project:

> The [traditional] historian offers this confused and anonymous European, who no longer knows himself or what name he should adopt, the possibility of alternate identities, more individualized and substantial than his own. But the man with historical sense [the genealogist] will see that this substitution is simply a disguise. Historians supplied the Revolution with Roman prototypes, romanticism with knight's armor, and the Wagnerian era was given the sword of a German hero — ephemeral props that point to our own unreality. No one kept them from venerating these religions, from going to Bayreuth to commemorate a new afterlife; they were free, as well, to be transformed into street-vendors of empty identities. The new historian, the genealogist, will know what to make of this masquerade. He will not be too serious to enjoy it; on the contrary, he will push the masquerade to its limit and prepare the great carnival of time where masks are constantly reapppearing. No longer the identification of our faint individuality with the solid identities of the past, but our "unrealization" through the excessive choice of identities. . . . "Perhaps, we can discover a realm where originality is again possible as parodists of God." In this, we recognize the parodic double of what the second of the *Untimely Meditations* called "monumental history": *a history given to reestablishing the high points of historical development and their maintenance in a perpetual presence, given to the*

recovery of works, actions, and creations through the monogram of their personal essence. But in 1874, Nietzsche accused this history, one totally devoted to veneration, *of barring access to the actual intensities and creations of life.* The parody of his last texts serves to emphasize that "monumental history" is itself parody. Genealogy is history in the form of a concerted carnival.[14]

Jameson's account of postmodernity betrays a nostalgia for History (as it is understood by Marx). Jameson's ephebes, however, celebrate the effacement of historicity and affect induced by the reduction of art and history to "blank parody." In their hands, postmodernity becomes the postmodern Left's version of the new Right's representation of the post–Cold War as "the end of history." Its representation of the contemporary occasion as devoid of historical resonance thus becomes the symptom of an impasse of thought and practice that lends itself to the ideological purposes of its adversary.

From the decentered perspective precipitated by what I have called the epistemic break that occurred in the 1960s, then, the "Jamesonian" representation of postmodernity seems to be blinded by its insight into the late capitalist detemporalization of history to the amnesiac and banalizing strategy of *accommodation*. This is the strategy, most subtly developed by the United States in the aftermath of the Vietnam War to pacify and domesticate the visible contradictions exposed by its virulent will to save Vietnam for liberal democracy, that has increasingly become the essential technology of power of neocapitalist imperialism. A postmodernism that remembers its historically specific origins as a *discursive practice* of resistance against a genocidal assault on a Third World people undertaken in the name of the ontological principles of humanist freedom discloses a different understanding of the logic of late capitalism. Such a retrieval implies not only that this logic is "the spatial logic of the simulacrum," of fragmentation, superficiality, depthlessness, pastiche, but that this totally disjunctive field of simulacra is a seductive *appearance*. As I have suggested, the Vietnam War bore genealogical witness to the continuous complicity between the post-World War II American (neoimperial) capitalist initiative in the "wilderness" of Vietnam and the rugged individualist entrepreneur of the late nineteenth century, the self-reliant "westering" frontiersman of the early nineteenth century (Manifest Destiny), the colonial pioneer, and the Puritan planter, whose errand in the wilderness was providentially (ontologically) ordained. To remember this epochal event — this first postmodern war, as Jameson has rightly identified it — is to estrange the "Jamesonian" representation of postmodernism. The fractured "field of stylistic and discursive heterogeneity without a norm" becomes the "look" — the re-presentation — produced by a recuperative reorganization of the operative functions of the American *logos* in the wake of its decentering in the 1960s. (This reorganization, it should be noted, is in the process of being reproduced in Europe as the EC.) The post–Vietnam War self-representation of "America" in the hegemonized terms of radical and untethered diversity is precisely intended to make such "postmodern" cultural production *appear* to correspond with the emancipatory imperatives of the decentering of the Vietnam era — that is, to *mask* the imperial agenda of the recuperated accommodational center in the soft features of a tolerant and ameliorative benevolence, that is, in the rhetoric of "development." This is tacitly the point Edward Said makes in recalling contemporary postcolonial criticism to the critical task demanded by the absolute affiliation between culture and imperialism:

> One can recognize new patterns of dominance, to borrow from Fredric Jameson's description of post-modernism, in contemporary culture. Jameson's argument is yoked to his description of consumer culture, whose central features are a new relationship with the past based on pastiche and nostalgia, a new and eclectic randomness in the cultural artifact, a reorganization of space, and characteristics of multinational capitalism. *To this we must add the culture's phenomenally incorporative capacity, which makes it possible for anyone in fact to say anything at all, but everything is processed either toward the dominant mainstream or out to the margins.*[15]

By way of the culturally induced forgetting of the event of Vietnam, the politically conservative wing of the dominant post–Cold War culture has been increasingly empowered to transform the earlier defensive imperative to heal the wound opened up in the American collective consciousness into the aggressive jeremiadic imperative to "kick the Vietnam syndrome." This has taken the form of a massive political offensive dedicated to the reaffirmation of the American version of the Occidental *(anthropo)logos* in the face of a multicultural initiative it represents as a discourse and practice of "political correctness" that threaten the triumphant end-of-history narrative allegedly worked out by the dialectical dynamics of Universal History. According to the logical economy of the "Jamesonian" version of postmodernity, we are compelled to conclude (as liberal humanists claim) that this reactionary cultural initiative of the political Right to reaffirm the metaphysical foundations of "Western" society by force is external to — a radical contradiction of — the decentered and fracturing dynamics of late capitalism. Which is to say, it splits a single problem into two distinct ones, each requiring radically different critical approaches. By thus occluding their continuous (onto)logic, it displaces critical focus from the question of being reinstigated by the *episteme*-shattering event of Vietnam to the question of politics.

Understood in terms of the accommodational strategy developed by liberal/late capitalism to pacify and domesticate the explosive relay of differences precipitated by the Vietnam War, the post–Cold War reactionary momentum does not constitute a project that contradicts or opposes — is external to and incommensurate with — this "liberal" accommodational process. Its call for the overt policing of the multicultural initiative in the name of "free inquiry" is seen, rather, as a symptom of the will to power inhering in the accommodational anthropo-logic of late capitalism. It is a power that is strategically held in hidden reserve until the relay of differential constituencies of civil society refuses its "spontaneous consent" to the late capitalist discourse of truth.[16]

It is to this new Holy Alliance — this logocentric imperial dominant that harnesses "*three* indissociable places or apparatuses of our culture": the political (the *classe politique*), the mass mediatic, and the academic — that Jacques Derrida bears witness in his recent engagement with Marx and Marxism. It is a witness, it should be noted, not only against the liberal democratic representation of the post–Cold War moment, but also against a certain disabling poststructuralist representation of the cultural dominant of the postmodern occasion to which he contributed:

> No one, it seems to me, can *contest* the fact that a dogmatics is attempting to install its worldwide hegemony in paradoxical and suspect conditions. There is today in the world a *dominant* discourse, or rather one that is on the way to becoming dominant, on the subject of Marx's work and thought, on the subject of Marxism (which is perhaps not the same thing), on the subject of the socialist International and the universal revolution, on the subject of the more or less slow destruction of the revolutionary model in its Marxist inspiration, on the subject of the rapid, precipitous recent collapse of societies that attempted to put it into effect at least in what we will call for the moment, citing once again the *Manifesto,* "old Europe" and so forth. This dominating discourse often has the manic, jubilatory, and incantatory form that Freud assigned to the so-called triumphant phase of mourning work. The

incantation repeats and ritualizes itself, it holds forth and holds
to formulas, like any animist magic. To the rhythm of a cadenced
march, it proclaims Marx is dead, communism is dead, very dead,
and along with it its hope, its discourse, its theories, and its practices. It says long live capitalism, long live the market, here's to the
survival of economics and political liberalism![17]

Indeed, Derrida goes out of his way, seemingly against a "Jamesonian" interpretation of the postmodern occasion, to emphasize the
indissoluble relatedness of these apparently different and difference-
producing cultures that have established this new post–Cold War
hegemony. In invoking a "certain spirit of Marx" — which, to give
parodic visibility to the adversary, he calls "hauntology"[18] — he also
stresses their ontologically enabled coherence. By this "certain spirit of
Marx," of course, Derrida means Marx's deconstructive/antiteleological
impulse that "Marxism" and capitalism mutually reified, named, and
buried but that, precisely with the finality of this burial, has come back
to haunt them. In a rhetoric that clearly refers to the essential terms
of the "Jamesonian" representation of late capitalist postmodernity,
Derrida writes:

> These apparatuses are doubtless complex, differential, conflictual,
> and overdetermined. But whatever may be the conflicts, inequal-
> ities, or overdeterminations among them, they communicate and
> cooperate at every moment towards producing the greatest force
> with which to assure the hegemony or imperialism in question.
> ... Now, this power [that *"conditions and endangers* any democ-
> racy"] ... cannot be analyzed or potentially combated, supported
> here, attacked there, without taking into account so many *spec-
> tral* effects, the new speed of *apparition* (we understand this word
> in its ghostly sense) of the simulacrum, the synthetic or pros-
> thetic image, and the virtual event, cyberspace and surveillance,
> the control, appropriations, and speculations that today deploy
> unheard-of powers. Have Marx and his heirs helped us to think
> and to treat this phenomenon? If we say that the answer to this
> question is at once *yes* and *no, yes* in one respect, *no* in another,
> and that one must filter, select, differentiate, restructure the ques-
> tions, it is only in order to announce ... the tone and the general
> form of our conclusions: namely that one *must assume the in-
> heritance* of Marxism, assume its most "living" part, which is to
> say, paradoxically, that which continues to put back on the draw-
> ing board the question of life, spirit, or the spectral, of life-death
> beyond the opposition between life and death.[19]

That is to say, one must recognize that it is metaphysical ontology — the *representation* of being *as total thing* to be *comprehended* (taken hold of) — that *informs* the "conflicts, inequalities, or overdeterminations" of these apparatuses of the postmodern occasion and that, in its inclusive imperatives, this ontology precludes the possibility of assuming the "most 'living' part" of the inheritance of Marx: the *question* of being-in-the-world, if not of being as such.

Because the "Jamesonian" version of postmodernity represents the contemporary world as "a field of discursive heterogeneity, without a norm," its project of "cognitive mapping" is inadequate to the task of criticism posed by the liberal democratic culture's representation of the end of the Cold War as the end of the cosmic narrative of history. No less than the cultural discourse of the humanist (and "Marxist" opponents of postmodernism), this neo-Marxist discourse for all practical purposes forgets "Vietnam": the epistemic decentering of the polyvalent imperial center of humanist (neo)capitalism.[20] Given its (contradictory) nostalgia for (a centered and normative) History — a metanarrative — in the face of what it takes to be the "posthistoricality" of the "postmodern period," the "Jamesonian" representation of postmodernity is necessarily limited to two more or less ineffectual options in addressing the imperial aspects of the contemporary occasion. One, recently exemplified by Christopher Norris and Terry Eagleton, is the recuperation of a Marx*ist* problematic that modern history has, perhaps decisively, delegitimized and rendered anachronistic. The other is the repetition of the end-of-history discourse of the political Right in terms of the radically relativist diagnosis of the contemporary occasion of the political Left and thus the annulment of criticism as struggle in favor of analysis. This option is exemplified by Michael Hardt's and Antonio Negri's neo-Marxist analysis of postmodernity, in which the center and periphery of the traditional imperial project are replaced by the free-floating center of free-market capital,[21] and, in an analogous way, by the diagnosis of the post–Cold War occasion by Bill Readings and other exponents of the view that transnational capitalism has decisively rendered the nation-state, in this case the American center, anachronistic.[22] As Edward Said has observed, this is tantamount to "a kind of fascination with the techniques of domination" in which "the site of resistance is eliminated."[23]

To be sure, the currently privileged "Jamesonian" version of postmodernism has contributed significantly to an oppositional understanding of the contemporary global occasion precisely by focusing its analysis on the rapid transformation since the Vietnam War of a national corporate capitalism to a global late or commodity capitalism.

Its acutely differentiated description of this complex new global terrain is indispensable to any effort that would resist late capitalism's culturally and sociopolitically disabling seductions. But this account of the postmodernism of postmodernity is blind to the essentially accommodational dynamics of this accelerating planetary process. It fails to see, that is, that this process has been one of strategically incorporating the contradictory and delegitimating differences (Others) precipitated by the "fulfillment" of the "benign" logic that justified the United States's intervention in Vietnam into (an instrumentalized version of) the American *logos*. Since the Vietnam War, the United States, understood as a nation-state, has indeed been eclipsed by the rise of transnational capitalism, but this does not mean that America is no longer an imperial center. It means, rather, that transnational capitalism has become "American" — an ontologically grounded comportment toward other "underdeveloped" worlds, from their way of perceiving reality to their political institutions, that assumes the latter's radical inferiority — and that its post–Cold War project is the "Americanization" of the planet.

As a consequence of its interpretation of the rise of transnational capital in binary opposite terms of the obsolescence of the nation-state, this version of postmodernity has also deflected its attention from the essential site of vulnerability in the discourse and practice of late capitalist democracy disclosed by this accelerating global strategy of accommodation. In expanding the circumference of the controlling anthropological center — the imperial periphery or frontier of the commanding metropolis, as it were — to incorporate an increasing number of historically specific subject positions, areas of lived experience, lifestyles, modes of cultural production, Third Worlds, and so on, hitherto censored, marginalized, excluded, or repressed by an older classical (bourgeois) democratic capitalism, the power of this center/capital has been increasingly attenuated to the point where the lines of its force, like those of the American army in Vietnam, have become gossamer-like threads: shown, that is, to be spectral. As W. B. Yeats put this rarefaction of the power of the imperial anthropologic enabled by the Renaissance (of Rome) in "The Second Coming" — a poem that, however one reads its political intentions, is as appropriate to the postmodern occasion as to the 1930s —

> Turning and turning in the widening gyre
> The falcon cannot hear the falconer;
> Things fall apart; the centre cannot hold;
> Mere anarchy is loosed upon the world.[24]

But this paradoxical attenuation of the power of the centered, imperial voice of anthropo-logy to be heard (and obeyed) — to interpellate
the postmodern subject — at the ever-widening periphery of its reach is
not the only consequence of the fulfillment of the logic of the *anthropologos*. In its self-induced solicitation of the imperial center, the liberal
democratic/capitalist problematic has, against its will — as in the more
violent case of the American intervention in Vietnam — been compelled
by the decentering and the impending disintegration of the imperial
circle to activate, at least in certain telling areas, the hidden and latent power it holds in reserve as long as its discursive practices are
spontaneously assented to as the truth, as long, that is, as it continues to "win the hearts and minds" of the Other. In Jacques Derrida's
rhetoric, the "center elsewhere" that hitherto did its coercive struc-
turalizing/interpellative work from "beyond the reach of free play" (of
criticism) has been compelled by its *own* logic to expose itself — to make
itself visible in the form of the overt use of its power at certain crucial
sites on the continuum of being. To invoke the trope of super-vision that
is endemic to the anthropological tradition, it has been compelled, that
is, to come down from its immured and immunizing meta-physical or
panoptic heights into the political *agora*.

I am referring specifically to the massive call by the political, journalistic, and academic Right for a politically administered policing action
taken in the name of protecting "free inquiry" against the multisituated
emancipatory initiative in the United States — not least in its colleges
and universities — that promises to transform a racially, ethnically, sex-
ually, economically, intellectually, and culturally stratified "democracy"
into a truly democratic social democracy. This last is, of course, the
multicultural initiative proleptically announced, if unachieved in fact,
by the decentering of the American Word and the disintegration of its
episteme and the ensuing knowledge explosion in the decade of the Vietnam War. It is the emancipatory initiative that the reactionary Right
(especially since the Reagan presidency) and certain nostalgic voices of
the Left — both Marxists like Terry Eagleton and reformist liberals like
Arthur Schlesinger and Richard Rorty — have represented not simply
as "Mere anarchy loosed upon the world," in which "The best lack all
conviction, while the worst / Are full of passionate intensity," but as a
totalitarian practice of political correctness that threatens the well-being
of the American body politic. This, *if* the references to metaphysics are
intended to be understood as continuous with, rather than as arbitrary
impositions on, the "fragmented" late capitalist terrain, is precisely the
revealing paradox that Terry Eagleton articulates about the Britain of
Margaret Thatcher in his inaugural lecture as Wharton Professor at Ox-

ford. I underscore "if" because Eagleton's neo-Marxist nostalgia for the old Marxist ontological center and his all-too-easy identification of all modes of decenteredness with "the commodity form" inhibit unqualified assent:

Culture [from the point of view of the dominant sociopolitical formation] must not simply generate itself up from what we do, for if it does we will end up with all the worst kinds of values. It must also idealize those practices, lend them some metaphysical support; but the more the commodity form levels all hierarchies of value, mixes diverse life forms promiscuously together and strikes all transcendence empty, the more these societies will come to deplete the very symbolic resources necessary for their own ideological authority.

This contradiction can be seen at almost every level of contemporary social life. If you erode people's sense of corporate identity, reducing their common history to the eternal now of consumerist desire, they will simply cease to operate effectively as responsible citizens; and so you will have to manufacture that corporate identity synthetically, in the shape of the heritage industry or imperial war. If you allow education to be invaded by the leveling, fragmenting commodity form, you will need all the more stridently to insist on basics, fixed canons, immutable standards. The more you commercialize the media, the more you will feel the need for poems that rhyme and say nice things about Lord Nelson. The more cheap black labour-power you exploit, the more you will feel inspired to preserve the unity and purity of the national culture. In all these ways, anarchy and autocracy, money and metaphysics, exchange value and absolute value, are both strangers and brothers, sworn foes and intimate bedfellows. So it is that the intellectuals of the New Right, having actively colluded with forms of politics which drain purpose and value from social life, then turn their horror-stricken countenances on the very devastated social landscape they themselves have helped to create, and mourn the loss of absolute value.[25]

As this radicalization of Eagleton's diagnosis of the contemporary historical occasion suggests, what the problematic informing the "Jamesonian" version of postmodernism renders invisible, in other words, is that the foundational discourse of the late capitalist extension of the Enlightenment's imperial logical economy now — in the aftermath of Vietnam — rings irretrievably hollow. It does not simply preclude seeing, at least clearly, what to someone outside the perimeter of its problematic is obvious and of crucial importance: that the discursive practice of late capitalist democracy has not been able, despite its amnesiac efforts to force the Vietnam War into the triumphalist Cold War narrative, to conceal or nullify the destructive contradictions inhering in its (onto)logical economy. This "Jamesonian" problematic continues to think the post–Cold War occasion in the re-presentational (enframing or spatializing or territorializing) terms of thinking laid down by its triumphant adversary. This is one significant reason why a postmodern discursive practice that would be adequate to the historically specific conditions of the contemporary global occasion must understand itself not as a *symptom* of the "simulacral" logic of late capitalism (the cultural dominant), but as an instrument of resistance committed to the critique and eventual overcoming of its Janus-faced discourse and practice.

The New Historicism and the Theorization of the Local

I would like to write the history of this prison, with all the political investments of the body that it gathers together in its closed architecture. Why? Simply because I am interested in the past? No, if one means by that writing a history of the past in terms of the present. Yes, if one means writing the history of the present.

— MICHEL FOUCAULT, *Discipline and Punish*

The representation of postmodernism implicit in the discourse of the New Historicism is, in my mind, more productive than the "Jamesonian" version insofar as it identifies itself with Michel Foucault's critical genealogy: not, that is, as a symptom of a "postmodern" period, but as a critical instrument that is intended to demystify the dominant neo-imperial discursive practices of this post–Cold War historical occasion. The New Historicist representation of postmodernism is preferable, that is, because, like Foucault's, it is intended to give back a history to those differential constituencies of the human community to whom History — including the ahistorical History of the postmodern Marxists — has denied a history.[26]

Foucault's and Said's critical genealogy acknowledges, in some enabling degree at least, the crucial role ontological representation plays in the construction of the disciplinary or metropolitan society (even if they subordinate it to cultural or sociopolitical structuration). The New Historicism, however, remains essentially disciplinary in its critical perspective. Though it focuses its countergaze on cultural history, it generally represents this history in the restricted terms of a pragmatic sociopolitics devoid of ontological moorings. That is to say, it is "against theory" in a way that disables criticism insofar as it represents "theory" in a binary opposition with a privileged practice without realizing that this kind of New Historicism is itself a totalizing theory that is oblivious to an interpretation of theory, deriving from Heidegger, that understands it as ontic-ontological: a seeing (*theoria*) that is simultaneously and always already a practice (praxis). As Paul Bové observes, the "against theory" discourse of the New Historicists constitutes a "neopragmatism" that, in fact, reinscribes the binarist ontology that it would demystify:

> "KBM" [the acronym Bové uses (derived from Stephen Knapp and Walter Benn Michaels) to identify a certain prominent strain of New Historicist discourse] make an argument against theory by assigning a Kantian conception of intuition to theory and, once having done that, assert that it cannot be held: "Theory in a nontrivial sense always consists in the attempt to 'stand outside practice in order to govern practice from without,' and this strong ('foundationalist') kind of theory is the kind whose coherence we deny."
>
> Indeed, the neopragmatist and antioppositional KBM position makes a fundamental error in its reductive binary thinking about the relations between "theory" and "practice." KBM argue that in theory there is "distantiation," whereas "practice" alone presents a sort of truth of or in immediacy, in action. This neopragmatism exists by virtue of a binary opposition that annuls theory in advance as folly. The fundamental problem with KBM, however, is that their dualisms are naive. The distantiation they assign as a quality to theory is, as sight, also an aspect of the "practical."[27]

One of the disabling consequences of this forced separation of practice from theory is the radical localization of history: the reduction of the global context precipitated by the postmodern occasion to the radically singular — and indifferent — event. More specifically, it reduces the global role America has always played to the national context, thus reinscribing itself within the very exceptionalist Americanist discourse that contemporary history has demystified.

The immediate source of this "oversight" is in part a too superficial reading of Foucault's and/or Said's genealogical texts and in part a categorical rejection of Heidegger's destruction of the ontotheological history of ontological representation probably on the dubious basis of a too hasty identification of Heidegger's (and Paul de Man's) philosophical discourse with totalitarian practice. (It is an identification, not incidentally, that, like that of certain neo-Marxists, paradoxically allies the New Historicists with all those liberal and conservative American humanists who have grasped the opportunity to take the offensive not only against the anti-"American" Heidegger, but also against the anti-"Americanism" of those thinkers such as Derrida, Lacan, Lyotard, Foucault, Althusser, Irigaray, and Spivak that Heidegger's philosophical discourse enabled or catalyzed.)[28] But the ultimate source of this oversight is the forgetting or repression of the epochally global disclosures precipitated by the self-destruction of the "disinterested" — and "exceptionalist" — Enlightenment logic informing American imperial practice, both in the United States and Vietnam, during the decade of the Vietnam War.

Like the blindness of the neo-Marxist version of postmodernism, the blindness of this pragmatist New Historicism is the consequence of a paradoxical formalism. It is the result of a theoretical distancing from specific history, the differential occasion that precipitates the will to resist the repressive/forgetful suprahistorical History that has increasingly determined truth and practice in the world throughout the history of the Occident. The blindness of the New Historicism to history, to put it specifically, is the consequence of the institutionalization not simply of the existential origins of Foucault's and Said's critical genealogy, but of the occasion bearing witness to the decolonization of a relay of Others, from being as such to the peoples of the Third World, hitherto colonized by the imperial panoptic economy of the modern Occidental *episteme*.

In occluding the site of ontological representation, the postmodernism of the New Historicists thus becomes inadequate to the conditions of the post–Cold War occasion. It retrogressively delimits critique to the site of culture understood as essentially sociopolitical, pragmatic, and national — emptied, that is, of ontological content. And in so doing, it precludes the perception that the "triumphant" post–Cold War culture has reverted to the overt invocation of universal ontological principles that, in fact, determined America's founding identity, rather than appealing in the usual pragmatic way to economic or sociopolitical practices, in the process of legitimizing its representation of the "new" global scene as a New World Order presided over by an elected America: *the very principles, in short, that the Vietnam War — and the poststructuralist theorization of its representation and conduct — decisively delegitimized by foregrounding the violence inhering in the exceptionalist American effort to "win the hearts and minds" of the Vietnamese people.*

This marginalization of the ontological site renders the postmodernism of the New Historicists inadequate to the conditions of the contemporary occasion in another related sense, one that pertains to the subject proper. To repeat my beginning, the epochal event of the Vietnam War — the occasion that enabled oppositional intellectuals in both the First and Third World to think the imperial ontological, cultural, and sociopolitical implications that the post–Cold War discourse would obliterate from memory — was the demystification and decentering of the *anthropologos*. This not only meant the decentering of the Enlightenment representation of being understood as Universal History. It also meant the decentering of the sovereign subject, which reflects the self-presence of a Being thus represented. It meant the disclosure that human identity — whether understood in terms of the individual or the nation, gender, race, ethnic nationality, or Man at large — is meta-physical, which is to say, a totalized, self-identical historical construct that is, in fact, grounded in nothing. This epochal break with the ontological principle of Identity, the metaphysical principle, more specifically, that posits Identity as the condition for the possibility of difference and not the other way around, is determinative in Michel Foucault's postmodern genealogical analysis of modern Occidental power relations (his exposure of the complicity between [Western] truth and power). And, despite an unwillingness to theorize it, this break also informs Edward Said's postcolonial rereading of the relation between culture and imperialism.[29] But this decentering of the (Enlightenment) subject that reveals it to be a historical fiction has been marginalized, if not entirely effaced, in the discursive practices of the New Historicists and the affiliated discourses vaguely called cultural criticism and postcolonial criticism.

This marginalization has been the consequence of a number of interrelated tendencies: the growing (American) pragmatist resistance to theory, the academic loss of nerve in the face of the existential imperatives of the decentering of the subject, the nationalist or racist resistance to "white" postmodernist writing, the nostalgic Left's representation of the decentering as a relativism that precludes practice, and, not least, the disengagement incumbent on the institutionalization of dissent. Whatever the causes, the marginalization of the postmodern demystification of the self-identical subject has been disabling. It has paralyzed — indeed, rendered irrelevant — the critical function of the New Historicism and its affiliated cultural and postcolonial discourses in the face of the horrifically paradoxical underside of the post–Cold War occasion: the occasion that has given rise to the ubiquitous and multisituated wars of Identity all-too-glibly represented as "Balkanization," as if such violence were endemic to that particular ("unimproved" or "underdeveloped") region of the world. I am not simply referring to Eastern Europe (the conditions of sociopolitical life in the former Central European communist bloc, Yugoslavia, and the Soviet Union), the

Middle East, and Africa. I am also referring to the West, particularly, but certainly not exclusively, to the United States (the conditions of socio-political life subsequent to the emergence in the post-Vietnam period of multiculturalism).

The first instance bears pervasive witness to the renewed spectacle of an old and virulent nationalism, ethnocentrism, and racism — a violent sociopolitics of Identity. This is the state of life in the newly decol-onized cultures of Eastern and Central Europe, Yugoslavia, and the Soviet Union, which have ironically reinscribed with a vengeance the very metaphysically legitimated principle of self-presence that Stalinist communism, by way of its apotheosis of the Party and the Proletariat as its principle of identity, employed to justify the brutal totalitarian or im-perial suppression and oppression of the different social, cultural, ethnic, and racial enclaves of these geopolitical spaces.[30] Similarly, postcolonial countries in the Middle East and Africa have reinscribed the very prin-ciple of identity that the imperial powers, by way of the apotheosis of the Western idea of civilization, employed to justify their cultural, eco-nomic, and political domination and exploitation of their spaces. These, too, as the examples of Iran, Iraq, and Algeria testify, manifest their "freedom" from colonial rule in a virulent identity politics expressed in bloodletting.

However asymmetrical the violence, the second instance — the analo-gous occasion in Western democratic societies — bears a similar witness. I am referring to the spectacle of an allegedly emergent emancipatory cultural politics that pits the social constituencies — blacks, Orientals, Jews, Latinos, women, gays, and the working-class — constituted and represented as "different," and monstrous, by the dominant culture against each other in an internecine struggle over which constituency is more justified in claiming the label of victim. This antagonism of essen-tialist subject positions, I suggest, is ultimately the legacy of the failure of the protest movement during the Vietnam decade (and the theorists who took on the task of conceptualizing that occasion) to think the relatively effective solidarity all-too-momentarily and spontaneously achieved by a multiplicity of differential social constituencies against the dominant — white, male, middle-class, adult, heterosexual — culture. The hegemonic regime of truth relies not only on the interpellated or subjected sub-ject — on, that is, the "sovereignty" of the ontological self — but also on the compartmentalization (individuation) and accommodation of op-pressed constituencies to a larger, essentialist, and identical whole in order to neutralize the possibility of collective resistance.

To think this ontological unthought of the Vietnam decade is to dis-cover the effective power inhering in a coalition of *identityless* identities.

I mean by this the *differential* subject positions that acknowledge the social/historical constitution of their identities and, therefore, that confront the question of justice and injustice, equality and inequality, not, as humanists do, on the basis of a universal (and monologic) ontological principle of self-presence, but *on the basis of the imbalance(s) of power obtaining in any historically specific occasion.*[31] It is to realize that only the solidarity of such a "union" of *differential* identities — of the "*historical* bloc," as Gramsci puts it — is capable of breaking through the seductive divide-and-conquer (disciplinary) discourse of hegemony, so brilliantly worked out by the founding fathers of the United States. To think the decentering of the subject that occurred in the Vietnam decade, in short, is to realize that such a solidarity of nonessentialist (spectral) identities is, more likely than any form of identity politics, to effect a transformation of the forces of resistance into a "new International" — and "America" into a truly multicultural social democracy.

This imperative to think the postmodern *polis* as a community of identityless identities — of specters precipitated by the ravages of the (Western) "Spirit," as it were — lies behind Jacques Derrida's effort to think the "new International" in terms of "a certain spirit of Marx." Having invoked Maurice Blanchot's "Marx's Three Voices" as exemplary of this kind of thinking, Derrida writes:

> Blanchot reminds us that we are asked by [the three voices of Marx], in the first place, to think the "holding together" of the *disparate* itself. Not to maintain together the disparate, but to put ourselves there where the disparate itself *holds together,* without wounding the dis-jointure, the dispersion, or the difference, without effacing the heterogeneity of the other. We are asked (enjoined, perhaps) to turn *ourselves* over to the future, to join ourselves in this *we,* there where the disparate is turned over to this singular *joining,* without concept or certainty of determination, without knowledge, without or before the synthetic junction of the conjunction and the disjunction. The alliance of a *rejoining* without conjoined mate, without organization, without party, without nation, without State, without property (the "communism" that we will later nickname the new International).[32]

However resonant its suggestiveness, Derrida's postmodern initiative to think the negative political imperatives precipitated by the fulfillment — and disintegration — of the imperial logic of the self-present subject positively, in terms of a spectral "new International" that overcomes the limits of a Marxism that remains tethered to the Enlightenment subject, is not unique, neither French nor Jewish. It is, rather, a pervasive international initiative, an initiative that, however symptomatically, has informed the postmodern countermemory, especially of the post-Vietnam occasion, not simply that of the "philosophical" consciousness — Antonio Gramsci, Hannah Arendt, Gilles Deleuze and Félix Guattari, Michel Foucault, Theodor Adorno, Jean-François Lyotard, Paul Virilio, Edward Said, Gayatri Spivak, for example — but also, if more intuitively, that of the creative imagination. One thinks especially of Thomas Pynchon's proleptic American version of Derrida's new Internationalist project in *Gravity's Rainbow,* where Tyrone Slothrop, one of the multitude of displaced victims of the post–World War II imperial "They," invokes the specter of his Puritan ancestor, William Slothrop — the exiled and nomadic author of the heretical pamphlet *Preterition,* in which he affirms the historical integrity of the "others," those who have been "passed over" by God's elected "Saints":

> Could he have been the fork in the road America never took, the singular point she jumped the wrong way from? Suppose the Slothropite heresy had had the time to consolidate and prosper? Might there have been fewer crimes in the name of Jesus, and more mercy in the name of Judas Iscariot? It seems to Tyrone Slothrop that there might be a route back — maybe that anarchist he met in Zurich was right, maybe for a little while all the fences are down, one road as good as another, the whole space of the Zone cleared, depolarized, and somewhere inside the waste of it a single set of coordinates from which to proceed, without elect, without preterite, without even nationality to fuck it up.[33]

It is this nonessential internationalist initiative that the New Historicism, in its tradition-induced indifference to the global implications of the decentered (American) subject, inadvertently blocks. Under the aegis of the New Historicism and cultural criticism in general, we encounter instead a "postcolonial" cultural politics that has forgotten or willfully bracketed the ontological decentering of the subject in the name of a pragmatic practice that defines itself "against theory." It thus manifests itself as either a free-floating formalism, an indifferent localism, or, most disablingly, an often bitter contention of essentialist subject positions the divisiveness of which, in keeping with the logic of division and mastery endemic to the disciplinary society, leaves the dominant culture and its imperial political institutions intact. It is to this exclusionary practice of identity politics, if not exactly of racial or ethnic cleansing, that the post–Cold War occasion bears massive witness. It is a politics that for all practical purposes is based on and justified by the self-present and "sovereign" metaphysical self. *It is, ironically, a politics, both domestic*

and global, the very ontological ground of which enabled the histor-
ical invention of the identities of these same emergent constituencies
the better to subject, dominate, and exploit them. This, to underscore
my argument, is the metaphysically grounded ruse to which early postmodern "theory" — now discarded as "anachronistic" by the "more
practice-oriented" oppositional discourses that have superseded it — has
borne witness. In short, the oppositional discourses that prevail in the
post–Cold War era have not attained the degree of *exilic* — and thus
spectral — consciousness that would be adequate to the task of deterring
liberal capitalist democracy.

Chapter 5

Thinking in the Interregnum
Prolegomenon to a Spectral Politics

In an intellectual hierarchy which constantly makes everyone answerable,
unanswerabilty alone can call the hierarchy by its name.
— THEODOR ADORNO, *Minima Moralis*

What I have argued in this book about the relationship between philosophy and imperialism is that the euphoric annunciation of the end of history and the advent of the New World Order by the deputies of the dominant American culture at the end of the Cold War is symptomatic of the achievement of the global hegemony of "America" understood not simply as a political order, but as a way of thinking. I have claimed that this triumphant "American" way of thinking is not exceptionalist, as it has always been claimed by Americans, especially since de Tocqueville's announcement of the advent of democracy in America, but European, which means metaphysical: an imperial thinking, whose provenance resides in Roman antiquity, that *sees* the being into which it inquires as a totalized spatial image, a "field" or "region" or "domain" to be comprehended, mastered, and exploited.

But this way of putting this imperial metanarrative, though necessary in the context of the amnesiac imperatives of thinking the Enlightenment as an epochal emancipatory moment in world history, is too general. It does not account for the historically specific transformation of this European mode of knowledge production accomplished in the wake of America's emergence as a global power: the fulfillment of the Enlightenment's "developmental model" in the effacement of the visible imperial *logos* informing traditional metaphysics by way of the apotheosis of the "objectivity" of empirical science and the advent of the classificatory table. Under the aegis of a triumphant America, the narrative economy of European metaphysics has come to its end in the form of a universal instrumentalism, a Man-centered thinking for which everything in time and space is *seen* as a "problem" that the larger comparative "picture" renders susceptible to a final and determinate solution.

191

In Heidegger's proleptic terms, European metaphysical thinking in the technological age dominated by America has become "Americanized," a "re-presentational"/"calculative" thinking or "planning" that has transformed the uncalculability of being at large into a planetary "world picture":

> "We get the picture" concerning something does not mean only that what is, is set before us, is represented to us, in general, but that what is stands before us — in all that belongs to it and all that stands together in it — as a system. "To get the picture" throbs with being acquainted with something, with being equipped and prepared for it. Where the world becomes picture, what is, in its entirely, is juxtaposed as that for which man is prepared and which, correspondingly, he therefore intends to bring before himself and have before himself, and consequently intends in a decisive sense to set in place before himself. Hence world picture, when understood essentially, does not mean a picture of the world but the world conceived and grasped as picture. What is, in its entirety, is now taken in such a way that it first is in being and only is in being to the extent that it is set up by man, who represents and sets forth. Wherever we have the world picture, an essential decision takes place regarding what is, in its entirety. The Being of whatever is, is sought and found in the representedness of the latter.[1]

Reconstellated into the context of this Heideggerian diagnosis of modernity, the American end-of-history discourse undergoes a resonant estrangement. What is euphorically represented as "good news" — the global fulfillment ("end") of the emancipatory promise of History — comes to be seen as the *Pax Metaphysica:* the colonization of the errant mind of humanity at large by a banal and banalizing thinking that has reduced *everything,* including human beings, to "standing [or disposable] reserve."[2] This "end of philosophy" in the form of a "triumphant" instrumentalist thinking that has reduced being to disposable commodity is everywhere manifest in the post–Cold War era. And, I suggest, its most telling symptom is the globalization of (American) English as the *lingua franca* of the "free market," which has as one of its most devastating consequences the "Americanization" not simply of the Western nation-states but of entire Third World cultures.

What for the purpose of my argument this global triumph of "American" thinking means is that even those who would oppose American global hegemony are, insofar as they remain indifferent to the ontological grounds of its sociopolitical practices, condemned to think their opposition according to the imperatives of the discursive practices they would oppose. They thus fulfill the expectation of the deputies of American culture who predict that "even nondemocrats will have to speak the language of democracy in order to justify their deviation from the single universal standard."[3] That is to say, the fulfillment of the European metanarrative in the globalization of American technological thinking, that is, the Americanization of the planet, has tacitly reduced opposition to a resonant silence.

It is in this sense that, with Heidegger, the intellectual who is attuned to the complicity between Western philosophy and imperialism is compelled to call this "age of the world picture" presided over by America a "destitute time" or, more suggestively, "a realm of in-between" — "the No-more of the gods that have fled and the Not-yet of the god that is coming."[4] In the context of the impasse of oppositional thinking, in other words, he/she is compelled to acknowledge the time of the post–Cold War occasion as an interregnum. This, for an opposition that limits resistance to the political, means a time of defeat. But for the oppositional thinker who is attuned to the *ontological exile* to which he/she has been condemned by the global triumph of technological thinking it also means the recognition that this exilic condition of *silence* constitutes an irresolvable *contradiction* in the "Truth" of instrumental thinking — the "shadow" that haunts its light — that demands to be thought. In the interregnum, the primary task of the marginalized intellectual is the re-thinking of thinking itself. And, as I have suggested, it is the event of the Vietnam War — and the dominant American culture's inordinate will to forget it — that provides the directives for this most difficult of tasks not impossible.

Thinking Dissemination and Diaspora

No Iris-like messenger, bringing the gift of speech, and with it the gift of reasoned argument and reasonable response, accompanies the philosophical shock, and the affirmation of Being, clearly corresponding to the element of admiration in Plato's wonder, needs faith in a Creator-God to save human reason from the speechless dizzy glance into the abyss of nothingness.   — HANNAH ARENDT, *The Life of the Mind*

The incommensurability between the United States's justification for its intervention in Vietnam and its totally instrumentalist planning and conduct of the war exposed the irreconcilable contradiction inhering in the liberal democratic/humanist discourse of "the free world." In Nietzsche's and Foucault's ironic terms, the Vietnam War revealed its "benignity" — the "sweetness and light" ostensibly deriving from classical Greece — to be an "Egyptianism," a comportment toward being that has as its fundamental purpose the pacification of any resistance to its truth discourse. It revealed that the real project of the anthropological discourse inherited by America from the European Enlightenment is the reification of the nothing that belongs to being for the purpose not simply of "comprehending" its ineffable and elusive errancy, but of rendering its various manifestations "practically assailable." This first postmodern war, in short, showed decisively that the benign discourse of Enlightenment Man must *end* in violence against the recalcitrant Other that does not answer to the dictates of its plenary anthropo-logic — sometimes, as in the case of America's intervention in Vietnam, taken to a genocidal extreme.

It is this radical contradiction that the American Cultural Memory's remembrance of the war has obsessively tried to forget. As I have shown, this inordinate amnesiac will to obliterate the disclosures of Vietnam has been the hidden ideological agenda not simply of the American media's representation of the war in its long aftermath, but of the intellectual deputies of the dominant post–Cold War culture, who have been compelled by their recuperative exceptionalist "Hegelian" metanarrative to negate — or sublate — the history of the Vietnam War in order to celebrate the advent of the end of history and the *Pax Americana*. What needs to be remarked about this victorious post–Cold War discourse is that in affirming its universal truth, its spokespersons are compelled to speak something different. What matters to them is *not* the historically specific event of the Vietnam War, but the globally triumphant *idea* of liberal capitalist democracy. Is it an accident that they insistently speak of the post–Cold War occasion in this way? What about this "not Vietnam"?

This is the first directive toward rethinking thinking in the interregnum. An oppositional discourse that would be adequate to the task of resisting the *Pax Americana* must first think this sublated negation of the contradiction positively. This is not to say that the disclosure of this directive to think the *nonbeing of* — that belongs to — the imperial discourse of instrumentalism is restricted to the event of the Vietnam War. It is, as Heidegger's earlier call to rethink the nothing that modern science "wishes to know nothing about"[5] suggests, the unthought directive precipitated by the devastations at the sites of language, the earth, and its peoples incumbent on the "planetary imperialism of technologically organized man."[6] In a formulation of this resonant disclosure that implicates "Americanism" with the advent of the "age of the world picture," Heidegger writes:

As soon as the gigantic in planning and calculating and adjusting and making secure [one of the most revealing symptomatic manifestations of which is the annihilation of space and time by means of the electronic revolution] shifts over out of the quantitative and becomes a special quality, then what is gigantic, and what can seemingly always be calculated completely, becomes, precisely through this, incalculable. This *becoming incalculable remains the invisible shadow that is cast around things everywhere when man has been transformed into subjectum* and the world into picture.[7]

But, I am suggesting, it was the decisiveness of the Vietnam War's disclosure of this ontological contradiction — the shadow — that has rendered the retrieval of Heidegger's call to rethink the *not* that haunts the discourse and practice of "Americanism" an urgent imperative of the post-Vietnam occasion.

Indeed, this is the pervasive, if only symptomatic, testimony of the early poststructuralist theory — enabled in large part by Heidegger's interrogation of modernity, particularly, his retrieval of the "nonbeing" of being — that in some fundamental sense had its origins in the self-destruction of the truth discourse of the Enlightenment during the Vietnam War or, more precisely, in the failure of the global protest movements it catalyzed (most notably in France, in Germany, in Czechoslovakia, and in Mexico) to effect essential and lasting transformations in their respective polities. I am referring, above all, to the various critiques of Western logocentrism that precipitated an acute and pervasive consciousness of the *marginal* — the radical Other — that is either accommodated to or banished from the totalizing circle articulated by the concentering imperial *logos* of Western metaphysics. Taking its point of departure from the language of the countermemory established by Nietzsche, a certain Freud, and Heidegger ("Dionysus," "the returned repressed," the "nothing"), these critiques gave this ubiquitous Other *of* the logocentric Same various names: "the other that remains other" (Emmanuel Levinas), "the negative" (Theodor Adorno), "the *différance*" (Jacques Derrida), "the aporia" (Paul de Man), "the *differend*" (Jean-François Lyotard), "the invisible of the visible" (Louis Althusser), "the deviant" (Michel Foucault), "the catachrestic remainder" (Gayatri Spivak), "the rhizomatic," the "deterritorialized," or "the nomadic" (Gilles Deleuze and Félix Guattari), "the hybrid," "the Third Space," or "the minus in the one" (Homi Bhabha), and so on. But what these various names for the radically marginal have in common is not simply that they testify to the global scope of the imperial logocentrism of modernity, but that they point to "something" *incalculable* that the imperial instrumentalist thought of American modernity cannot "comprehend" and thus contain, indeed, to the shadow, as it were, that belongs to its dedifferentiating — colonizing — light. As the metaphorics that everywhere in this early postmodern theory accompanies these names, they testify to the *specter* — that which, to the metaphysical eye, *is not* — that menaces the triumphalist thinking of American modernity.

It is, further, this symptomatic *awareness* of the spectrality of the "not" that belongs to but cannot be seen or said by the "triumphant" thought of the age of the world picture that renders this early postmetaphysical thinker an "ontological exile" from the solar "at-homeland." Aware of the global colonization of originative thinking by the total technologization of "enlightening" thought, this thinker becomes, in Heidegger's resonant term, *der Abgeschiedene*, "the one apart":[8] he is the "ghostly" (*geistlich*) stranger ("LP," 177)[9] who wanders "at the fringe of the technically-economically oriented world of modern mass existence" ("LP," 196) listening to the silence (the unsayable) its saying has precipitated as self-destructive contradiction. Indeed, in thus reverting *knowingly* to precisely the condition of the "undomiciliated" or "wandering" or "nomadic" Other that enabled and justified the "civilizing/colonizing" truth discourse of the Occident, this ontological nomad in "the realm of the Between" (*Abgeschiedenheit:* "apartness") becomes the invisible "ghost" who, in his/her refusal to be answerable to the saying of the homeland, silently haunts its imperial authority. In Derrida's "Marxian" version of this "nonbeing" that activates anxiety (that which has no-thing as its object) in the homeland, he/she becomes the *"revenant"* — the interred "specter" who returns to *"visit"* the *"visitor."*[10]

It is, as I have suggested, this ontological "specter" that the "more worldly" oriented critical discourses that have superseded early poststructuralist theory are blinded to by their finally "reformist" cultural politics. And it is this oversight that renders their political marginality not exilic enough to be adequate to the conditions of the global post–Cold War occasion.

In interpreting Heidegger's antimetaphysical discourse and that of the poststructuralism it catalyzed in terms of the spectrality that produces anxiety in the dominant culture, I do not want to suggest that they, unlike the oppositional discourses that have interred them as counterproductive or obsolete, are, *as such,* viable agents of resisting the neoimperialism of the *Pax Americana*. Though this body of antimetaphysical thought (I realize that this way of putting it is reductive of specific differences) foregrounds the specter that menaces the truth discourse of Western modernity, it does not, with the exception of Heidegger and perhaps the late Derrida, adequately perceive that the imperative of the disclosure of the specter is the rethinking of thinking itself. That is to say, its witness to the specter, as the *metaphorical* way in which the spectral is articulated suggests, remains symptomatic and thus inadequately thought. More importantly, just as the dominant oppositional discourses — whether those of neo-Marxism, the New Historicism, feminism, cultural critique, black criticism, or postcolonial criticism — discount or tend to slide over the *ontological* question provoked by the annunciation of the end of history in their over-determination of the political site, this poststructural discourse, with the exception of the late Derrida, discounts or tends to slide over the *political* question provoked by the annunciation of the *Pax Americana*. More accurately, it fails to perceive and thus to think the *indissoluble* affiliation between the question of being and the question of the *polis,* theory, and praxis.

If, however, we forcibly dislocate the pervasive, if symptomatic, disclosure of the specter out of the ontological matrix where it has been embedded in the discourse of poststructuralism and reconstellate it into the specific political history of the 1960s — particularly, the military strategy of the Vietnamese insurgents — its meaning undergoes a productive estrangement. The genocidal violence perpetrated by the United States against the Vietnamese people and their land in the name of the "free world" not only exposed the European origins of the myth of American exceptionalism. It also exposed the metaphysical principle of decidability informing this grand imperial narrative. And it was in some sense the recognition of this arrogant American intolerance of undecidability that the Vietnamese Other exploited to abort the goals of the cultural and political armies of a much more powerful United States. That strategy, it will be recalled, which has been aptly called "*guerrilla* warfare" in the annals of Western military history, refused to accommodate itself — to be "answerable" — *to* the European concept of warfare: the binary "frontal engagement" of opposing visible armies whose story would end in a "decisive victory." Instead, these Vietnamese insurgents resorted to a "barbarian" strategy. They resisted invasion of their Asian homeland not by direct confrontation, but by an invisible nomadic mobility — a "spectral" tactics, as it were — that reversed the see-er/seen binary of Western imperialism and in so doing demolecularized the more formidable invading army and reduced its otherwise invincible war machine to utter ineffectiveness.

This disclosure of the Achilles' heel of the Western imperial project constitutes the second directive of the Vietnam War for the task of rethinking thinking in the American age of the world picture, more specifically, for the articulation of a theory of resistance against the *Pax Metaphysica* that is simultaneously a practice of political resistance against the *Pax Americana*. In reconstellating the Vietnamese strategy into the postcolonial context, we not only discover the hitherto overlooked connection between the spectral ontological Other precipitated by the fulfillment of the logical economy of Western metaphysics in the "Americanization" of the planet and the multitude of displaced political Others — the "nonexistent" beings — precipitated by the fulfillment (the coming to its "end") of the project of Western imperialism at large. In recognizing the indissoluble relationship between these two hitherto disparate Others, we are also compelled to appropriate the "eccentric" Vietnamese strategy of "unanswerability" that defeated America as a directive for thinking the positive emancipatory possibilities of the postcolonial occasion, that is, of the vast and various population of people unhomed by the depredations of Western imperialism.

This effort to theorize an "eccentric" adversarial political strategy of unanswerability from the global demographic shifts incumbent on the fulfillment of the imperial project has, is fact, already been inaugurated by Edward Said at the close of *Culture and Imperialism,* if only in a tentative way. Symptomatically, if not fully, conscious of the implications of the interregnum for thinking, Said, like Salman Rushdie in his fiction, takes his point of departure in this theoretical initiative from his exilic experience as émigré — as an irreversibly "unhoused" Other whose difference is indissolubly related to, indeed, was produced by, the colonizing (at-homing) imperatives of Occidental imperialism. In so doing, he invokes a theoretical motif that was fundamental to but inadequately thought by the early postmodernists (Heidegger, Derrida, Lyotard, for example) who overdetermined the decentering of the Occidental *logos,* a motif that Said finds thought in some degree by Paul Virilio (*L'Insecurité du territoire*), Gilles Deleuze and Félix Guattari (*Thousand Plateaus*), and Theodor Adorno (*Minima Moralia*), among others. I am referring to the possibilities not only for refuge but for political resistance and emancipation that, according to Said, are paradoxically inherent in the unhomed, estranging, and dereifying mobility — the spectral political being, as it were — of the displaced persons, the migrants, and the historyless Others of the imperial Occident who, in the postcolonial era, exist "between domains, between forms, between homes, and between languages." These are the possibilities of e-mergence precipitated on a global scale by the thinning out or occasional breaking of the lines of force that, by way of cultural familiarization, domestication, and pacification, have historically bound the periphery to the metropolitan center/homeland. I have quoted a passage from Said's all-too-brief summation of his oppositional postcolonial project in chapter 2, but the resonant suggestiveness precipitated by the reconstellation of the estranged political perspective he overdetermines into the ontological context I have inferred from the decentering and disarticulating guerrilla strategy of the nomadic Vietnamese insurgents warrants its retrieval at this culminating point of my argument:

> It is no exaggeration to say that liberation as an intellectual mission, born in the resistance and opposition to the confinements and ravages of imperialism, has now shifted from the settled, established, and domesticated dynamics of culture to its unhoused, decentered, and exilic energies, energies whose incarnation today is the migrant, and whose consciousness is that of the intellectual and artist in exile, the political figure between domains, between forms, between homes, and between languages. From this perspective then all things are indeed counter, original, spare, strange. From this perspective also, one can see "the common consort dancing together" contrapuntally. And while it would be the rankest Panglossian dishonesty to say that the bravura performances of the intellectual exile and the miseries of the displaced person or refugee are the same, it is possible, I think, to regard the intellectual as first distilling then articulating the predicaments that disfigure modernity — mass deportation, imprisonment, population transfer, collective dispossession, and forced immigration.

Having thematized the estrangement latent in the exilic condition of the émigré — the uncanny ability to see what from the point of view of the imperial discourse of the dominant culture is otherwise invisible — Said goes on to invoke the exemplary migrant discourse of the exiled German intellectual Theodor Adorno: " 'The past life of emigrés is, as we know, annulled,' says Adorno in *Minima Moralia*, subtitled *Reflections from a Damaged Life....* Why? *'Because anything that is not reified, cannot be counted and measured, ceases to exist'* or, as he says later, is consigned to mere *'background.'* " In the Heideggerian/Derridian rhetoric I have emphasized in my effort to think the implications of ontological imperialism, the émigré becomes the spectral *Abgeschiedene* in the "realm of the Between" who haunts the Being of the imperial culture that has reduced him/her to nonbeing. Said rightly acknowledges "the disabling aspects of this fate." But it does not blind him, as it does so many "progressive" postmodern or postcolonial thinkers, to "the virtues or possibilities" of this spectral marginalization. They are — and here Said announces the post-postmodern and -postcolonial project of the interregnum — "worth exploring." "Adorno's general pattern," he writes, "is what in another place he calls the 'administered world' or, insofar as the irresistible dominants in the culture are concerned, 'the conscious-ness industry.' There is then not just the negative advantage of refuge in the emigré's eccentricity; there is also the positive benefit of challeng-ing the system, *describing it in a language unavailable to those it has already subdued.*"[11]

Admittedly, the possibilities for this "freedom from exchange" — this "last refuge" from the globalization of late capitalism — that Said prof-fers as an alternative to the existing oppositional discourses are, like Adorno's, the *minima moralia* of a damaged political life, and, in its em-phasis on survival, his alternative lacks the force of a truly positive hope. But if, as the resonant doubleness of the language I have italicized am-ply warrants, the terms of his global elaboration of these postcolonial possibilities are reconstellated into the occasion of the struggle of the Vietnamese people against American imperialism in the 1960s, one need not, at least on this count, be quite as pessimistic as Adorno and Said about the role of the intellectual in the global post–Cold War period I have called the interregnum, without at the same time succumbing to "the rankest Panglossian dishonesty." For, to reiterate, it was pre-cisely the Vietnamese's exploitation of the very ontological conditions of their enforced confinement by a formidable imperial culture that es-tranged that colonized space and, in so doing, disintegrated *both* the cultural narrative *and* the decisive end-oriented imperial practice this narrative was designed to enable. The powerless Vietnamese masterfully transformed the United States's arrogant and clamorous strategy to re-duce the unaccountable and immeasurable Other to nonexistent status or, to invoke Adorno's language, to consign its spectral Otherness to "mere background" in its metanarrative — which is to say, to *silent invisibility before the panoptic imperial gaze* — into a powerful polyva-lent de-structive and e-mancipatory (projective) weapon. And it was this transformation of the debilitating, that is, passivizing and silencing, ef-fects of reification that enabled this "damaged" Third World country — *precisely by way of its spectral invisibility* — to disable the otherwise irrefragable operations of reification and thus to defeat the most power-ful nation in the history of the world.[12] To think the spectral as the menacing precipitate of the indissoluble relationship between the *Pax Metaphysica* and the *Pax Americana:* this, not the "reformist" initiative of those liberals like Sacvan Bercovitch and Richard Rorty whose oppo-sitional discourse continues to be answerable to the imperial language informed by the *idea* of America, is the resonantly silent imperative of the interregnum, especially for American intellectuals of the Left.[13]

This appeal to contemporary American intellectuals to think the no-madic political émigré who haunts the post–Cold War New World Order simultaneously with the ontological specter that postmetaphysical European theorists[14] have thematized as the paradoxical consequence of the fulfillment of the logical economy of Western philosophy is an ap-peal to think America globally. And it no doubt will be criticized by those nation-oriented American intellectuals to whom it is addressed as "traveling theory," the importation of a foreign interpretive discourse into a historically specifically American context.[15] Lest this vestigial American exceptionalist conclusion be drawn, let me finally invoke the testimony of an American writer — one to whom Said often refers, but only in passing — whose work at large, as I have shown elsewhere,[16] is decisively pertinent to the occasion of the Vietnam War and its af-termath. For this American writer's testimony not only anticipates in a fundamental way the essence of the American intervention in Viet-nam — the essentially imperial ontological/cultural origins and character of its Adamic errand in the Vietnamese wilderness. It also constitutes a prolepsis of the essence of the Vietnamese resistance and, above all, of the adversarial strategy of "refusal" — of spectral "unanswerabil-ity" — that, as all these postmetaphysical European theorists as well as Said imply, is more than any other adequate to the task of "deter-ring" the global pretensions of "America" in the post–Cold War era. I am referring to the radically exilic witness of Herman Melville, of what, to underscore its spectral ec-centricity, I have called his "errant art," a negational or antinarrative strategy that was deliberately intended to call the metaphysically ordained uni-directionality of America's excep-tionalist imperial project into question. Thus, for example, in "Bartleby, the Scrivener," this ghostly preterite's resonant silence — his refusal to respond in kind to the reifying and reified "premises" of American Wall Street logic (to be "counted and measured" by "the adminis-tered world," as it were) — utterly confounds, derails, and neutralizes its "unerring" and vaunted practical efficacy. Thus also in *Moby-Dick*, Ishmael's errant narrative — its endlessly differentiating and deferring language — comes to be understood not simply as an alternative to the "unerring" discourse of the dominant American culture. As in the case of Bartleby's minimalist "I prefer not to," his maximalist "white" or "unnaming" saying also comes to be understood as the most effective means of rendering impotent the positive globally oriented power that proceeds from a totalizing "monomaniacal" naming, a stridently vo-cal Ahabian saying that reifies the unnameable whiteness of being in order to make it "practically assailable."[17] Indeed, as *Pierre, Israel Pot-ter, The Confidence-Man,* and *Billy Budd* make manifest, this effort to think positively the nothing that the exceptionalist global discourse of America will have nothing to do with — this effort to get "a voice out of silence"[18] — constitutes the supreme theme of this unhomed American writer's fiction. Melville's American project, in fact, has more in common with Heidegger's and the European poststructuralists' than it has with that of the American intellectuals who are "against theory" because it is foreign to American culture.[19]

The Silent Voice of the Specter: A Recapitulation

> If he loves justice, the "scholar" of the future, the "intellectual" of tomorrow should learn it from the ghost. He should learn to live by learning not how to make conversation with the ghost but how to talk to him, with her, how to let them speak or how to give them back speech, even if it is in oneself, in the other, in the other in oneself: they are always *there*, specters, even if they do not exist, even if they are no longer, even if they are not yet.   — JACQUES DERRIDA, *Specters of Marx*

The specter of Vietnam continues to haunt "America" in the post–Cold War era, despite the obsessive effort of the American Cultural Memory to inter it once and for all in the innocuous past. What this globally resonant event's refusal to be answerable to the national will to forget it seems to be saying to oppositional critics who have not heeded its silent voice is that it is now — at the moment the West represents the end of the Cold War as the end of history and the advent of the New World Order — high time to abandon the word "Postmodernism." For it has been drained of virtually all ontological content — an emptying epitomized by its reduction by the culture industry, the neo-Marxist diagnosticians of late capitalism, and the culture and postcolonial critics to a free-floating (or posthistorical) late capitalist acronym, "Pomo." It is a name, that is, that has essentially forgotten its provenance in the terrible devastation of Vietnam by an imperial nation that has assumed the civilizing mission of a decadent Europe as its "exceptionalist" burden ordained by History. Perhaps, to put it positively, this silent voice of the *revenant* is saying that those who would resist the triumphalist post–Cold War discourse would be better served by rethinking the cultural and political implications of the Vietnam War — its global reach — in the now-unfashionable ontological terms originally invoked by such continental intellectuals as Derrida, Lacan, Lyotard, Lacoue-Labarthe, Nancy, Althusser, Deleuze, and Foucault: those inaugural post-"Heideggerian" thinkers whom the rise to prominence of postmodernist Marxism, New Historicism, cultural studies, and postcolonial criticism has marginalized, if not entirely superseded. These were the inaugural theorists of the Occidental *logos* who began the project of thinking the decentering that came all too gratuitously — and misleadingly — to be called "postmodern." I am referring specifically to their communal and insistent interrogation of the discourse of Man or, to appropriate the title of an "untimely" (dis)seminal lecture Derrida delivered at an international philosophical colloquium in New York in 1968 — at the height of American violence in Vietnam — on "the ends of man."[20]

In this historically resonant phrase, Derrida is invoking the double meaning of Heidegger's representation of the modern (anthropological) age as the "end of philosophy": the fulfillment-*and*-exhaustion of the restricted (teleo)logical economy of the Western philosophical tradition in the "age of the world picture" (*die Zeit des Weltbildes*). This, it will be recalled, is the age in which visual perception — thinking being at large as mappable territory — achieves planetary hegemony, the age that has totally reduced and accommodated the differences that time always already disseminates to totalized image. It is the age, to put it specifically, that has enframed (*gestelt*) and reified (the be*ing* of) being into a banalized standing reserve (*Bestand*). In this dark age, as is everywhere — globally — manifest in the discourse and practices of the accomplished enlightenment, everything, including human being, is disposable. That which "counts" has utility; when its utility is used up, it is ruthlessly discarded. It is, to risk an invidious comparison, to this world-devastating depthlessness of thinking in modernity, I suggest, that Hannah Arendt is referring when, in her last, great, unfinished book, she reinvokes her controversial attribution of Adolph Eichmann's evil to the banality of this common mind as that which instigated her effort to rethink thinking:

> The immediate impulse [for "my preoccupation with mental activities" in *The Life of the Mind*] came from my attending the Eichmann trial in Jerusalem. In my report of it I spoke of "the banality of evil." Behind that phrase, I held no thesis or doctrine, although I was dimly aware of the fact that it went counter to our tradition of thought — literary, theological, or philosophical — about the phenomenon of evil. Evil, we have learned, is something demonic. . . . However, what I was confronted with was utterly different and still undeniably factual. I was struck by a manifest shallowness in the doer of his deeds that made it impossible to trace the uncontestable evil of his deeds to any deeper level of roots or motives. The deeds were monstrous, but the doer . . . was

quite ordinary, commonplace, and neither demonic nor monstrous. There was no sign in him of firm ideological convictions or of specific evil motives, and the only notable characteristic one could detect in his past behavior as well as in his behavior during the trial...was something entirely negative: it was not stupidity but *thoughtlessness*.[21]

Given this utterly reduced condition of thinking, the "ends of man" thus points to the (self)dis-closure of that spectral force field of differences that the "truth" of the age of the world picture cannot finally contain within its imperial circumference. The moment that the structuralist logic of the discourse of modern anthropology reaches its limits — achieves closure — means, finally, the delegitimation of the ("disinterested" or "objective") truth discourse of Occidental humanism. This, it must be remembered, is the post-Enlightenment "anthropology" that, under the allotropic names of "the free world" or "liberal [American] democracy," has come to be represented in the aftermath of the Cold War and the "kicking of the Vietnam syndrome" as "the end of history" by the spokespersons of "America."

In the face of this triumphalist ontological representation of the contemporary occasion — which is to say, this astonishingly amnesiac historical memory — would not a "postcolonial" opposition be better served by discarding the worn-out, ontologically empty word "postmodernism"? Would it not, further, be preferable to undertake the postcolonial project by thinking the dangerous political occasion called "the New World Order" in the resonant spectral terms recalled by Derrida's early effort to think the "ends of man" in the context of the Vietnam War? This, at any rate, is the suggestive oppositional project Derrida proposes in *Specters of Marx,* his most recent and most political repetition of the "Heideggerian" effort of ontological retrieval, in the wake of the dominant liberal/capitalist culture's proclamation at the end of the Cold War of the death and burial of Marx and its euphoric announcement of the "gospel," "the good news" that has been brought into being by the dialectical labor of History in the "fullness of time."[22] And, as I have suggested by pointing to its affiliation with Said's invocation of the political émigré, it is a proposal that demands urgent attention. Indeed, it is the imperative of thinking in the interregnum, given the apparent indifference of postmodern/postcolonial criticism, which restricts its understanding of the new globalism to the untethered flow of transnational capital, to this other, equally pervasive, nationalist globalism, which represents the present post–Cold War moment not simply as the end of History, but as the triumph of "America" as well.

If, as I have suggested, this alleged "good news" is understood, as I think it should be, as the triumphant annunciation of a fully realized imperial and banalizing project of thinking, of an "advent," as it were (the *Pax Metaphysica*), as well as the completed imperial and banalizing project of sociopolitics (the *Pax Americana*), then it becomes the task of a "postcolonial" opposition not simply to retrieve the differential event that the announcement of "good news" has had to obliterate in order to legitimize the planetary truth of liberal capitalist democracy. (It should not be overlooked that this end-of-history discourse repeats in *thought* the violence in *practice* to which the American officer in Vietnam synecdochically referred when he declared that "[w]e had to destroy Ben Tre in order to save it.")[23] It also becomes a postcolonial opposition's task to *think* that repressed event in terms of the implications of its persistent and anxiety-provoking spectral afterlife for a way of thinking capable of disarticulating or molecularizing the inordinate positive power of the triumphant imperial discourse.

It has not been my purpose in this book to undertake this rethinking of thinking, though I want to emphasize that what I have said in the preceding chapters makes it clear that this initiative would benefit by attuning itself to the de-structive (or decentering) project Heidegger inaugurated in *Being and Time* in the wake of the forgetting of the *Seinsfrage* (which is to say, of the closure of philosophy) and that Derrida and Foucault, in different ways, extended and modified. Finally, however, it is not so much to theory as such that the project to rethink thinking in the interregnum must look as it is to the violence of the history of the Occidental thought and practice I have retrieved. This history, bathed in innocent blood, emphatically suggests that such a thinking must take its point of departure from the self-de-struction of the discourse of Man in the Vietnam War — the event that synecdochically and decisively disclosed not only the *essential* complicity of Occidental thought with imperial practice, but also the essential affiliation between the dissemination inhering in its Word and the diasporic consequences of the fulfillment of its Word's logic. To "repeat" my beginning after a long detour, it must take its positive point of departure from the negative force — the "decentered" or, in the allotropes of Edward Said and Gilles Deleuze and Félix Guattari, the "unhoused" or "deterritorialized" or "diasporic" or "nomadic" energies — released into history as haunting specters by the fulfillment of this European Word's reifying or spatial, which is to say, imperial, logic. This task reflects the poverty — the "damaged life" — of the exiled intellectual in the interregnum. Having learned from its fate at the *hands* of the colonial regime of truth, however, such a differential/exilic thinking of the *Abgeschiedene*, unlike

the modes of opposition that sanguinely continue to think in the ontological terms prescribed by the master discourse, is not only enabled
to refuse to play by the rules of its imperial logic. It is also enabled to
transform this negative condition into a positive force of resistance. As
I hope these chapters have shown, such a strategic "nomadic" thinking,
more than any other that is currently available, will be adequate to the
task of writing the history of the present and, though it may in the end
be the same thing, of deterring liberal capitalist democracy and the *Pax
Americana.*

But, it needs to be underscored, the self-de-struction of the imperial
truth discourse of the post-Enlightenment incumbent on the fulfillment
of its ontologic should not merely be thought in terms of resisting an oppressive and banalizing tradition. For this dis-closure of its plenary circle
also and simultaneously releases *pro-jective* possibilities. To think positively the spectral Other that haunts Occidental thought — "the shadow
that the light of Being has not been able to illumine," in Enrique Dussel's resonant formulation[24] — is, therefore, to open up the possibility
of a different idea of the *polis* from that envisioned by the metaphysical (and Roman) West. It is, finally, to bring into being (to liberate) the
thought of a differential polity, a polity in which the dialogue that is
the essential condition of our mortal being-with takes place not in the
seductive paradisal realm to which it has, in fact, been strategically confined by liberal democracy, but in *this* unequal world, where imbalance
of power — and injustice — always rules.

Notes

Introduction

1. Alexis de Tocqueville, *Democracy in America,* 2 vols., trans. Henry Reeve, rev. Francis Bowen (New York: Vintage, 1990), 6.

2. De Tocqueville, *Democracy in America:* "Their implacable prejudices, their uncontrolled passions, their vices, and still more, perhaps, their savage virtues, consigned them to inevitable destruction" (1:25).

3. Francis Fukuyama, *The End of History and the Last Man* (New York: Free Press, 1992). This book constitutes an expansion of the argument of Fukuyama's earlier, highly publicized essay, "The End of History," published in the neoconservative journal *National Interest* 18 (summer 1989): 3–18. Fukuyama invokes Hegel's and Kojève's Universal History as his theoretical source, but as his insistent references make clear, his ultimate source, as it has been for virtually every intellectual spokesman for liberal democratic America's global mission, is de Tocqueville's *Democracy in America:* "[T]he overtly democratic nature of the American founding was responsible for the formation of the democratic American of later generations, a human type (so brilliantly described by Tocqueville) which has not existed before in the course of history (*End of History,* 222).

4. Richard Haass, *The Reluctant Sheriff: The United States after the Cold War* (Washington, D.C.: Institute of Foreign Affairs, 1997).

5. See especially Sacvan Bercovitch, *The American Jeremiad* (Madison: University of Wisconsin Press, 1978); Richard Drinnon, *Facing West: The Metaphysics of Indian-Hating and Empire-Building* (Minneapolis: University of Minnesota Press, 1980); and Donald Pease, "New Americanists: Revisionist Interventions in the Canon," in Pease, ed., *New Americanists,* a special issue of *boundary* 2 17 (spring 1990): 1–37.

6. Tom Engelhardt, *The End of Victory Culture: Cold War America and the Disillusioning of a Generation* (New York: Basic Books, 1995).

7. James W. Ceaser, *Reconstructing America: The Symbol of America in Modern Thought* (New Haven: Yale University Press, 1997).

8. Arthur Schlesinger, *The Disuniting of America: Reflections on a Multicultural Society* (New York: W. W. Norton, 1998); Richard Rorty, *Achieving Our Country: Leftist Thought in Twentieth-Century America* (Cambridge, Mass.: Harvard University Press, 1998).

9. Bart Moore-Gilbert, *Postcolonial Theory: Context, Practices, Politics* (London: Verso, 1997), 50. Of the many critiques of Said's totalizing tendency, see especially Dennis Porter, "*Orientalism* and Its Problems" (1983), reprinted in *Colonial Discourse and Post-colonial Theory,* ed. Patrick Williams and Laura Chrisman (New York: Columbia University Press, 1994); James Clifford, "On *Orientalism,*" in *The Predicament of Culture: Twentieth-Century Ethnography, Literature, and Art* (Cambridge, Mass.: Harvard University Press, 1988); Lisa

Lowe, *Critical Terrains: French and British Orientalisms* (Ithaca, N.Y.: Cornell University Press, 1991); and Aijaz Ahmad, "*Orientalism* and After: Ambivalence and Metropolitan Location in the Work of Edward Said," in *In Theory: Classes, Nations, Literatures* (London: Verso, 1992), 159–219.

1. The Ontological Origins of Occidental Imperialism

1. Robin Blackburn, ed., *After the Fall: The Failure of Communism and the Future of Socialism* (London: Verso, 1991); Bernd Magnus and Stephen Cullenberg, eds., *Whither Marxism? Global Crises in International Perspective* (New York: Routledge, 1995); Charles Derber (with Karen Marie Ferroggiaro, Jacqueline A. Ortiz, and James A. Vela-McConnell), *What's Left? Radical Politics in the Postcommunist Era* (Amherst: University of Massachusetts Press, 1995).

2. I adopt this term from Martin Heidegger, *An Introduction to Metaphysics*, trans. Ralph Manheim (New Haven: Yale University Press, 1959), to avoid the pluralistic connotation of "dialogue." In an *Auseinandersetzung* the object of the dialogue is not the reconciliation of opposites. The antagonistic positions involve a *belongingness in strife* and are undertaken to achieve *presencing* (not Presence): "The *polemos* [in Heraclitus's Fragment 53] is a conflict that prevailed prior to everything divine and human, not a war in the human sense. . . . In the conflict (*Aus-einandersetzung*, setting apart) a world comes into being. (Conflict does not split, much less destroy unity, it is a binding-together, *logos. Polemos* and *logos* are the same)" (ibid., 62).

3. In this transdisciplinary project, I take my lead from Heidegger's suggestive, but inadequately thought, critique of disciplinarity, especially in his essay "The Anaximander Fragment," in *Early Greek Thinking*, trans. David Farrell Krell and Anthony A. Capuzzi (New York: Harper and Row, 1975). In this neglected essay, Heidegger rejects the prevailing assumption that the Anaximander Fragment "strives after scientific knowledge concerning the demarcated realm of nature." And with the "collapse of this presupposition," "another assumption becomes superfluous, namely, that at this time [in pre-Socratic Greece] ethical or juridical matters were interpreted in terms of the disciplines we call 'ethics' and 'jurisprudence.' Denial of such boundaries between disciplines does not mean to imply that in early times law and ethicality were unknown. But if the way we normally think within a range of disciplines (such as physics, ethics, philosophy of law, biology, psychology) has no place here — if boundaries between these subjects are lacking — then there is no possibility of trespass or of the unjustified transfer of notions from one area to another. Yet where boundaries between disciplines do not appear, boundless indeterminacy and flux do not necessarily prevail: on the contrary, an appropriate articulation of a matter purely thought may well come to language when it has been freed from every oversimplification" (21–22). See also Martin Heidegger, "Letter on Humanism," trans. Frank A. Capuzzi, in *Basic Writings*, ed. David Farrell Krell (New York: Harper and Row, 1977), 232–33.

4. Michel Foucault, *Discipline and Punish: The Birth of the Prison*, trans. Alan Sheridan (New York: Pantheon, 1977), 169. For a fuller treatment of this motif in Foucault's genealogy of the disciplinary society, see chapter 2 above.

5. Jacques Derrida, "Structure, Sign, and Play in the Discourse of the Human Sciences," in *Writing and Difference*, trans. Alan Bass (Chicago: University of Chicago Press, 1978), 288.

6. Foucault, *Discipline and Punish,* 205.

7. My use of the word "metaphysics" to refer to an orientation toward differential being that facilitates its mastery and colonization derives from a certain spirit of Heidegger. It is to be distinguished, therefore, from Emmanuel Levinas's use of the same term. The mode of inquiry I am calling "metaphysical imperialism" is called by Levinas — and by Derrida — "ontological imperialism" (Emmanuel Levinas, *Totality and Infinity: An Essay on Exteriority,* trans. Alfonso Lingis [Pittsburgh: Duquesne University Press, 1969], 44). For Levinas (and Derrida) ontology is ideological; for me it is a neutral term referring to inquiry into the question of being. Metaphysics, on the other hand, is for Levinas — strangely — the "beyond of totality" (23), the *"absolutely other"* (33), "the transcendence, the welcoming of the other by the same, of the Other by me," and "is concretely produced as the calling into question of the same by the other, that is, as the ethics that accomplished the critical essence of knowledge." As such, "metaphysics precedes ontology" (43). See Robert Young, *White Mythologies: Writing History and the West* (New York: Routledge, 1990), 15.

Levinas identifies Heidegger's thought with this "ontological imperialism" (46–49) that has its origins in Greece. I have chosen, despite the ambivalences in his thought, to focus on Heidegger's confrontation with the question of the relationship between the Western philosophical tradition and imperialism rather than on Levinas's profoundly suggestive analogous critique of the Western philosophical obsession with totality. I do not discount the Levinasian critique of Heidegger's thought vis-à-vis being (though Levinas, as I will show, overlooks an equally anti-"ontological" strain in Heidegger's "Greek" discourse: his insistent invocation of the *Auseinandersetzung* and his meditation on Western language and imperialism in the *Parmenides,* for example). But I want to invoke the very gestures vis-à-vis the Other in Heidegger's thought that clearly catalyzed Levinas's own thought. Further I want to eschew certain recuperative (Judaic) religious resonances that inhere in Levinas's very definition of metaphysics. This reasoning applies as well to the equally provocative Levinasian "metaphysics" — the liberation theology — of Enrique Dussel (*Philosophy of Liberation,* trans. Aquilina Martínez and Christine Morkovsky [Maryknoll, N.Y.: Orbis Books, 1985], 48–49).

8. Martin Heidegger, "What Is Metaphysics?" trans. David Farrell Krell, in *Basic Writings,* ed. Krell (New York: Harper and Row, 1977), 109; my emphasis.

9. Hannah Arendt, *The Human Condition* (Chicago: University of Chicago Press, 1958), 257–68.

10. Martin Heidegger, *Being and Time,* trans. John Macquarrie and Edward Robinson (New York: Harper and Row, 1962): "If the question of Being is to have its own history made transparent, then this hardened tradition must be loosened up, and the concealments which it has brought about must be dissolved. We understand this task as one in which by taking *the question of Being as our clue,* we are to *destroy* the traditional content of ancient ontology [*Destruktion des überlieferten Bestandes der antiken Ontologie*] until we arrive at those primordial experiences in which we achieved our first ways of determining the nature of Being—the ways which have guided us ever since" (44).

11. Heidegger, "What Is Metaphysics?" 103.

12. Plato, *Phaedrus and the Seventh and Eighth Letters,* trans. William Hamilton (Harmondsworth, England: Penguin, 1973), 57.

13. In virtually all cultural materialist or postcolonial criticism that in some degree recognizes the polyvalency of the imperial project, the "literal" (given) meaning of the word "colonization" is reserved for the economic/political/racial act of conquest and exploitation of the indigenous Others of geographical spaces at the periphery of Europe. In referring to the conquest and exploitation of other sites on this continuum, such as being or the subject or language or women, as "colonization" (the reference, significantly, is never to the continuum as a whole), this criticism invariably qualifies the name by putting quotation marks around it and/or by referring to it as metaphorical. In this discourse, in other words, the colonization of being, of the subject, of language, or of women — and the act of resistance or decolonization — is superstructural to the privileged "literal" economic/political base. A telling example of this pervasive but invisible kind of imperial anti-imperialism can be found in Bill Ashcroft, Gareth Griffiths, and Helen Tiffin, *The Empire Writes Back: Theory and Practice in Post-colonial Literatures* (London: Routledge, 1989), in a section titled "Feminism and Post-colonialism." Unaware of, or probably indifferent to, the etymological provenance of the word "colonialism" (see chapter 2), they write: "Women in many societies have been relegated to the position of 'Other,' marginalized and, in a metaphorical sense, 'colonized,' forced to pursue guerrilla warfare against imperial domination from positions deeply imbedded in, yet fundamentally alienated from, that *imperium*" (174).

14. This distinction is fundamental from beginning to end in Heidegger's discourse. See especially *Being and Time,* 43; "On the Essence of Truth," trans. John Sallis, in *Basic Writings,* 118–22; and "On the Origins of the Work of Art," trans. Albert Hofstadter, in *Basic Writings,* 153–54.

15. In its encyclopedic range of reference of both primary and secondary materials, Martin Jay's *Downcast Eyes: The Denigration of Vision in Twentieth-Century French Thought* (Berkeley: University of California Press, 1993) constitutes a useful compendium of the discourse circulating around the primacy of vision (the eye) in the Western tradition. But I find significant, indeed, disabling, problems with his influential book, not the least of which is the unsaid that results from an ideological bias (broadly Habermasian) that, though admitted, is always in contention with its (objective) encyclopedic pretensions. As Jay notes at the outset, his massive research project into the (basically poststructuralist) French critique of the Occidental privileging of vision in knowledge production is carried out from the point of view of an ocularcentric perspective: "I remain unrepentantly beholden to the ideal of illumination that suggests an Enlightenment faith in clarifying indistinct ideas. To make matter's worse, I will employ a method that unapologetically embraces one of the antiocularcentric discourse's other major targets, a synoptic survey of an intellectual field at some remove from it" (17).

Jay qualifies this assertion by appropriating Hans-Georg Gadamer's "fusion of horizons" in behalf of the historian's achievement of "a communicative interaction" with the past. But this appropriation of "a less totalizing [metaphor] than synopsis" does not save him from the charge he anticipates but would disarm by this qualification. The fact is that his "ocularcentric perspective" does indeed compel him to overlook or to minimize, if not repress, not only the polyvalent violent ideological practices enabled by this ocularcentrism, but also recent studies, like mine and other "poststructuralist" or neo-Marxist critics, that in some degree or other thematize the multisituated violence of the ocularcentric regime.

Despite his disclaimer, Jay's study is indeed guilty of the very metaphysical/cultural imperialism that, according to the French texts he analyzes, is inscribed in the discourse of modernity. This blindness of Jay's ocularcentric oversight is manifest everywhere in his text, but the most significant and most symptomatic are the following: (1) It fails to see the major role that the Roman translation of an originative Greek truth (*aletheia*) to the derivative (retro-spective oriented) *veritas* (the adequation of mind and thing) plays in the establishment of European ocularcentrism, a failure that also results in misleadingly locating the enabling origin of the modern "scopic regime" in the instrumental reason of the Enlightenment. (2) It fails to see the indissoluble affiliation between the metaphorics of vision (and light) and other tributary systems — the center/periphery, planting, and, not least, the metaphorics of reification/closure (com-prehension as "taking hold of"). As the opening paragraph of his book charmingly demonstrates, Jay is aware of the pervasiveness of visual metaphors in the everyday language of knowledge production in Occidental societies. But he does not recognize the inordinate degree to which this ubiquitous visual metaphorics enables the equally pervasive metaphorics of grasping/bringing to closure (the being that is in essence ungraspable and unclosable). (3) It fails to see the decisive degree to which this relay of metaphorics is inscribed not simply in the vocabularies of Western languages, but also, and more tellingly, in their grammars and structures, from the sentence to the narrative.

Focusing the attention of his research almost entirely on literal references to vision, Jay indicates virtually no awareness, for example, that it is the privileged eye that is imperially at work in the structuration of the philosophical, scientific, or literary texts of the European canon. A telling example of this reductive literal-mindedness is the following commentary on Hegel's philosophy: "German Romanticism, for all its nocturnal preoccupations and fascination with the musicalization of poetry, was not without a similar visual moment. Philippe Lacoue-Labarthe and Jean-Luc Nancy have pointed to what they call 'eidaesthetics' in the theory of the Jena Romantics, the yearning for a plastic representation of the idea. Georg Wilhelm Friedrich Hegel's defense of 'imageless truth,' his recognition that philosophical reflection [*sic*] need not be based on its visual counterpart, was in part a critique of this Romantic hope." And in a footnote he adds, ostensibly with Hegel's invocation of the "imageless truth" of philosophy in mind, "The issue of the visual in German Idealism as a whole is beyond our scope, but its exploration would doubtless contribute to an understanding of the roots of the twentieth-century interrogation of ocularcentrism" (110). Jay's blindness to the *meta*narrativity of Hegel's philosophical discourse, most visibly evident in *The Philosophy of History* — which is to say, its absolute reliance on the panoptic mind's eye — is underscored by his surprising omission of reference to Jacques Derrida's genealogy of Hegel's dream of the "imageless truth" in "White Mythology": his powerful demonstration, by way of highlighting the visual metaphorics of Hegel's metaphysics, that this "universal" veridical "truth" is the mature *end* of the dialectic historical process that, by way of the *Aufhebung,* does not annul visual figuration (metaphor in general and the gaze in particular) — and its Eurocentric imperial project — but totalizes, interiorizes, and naturalizes (conceals) it as "the truth of [European] philosophy": "Philosophical discourse — as such — describes a metaphor which is displaced and reabsorbed between two suns [or two eyes]. This *end* of metaphor is not interpreted as a death or dislocation, but as an interiorizing anamnesis (*Erinnerung*), a recollection of meaning, a *relève* of living metaphoricity into a living state of properness. This is the irrepressible philosophical desire to summarize-interiorize-dialecticize-master-*relever* the metaphorical division between the origin [in the East] and itself [the West], the Oriental difference" (269).

16. This way of putting the genealogy of Occidental education is intended to suggest that the received interpretation of Plato's allegory of the cave is one that has been mediated through the eyes of (imperial) Rome and thus is not, in its apotheosis of light, a decisive reading. See Martin Heidegger, "Plato's Doctrine of Truth," trans. John Barlow, in *Philosophy in the Twentieth Century,* vol. 3, ed. William Barrett and Henry D. Aiken (New York: Random House, 1962), 251–69. Virtually all recent commentators on Western ocularcentrism trace the West's privileging of the eye back to Greece and especially to Plato. They entirely overlook Heidegger's fundamental differentiation of the Greeks' and Romans' understanding of the relationship between vision and knowledge, even as some commentators indicate awareness of a certain insistent ambiguity in the Greek understanding. See, for example, Martin Jay, "The Noblest of the Senses: Vision from Plato to Descartes," in *Downcast Eyes,* 28–82; David Michael Levin, *The Opening of Vision: Nihilism and the Postmodern Situation* (New York: Routledge, 1988); and Levin, ed., *Modernity and the Hegemony of Vision* (Berkeley: University of California Press, 1993), especially Levin's introduction, 1–29, and his "Decline and Fall: Ocularcentrism in Heidegger's Reading of the History of Metaphysics," 186–217. Though Heidegger early on gives the impression that the ontotheological tradition begins with Plato's "correction" of the pre-Socratics, he simultaneously, as in the very first paragraph of *Being and Time,* distinguishes Plato (and Aristotle) from those who come after: "[The question of Being] is one which provided a stimulus for the research of Plato and Aristotle, only to subside from then on as *a theme for actual investigation.* What these two men achieved was to persist through many alterations and 'retouchings' down to the 'logic' of Hegel. And *what they wrested with the utmost intellectual effort from the phenomena,* fragmentary and incipient though it was, has long since become trivialized" (21; my emphasis). In his later work, it is to Rome that Heidegger assigns the origin of this process of trivialization, which is to say, its reduction of the originative thinking of the Greeks to a derivative, calculative project, a retro-spective thought that begins from the end.

17. In his essay on Levinas, "Violence and Metaphysics: An Essay on the Thought of Emmanuel Levinas," in *Writing and Difference,* Derrida, like Levinas, locates the origin of philosophy as such — that is, logocentrism — in Greece. Thus, he also includes Heidegger in the philosophical tradition, since the latter identifies himself with Greek thinking. Explicating Levinas, he writes in total sympathy: "These three motifs [the Greek source of philosophy; the "reduction of metaphysics" (understood as a thought of alterity); and the consequent annulment of the ethical in Husserl's and Heidegger's "ontological"

thought] arrayed at the unique source of the unique philosophy would indicate the only possible direction to be taken by any philosophical resource in general. Any possible dialogue between Husserlian phenomenology and Heideggerian 'ontology...' can be understood only from within the Greek tradition. At the moment when the fundamental conceptual system produced by the Greco-European adventure is in the process of taking over all of humanity, these three motifs would predetermine the totality of the logos and of the worldwide historico-philosophical situation. No philosophy could possibly dislodge them without first succumbing to them, or without finally destroying itself as philosophical language. At a historical depth which the science and philosophies of history can only presuppose, we know that we are consigned to the security of the Greek element; and we know it with a knowledge and confidence which are neither habitual nor comfortable but, on the contrary, permit us to experience torment or distress in general. For example..., [w]hen Heidegger says that 'for a long time, too long, thought has been desiccated,' like a fish out of water, the element to which he wished to return thought is still — already — the Greek element, the Greek thought of Being, the thought of Being whose irruption or call produced Greece" (82).

This early statement constitutes a persuasive — and overlooked — identification of Western philosophy with its global imperial project. And there is, further, some justification for identifying Husserl's and Heidegger's thought with it. But what Derrida, like Levinas, overlooks, in a way that, it seems to me, distorts a massive and important motif in Heidegger's thinking, is Heidegger's reiterated insistence on the profound difference between Greek and Roman thinking, which could be taken to mean that, for Heidegger, European thinking as such — that is, "philosophy" — begins not with Greece, but with the translation of Greek *aletheia* into Roman *veritas* and that, therefore, the idea of Europe (and the violence it compels) has its origins in Rome. See chapter 3 above.

The question as to why both Derrida and Levinas do not address this reiterated distinction, which, after all, is a foundational motif in Heidegger's, if not in Husserl's, discourse on the ontotheological tradition, needs to be thought. On this crucial matter, see Vassilis Lambropoulos's important *The Rise of Eurocentrism: Anatomy of Interpretation* (Princeton, N.J.: Princeton University Press, 1993). In this book, Lambropoulos undertakes an encyclopedic exploration of the history of the ideological struggle between "Hellenism" and "Hebraism" over the identity of Europe. In a way that provocatively estranges the received view of Derrida, Lambropoulos argues with some force that Derrida's deconstructive thinking (like Levinas's) partakes in this ideological struggle in a fundamental way: "What has made the banality of Derridean theory attractive is its playful reliance on the Hebraic-Hellenic dichotomy. Given the philosophical tradition to which the author subscribes, the belief in a vicious Hellenic dominance and a benevolent Hebraic otherness becomes inevitable. He has turned the standard distinction, however, into a dogma, making it the central topic of his investigation, the pivotal concept of his views, the fundamental issue of his writings. Over and over again, he resorts to it, reducing any distinction to a difference and every difference to the infinite and yet imperceptible distance between the two terms, which are confronted and contrasted in an endlessly absorbing array of variations: presence-absence, seeing-hearing, speech-writing, plenitude-lack, voice-silence, and here eschatology-difference. They are all perfect and contagious, appealing to both traditional structuralist dispositions and radical poststructuralist aspirations" (228–29).

18. See Raymond Williams, *Marxism and Literature* (Oxford: Oxford University Press, 1977), 128–35.

19. Hannah Arendt, *Eichmann in Jerusalem: A Report on the Banality of Evil* (New York: Penguin, 1964).

20. See Richard Rorty, *Philosophy and the Mirror of Nature* (Princeton, N.J.: Princeton University Press, 1979).

21. All these locutions no doubt derive from the more abstract philosophical concept "theory," from the Greek *thea* (view) or *theoros* (spectator) and ultimately from *theos* (god; Latin, *Deus*). Or, rather, I suggest, they derive from a Romanized reduction of an original ambiguity to a certain seeing/objectification parallel to the reduction of the Greek *aletheia* to *veritas*. For Heidegger's reading of the quite different Greek understanding of the "theory"/*theos* relationship, see *Parmenides*, trans. André Schuwer and Richard Rojcewicz (Bloomington: Indiana University Press, 1992), 103–10.

22. Jacques Derrida has also pointed to the visual origins of this violent phenomenological thinking, the etymology of which discloses the relationship between seeing and speech (*phos*, "light"; and *phone*, "voice") and their complicity with logocentrism. See especially *Speech and Phenomena and Other Essays on Husserl's Theory of Signs*, trans. David B. Allison (Evanston, Ill.: Northwestern University Press, 1973). Derrida includes Heidegger's phenomenology in this indictment. See Jacques Derrida, "The Ends of Man" and "*Ousia* and *Grammé*: Note on a Note from *Being and Time*," in *Margins of Philosophy*, trans. Alan Bass (Chicago: University of Chicago Press, 1982), 123–33 and 31–67, respectively. However, Heidegger's invocation of the etymological elements of "phenomenology" — *phone/phos* — must be understood in their erased sense. See William V. Spanos, "The Indifference of *Différance*: Retrieving Heidegger's Destruction," in *Heidegger and Criticism: Retrieving the Cultural Politics of Destruction* (Minneapolis: University of Minnesota Press, 1993), 109ff.

23. For a side of this imperative of the dominant order that is even darker than that implied by contempt, see Jacques Derrida's summarization of his encounter with *The New York Review of Books* and its chosen deputies over the issue of Richard Wolin's translation and publication of Derrida's "Heidegger, the Philosopher's Hell: An Interview," in *The Heidegger Controversy: A Critical Reader* (New York: Columbia University Press, 1991). Derrida's summarization is in "The Work of Intellectuals and the Press (The Bad Example: How *The New York Review of Books* and Company Do Business," in *Points... : Interviews, 1974–1994,* ed. Werner Hamacher and David E. Wellbery and trans. Peggy Kamuf et al. (Stanford, Calif.: Stanford University Press, 1995), 422–53.

24. The carnivalesque critique of the language of simplification sponsored by John Locke, Bishop Thomas Sprat, and the Royal Society at the outset of the British Enlightenment is at the core of Laurence Sterne's novel *Tristram Shandy*. In this novel, Sterne exposes the disciplinary will to power over intellectual errancy inhering in this language of "common sense" by way of thematizing its rigid spatiality, its polyvalent imperial reductiveness, a reductiveness that manifests itself especially in language, the *socius,* and the international polity (the British Empire):

If I mend at this rate, it is not impossible — by the good leave of his grace
of *Benevento's* devils — but I may arrive hereafter at the excellency of
going on even thus;

which is a line drawn as straight as I could draw it, by a writing-master's
rule, (borrowed for that purpose) turning neither to the right hand or to
the left.

This *right line,* — the path-way for Christians to walk in! say divines —
— the emblem of moral rectitude! says *Cicero* —
— The best *line* ! say cabbage planters — is the shortest line, says
Archimedes, which can be drawn from one given point to another — ...
— What a journey!

Pray can you tell me, — that is, without anger, before I write my chapter upon straight lines — by what mistake — who told them so — or
how it has come to pass, that your men of wit and genius have all along
confounded this line, with the line of *GRAVITATION.*

It is no accident that Sterne's elusive fiction, which traditionalists have, from the
beginning, called "excessive," "monstrous," "exorbitant," "fantastic," has become a prototype of the open-ended novel and a "model" of differential writing
for the literary postmodernists.

25. Martin Heidegger, "The Question concerning Technology" in *The Question concerning Technology and Other Essays,* trans. William Lovitt (New York:
Harper and Row, 1977), 26–27; Foucault, *Discipline and Punish,* 135–38.

26. See especially Heidegger, *Parmenides;* Levinas, *Totality and Infinity;* and
Derrida, "Violence and Metaphysics," 79–153.

27. By "the spatialization of time" I mean something quite different from
that postmodern condition that Fredric Jameson characterizes in *Postmodernism, or The Cultural Logic of Late Capitalism* (Durham, N.C.: Duke University
Press, 1991) as the pure decentered space of simulacra: a pastiche of surface
references to the past devoid of directionality, of affect, and thus of effective history. For my critique of the "Jamesonian" diagnosis of the postmodern occasion
as the fulfillment of the logic of late capitalism, see chapter 4 above.

28. Jean-Paul Sartre, *Being and Nothingness: An Essay in Phenomenological Ontology,* trans. Hazel Barnes (New York: Citadel Press, 1964), 406; see
also 228–79. Sartre's *le regard* becomes, in fact, a pervasive motif of his fiction and drama from the time of *Nausea,* trans. Lloyd Alexander (New York:
New Directions, 1964 [1938]): his characterization of Dr. Rogé, whose "direct
look puts everything in its place" (66), and of the portraits of the supervisory
founding bourgeois fathers and guardians of Bouville in the Salon Bordurin-
Renaudas (82–94). See also Henri Bergson, *Time and Free Will: An Essay on the
Immediate Data of Consciousness,* trans. F. L. Pogson (New York: Macmillan,
1910).

29. This "Heideggerian" interpretation of the spatialization of time has
it provenance in Søren Kierkegaard's critique of the dialectical/interiorizing/
comprehensive Hegelian recollection (*Er-Innerung*): "The life in recollection is
the most complete life conceivable," the aesthete A observes, "recollection sat-
isfies more richly than all reality, and has a security that no reality possesses.
A recollected life-relation has already passed into eternity and has no more
temporal interest" (Kierkegaard, *Either/Or,* vol. 1, trans. David F. Swenson, Lil-

lian M. Swenson, and Walter Lowrie, with revisions by Howard A. Johnson [Garden City, N.Y.: Anchor Books, 1959], 31–31). Kierkegaard, like Heidegger after him, is acutely aware of the spatial metaphor in the word "recollection": the re-collection and interiorization into ideal image of the plenary state prior to its fragmentation and scattering with the fall into time. For an amplification of this genealogy, see William V. Spanos, "Heidegger, Kierkegaard, and the Hermeneutic Circle," in *Heidegger and Criticism,* 61–68. This metaphysical imperative to "recollect" informs as a deep structure the collecting and classifying of specimens of flora and fauna in the "New Worlds," the obsessive activity described in those eighteenth- and early nineteenth-century travel books that are now being identified with the imperial project proper. See, for example, Mary Louise Pratt, *Imperial Eyes: Travel Writing and Transculturation* (New York: Routledge, 1992).

30. Unlike Hegel, whose metaphysical/recollective or "reflective" perspective is a disinterestedness that manifests itself as a totalizing ontological imperialism, Kierkegaard (and Heidegger after him) opts for a knowledge of being that is precipitated by being existentially *interested* or by being-in-the-world and is thus always "partial": "Reflection is disinterestedness. Consciousness [life] is relationship, and it brings with it interest or concern [Heidegger's *Sorge*]; a duality which is perfectly expressed with the pregnant double meaning by the word 'interest' (Latin *inter esse,* meaning (i) 'to be between,' (ii) 'to be a matter of concern')" (Kierkegaard, *Johannes Climacus or De Omnibus Dubitandum Est and a Sermon,* trans. T. H. Croxall [Stanford, Calif.: Stanford University Press, 1958], 151–52).

31. To suggest how pervasive the contemporary critique of this retrospective mode of interpretation is, it is worth invoking the witness of a number of postmodern theorists. Roland Barthes, for example, calls this retrospective mode the "preterite, which is the corner stone of Narration, always signifies Art; ... a part of a ritual of Letters" (*Writing Degree Zero and Elements of Semiology,* trans. Annette Lavers and Colin Smith [Boston: Beacon, 1968], 30). Mikhail Bakhtin calls it the "memorializing mode," which "serves the future memory of the past, ... a world that is always opposed in principle to *any merely transitory past*" ("Epic and Novel," in *The Dialogic Imagination* [Austin: University of Texas Press, 1981], 18–19). And Louis Althusser, with the Hegelian dialect — and a certain Hegelian Marxist interpretive perspective in mind — calls it "philosophy in the future anterior" (54) or the "analytico-teleological method" (60) ("On the Young Marx," in *For Marx,* trans. Ben Brewster [London: Verso, 1977]).

32. Emmanuel Levinas represents Odysseus's journey as simply a circular movement that reflects his and the Greeks' obsessive imperial centeredness: their nostalgia — their painful yearning (*algos*) for the homeland (*nostos*). This interpretation constitutes a reduction (no less violent than the traditional, Hellenist, representation it is opposing) of the productive errancy so fundamental to Greek poiesis and thinking. It is a representation that repeats a fundamental motif of modern Jewish cultural criticism that includes Erich Auerbach ("Odysseus' Scar," in *Mimesis: The Representation of Reality in Western Literature,* trans. Willard Trask [Princeton, N.J.: Princeton University Press, 1953]); Max Horkheimer and Theodor Adorno (*Dialectic of Enlightenment,* trans. John Cumming [New York: Seabury Press, 1972]); and, with a twist, Walter Benjamin

("Franz Kafka," in *Illuminations*, trans. Harry Zohn [New York: Schocken, 1969], 111–40). And, I suggest, this representation is intended to force the *Odyssey* into the Hebraism/Hellenism opposition that is the ground of Levinas's equation of the "infinite Other" of the West with Judaism. As Vassilis Lambropoulos has observed about Levinas's opposition of the story of Abraham's departure from "his fatherland forever" to "the myth of Ulysses returning to Ithaca," "Levinas believes that Odysseus' adventure is circular; his career, which is but a return home, represents the central concern of Greek and most Western thought, from Parmenides to Heidegger: the search for self, truth, and Being as the *algos* of *nostos*. Philosophy [including Heidegger's] has long aspired to the totality of homeliness, the ideal of at-homeness (*Heimatlichkeit*) in one's entire existence, and has found its model in the Greek objective (self)representation. . . . In this search for dwelling, symbolized by the travel back to Ithaca, Levinas detects the incurable nostalgia for the same. 'Philosophy's itinerary remains that of Ulysses, whose adventure in the world was only a return to his native island — a complacency in the Same, an unrecognition of the other'" (*Rise of Eurocentrism*, 215–16; the quotations from Levinas are from "On the Trail of the Other," trans. Daniel J. Hoy, *Philosophy Today* 10 [1968]: 34–45; and "Meaning and Sense," in *Collected Philosophical Papers*, trans. Alphonso Lingis [Dordrecht: Martinus Nijhoff, 1987], 91). The introduction of Virgil's correction of Homer in the *Aeneid* into the equation estranges Levinas's foundational thesis.

33. Richard Waswo, *The Founding Legend of Western Civilization: From Virgil to Vietnam* (Hanover, N.H.: Wesleyan University Press, 1997): "[The history of the West's appropriation of the story of Aeneas and his exiled Trojan band] is the history of a plot that is continually enacted both in language and in the world. The story that contains the plot together with the later versions of the plot in ostensibly nonfictional discourses constitute one of the 'grand narratives' that Jean-François Lyotard has assured us are dead in our postmodern age. I shall try to show that the report of this story's death is premature, that we still, to some extent, are *inside* this story, that we (members of occidental culture) have internalized it — or it us" (xiii).

34. See Marilynn Desmond, *Reading Dido: Gender, Textuality, and the Medieval "Aeneid"* (Minneapolis: University of Minnesota Press, 1994).

35. Tzvetan Todorov, *The Conquest of America*, trans. Richard Howard (New York: Harper Collins, 1984), 22–23.

36. Cotton Mather, *Magnalia Christi Americana, Books I and II*, ed. Kenneth B. Murdock (with the assistance of Elizabeth W. Miller) (Cambridge, Mass.: Harvard University Press, 1977).

37. See Sacvan Bercovitch, *The American Jeremiad* (Madison: University of Wisconsin Press, 1978); and Wai-chee Dimock, *Empire for Liberty: Melville and the Poetics of Individualism* (Princeton, N.J.: Princeton University Press, 1989). Dimock's disclosure of the perennial complicity of the promise/fulfillment narrative (its spatialization of time), which was inscribed as a deep structure in the collective American consciousness since the Puritans, with the American imperial project is especially telling. In the process of her reading Herman Melville's *Moby-Dick*, she writes: "Prophecy in *Moby-Dick* is a territorial enterprise. To be a prophet one must survey the future, with an eye to ownership. . . . Prophecy in *Moby-Dick* enlarges upon the past. But that too is what one should expect

from a spatial ordering of time. Indeed, the future is knowable to the prophets only because it has been converted into a spatial category, part of a known design. Prophets are prospectors and colonizers because they are emissaries of the known, because their mission is to expand and assimilate, to annex the 'wilderness of untried things' into the domain of the existing. They can function as prophets only by reducing the potentiality of sequence to the legibility of design, only by reading time as space.

In that regard Melville's prophets are perhaps less prophets of the future than spokesmen for their own age, for spatialized time was the very condition for Manifest Destiny. What Albert Weinberg calls America's 'geographical determinism' operated by equating geography with destiny, an equation that, in conflating time and space — in harnessing time to space — at once recomposed time and incorporated it as a vehicle for spatial aggrandizement. The familiar strategy for antebellum expansionists was to invoke some version of 'Providence,' whose plans for the future happened to coincide exactly with America's territorial ambitions. American expansion in space and providential design in time turned out to be one and the same" (132–33). As I have argued elsewhere, however, Dimock's attribution of this complicity to Herman Melville is questionable. In *The Errant Art of* Moby-Dick: *The Cold War, the Canon, and the Struggle for American Studies* (Durham, N.C.: Duke University Press, 1995), I suggest, on the contrary, that it was precisely this complicitous relationship between American spatialization, prophecy, and empire that Melville intended to expose in *Moby-Dick*.

38. Sartre, *Nausea*, 39–40. More recently, Edward W. Said has made the same claim in his analysis of Joseph Conrad's *The Heart of Darkness*, but in terms that, far more than Sartre's, reflect the realistic novel's complicity with the imperial project (see Said, *Culture and Imperialism* [New York: Alfred Knopf, 1993], 69–70). My "Sartrian," that is, ontological, identification of the novel with imperialism should not, however, be understood as different from Said's sociopolitical equation. As I will suggest in chapter 2, they are indissolubly related.

39. Derrida, "Structure, Sign, and Play," 278.

40. See Foucault, *Discipline and Punish,* 174.

41. Geffrey Whitney, *A Choice of Emblems,* ed. Henry Green (New York: Benjamin Blom, 1967 [1586]), 229.

42. Mungo Parks, *Travels in the Interior of Africa* (1860 edition), quoted in Pratt, *Imperial Eyes,* 77–78 (Park's emphasis). According to Pratt, what saves Parks in this dire moment of crisis is "a naturalist's epiphany" (77): "The man of sensibility, in the hour of his need, looks *through* the language of science and finds the alternative spiritual understanding of nature as image of the divine. If Barrow's invasion of the Bushman camp provoked a breakdown in the language of science, Park's emotional bootstrapping here is a triumph of the language of sentiment and its protagonist, the individual" (78). This insight, which makes visible the official collective motive of the quest into the "heart of darkness" that informs the "personal experience," constitutes the beginning of a productive analysis of the way sentimental and individualist (private) travel literature like Park's lent its hegemonic authority massively to the economic economy of the imperial project. But Pratt overlooks Park's "epiphany" — the resonant historical and ideological implications of its theoptic metaphorics. She thus misses not

only the indissoluble relationship between the emergent classificatory scientific project of the state and the older, and the more deeply inscribed, (hegemonic) theoptic discourse, but also the ontological source of the enormously persuasive power of these "private' discourses vis-à-vis the European encounter with the "dark" continents.

43. This official figure conflates the American Puritans' providential design enabling and determining their "errand in the wilderness" and the imperial Roman project so basic to the self-definition of the founders of the American republic in the eighteenth century. This emblem, intended to symbolize the cultural identity of America, symptomatically captures its ideological itinerary in the secularized post-Revolutionary period. It also reflects the historical relationship between Puritanism and capitalism as it has been analyzed by Max Weber in *The Protestant Ethic and the Spirit of Capitalism*, trans. Talcott Parsons (New York: Scribner's, 1958); see Spanos, *Errant Art*, 101–2, 208–11, 214–15. This synecdochic history should make forcefully clear the genealogy of the post–Cold War discourse of the New World Order.

44. John Berger, *Ways of Seeing* (London: Penguin, 1972), 16.

45. I am indebted to John Barrell, "The Public Prospect and the Private View: The Politics of Taste in Eighteenth-Century Britain," in *Reading Landscape: Country-City-Capital,* ed. Simon Pugh (Manchester, England: Manchester University Press, 1990), for this extension of the metaphorics of the "prospect" into the eighteenth-century English representation of landscape. The passages from Reynolds and Campbell are quoted in Barrell's book on pp. 24 and 27, respectively. See Sir Joshua Reynolds, *Discourses on Art,* 2d ed., ed. Robert R. Wark (New Haven: Yale University Press, 1975), 44; and George Campbell, *The Philosophy of Rhetoric* (London, 1776), 1:5. Though Barrell is aware of the generality of this "prospective," he nevertheless limits his analysis of its ideological operations to its function as an aesthetic/cultural paradigm (taste) that legitimizes an ethical national politics: that of the public as opposed to the private man. Barrell does not address the question of the genealogy of this important aesthetic/cultural/political motif. As a result, he fails to see its indissoluble relationship to the emergent British imperial project. That is, he fails to observe that this land-owning "public man," whose prospective gaze dominates and orders the "wild" scene below, is pervasively represented in eighteenth-century English public discourse and art as a Roman, a republican admittedly, but a patrician and exponent of the Roman colonization of the barbaric peoples beyond the metropolitan periphery. This omission in Barrell's essay is partially filled by another, otherwise affiliated, essay in this volume: David H. Solkin, "The Battle of the Ciceros: Richard Wilson and the Politics of Landscape in the Age of John Wilkes," 41–65.

46. The most devastating epitomization and critique of the ideological agenda of the panoptic gaze informing the perspective art and cartography inaugurated in the Renaissance and consciously developed into an instrument of power in the Enlightenment is William Blake's *Newton*. This etching depicts the English author of *The Optics* seated on a slab, naked, bending over and staring fiercely at a scroll and drawing a circle around it with a compass. Blake's caption reads: "All that we saw was owing to your metaphysics." *Newton*, which clearly alludes to the emblematic tradition I am thematizing, repeats Blake's "Ancient of Days," which represents "Urizen," the deity of the Enlightenment, kneeling

over the void and, like Newton, drawing a circle around it with an extended compass.

47. See Rennsalaer W. Lee, *Ut Pictura Poesis: The Humanistic Theory of Painting* (New York: Norton, 1924).

48. William Shakespeare, *Troilus and Cressida*, 1.3.86–96. See E. M. W. Tillyard, *The Elizabethan World Picture* (London: Chatto and Windus, 1945), 7–9.

49. John Milton, *Paradise Lost*, in *The Student's Milton*, ed. Frank Allen Patterson (New York: Appleton-Century-Crofts, 1933), 11.376–88.

50. See Diderot, "Prospectus" (November 1750); reprinted in Jean Le Rond D'Alembert, *Preliminary Discourse to the Encyclopedia of Diderot*, trans. Richard N. Schwab and Walter E. Rex (Indianapolis: Bobbs-Merrill, 1963), 106–40.

51. Daniel Defoe, *Robinson Crusoe*, ed. Michael Shinagel, 2d ed. (New York: Norton Critical Edition, 1994), 47.

52. Defoe, *Robinson Crusoe*, 48–49.

53. Pratt, *Imperial Eyes*, 61.

54. Michel Foucault, "The Life of Infamous Men," in *Michel Foucault: Power, Truth, Strategy* (Sydney, Australia: Feral Press, 1979), 90–91. See also William V. Spanos, "Percy Lubbock and the Craft of Supervison," in *Repetitions: The Postmodern Occasion in Literature and Culture* (Baton Rouge: Louisiana State University Press, 1987), 149–88; and Mark Seltzer, "*The Princess Casamassima*: Realism and the Fantasy of Surveillance," in *American Realism*, ed. Eric Sundquist (Baltimore: Johns Hopkins University Press, 1982); reprinted in Seltzer, *Henry James: The Art of Power* (Ithaca, N.Y.: Cornell University Press, 1984). Nor should it be supposed that this optical figure is restricted to nineteenth-century realistic fiction, whose ontological source is the "observational" empiricism of modern science. For it also informs the antirealist literary art and, especially, the literary critical discourse of high modernism: its privileged "autotelism" or "spatial form," for example, which finds its most telling expression in T. S. Eliot's modernist formulation of the perennial European binary opposition between the "Beautiful" and the Sublime. I am referring to his notion of the objective correlative, "a set of objects, a situation, a chain of events" that constitutes "the formula of that *particular* emotion [that would be expressed in art]; such that when the external facts, which must terminate in sensory experience, are given, the emotion is immediately evoked." This is the totalized structure that would contain within the subjective eye's circumference the "excess" — the differential and otherwise "baffling" force — that "escaped" Shakespeare's defective gaze in *Hamlet*. See T. S. Eliot, "Hamlet and His Problems," in *Selected Essays* (New York: Harcourt, Brace, 1950), 17–19.

55. Pratt, *Imperial Eyes*, 202–8. See also Edward Said, *Orientalism* (New York: Vintage Books, 1979); and David Spurr, *The Rhetoric of Empire: Colonial Discourse in Journalism, Travel Writing, and Imperial Administration* (Durham, N.C.: Duke University Press, 1993), 17–19.

56. Derrida, "Structure, Sign, and Play," 280.

57. For a classic example of the unexamined invocation of the circle to represent the ideals of beauty and perfection that have determined English literary/cultural history (up until the "dissociation of sensibility" in the eighteenth century), see Marjorie Hope Nicholson, "The Circle of Perfection," in *Breaking*

the Circle: Studies in the Effect of the "New Science" on Seventeenth-Century Poetry, rev. ed. (New York: Columbia University Press, 1960), 45–80. Like her master, E. M. W. Tillyard, in *The Elizabethan World Picture,* Nicholson reflects the conservative humanist nostalgia for the ordered organic cosmos of medieval Europe as that cosmos was self-consciously mirrored by the Christian humanist Metaphysical Poets. She represents the poets of the Augustan Age as "breaking the circle" by succumbing to the seduction of the "New Science." The consequent of this break was the "dissociation of sensibility" and the forgetting of the enabling polyvalent system of correspondences intrinsic to the cosmic circle of perfection. This representation of eighteenth-century English poetry and culture constitutes a misreading of its difference from the Metaphysical Poetry that preceded it. Nicholson interprets as a radical epistemic break what in fact was an Enlightenment supplementation — the "substitution of one center for another" — of the metaphysical circle that was called into doubt by the New Science.

58. See Rob Wilson, *American Sublime: The Genealogy of a Poetic Genre* (Madison: University of Wisconsin Press, 1991).

59. See Rudolph Wittkower, *Architectural Principles in the Age of Humanism* (London: Alec Tiranti, 1952): "With the Renaissance revival of the Greek mathematical interpretation of God and the world, and invigorated by the Christian belief that Man as the image of God embodied the harmonies of the Universe, the Vitruvian figure inscribed in a square and a circle became a symbol of the mathematical sympathy between microcosm and macrocosm. How could the relation of Man to God be better expressed, we feel now justified in asking, than by building the house of God in accordance with the fundamental geometry of square and circle?" (15).

60. As David H. Pickney (*Napoleon III and the Rebuilding of Paris* [Princeton, N.J.: Princeton University Press, 1958]) makes amply clear, Haussmann's Paris was, in some fundamental way, a response to the insurrectionary momentum of 1848. The rebuilding of the city, that is, like its literary allotrope, the emergent realist novel, was intended, above all, to enable light — and the policing eye — to penetrate into the miasmic darkness that hitherto characterized the potentially revolutionary urban spaces in which the working poor lived.

61. For a brief history of the cultural politics informing the ideal of the circular city, see William V. Spanos, *The End of Education: Toward Posthumanism* (Minneapolis: University of Minnesota Press, 1993), 33–35.

62. Wittkower, *Architectural Principles,* 18; see also E. A. Gutkind, *Urban Development in Western Europe: France and Belgium* (New York: Free Press, 1970), vol. 5 of *International History of City Development,* 8 vols. (1964–72); and Norman J. Johnston, *Cities in the Round* (Seattle: University of Washington Press, 1983).

63. See the chapter titled "Humanist Inquiry and the Politics of the Gaze," in Spanos, *End of Education,* 25–63.

64. See, for example, Said, *Orientalism;* Pratt, *Imperial Eyes;* and Spurr, *Rhetoric of Empire,* 13–27.

65. Foucault, *Discipline and Punish,* 205; my emphasis.

66. Enrique Dussel, *Philosophy of Liberation,* 5–6; my emphasis.

67. Michel Foucault, "Questions on Geography," in *Power/Knowledge: Selected Interviews and Other Writings, 1972–1977,* ed. Colin Gordon (New York: Pantheon Books, 1980), 69.

68. Heidegger, *Parmenides,* 60.

69. See, for example, Francis Jennings, *The Invasion of America: Indians, Colonialism, and the Cant of Conquest* (Chapel Hill, N.C.: University of North Carolina Press, 1975); Richard Slotkin, *Fatal Environment* (New York: Athenaeum, 1985); Slotkin, *Regeneration through Violence* (Hanover, N.H.: Wesleyan University Press, 1973); Peter Hulme, *Colonial Encounters: Europe and the Native Caribbean, 1492–1797* (New York: Routledge, 1986); Pratt, *Imperial Eyes;* Spurr, *Rhetoric of Empire;* and Waswo, *Founding Legend.*

70. Hulme, *Colonial Encounters,* 156–57. Already in the very discourse of early colonialism—the empowering differentiation between the Europeans who "inhabit," "occupy," and "domicile" a territory and those who wander errantly through it as spectral nomads — there resides paradoxically a means of resistance to Occidental imperialism: the colonial's refusal to be answerable to the representational/calculative terms of the dominant imperial discourse. See chapter 5 above.

71. Hulme, *Colonial Encounters,* 157–58. These examples of the early colonialist representation of the native inhabitants of the "New World" could be extended at length. See Waswo (*Founding Legend*), who grounds his history of Western imperialism on the binary opposition between agricultural communities (those that cultivate the land) and nomadic peoples: "Opposed to cultivation, which is civilized, is savagery, which isn't. And what is savage (*silvestris, silva*) is literally 'of the woods.' It is land and people that remain uncultivated. To be *uncultus* is to be savage, rude, and dumb. Our languages thus encode the forms of fear and contempt felt by a settled agricultural community for other modes of material and social organization" (6).

72. The binary opposition between "improved" and "unimproved" is ubiquitous in the discourse of colonialism. A notable instance of the commonplace use of this trope from the American colonialist context can be found in the writing of the eminent nineteenth-century American historian Francis Parkman: "There is nothing progressive in the rigid, inflexible nature of the Indian. He will not open his mind to the idea of improvement" (*The Conspiracy of Pontiac* [New York: Library of America, 1991], 1:500; see also 459 and 584). Not accidentally, in Parkman, as in virtually all colonialist discourse, this rhetorical opposition is invariably affiliated with the adulthood/childhood and nomadic/"domiciliated" binary (see *Conspiracy of Pontiac,* 458, 517, for example).

73. This representation of America's genocidal war against the hopelessly unimprovable Indians is, for example, fundamental in the fiction of James Fenimore Cooper (see especially *The Pioneers* [1823] and *The Last of the Mohicans* [1826] and the historiography of Francis Parkman: "To reclaim the Indians from their savage state has again and again been attempted, and each attempt has failed. Their intractable, unchanging character leaves no other alternative than gradual extinction, or abandonment of the western world to eternal barbarism; and of this and other similar plans, whether the offspring of British or American legislation, it may alike be said that sentimental philanthropy will find it easier to cavil at than to amend them" (*The Conspiracy of Pontiac,* 732).

74. See Spurr, *Rhetoric of Empire,* 28–42.

75. Pratt, *Imperial Eyes,* 61.

76. Enrique Dussel, *The Invention of the Americas: Eclipse of the "Other"*

and the Myth of Modernity (New York: Continuum, 1995), 20–21; the quotation from Hegel in Dussel's text derives from G. W. F. Hegel, *The Philosophy of History,* trans. J. Sibree (New York: Dover, 1956), 101. In *The Philosophy of History,* Hegel writes: "Universal history...shows the development of the consciousness of Freedom on the part of Spirit, and the consequent realization of that Freedom. This development implies a gradation — a series of increasingly adequate expressions or manifestations of Freedom, which result from its Idea. The logical, and — as still more prominent — the *dialectical* nature of the Idea in general, viz. that it is self-determined — that it assumes successive forms which it successively transcends; and by this process of transcending its earlier stages, gains an affirmative, and, in fact, a richer and more concrete shape; — this necessity of its nature, and the necessary series of pure abstract forms which the Idea successively assumes — is exhibited in the department of *Logic*" (63; see also 54–55).

77. See Henry Nash Smith, *Virgin Land: The American West as Symbol and Myth* (New York: Vintage, 1950). The enormous influence, until recently, of this founding classic of American literary and cultural studies testifies to the continuing power of this metaphor long after its introduction in the "age of exploration." It was not until the mid-1970s, in the wake of the Vietnam War, that this metaphorics came to be interrogated. See, for example, Slotkin, *Regeneration through Violence;* Slotkin, *Fatal Environment;* and Richard Drinnon, *Facing West: The Metaphysics of Indian-Hating and Empire-Building* (Minneapolis: University of Minnesota Press, 1980). For a more recent and thus more theoretically informed analysis of the imperial violence hidden in the benign rhetoric emanating from this metaphorization of America, see Donald Pease, "New Americanists: Revisionist Interventions in the Canon" in Pease, ed., *New Americanists,* a special issue of *boundary 2* 17 (spring 1990): 1–37; and, not least, Hulme, *Colonial Encounters:* "Absence of true 'settlement' left the land *virgin:* probably no single word has had to bear so heavy a weight in the construction of American mythology from the moment when, in Samuel Eliot Morison's immortal words, 'the New World gracefully yielded her virginity to the conquering Castilians.' The novelty of America was always perceived in overtly sexual terms. To speak of the 'maidenhead' of Guiana or Virginia was to condense into one potent image the absence of significant native agriculture and the joyful masculine thrust of Elizabethan expansion" (159).

78. Michel Adanson, *Cours d'histoire naturelle* (1845 ed.), 4–5; quoted in Michel Foucault, *The Order of Things: An Archeology of the Human Sciences* (New York: Vintage Books, 1973), 148; see also Pratt, *Imperial Eyes,* 30–31.

79. This reliance on the metaphorics of Adamic naming to justify the appropriation of American space from the native inhabitants has been well documented by the New Americanists. These critics invoke this Adamic history to demonstrate the complicity with American (Cold War) imperialism of such founders of the Americanist "field imaginary" as Perry Miller, *Errand in the Wilderness* (Cambridge, Mass.: Harvard University Press, 1958); R. W. B. Lewis, *The American Adam: Innocence, Tragedy, and Tradition in the Nineteenth Century* (Chicago: University of Chicago Press, 1955); Henry Nash Smith, *Virgin Land;* Quentin Anderson, *The Imperial Self: An Essay in American Literary and Cultural History* (New York: Random House, 1970). See especially Slotkin, *Fatal Environment;* Bercovitch, *American Jeremiad;* Drinnon, *Facing*

West; Tom Engelhardt, *The End of Victory Culture: Cold War America and the Disillusioning of a Generation* (New York: Basic Books, 1995); and Spanos, *Errant Art.*

80. D'Alembert, *Preliminary Discourse,* 46–47.

81. Ezra Pound, "Canto LIX," in *The Cantos* (New York: New Directions, 1970), 324. Pound, of course, along with other postmodern American poets, not least Charles Olson, glorifies this kind of map — best exemplified by Hanno the Phoenician (the *periplus* of his journey around the northwest coast of Africa [ca. 425 B.C.] and Juan de la Cosa, Columbus's cartographer. For Pound and Olson, these *periploi* are the expression of an unmediated being-there. As such they are preferable not only over earlier maps of sedentary academics such as the map of the world of Martin Behaim (1492), which shows no land between Europe and Cipangu (Japan), but also over later maps of the "New World" based on Mercator's projections. Despite their fundamentally anticolonialist stance, Pound and Olson fail to observe that the "immediate" representations of the *periplus,* including the synecdochic pictures of the grotesque denizens of the waters and the land they encounter, are images of the "Other" projected from a Eurocentric perspective. See Pound, "Canto XL," in *The Cantos,* 199–201; and Olson, "On First Looking Out through Juan de la Cosa's Eyes," in *The Maximus Poems,* ed. George Butterick (Berkeley: University of California Press, 1983), 81–84. In the context of the kind of panoptic modern mapping that Pound and Olson were opposing, however, the pre-Enlightenment *periplum* can be seen not simply as an imperfectly developed instrument of European imperialism, but, in its relative immediacy, as embodying a contradiction that could be read as deconstructing the imperial project.

82. Michel Foucault, *The Birth of the Clinic: An Archaeology of Medical Perception,* trans. A. M. Sheridan Smith (New York: Vintage Books, 1975), 89.

83. The crucial importance of this distinction between the map as *periplum* and as table for the global imperial project is forcefully conveyed by the passage from Daniel Defoe's *The Compleat English Gentleman* (1730) that constitutes one of the epigraphs of Mary Louise Pratt's chapter on the complicity of the "Linnaean" system of classification with the construction of what she calls "a European global or planetary subject": "[He may] make a tour of the world in books, he may make himself master of the geography of the universe in the maps, atlases and measurements of our mathematicians. He may travel by land with the historians, by sea with the navigators. He may go round the globe with Dampier and Rogers, and kno' a thousand times more doing it than all those illiterate sailors" (Pratt, *Imperial Eyes,* 16). Commenting on this passage, Pratt writes, "As Defoe's terms make clear, this world historical subject is European, male, secular, and lettered; his planetary consciousness is the product of his contact with print culture and infinitely more 'compleat' than the lived experiences of sailors" (ibid., 30).

84. Foucault, *Discipline and Punish,* 148.

85. Ibid., 169.

86. That Foucault's sustained effort to think the political implications of the Enlightenment's spatialization of knowledge in terms of territory or region or domain inevitably leads him to the question of imperialism is clearly suggested in his final remarks in the previously cited interview with the Marxist geographers, "Questions on Geography": "The longer I continue, the more it seems to me that the formation of discourses and the genealogy of knowledge need to

be analyzed, not in terms of types of consciousness, modes of perception and forms of ideology, but in terms of tactics and strategies of power. Tactics and strategies deployed through implantations, distributions, demarcations, control of territories and organizations of domains which could well make up a sort of geopolitics where my preoccupations would link up with your methods. One theme I would like to study in the next few years is that of the army as a matrix of organization and knowledge; one would need to study the history of the for-tress, the 'campaign,' the 'movement,' the colony, the territory. Geography must indeed necessarily lie at the heart of my concerns" (77).

87. According to tradition, Alexander the Great undertook his conquest of India accompanied by savants who were commissioned to record the character-istics of the geography and peoples beyond the "known world" (*oikoumene*). For example, Pliny the Elder, a Roman, says that the most prestigious of these was Aristotle himself, though there is no evidence to support this claim. Most of the Greek texts of "Indography" resulting from this expedition or from its aftermath have been lost. But their work is preserved in representational form, above all, by Pliny (*Natural History*) and the colonized Greek Strabo of Ama-seia (*The Geography*). Both of these writers, not incidentally, could be described, despite the fact that their geographies are based primarily on "scholarship" rather than active traveling, as the Roman precursors of the travel writing of the Enlightenment. Read in the context of the contemporary interrogation of representation, these "Roman" accounts of earlier Greek travel writing be-tray an effort, analogous to Virgil's vis-à-vis Homer's *Odyssey,* to correct *ta Indika* (the Indian writing) of the early Greeks consonant with the aims of em-pire. They disclose, against themselves, as in the case of Pliny's commentary on Aristotle's participation in Alexander's expedition, that this early Greek travel literature is not simply erratic and unsystematic — "fabulous" — but also re-markably untainted by Hellenocentric prejudices. For further commentary on this geographical tradition, see chapter 2 above.

88. Said, *Orientalism,* 83.

89. Ibid., 86.

90. Anders Sparrman, *A Voyage to the Cape of Good Hope* (London: J. and G. Robinson, 1785). See Pratt's insightful reading of this book in *Imperial Eyes,* 50–57.

91. Pratt, *Imperial Eyes,* 39. For another useful "Foucauldian" analysis of the complicity of the visual/classificatory perspective with the imperial project, this time focusing on the traveler-reporter, see Spurr, *Rhetoric of Empire,* especially the chapter titled "Surveillance," 13–27.

92. Dussel, *Philosophy of Liberation,* 15.

93. Louis Althusser, "Ideology and Ideological State Apparatuses (Notes to-ward an Investigation)," in *Lenin and Philosophy,* trans. Ben Brewster (London: Monthly Review Press, 1971), 180–81.

94. Foucault, *Discipline and Punish,* 194. For Foucault's definition of "the repressive hypothesis," see *The History of Sexuality, Part I: An Introduction,* trans. Robert Hurley (New York: Pantheon Books, 1978), 10. For his exten-sion of the analysis of "the repressive hypothesis" to include other sociopolitical sites besides the sexual that he is addressing here, see *Power/Knowledge,* 109–33. See also William V. Spanos, "Heidegger and Foucault: The Politics of the Commanding Gaze," in *Heidegger and Criticism,* 168–74.

95. Heidegger, *Parmenides,* 44; henceforth cited as *P* in the text. In the following passages I have modified the translation to emphasize certain meanings that it obscures.

96. I have bracketed the German verb *heissen,* which means not only "enjoin, command, bid, order, direct," but also "to name, call, denominate," in order to suggest its remarkable proximity with Althusser's analysis of ideology as the "interpellation" (or "hailing") of individuals as (subjected) subjects by an "Absolute Subject."

97. Martin Heidegger, "The End of Philosophy and the Task of Thinking," in *Basic Writings;* first published in *Zur Sache des Denken* (Tübingen: Max Niemeyer Verlag, 1969), 327. See also Heidegger, "A Dialogue on Language," in *On the Way to Language,* trans. Peter D. Hertz (San Francisco: Harper and Row, 1977): "That temptation [of the East 'to rely on European ways of representation and their concepts'] is reinforced by a process which I would call the complete Europeanization of the earth and man" (15).

98. Martin Heidegger, "The Age of the World Picture," in *The Question concerning Technology,* 115–54.

99. Heidegger, "The Question Concerning Technology," 15–28. The pertinence of Heidegger's critique of the global triumph of technology to the postcolonial critique of imperialism, particularly of his identification of the gaze, classification, and enframing, is suggested by David Spurr in *The Rhetoric of Empire.* Commenting on a number of journalistic texts treating the contemporary African character that exemplify the "survival of colonial discourse in the postcolonial era" (61), Spurr writes: "The weakness of African character [as represented in these texts] is not something discovered or revealed to a pure, unfettered eye, but rather is determined by the logical order followed by Western observation and by the system of classification that governs the procedures of observation. In other words, the order that classifies non-Western peoples according to the paradigm of modernization contains within it, already and as a given, the judgment of their character. Yet the emphasis on observable phenomena obscures the way in which such observation is ordered in advance, a misrecognition that allows interpretation to pass for objective truth. Classification is a form of what Heidegger calls 'enframing' — the process by which the mind transforms the world into an object. Yet 'enframing disguises even this, its disguising'" (71; see also 184–85). Unfortunately, Spurr does not elaborate this important insight into a recognition of the pertinence of Heidegger's destruction of the metaphysical discourse of the Western philosophical tradition to the post–Cold War occasion. As a result, he represents "the rhetoric of empire" in terms of its "survival" in the postcolonial era, thus obscuring the far older genealogy of this rhetoric and deflecting attention away from its centrality in the post–Cold War moment of the postcolonial occasion.

100. Francis Fukuyama, *The End of History and the Last Man* (New York: Free Press, 1992), 45; my emphasis.

101. Richard Haass, *The Reluctant Sheriff: The United States after the Cold War* (Washington, D.C.: Institute of Foreign Affairs, 1997).

102. Martin Heidegger, "Language in the Poem: A Discussion on Georg Trakl's Poetic Work," in *On the Way to Language,* 170ff.

103. Dussel, *Philosophy of Liberation,* 14. In his more recent book, *The Invention of the Americas,* Dussel implicates the Habermas of *The Philosophical*

Discourse of Modernity in this Eurocentric "classic ontology of the center" insofar as Habermas, like Hegel, completely overlooks 1492 and the Spanish conquest of America in his representation of the origins of modernity (*Invention of the Americas*, 25–26, 129–30).

2. Culture and Colonization

1. Edward W. Said, "Secular Criticism," in *The World, the Text, and the Critic* (Cambridge, Mass: Harvard University Press, 1983), 21–22.

2. I want to make it clear at the outset that I have chosen to confront Edward Said in an *Auseinandersetzung* precisely because of my great admiration for his work, because his writing continues to be the strongest and most provocative in the field of studies that goes under the name of "postcolonial" criticism.

3. The recent "revival" of the "classics" in the context of the debates over the postcolonial and multicultural initiatives and the renewed concern about the cultural identity of the ancient Greeks as an ideological issue in philosophers like Martin Heidegger, Hannah Arendt, Emmanuel Levinas, Jacques Derrida, and Philippe Lacoue-Labarthe, in historians of culture like Martin Bernal and Mary Lefkowitz, and in social historians like Vassilis Lambropoulos and Gregory Jusdanus, bears symptomatic witness to the contemporary urgency of this genealogical project.

4. Martin Heidegger, "On the Essence of Truth," trans. John Sallis, in *Basic Writings* ed. David Farrell Krell (New York: Harper and Row, 1977), 120.

5. Martin Heidegger, "The Origin of the Work of Art," in *Basic Writings,* 154; Heidegger's emphasis.

6. Martin Heidegger, introduction to *Being and Time,* in *Basic Writings,* 66.

7. What is usually missing from accounts of Althusser's concept of the problematic is analysis of the visual metaphorics he employs to define its "imperial" operations. Such analysis would show the remarkable affiliation between Althusser's understanding of the capitalist problematic and Heidegger's ontological understanding of the post-Enlightenment's representation of truth as *veritas:* their common disclosure that the truths they are interrogating are the consequence of the spatialization or structuration of temporality or, rather, the differences that temporality disseminates. In other words, there is nothing outside the truth that the problematic makes visible. Everything outside the problematic is invisible — or, in Emmanuel Levinas's and Enrique Dussel's terms, is without being. As Althusser puts this disablingly overlooked imperial "oversight" of the problematic: "It is the field of the problematic [which *sees itself* in the objects or problems it defines] that defines and structures the invisible as the defined excluded, *excluded* from the field of visibility and *defined* as excluded by the existence and peculiar structure of the field of the problematic. . . . These new objects and problems are necessarily *invisible* in the field of the existing theory, because they are not objects of this theory, because they are *forbidden* by it — they are objects and problems necessarily without any necessary relations with the field of the visible as defined by this problematic. They are invisible because they are rejected in principle, repressed from the field of the visible: and that is why their fleeting presence in the field when it does occur (in very peculiar and symptomatic circumstances) *goes unperceived,* and becomes literally an un-

divulgeable absence — since the whole function of the field is not to see them, to forbid any sighting of them. Here again, the invisible is no more a function of *a subject's sighting* than is the visible: the invisible is the theoretical problematic's non-vision of its non-objects, the invisible is the darkness, the blinded eye of the theoretical problematic's self-reflection when it scans its non-objects, its non-problems without seeing them, *in order not to look at them*" ("From *Capital* to Marx's Philosophy," in Althusser and Étienne Balibar, *Reading* Capital [London: Verso, 1970], 26).

8. Unlike Heidegger, who asks, "What about the nothing?" that *veritas* "wishes to know nothing about" (is blind to), who, in other words, insists on thinking the nothing positively, Althusser does not explicitly call for thinking the positive possibilities of the invisible that shadows the problematic. The crucial imperative to think this spectral nothing that haunts the visible will be the topic of the last chapter of this book. For an amplification of the relationship between Heidegger's and Althusser's interrogation of Western ocularcentrism, see William V. Spanos, "Althusser's Problematic in the Context of the Vietnam War: Towards a Spectral Politics," *Rethinking Marxism* 10 (fall 1998): 1–21.

9. I am referring to Nietzsche's critique of the classical German representation of Greek tragedy, which privileges the Apollonian principle of structuration in a polar opposition to Dionysian force (which is to say, a Roman interpretation of Greek tragedy — and culture). In opposition, Nietzsche's interpretation overdetermines Dionysian force or, more precisely, renders Dionysian force the condition for the possibility of Apollonian structuration: "It is Apollo who tranquilizes the individual by drawing boundary lines, and who, by enjoining again and again the practice of self-knowledge, reminds him of the holy, universal norms. But lest the Apollonian tendency freeze all form into Egyptian rigidity, and in attempting to prescribe its orbit to each particular wave inhibit the movement of the lake, the Dionysian flood tide periodically destroys all the circles in which the Apollonian will would confine Hellenism" (*The Birth of Tragedy and the Genealogy of Morals,* trans. Francis Golffing [Garden City, N.Y.: Anchor Books, 1956], 65). See also Nietzsche, *The Gay Science,* trans. Walter Kaufmann (New York: Vintage Books, 1974): "The degree of the historical sense of any age may be inferred from the manner in which this age makes *translations* and tries to absorb former ages and books.... [H]ow forcibly and at the same time how naively [Rome] took hold of everything good and lofty of Greek antiquity, which was more ancient! How they translated things into the Roman present!...They did not know the delights of the historical sense; what was past and alien was an embarrassment for them; and being Romans, they saw it as an incentive for a Roman conquest. Indeed, translation was a form of conquest. Not only did one omit what was historical; one also added allusions to the present and, above all, struck out the name of the poet and replaced it with one's own — not with any sense of theft but with the very best conscience of the *imperium Romanum*" (137–38).

10. For an account of Johann J. Winckelmann's enormous influence on British "Victorian humanist Hellenism," see Frank M. Turner, *The Greek Heritage in Victorian Britain* (New Haven: Yale University Press, 1981). Turner's ground-breaking study, especially his interpretation of Winckelmann's reading of classical Greek sculpture (*Thoughts on the Imitation of Greek Art in Painting and Sculpture* [1755] and *The History of Ancient Art* [1764]) and its

effect on British humanist writers and artists from Sir Joshua Reynolds to Matthew Arnold and after, goes far to corroborate Heidegger's passing reference to Winckelmann's — and the later German writers' — Romanization of Greek art: "[Winckelmann's] interpretation of the classical restraint and harmony in fifth — and fourth — century sculpture derived from his reading of the literature of that period rather than from examination of its sculpture. The statues with which he was actually acquainted were Hellenistic" (40). Again, "Winckelmann had... contended... that the achievement of ideal beauty had occurred only during the highest stage of Greek art. Following in detail the scheme of art history set forth by Quintilian and Cicero, Winckelmann portrayed four periods in the development of Greek sculpture.... British critics later repeated this same pattern in their accounts of the rise and fall of Greek art. Its origin in the ancient [Roman] critics of art, and Winckelmann's repetition of the scheme, convinced them of its validity" (43).

11. Martin Heidegger, "Letter on Humanism," trans. Frank A. Capuzzi and J. Glen Gray, in *Basic Writings*, 200–201.

12. Quoted in Claude Nicolet, *Space, Geography, and Politics in the Early Roman Empire* (Ann Arbor: University of Michigan Press, 1991), 111–12.

13. Ibid., 72–73.

14. Aristotle, *The Politics*, trans. Ernest Barker (Oxford: Oxford University Press, 1948), 3.

15. According to recent findings, the population of Athens immediately before the Peloponnesian War (431 B.C.) consisted of the following percentages: free citizens, 42–48 percent; *metoikoi*, free but without citizen's rights, 7.5 percent; and slaves, 50 percent (*History of the Greek City-State* [Athens: University of Athens Press, 1990]).

16. Euripides, *Iphigenia in Aulis*, trans. Charles Walker, in *The Complete Greek Tragedies*, vol. 4, ed. David Grene and Richmond Lattimore (Chicago: University of Chicago Press, 1958), 290–91; hereafter cited in the text as *IA*.

17. The finality with which the European tradition has subscribed to the binary opposition between the Greeks and the barbarians voiced by Agamemnon — and appropriated by Aristotle — is suggested even in the translations of Euripides' text. Thus, for example, Arthur S. Way, the translator of Euripides' plays in the Loeb Classical Library, construes the word *gamon* (marriage) in these lines from Iphigenia's speech as "rape": "What part have I in Paris' rape of Helen?" (*Euripides* [Cambridge, Mass.: Harvard University Press, 1912], 1:115).

18. See Margaret Williamson, "A Woman's Place in Euripides' *Medea*," in *Euripides, Women, and Sexuality*, ed. Anton Powell (London: Routledge, 1990, 16–31). In this suggestive essay, Williamson focuses on Medea's futile effort to break out of the private sphere, the *oikos*, which is the space of women and the language appropriate to it, into the public sphere, the *polis*, which is the domain of manly action and the speech proper to it. This futile effort is reenacted in *Iphigenia in Aulis*. But in both cases, each in its own way, this very futility accomplishes the delegitimation of the dominant patriarchal/ethnocentric culture.

19. It is, by now, a commonplace of Euripides criticism that the deus ex machina that miraculously "saves" Iphigenia at the last moment was a later interpolation for which Euripides was not responsible. Thus, for example, Charles

Walker, the translator of the *Iphigenia* for the University of Chicago Press's edition of *The Complete Greek Tragedies,* following "the practice of most modern translators (Schiller among them)," omits this "happy ending," relegating it to an appendix (214). If, however, one resists reading the *Iphigenia* from the retrospective *end* prescribed by the "Latin" West's historical appropriation of the binary opposition between the Greeks and the barbarians, it will be seen that this deus ex machina is essential to the paradoxical — that is, deconstructive — logic that informs Euripides' play.

20. I am indebted to my student Assimina Karavanta for alerting me to the pertinence of the ironies of the *Iphigenia* and the *Medea* that call into question Aristotle's appropriation of Euripides in his *Politics.* As she put it in a letter dated May 23, 1997: "Iphigenia repeats Agamemnon's justification of the Trojan expedition — 'It is / A right thing that Greeks rule barbarians, / Not barbarians Greeks.... And why? They are bondsmen and slaves, and we, / Mother, are Greeks and are free' — not in order to reenforce the alleged necessity of the expedition but to turn her slaughter into a sacrifice, the space of torture into the space of her own performance. So she, as a woman, an 'other' to the military center of decisions, employs its own argument about the superiority of Greeks over the Trojans — against itself. For, paradoxically, it is a woman who utters this ideal, the woman about to be slaughtered for the fulfillment of this ideal. The fact that it is she who utters it renders the statement suspect and ironic. If the Greeks are [so] 'civilized' and superior to the brutal 'others,' why is it that a Greek father is about to kill his own daughter? And it is, again, a deus ex machina that saves Iphigenia from her father's hand without resolving the conflict created by the utterance put in Iphigenia's mouth, a conflict pertinent to the tension that inhabits the heart of the city/audience of the play — and of the contemporary Athenian *polis.*"

21. What I have said about the *Iphigenia* should not be read as an exception to the Euripidean rule. It applies as well to several of Euripides' plays, not least the *Medea,* to which Aristotle may also be referring. Jason's famous speech justifying his abandonment of Medea — a women, like Iphigenia, but also a barbarian — for Creon's Greek daughter repeats Agamemnon's (and Aristotle's) binarist ethnocentric argument (see Euripides, *The Medea,* trans. Rex Warner, in *The Complete Greek Tragedies,* vol. 1, ed. David Grene and Richmond Lattimore [Chicago: University of Chicago Press, 1955], 76):

> In so far as you helped me, you did well enough.
> But on this question of saving me, I can prove
> You have certainly got for me more than you give.
> Firstly, instead of living among barbarians
> You inhabit a Greek land and understand our ways,
> How to live by law instead of the sweet will of force.
> And all the Greeks considered you a clever woman.
> You were honored for it; while, if you were living at
> The ends of the earth, nobody would have heard of you.

In the dramatic context, Jason's invocation of the binary opposition between Greek and barbarian reveals itself not as the affirmation of a Greek ideal threatened by the irrationality of a woman/barbarian, but, as his instrumental logic suggests, as a calculative rhetorical strategy intended to "prove" the justness of his abandonment of his "barbarian" wife for a more prestigious position in the Greek *polis*. And he relies on this polyvalent "Greek" binary logic to bereave Medea of a language capable of countering his justification. Jason's appeal to the hegemonic discourse of the Greek *polis* renders Medea, like Iphigenia, homeless, an *Abgeschiedene*. But it is precisely her consciousness of her condition as foreigner or specter, as it were — the condition of silence precipitated by Jason's binary logic — and her refusal to be accommodated that Euripides thematizes as that which Jason's *logos* cannot account for, as that which haunts the *logos* informing that polyvalent imperial logic. In thus foregrounding Medea's enforced reduction to "silence" in the face of Jason's brutal civility, Euripides also points to that logic's superficiality — and demise. For in depriving this barbarian/woman of any other linguistic recourse, Jason's hegemonic discourse renders Medea's terrible revenge against Jason and the Greek *polis* understandable, if not an act of justice: "They [the children of Jason and Medea] died," Medea tells Jason, near the end of the play, "from a disease they caught from their father" (105). And, as in the case of the deus ex machina that saves Iphigenia, the "anticlimactic" flight of Medea in a chariot drawn by winged dragons at the end of the play underscores the force of this judgment.

22. David Spurr, *The Rhetoric of Empire: Colonial Discourse in Journalism, Travel Writing, and Imperial Administration* (Durham, N.C.: Duke University Press, 1993), 102–3.

23. Although Plato and Aristotle strive to achieve a metaphysical vision of being, their mode of inquiry was not, as Heidegger everywhere insists, finally metaphysical in the strict sense. Insofar as they asked the *question* of being (*die Seinsfrage*), it was not imperial: a derivative, that is, circular, process in the sense of beginning from the end (in both meanings of the word). It was, rather, like that of the pre-Socratics, originative, which is to say, hermeneutic or phenomenological: "But the question touched upon here [the question of being, which 'has today been forgotten'] is hardly an arbitrary one. It sustained the avid research of Plato and Aristotle but from then on ceased to be heard *as a thematic question of actual investigation*. What these two thinkers gained has been preserved in various distorted and 'camouflaged' forms down to Hegel's *Logic:* and what then was wrested from phenomena by the highest exertion of thinking, albeit in fragments and first beginnings, has long since been trivialized" (Heidegger, introduction to *Being and Time*, 42).

24. Spurr, *Rhetoric of Empire*, 103. See also Peter Mason, *Deconstructing America: Representations of the Other* (London: Routledge, 1990): "The grid according to which Herodotus places these peoples [the 'monstrous human races' beyond the *oikoumene*] can be shown to be Greek-centered: Greece is 'the domain of measure, while the extremities of the earth are the domain of extreme riches (gold) and of the extremely bizarre' (P. Lévêque and P. Vidal-Naquet, *Clisthène l'Athénien*, Annales Littéraires de l'Université de Besançon, Vol. 65, Les Belles Lettres, Paris: 1973: 81 n.1). Increasing geographical remoteness is coupled to remoteness in terms of dietary practices, sexual customs, and cultural faculties,... a schema which is followed by Herodotus' successors too.... The symmetrical play of oppositions by which this grid is organized... suggests that the ethnographical details furnished by Herodotus should be seen rather in the light of differences which are 'good to think with,' and that it is more rewarding to examine these patterns in the light of Greek thought about non-Greeks than

to try to track down the 'lost tribes' which might be supposed to conform to such descriptions" (75). In demonstrating the applicability of ancient ontologically grounded models of colonialism — specifically, that which measures the worth of races increasingly remote from the privileged center — to the discourse of "America" from the age of exploration to the Enlightenment, Mason's book constitutes a valuable contribution to a "postcolonial" scholarship that more or less restricts the genealogy of modern imperialism to the age of exploration and after. However, as his reading of Herodotus's peripatetic perspective as a fixed "Greek" center suggests, Mason, like Spurr and most other postcolonial commentators, elides the radical difference between the Greek and the Roman perspective on the distant Other. He thus obscures the origins of the discursive regularity that brings Europe (and its history) and imperialism into identity.

25. Herodotus, *The Histories,* trans. Aubrey de Selincourt and A. R. Burn (Harmondsworth, England: Penguin, 1972), 4.282; translation modified. Commenting on the problem posed by this passage from Herodotus, Jean-Pierre Vernant argues that the Milesian philosophers, especially Anaximander, represented the cosmos (Being) on the model of a *polis* in which "the social space was a centered space — common, public, egalitarian, and symmetrical — but also secularized, intended for confrontation, debate, and argument." Vernant assumes that Herodotus's view was thus an exception to the rule, rather than the norm. Sliding over Herodotus's mockery (and the ambiguity in Anaximander's representation of the cosmos — an ambiguity that Heidegger will later thematize by suggesting that Anaximander's cosmos was informed by a decentered center), he adds, "In another passage Herodotus reveals the institutional and political background of this geometrization of physical space, which in his opinion had been carried too far: after disaster had befallen the Ionians, they all gathered at the Panionion. First Bias of Priene, one of the sages, advised that they form a joint fleet to sail to Sardinia and found there a single Panionian city. Thales of Miletus was the next to speak. He proposed that they have a single council ... and locate its seat at Teos, since that island was at the center of Ionia. . . . [T]he other cities would continue to be inhabited, but would henceforth be in the position of outlying demes incorporated into a single *polis*" (*The Origins of Greek Thought* [Ithaca, N.Y.: Cornell University Press, 1982 (1962)], 127–28; the passage from Herodotus Vernant is summarizing is from *The Histories,* 1.109).

26. Charles Olson, "Letter 23," in *The Maximus Poems* (Berkeley: University of California Press, 1983), 104; see Ann Charters, ed., *The Special View of History* (Berkeley, Calif.: Oyez, 1970), 20; see also 26.

27. Martin Bernal, *Black Athena: The Afroasiatic Roots of Classical Civilization* (New Brunswick, N.J.: Rutgers University Press, 1987), 1:113. Plutarch's representation of Herodotus as barbarian-lover occurs in *On the Malice of Herodotus,* trans. L. Pearson and F. H. Pearson, vol. 11 of *Plutarch's Moralia,* 15 vols. (Cambridge, Mass.: Harvard University Press, 1965), 22. Bernal's thesis, that the received interpretation of Greek antiquity (what he calls "the Aryan Model") is an invention of Enlightenment Eurocentrism and racism and that it constitutes a radical departure from "the Ancient Model," which assumed that "Greek culture had arisen as the result of colonization, around 1500 B.C., by Egyptians and Phoenicians who had civilized the native inhabitants," has its point of departure in Herodotus. For his reading of Herodotus's "multicultural" disposition, see especially *Black Athena,* 1:98–101, 112–20.

28. James S. Romm, *The Edges of the Earth in Ancient Thought* (Princeton, N.J.: Princeton University Press, 1992), 48. See also, Peter Mason, *Deconstructing America.*

29. Romm, *Edges of the Earth,* 55. See also James Redfield, "Herodotus the Tourist," *Classical Philology* 80 (April 1985): 97–118. Though Redfield's position on Herodotus's status is ambiguous (he refers to him as a "cultural relativist" and an ethnocentric ethnographer), his reading of the account of the Persian Wars in *The Histories* suggests at least that Herodotus was minimally skeptical about the ethnocentric center/periphery paradigm. For in this reading Redfield interprets the defeat of the Persians by the Greeks not as an imperial triumph, but as a warning to the victors against assuming the center/periphery perspective that culminated in the demise of the Persian empire: "It is tempting to . . . think that for Herodotus and his audience in the mid-fifth century the tyrannical Athenian empire was the moral heir of the Persian, threatened with the same moral collapse" (115).

30. See especially Claude Nicolet, "'The Geographical' Work of Augustus" and "The Administrative Organization of Space: Urban Regions and Italian Regions," in *Space, Geography, and Politics,* 171–207.

31. Nicolet, *Space, Geography, and Politics,* 194; the quotation from Vitruvius is from *The Ten Books of Architecture,* 6.1.10–12.

32. See Michel Foucault, *Discipline and Punish: The Birth of the Prison,* trans. Allen Sheridan (New York: Pantheon, 1977), 173–74, 214–15; see also A. E. Gutkind, *Urban Development in Western Europe: France and Belgium* (New York: Free Press, 1970), vol. 5 of *International History of City Development,* 8 vols. (1964–72); and Norman J. Johnston, *Cities in the Round* (Seattle: University of Washington Press, 1983). Both Gutkind and Johnston represent the military and disciplinary use to which the paradigm of the circular city was put after the Renaissance as the betrayal of the ideal envisaged by the humanists such as Alberti and Campanella. Inscribed by their humanist perspective on the circle, they fail to see, as Foucault does not, that this architectural model of beauty is also the model of the domination.

33. Romm, *Edges of the Earth,* 108.

34. According to Éliane Escoubas in an important essay written after the publication of Victor Farias's *Heidegger et le nazisme* (1987), which inaugurated the now-pervasive humanist identification of Heidegger's philosophical thought at large with Nazi practice, the *Parmenides* lectures constitute the *"texte-charnière"* of Heidegger's *" 'explication' avec"* — his dissociation from, and rejoinder to, German National Socialism ("Heidegger, la question romaine, la question impériale: Autour du 'Tournant,' " in *Heidegger: Questions ouvertes,* ed. Éliane Escoubas [Paris: Editions Osiris, 1988], 173–88). For my account of the significance of the *Parmenides* lectures in the debate over the politics of Heidegger's thought, see *Heidegger and Criticism: Retrieving the Cultural Politics of Destruction* (Minneapolis: University of Minnesota Press, 1993), especially the chapters titled "Heidegger and Foucault: The Politics of the Commanding Gaze," 144–49, and "Heidegger, Nazism, and the 'Repressive Hypothesis,' " 222–30.

35. Martin Heidegger, *Parmenides,* trans. André Schewer and Richard Rojcewicz (Bloomington: Indiana University Press, 1992), 40–45.

36. Foucault, *Discipline and Punish,* 205.

37. Edward W. Said, *Culture and Imperialism* (New York: Alfred Knopf, 1993), 26, 41, 278. Said is right in claiming that Foucault's work overdetermines the European sphere at the expense of its colonial interests. I would, nevertheless, question Said's assertion that Foucault "ignor[es] the imperial context of his own theories" in favor of a swerve "away from politics entirely," motivated perhaps by "his disenchantment with both the insurrections of the 1960s and the Iranian Revolution" (278).

38. Foucault, *Discipline and Punish*, 146.

39. Ibid., 169. It is not only the pervasiveness of what Foucault calls "the Roman reference" in *Discipline and Punish* that attests to his awareness of the relationship between the operation of the panoptic diagram and the imperial project. As I have suggested in chapter 1, this awareness is also borne witness to by Foucault's insistent demonstration that, in the wake of the Enlightenment, the knowledge of the knowledge/power nexus he insistently interrogates is represented as "territory," "region," or "domain," that is, in terms that are borrowed from and in turn lend themselves to the modern imperialist project. See his interview with the Marxist editors of the geographical journal *Hérodote*, "Questions on Geography," in *Power/Knowledge: Selected Interviews and Other Writings, 1972–1977*, ed. Colin Gordon (New York: Pantheon, 1980), 63–77. See also Edward W. Said, *Orientalism* (New York: Vintage Books, 1979), esp. 79–92. Here, in a discussion of Napoleon's Egyptian expedition, Said amplifies on Foucault's brief remarks on Napoleonic imperialism by adding textual tactics (knowledge production) to the military discipline and training in good citizenship that are continuous with colonization.

40. Antonio Gramsci, *Selections from the Prison Notebooks*, ed. and trans. Quintin Hoare and Geoffrey Nowell Smith (New York: International Publishers, 1971): "The intellectuals are the dominant group's 'deputies' exercising the subaltern functions of social hegemony [in the sphere of 'civil society'] and political government [in the sphere of ['political society']. These comprise: (1) The 'spontaneous' consent given by the great masses of the population to the general direction imposed on social life by the dominant fundamental group; this concept is 'historically' caused by the prestige (and consequent confidence) which the dominant group enjoys because of its position and function in the world of production. (2) The apparatus of state coercive power which 'legally' enforces discipline on those groups who do not 'consent' either actively or passively. *This apparatus is, however, constituted for the whole of society in anticipation of moments of crisis of command and direction when spontaneous consent has failed*" (12).

41. Heidegger, *Parmenides*, 41; see also 45.

42. Tacitus, *Agricola*, trans. M. Hutton, rev., R. M. Ogilvie, in *Agricola, Germania, Dialogus*, Loeb Classical Library, vol. 35 (Cambridge, Mass.: Harvard University Press, 1970), 64–67.

43. Strabo, *The Geography*, 3.2.14–15.

44. See note 23 above.

45. Claude Lévi-Strauss, *The Savage Mind* (Chicago: University of Chicago Press, 1966), 23–24.

46. Plutarch, "Cato the Elder," in *Makers of Rome*, trans. Ian Scott-Kilvert (London: Penguin, 1965), 146. The evidence of the Romans' distrust of Greek philosophy in the name of an austere discipline is pervasive in both the Repub-

lican and imperial discourses. In the *Agricola,* for example, Tacitus writes of the education of his subject, "I remember how he used himself to tell that in early life he was inclined to drink more deeply of philosophy than is permitted to a Roman and a Senator, had not his mother's discretion imposed a check upon his enkindled and glowing imagination: no doubt his soaring and ambitious temper craved the beauty and splendour of high and exalted ideals with more ardour than prudence. Soon came reason and years to cool his blood: he achieved the rarest of feats; he was a student, yet preserved a sense of proportion" (33). As H. Mattingly, the translator of the *Agricola* in the Penguin edition (Tacitus, *On Britain and Germany* [Harmondsworth, England: Penguin, 1948]), observes in a note about this passage: "The Romans from old distrusted philosophy as an enemy of the active life. In 155 B.C. the Senate ordered all Greek philosophers to leave Rome. Under the Empire, philosophy was sometimes a cover for opposition to Government, and was resented as such. Domitian expelled philosophers from Rome in A.D. 93, possibly also earlier in A.D. 88–89." For an extended account of this highly serious official fear of (the "play" of) Greek philosophy, especially in the imperial period, see Ramsey MacMullen, *Enemies of the Roman Order: Treason, Unrest, and Alienation in the Empire* (London: Routledge, 1992 [1966]). See also Mikhail Bakhtin, "From the Prehistory of Novelistic Discourse," in *The Dialogic Imagination: Four Essays,* trans. Caryl Emerson and Michael Holquist (Austin: University of Texas Press, 1981): "Those upon whom the transmission of this heritage [of laughter] depended were agelasts [ideologues of 'high seriousness,' from the Greek 'one who doesn't laugh'] who elected the serious word and rejected its comic reflections as a profanation (as happened, for example, with numerous parodies on Virgil)" (58–59).

47. David Quint, *Epic and Empire: Politics and Generic Form from Virgil to Milton* (Princeton, N.J.: Princeton University Press, 1993), 29. Where I disagree with Quint's otherwise brilliant reading of the *Aeneid* is in his interpretation of Aeneas's father, Anchises, as the Trojan/Roman past that Augustus/Aeneas must reject in order to forestall repeating civil war. Quint writes: "However wrenching the death of Anchises may be for Aeneas, it provides in its context a reassuring image of generational continuity: the Roman stalk will succeed to a future where other heroic lines have failed. And with its parade of replica Troys — each successively and more explicitly revealed to be a place of death — the fiction of Book 3 insists that this future can only be reached if the Trojans relinquish their past and its memories, if they can escape from a pattern of traumatic repetition. Anchises appears to embody that past, as the representative of an older generation too much part of a former Troy to begin anew" (61). This interpretation of the Augustan ideology informing Virgil's retrospective vision of Roman history misses the clear symbolization of Aeneas as "saving remnant," that is, as *relic-* or *seed-bearer,* and thus the ontological *ground* or *logos* of the Augustan imperial myth, the *imperium sine fini.* For a provocative study of Virgil's and the "Virgilian" tradition's patriarchal/imperial representation of the African Dido, see Marilynn Desmond, *Reading Dido* (Minneapolis: University of Minnesota Press, 1994).

48. See David Spurr's analysis of this aspect of the rhetoric of imperialism in his chapter titled "Eroticization," in *Rhetoric of Empire,* 170–83. It is not Spurr's intent to establish the genealogy of this rhetoric, though it is clear that

he assumes its origins to be in the Enlightenment. This failure to be historical enough may account for his failure to perceive the affiliation of the eroticization of extraperipheral space in the discourse of modern imperialism with the metaphorics of seed/planting, and also of this last with the metaphorical systems emanating from the figures of light/dark and center/periphery.

49. George Orwell, *Burmese Days* (New York: Harvest Books, 1962), 48; hereafter cited in the text as *BD*.

50. Geoffrey of Monmouth, *The History of the Kings of Britain,* trans. Lewis Thrope (Harmondsworth, England: Penguin, 1988). For an extended discussion of this genealogy, see Richard Waswo, *The Founding Legend of Western Civilization: From Virgil to Vietnam* (Hanover, N.H.: Wesleyan University Press, 1997), 55–63.

51. Quoted in Philip Guedalla, *Palmerston: 1784–1863* (New York: Putnam's, 1927), 332–33. David Pacifico (or the Chevalier Pacifico, as he called himself) was a Spanish Jew born in Gibraltar and thus a British subject, despite being a naturalized citizen of Portugal. In 1847, a Greek mob broke into, ransacked, and burned his house, believing (erroneously) that Pacifico had been instrumental in the banning of the traditional burning of an effigy of Judas at Easter time. The so-called Don Pacifico affair was precipitated when Lord Palmerston, the imperialist British foreign secretary, sent the British navy into Piraeus, the port of Athens, on the pretext of protecting the rights of a British subject, but, in fact, to reinforce the credibility of imperial British power in the Mediterranean, especially to the new Greek government and its French and Russian "protectors." Palmerston was forced by the opposition to defend his actions in this affair before the British Parliament. At the end of a four-day debate, he gave a chauvinistic speech appealing to the civilized glories of British law against the barbarism of "almost every country of Europe" that "resulted in the greatest victory of [his] career" (Jasper Ridley, *Lord Palmerston* [London: Constable, 1970], 385).

52. Michel Foucault, "Nietzsche, Genealogy, History," in *Language, Counter-memory, Practice: Selected Essays and Interviews,* ed. Donald F. Bouchard, trans. Donald F. Bouchard and Sherry Simon (Ithaca, N.Y.: Cornell University Press, 1977), 161.

53. The "Romanism" informing the discourse and practice of British imperialism should not be restricted to the influence of the humanistic pedagogy of the British public school system. It is also, perhaps, above all, the construction of the classical scholarship of Victorian and post-Victorian humanists, not least of those like the editors and translators of the Penguin Classics (under the general editorship of E. V. Rieu). As in the case of H. Mattingly, the translator and editor of Tacitus's *Agricola* and *Germania* (Harmondsworth, Eng.: Penguin, 1948), in the aftermath of World War II and the beginning of the disintegration of the British Empire, these classical scholars, until recently, systematically represented the literature, philosophy, and history of Rome from the sympathetic perspective of their own analogous metropolitan culture: "Tacitus was one of those Italians of the sound old stock who brought to the service of the Empire a loyalty and devotion that recalls the best days of the Republic. It was the destiny of Rome to rule the world, the destiny of the high-born Roman to share in the great task; and Rome now meant not the city only, but Italy as well. We may think of Tacitus as something like an officer of the Indian army and an Indian Civil Servant

rolled into one. He has a passionate belief in the 'career' as the one thing in life that matters.... There is enough in common between his age and ours for us to sympathize with his problems. The Roman Empire is ... nearer to us spiritually than our own country in the Middle Ages" (Mattingly, *Tacitus on Britain and Germany,* 8–10).

54. Said, *Culture and Imperialism,* 68–70; hereafter cited in the text as *CI.* The passage from Conrad to which Said is referring occurs in *Heart of Darkness,* ed. Robert Kimbrough, rev. ed. (New York: Norton Critical Editions, 1988), 10–11.

55. Conrad, *Heart of Darkness,* 10.

56. This resonant phrase is from Jupiter's reassuring speech to Venus in book 1 of Virgil's *Aeneid,* in which he promises the founding of Rome (the new Troy) by Aeneas and the establishment of the Roman Empire (and the *Pax Romana*) in the fullness of time (i.e., the time of Virgil and Augustus): "His ego nec metas tempora pons: imperium sine fine dedi" (To Rome I set no boundary in space or time. I have granted it dominion and it has no end) (Virgil, *The Aeneid,* trans. W. F. Jackson Knight [Harmondsworth, England: Penguin, 1956], 1.283–84). See also the *Res Gestae* of Augustus, to which, as Claude Nicolet observes, "we owe the clearest and most striking *expression*" of the idea that the reign of Augustus entailed "the accomplishment of a divine will that has assigned to Rome the destiny of conquering, of dominating, but also of pacifying and organizing the whole world: *tu regere imperio populos, Romane, memento* (Virgil, *Aeneas,* 6, 851). Imperial Rome, that is the Rome of the empire (territorial), and Rome of the emperor (who governs), 'absorbs in its fate the fate of mankind' " (Nicolet, *Space, Geography, and Politics,* 15).

57. Strabo, *The Geography,* Loeb Classical Library, vol. 2, trans. H. L. Jones (Cambridge, Mass.: Harvard University Press, 1988 [1854]), 3.77–79. This passage from Strabo is also quoted by V. Y. Mudimbe, "The Power of the Greek Paradigm," *South Atlantic Quarterly* 92, no. 2 (spring 1993): 379–80; reprinted in Mudimbe, *The Idea of Africa* (Bloomington: Indiana University Press, 1994). In this brilliant and important genealogical essay, Mudimbe goes far to substantiate the priority I attribute to ontological representation in the modern colonial project and to classical antiquity as the source of the naturalized discourse of modern colonialism. My disagreement with Mudimbe lies in his characteristic conflation of the discursive practices of Greece and Rome, in, that is, his tracing of the imperial paradigm of the center and periphery to Greece — specifically to Herodotus — rather than to Rome. Mudimbe reads the Roman (Pliny) and late (Hellenistic) or Romanized Greek historians and geographers (Strabo and Diodorus Siculus, for example) back into Herodotus's *History.* He thus distorts a certain originary (or de-centered) impulse in Herodotus that, as I have suggested earlier in this chapter, is essentially foreign to the characteristically derivative — and ethnocentric — discourse of his Hellenistic and Roman successors. Strabo, for example, who acknowledges his very heavy dependency on Posidonius (135–50 B.C.), who, in turn, put his encyclopedic knowledge of the barbarian world to the service of his friend, Pompey, insistently asserts the ideological function of geography: "The greater part of geography subserves the needs of states; for the scene of the activities of states is land and sea, the dwelling-place of man" (*Geography* 1.1.16 [30]). Indeed, as Claude Nicolet notes in *Space, Geography, and Politics:* "It is not a coincidence that the most complete geographic

work handed down from antiquity, that of Strabo, is from the Augustan period. Written by a historian and scholar, the work is a genuine survey of all the traditions of geographic writings. It is essentially from Strabo that we have knowledge of most of his predecessors: Erotosthenes, Hipparchus, Artemidoros, or Posidonius.... More striking yet, it gives a global vision of the world (and even the concurrent hypotheses in use) and the place the Romans assigned to themselves. This geography, by an Asian Greek who was in favor at Rome, is proclaimed openly as a 'political geography' written mainly for the use of the ruling groups and destined to give an account of the state of the world (considered as satisfactory) at the beginning of Tiberius's reign; opened, on the one hand, by recent and direct commercial links with India, closed, on the other, by the *pax romana*" (8; see also 47 and esp. 72–74). See also H. L. Jones's introduction to the Loeb edition: "As for his political opinions, [Strabo] seems to have followed Polybius in his profound respect for the Romans, with whom, apparently, he is in entire sympathy; he never fails to show great admiration, not only for the political grandeur of the Roman Empire, but for its wise administration as well" (xix–xx). Nicolet, however, like Jones, tends (his rhetoric is always uncertain when it comes to the question of the "relation" between the two) to interpret the Greek geographical writing before Strabo and Pliny as underdeveloped rather than as different — characterized by a "noncartographical mentality" (73). In reading the history of Hellenistic or Roman writers back into Herodotus's history, Mudimbe, in other words, overlooks — and annuls — the originative interest of Herodotus's *interesse,* his peripatetic being-in-the-midst, in favor of representing it as calculation. Despite the force of the Heideggerian rethinking of the provenance of humanist modernity, the crucial distinction I have made throughout this chapter between Greece and Rome is, admittedly, one that needs to be more fully supported by historically specific evidence. This would also require addressing the evidence of Martin Bernal's monumental work *Black Athena.* I believe, however, that a case could be made for the view that a certain aspect of Bernal's revisionist history of the Occidental representation of classical Greece, especially his heavy reliance on Herodotus, could be invoked as evidence of the distinction I am suggesting between Greek and Roman culture. I am referring to that thrust of Bernal's thesis that posits Greece not as opposed to Egyptian/African culture (the Enlightenment's Arianized representation initiated by German classical scholarship), but as decisively open to cultural exchange with Egypt/Africa. At any rate, the force of Heidegger's linguistically derived distinction between Roman and Greek culture has definitively foreclosed the all-too-familiar option to identify Greece and Rome in any account — sympathetic or adversarial — of Occidental cultural history.

58. See also Lennard Davis, *Resisting Novels: Ideology and Fiction* (New York: Methuen, 1987), especially chapter 3, " 'Known Unknown' Locations: The Ideology of Place," 52–101.

59. Conrad, *Heart of Darkness,* 10.

60. I am indebted to V. Y. Mudimbe for the extension of the preceding etymological analysis of the words "culture and colonization" to include the *agros,* though the reservations concerning his reading of Herodotus I expressed in note 57 apply here as well: "On the basis of his travels and knowledge, Herodotus mocked the naivete of ancient geographers, but not the enterprise itself or its utility. His geography locates *barbaroi* and *agrioi* in their respective 'places' and,

at the same time, articulates a cultural and metaphoric geography (an arrangement of *muthoi* or stories he heard) on top of the first. His method for this second level of narration is one of *reservatio mentis*. He notes: 'I will not say that this or that story is true....' The *barbaroi* and the *agrioi* are part of the general vocabulary of the Greek *politeia*. The first basically means 'foreigner,' and designates a non-Greek speaker. The second signifies 'wild, savage' and is etymologically related to *agros*, 'field.' As such *agros* is, specifically, in a relation of opposition to the household or *oikos*, 'a dwelling place' symbolizing family ties.... *Oikos* implies also the meaning of 'home-city,' that of 'belonging to a community' (defined by a tradition, a culture, or a condition). This is well actualized in one of its parent words, *oikoumene*, which designates the inhabited region of the Greeks in opposition to barbarian countries and, by extension, all the inhabited world known by the Greeks. In brief, in its opposition to the paradigmatic and ethnocentric values of *oikos* (*domus* in Latin), *agros* is the exact counterpart of the Latin *foresticus* and *salvaticus*" ("Power of the Greek Paradigm," 372–73).

I cannot respond fully to this etymology here. It will have to suffice to invoke *georgos*, the much more fundamental ancient Greek word for "cultivating the earth," which suggests a Greek practice (*ourgos*) vis-à-vis the earth (*gea*) quite other, in its reciprocality, than that unidirectional violence implied by the Latinate "agriculture," and to point out Mudimbe's all-too-easy identification of the Greek *oikos* with the Latin *domus*, the source of such modern imperial words as "dominate," "domesticate," "dominion," and so forth, suggesting in this way that he may be ventriloquizing the Roman (imperial) representation of the Greek *agrioi/barbaroi* back into these terms. The "parent" Greek word, *oikoumene*, from which the English word "ecumenical" derives, constitutes, I would suggest, a far looser sense of community than the Roman "home-city" would tolerate. See Martin Heidegger, "Building Dwelling Thinking" and "...Poetically Man Dwells," trans. Richard Hoftstadter, in *Poetry, Language, Thought* (New York: Harper and Row, 1971), 143–62 and 211–29, and Hannah Arendt, *The Human Condition* (Chicago: University of Chicago Press, 1958). Further, as Heidegger has also pointed out in the *Parmenides* lectures, "earth" had a decisively different meaning for the Romans than it did for the Greeks. The Latin word *terra*, like so many Roman translations of Greek words, constitutes a reduction of the Greek *gea* to the ideological one-dimensionality of the imperial project. Suggesting the affiliation between the Greeks' comportment toward the earth and their understanding of truth as *a-letheia*, as unconcealment that always already *belongs* with *lathos*, Heidegger writes: "The earth is the in-between, namely between the concealment of the subterranean and the luminosity, the disclosiveness, of the supraterranean (the span of heaven, *ouranos*). For the Romans, on the contrary, the earth, *tellus, terra*, is the dry, the land as distinct from the sea; this distinction differentiates that upon which construction, settlement, and installation are possible from those places where they are impossible. *Terra* becomes *territorium*, land of settlement as realm of command. In Roman *terra* can be heard an imperial accent, completely foreign to the Greek *gea* and *ge*" (*Parmenides*, 60). To recall my discussion of the complicity of Enlightenment ontology — its reduction of the knowledge of being to "field" or "region" or "realm" or "domain" or "territory" (to be "mastered") — with the imperial project proper: the Roman reduction of the Greek *a-letheia* to *veritas* manifests itself in an interpretation of the earth in which the earth as *territory* appeals to the Rome to be colonized. From here it is a short step to the accommodation of the culture/colonization nexus to the (Roman) imperial project.

61. Plutarch, "The Life of Romulus," in *The Lives of the Noble Grecians and Romans,* trans. John Dryden, rev. Arthur Hugh Clough (Philadelphia, n.d.), 1.47.

62. Richard Waswo bears witness to the ubiquity of the Roman reference in *Founding Legend,* which traces the history of the imperial uses to which the West has put the Roman representation of the story of Aeneas: "The story was popularly regarded as actual history from the earliest Roman historians in the third century B.C. until the eighteenth century of our era. In all its versions [these include not only the chronicle and literary redactions of Virgil, Nennius, Geoffrey of Monmouth, Annias of Viterbo, Jean Lemaire de Belges, Luíz de Camoëns, Pierre de Ronsard, Edmund Spenser, but also the national historiography (William Roberston), literature (Alexander Pope, Joseph Conrad, and E. M. Forster) and cinematic production (John Ford) that, though abandoning overt reference to the story, nevertheless reproduced its structure] its point is to repeat, for whatever given locality or ruling house in western Europe, the founding of Rome by Aeneas — making the subsequent founders his lineal descendants (or inventing other Trojan survivors) and putting them through the identical trajectory of wandering from east to west until they come into possession of the promised land.... What kind of a story is this, that selects a cultural origin that is always already destroyed? For there is no doubt that what the homeless Trojans are bringing to the west is nothing less than civilization itself. The 'empire without end...' that Jupiter has given to the Roman heirs of the wandering Trojans includes the transplantation of all arts and sciences, the bringing of a total culture. Celebrated in the Middle Ages as the *translatio imperii et studii,* this 'transmission of empire and learning' is the central vision that the occident has of itself" (1–2).

What is missing in Waswo's otherwise powerful cultural analysis of the anatomy of Western imperialism is any overt reference to the ontological provenance of the myth of Aeneas (and the metaphors that inform it) and, not least, an adequate discussion of the distinction he implies between Greek and Roman antiquity. I am indebted to Vassilis Lambropoulos for alerting me to the existence of this book. Unfortunately, I came to it only after I had completed mine.

63. For my argument about the centrality of the Roman imperial model in the formation of Nazi Germany, see William V. Spanos, "Heidegger and Foucault: The Politics of the Commanding Gaze," in *Heidegger and Criticism,* 140–50. See also Philippe Lacoue-Labarthe, *Heidegger, Art, and Politics: The Fiction of the Political,* trans. Chris Turner (Oxford: Basil Blackwell, 1990), 73–74.

64. Sacvan Bercovitch, *The American Jeremiad* (Madison: University of Wisconsin Press, 1978). Bercovitch traces the ideological origin of the historical itinerary of America "from visible saint to American patriot, sacred errand to 'manifest destiny,' colony to republic to imperial power" (92), back to the Puritan biblical exegetes who accommodated Patristic figural or typological interpretation (which was fundamental in justifying the Holy Roman Empire) to legitimize their expansive New England theocracy. As persuasive as his argument

is, it nevertheless fails to indicate the degree to which both the medieval exegetes and the American Puritans also resorted to the Roman providential/imperial model, above all, the narrative of the saving remnant embodied in Virgil's *Aeneid* to justify their "imperial" projects. Thus he also obscures the Federalists' conflation of the imperial Roman with the biblical figural narrative of the saving remnant in their effort to articulate a hegemonic discourse — a discourse of national consensus — vis-à-vis Empire. To focalize what in Bercovitch is merely a suggestion, I quote the following passage on Cotton Mather's influential, indeed enabling, text *Magnalia Christi Americana* (1702), which one finds buried in a footnote in Bercovitch's study: "Mather's millennarianism at this time is worth special emphasis because the *Magnalia* has so often been read as a cry of despair. . . . The significance of those deliverances are indicated by the title of the last section of this last Book, 'Arma Virosque Cano,' a title that recalls the Virgilian invocation with which Mather opens the History (as well as the numerous echoes from the *Aeneid* thereafter), and so suggests the epic proportions of his narrative. For Mather, of course, New England's story not only parallels but supersedes that of the founding of Rome [by the saving remnant], as his literary 'assistance' from Christ excels the inspiration of Virgil's muse, as the 'exemplary heroes' he celebrates resemble but outshine the men of Aeneas' band — not only as Christians but as seafarers and conquerors of hostile pagan tribes — and, more spectacularly, as the millennium toward which the Reformation is moving provides the far more glorious antitype of the Augustan *Pax Romana*. Undoubtedly, the proper title for Mather's work is the exultant one he gave it: *Magnalia Christi Americana*, 'The Great Acts of Christ in America' " (87). The recurrence of the Puritan formula "to build a City on the Hill" in the public speeches of President Ronald Reagan referring to the historical destiny of the United States was thus no accident. However sedimented and trivialized by his hegemonic rhetoric of consensus, the logocentric/imperial narrative, from saving remnant — bearer of the seminal seed or relic and its planting in the western wilderness — to the *Pax Americana* it brings to culmination, continues to resonate in his representative "American" discourse.

65. See Vassilis Lambropoulos, *The Rise of Eurocentrism* (Princeton, N.J.: Princeton University Press, 1993), in which Lambropoulos reads the construction of the identity of Europe as an ideological struggle between "Hellenism" and "Hebraism" that culminates in the present age of interpretation in the triumph of the latter.

66. Waswo, *Founding Legend*, 29–37. Waswo's analysis of the primary texts of this history is detailed and, in my mind, decisive.

67. Sir Philip Sidney, *A Defence of Poetry*, ed. J. A. Van Dorsten (Oxford: Oxford University Press, 1996), 33.

68. Ibid., 47–48. Sidney's quotation derives from Horace's *Epistles* (1.2.4), where the latter tells his friend Lollius that Homer is a better teacher of ethics than both Chrysippus and Cantor. This passage is a striking example in European literary criticism of what Heidegger says about the Roman translation of originative Greek thinking to a derivative/circular mode. It is also worth observing that Sidney's representation of Virgil's Aeneas following the defeat of the Spanish Armada is, as we shall see, virtually repeated three centuries later by T. S. Eliot's in the aftermath of the defeat of Nazi Germany (and the emergence of the Cold War).

69. As Frank M. Turner observes in *The Greek Heritage in Victorian Britain,* his magisterial history of the "uses" to which classical Greece was put by Victorian English intellectuals, Homer's epics were read in terms of the typological hermeneutics of the Patristic Fathers, sometimes in ways that merely suggest this exegetical model, but often, especially since the Tractarian Movement at Oxford, quite consciously and specifically: "The reading of the Homeric epics as 'a secular Bible of mankind' [probably precipitated by Henry Nelson Coleridge, the nephew and son-in-law of the poet, whose *Introduction to the Study of the Greek Classic Poets* (1830) was the first post-Romantic period study of the subject and may properly be regarded as the earliest Victorian commentary on Homer] was in part an evaluation of the patristic embracing of pagan civilization for Christian purposes. However, this mode of interpretation also reflected the anxiety of Victorian Christians over the secularization of history by non-Christian writers. If portions of Homeric and Greek culture could be drawn into providential history or could be understood as illustrating Christian truth, then all history and not just that recorded in the Bible could be regarded as prescriptively sacred. This effort might well be considered the historical equivalent of Carlyle's metaphysical natural supernaturalism. Just as Carlyle had discerned the wonder and splendor of the supernatural within finite physical nature, so the writers who linked the Greeks and the Hebrews found evidence of divine dispensation and perhaps even of revelation, in secular history" (156). Despite the "empirical" scholarship of George Grote, who interpreted the Homeric texts to conform to the liberalism of the Utilitarians, this Anglican "prefigurative" hermeneutics prevailed throughout the Victorian era. It informed the learned commentary of William E. Gladstone, whose work on Homer constituted "for better or for worse... the single most extensive body of Victorian Homeric commentary" (160), and numerous other Anglican scholars. However attenuated the "sacred" dimension of their scholarship, it also informed the classical studies of a more "secular" tradition culminating in Gilbert Murray's *The Rise of the Greek Epic* (1907). Turner makes no reference to the importance of Virgil's *Aeneid* in this prefigurative reading of Homer. If, however, the fundamental role this Roman text played in the exegetical practice — and politics — of the Patristic Fathers is remembered, the mediating function of the *Aeneid* I am attributing to the Victorian interpretation of Homer will become apparent.

70. The German scholarship on which Arnold relies for his understanding of the Greek spirit is precisely that which, according to Heidegger, remains Roman. See Turner, *Greek Heritage:* "[Arnold's] Greeks were not ancient Hellenes but a version of humanity largely conjured up in the late-eighteenth century German literary and aesthetic imagination" (21; see also 40–41).

71. Matthew Arnold, "Numbers; or, The Majority and the Remnant," in *The Complete Prose Works,* ed. R. H. Super (Ann Arbor: University of Michigan Press, 1974), 10:147.

72. Charles Augustin Sainte-Beuve, *Étude sur Virgile: Suivre d'une étude sur Quintin de Smyrne* (Paris: Garnier Freres, 1857).

73. T. S. Eliot, "Ulysses, Order, and Myth," *Dial* (1923), reprinted in *Selected Prose,* ed. Frank Kermode (New York: Harcourt Brace Jovanovich, 1975), 175–78.

74. Matthew Arnold, "On the Modern Element in Literature," in *Complete Prose Works,* 1:20; my emphasis. It should not be overlooked in this respect that

Arnold's British humanism is also informed by the racist thought of his time. Derived essentially from nineteenth-century German scholarship, this thinking privileged Indo-European over Semitic and other racial stock and was appropriated by European powers to justify their imperial projects. See Frederick E. Faverty, *Matthew Arnold the Ethnologist* (Evanston, Ill.: Northwestern University Press, 1951), 182–85. I am indebted to Gerald Graff for referring me to this text. In thus relying on German classical scholarship, Arnold's classicism constitutes a significant instance of what Martin Bernal calls "the Aryan Model," that Eurocentric — and racist — representation of ancient Greek culture by Enlightenment Europe that discarded a much older scholarly tradition ("the Ancient Model") that acknowledged the profound influence of the Phoenicians and Egyptians: "For 18th- and 19th-century Romantics and racists, it was simply intolerable for Greece, which was seen not merely as the epitome of Europe but also as its pure childhood, to have been the result of the mixture of native Europeans and colonizing Africans and Semites. Therefore the Ancient Model had to be overthrown and replaced by something more acceptable" (*Black Athena,* 1:2). It is not within the scope of my study to address Bernal's controversial thesis, though it should be clear from this chapter that I am in agreement with his identification of the prevailing representation of classical Greek culture with a racist ideology and with his thesis that classical Greece was far more "multicultural" than the Aryan Model allows. What I find disablingly limited in Bernal's study is its overstatement of his thesis. I mean (1) his tendency to reinscribe in reverse the binary logic of the Aryan Model by way of "Hebraizing" the Greeks, and (2) his obliviousness to the role that Roman civilization—precisely its colonization of the "errancy" of Greek thinking and the cultural pluralism to which it gave rise—has played in the construction of the Aryan Model and the modern European identity.

75. See Frank Kermode, *The Classic: Literary Images of Permanence and Change* (Cambridge, Mass.: Harvard University Press, 1983).

76. Arnold derives the metaphor of "sweetness and light" from Jonathan Swift's parable of the spider and the bee in *The Battle of the Books:* "As for us, the Ancients, we are content with the bee, to pretend to nothing of our own beyond our wings and our voice, that is to say, our flights and our language. For the rest, whatever we have got has been by infinite labor, and search, and ranging through every corner of nature; the difference is that instead of dirt and poison, we have rather chose to fill our hives with honey and wax, thus furnishing mankind with the two noblest things, which are sweetness and light" (*A Tale of a Tub and Other Works,* ed. Angus Ross and David Woolley [Oxford: Oxford University Press, 1986], 113). What needs to be emphasized in recalling the genealogy of Arnold's metaphor for Greek culture is that Swift's representation of the "Ancients" occurs in a text that is profoundly Roman in its provenance.

77. Cicero, *De Officiis,* 1.24. Here, as elsewhere in his typically derivative Roman discourse, Cicero celebrates self-sacrifice in behalf of one's country.

78. Horace, *Odes,* 3.2.

79. *The Collected Poems of Wilfred Owen,* ed. C. Day Lewis (New York: New Directions, 1964), 55. As the editor notes, "BM [British Museum Manuscript] has two drafts, the earlier of which gives, beneath the title, *To Jessie Pope etc.* (cancelled), and *To a Certain Poetess.* HO [Harold Owen Manuscript] has two drafts, one subscribed *To Jessie Pope etc.,* the other, *To a Certain Poetess.*"

But it is clear from this and so many other poems of Owen's that the "you" he addresses here is meant to signify the custodians of the British heritage who have inscribed the hegemonic lie in the mind of a friend — indeed, a woman who ought to know better.

80. Chinua Achebe, *Things Fall Apart* (Oxford: Heinemann 1958), 124–25. For a powerful dramatization, written from a postcolonial feminist perspective, not only of the insidious effects of this neocolonialist strategy of "blaming the victim," but also of the positive possibilities of resistance inhering in the silenced Other that is its consequence, see Ama Ata Aidoo's neglected play, *Anowa,* in *The Dilemma of a Ghost and Anowa* (Essex, England: Longman, 1995).

81. For Eliot's critique of Arnold, see "Arnold and Pater," in *Selected Essays,* 382–93; "Matthew Arnold," in *The Use of Poetry and the Use of Criticism* (London: Faber and Faber, 1964), 103–19; and "The Three Senses of Culture," in *Notes towards the Definition of Culture* (New York: Harcourt Brace, 1949), 619–32.

82. Theodor Haecker, *Virgil, Father of the West,* trans. A. W. Wheer (London: Sheed and Ward, 1934). See Eliot, "Virgil and the Christian World," in *On Poetry and Poets* (London: Faber and Faber, 1957), 123, 125; hereafter cited in the text as "VCW"; see also Eliot's "The Unity of European Culture: An Appendix," in *Notes towards the Definition of Culture.* In this appendix, which consists of three radio broadcasts to the German people immediately after World War II, Eliot refers to Haecker as "that great critic and good European" (120).

83. T. S. Eliot, "What Is a Classic?" in *On Poetry and Poets,* 61; hereafter cited in the text as "WC." The inordinate importance Eliot, like Hegel, gives to the word "maturity" (and the genetic or developmental model it reflects) in his formulation of the idea of the Classic is suggested in the following passage from "WC": "If there is one word on which we can fix, which will suggest the maximum of what I mean by the term 'a classic,' it is the word *maturity.* . . . A classic can only occur when a civilization is mature; when language and a literature are mature; and it must be the work of a mature mind" (55).

84. Erich Auerbach, "Figura," in *Scenes from the Drama of European Literature,* trans. Ralph Manheim (New York: Meridian Books, 1959), 53–54. This hermeneutics of the *figura* is, of course, the teleological hermeneutics perfected by the Patristic exegetes (and employed by Dante, among many other medieval poets and painters, to accommodate radical temporal/historical transformations to the providential design of the abiding *Logos,* more specifically, the differential events of the Old Testament to the New). As I have shown at length in *Modern British Verse Drama and the Christian Tradition: The Poetics of Sacramental Time* (New Brunswick, N.J.: Rutgers University Press, 1967), the structure of Eliot's plays is determined essentially by this Patristic prefigurative hermeneutic tradition. What I was not aware of at that time was the degree to which the related tropes — Virgil, the Roman Empire, and the *Pax Romana* — are at play in the discourse of the Patristic Fathers, in the Anglican theologians of the Victorian (which is to say imperial) period of modern British history, and in Eliot's postconversion prose, poetry, and drama.

As Michel Foucault has shown, modern secular literary criticism, especially its methods for defining an author or, rather, for determining the configuration of the author from existing texts, derives from this medieval exegetical tradition. See "What Is an Author?" in *Language, Counter-memory, Practice,* 127–29. The seduction of the promise/fulfillment structure of Patristic exegesis is not limited to politically conservative critics like T. S. Eliot, however. For a telling example of the hold this totalizing historical structure continues to have on contemporary Marxist critics, see Fredric Jameson, *The Political Unconscious: Narrative as a Socially Symbolic Act* (Ithaca, N.Y.: Cornell University Press, 1981), 28ff.

85. Arnold, "Modern Element," 31.

86. What Eliot implies about Homer's "immaturity" in his remarks on the *Odyssey* and the *Iliad* is made explicit by his Christian humanist colleague C. S. Lewis in his famous essay "Virgil and the Subject of Secondary Epic," in *A Preface to Paradise Lost,* reprinted in *Virgil: A Collection of Critical Essays,* ed. Henry Steele Commager (Englewood Cliffs, N.J.: Prentice Hall, 1966): "With Virgil European poetry grows up. For there are certain moods in which all that had gone before seems, as it were, boy's poetry, depending both for its charm and for its limitations on a certain naivety, seen alike in its heady ecstasies and in its heady despairs" (66). This developmental model also informs Erich Auerbach's very influential representation of Greek literature in *Mimesis: The Representation of Reality in Western Literature,* trans. Willard R. Trask (Princeton, N.J.: Princeton University Press, 1954); see especially, "Odysseus's Scar," 3–23. As Vassilis Lambropoulos has shown, this reduction of Greek literature to the status of immaturity is in part the consequence of Auerbach's reduction of the history of the Western representation of reality to a binary opposition between the Greek and the Hebraic understanding of being. See Lambropoulos, *Rise of Eurocentrism,* 3–24.

87. Virgil, *The Aeneid,* trans. C. Day Lewis (Garden City, N.Y.: Doubleday Anchor Books, 1953), 1:256–63, 283–300. See also Anchises' speech to Aeneas, 6.761–862. On the relationship between the teleological structure of Virgil's *Aeneid* and Augustan imperialism, see Quint, "Repetition and Ideology in the *Aeneid,*" in *Epic and Empire,* 50–96.

88. Francis Fukuyama, *The End of History and the Last Man* (New York: Free Press, 1992), xiii; see also chapter 1, "Our Pessimism," 3–12.

89. During and after the war, Eliot participated systematically in a "think tank" called "The Moot," which was founded by the Anglican theologian J. H. Oldham and sponsored by the Anglican Church. This group met periodically during this time to read papers on and discuss the fate of Europe in the aftermath of World War II. Besides Eliot, it included such prominent figures as the English theologian and fellow and dean of King's College, Cambridge, A. R. Vidler; the literary critic Middleton Murray; the German sociologist Karl Mannheim; and others. It was these sessions that precipitated Eliot's *Notes towards the Definition of Culture,* the book that won him the Nobel Prize in 1948, and Mannheim's, *Diagnosis of Our Time: Wartime Essays of a Sociologist* (Chicago: University of Chicago Press, 1953). See especially Mannheim's "Towards a New Social Philosophy: A Challenge to Christian Thinkers by a Sociologist," the essay that, as Eliot acknowledges in *Notes,* most influenced his thinking about the postwar order. See also Ved Mehta, "The New Theologians, II — The Ekklesia," *New Yorker,* November 20, 1965.

90. The inordinate influence of the philosopher Leo Strauss on the neoconservative initiative in America is documented in Shadia B. Drury, *Leo Strauss and the American Right* (New York: St. Martin's, 1997).

91. Jacques Derrida, *Specters of Marx: The State of the Debt, the Work*

of Mourning, and the New International, trans. Peggy Kamuf (New York: Routledge, 1994), 64; hereafter cited in the text as *SM.*

92. Karl Marx and Frederick Engels, *The Communist Manifesto* (New York: International Publishers, 1948), 8.

93. See Vasilis Lambropoulos, "Writing the Law," in *Rise of Eurocentrism,* 215–31.

94. Fredric Jameson, "Marx's Purloined Letter," *New Left Review* 209 (January/February 1995): 96. A cursory review of Eliot's editorial contributions to *The Criterion* will reveal the inordinate degree to which the Virgilian reference presides. See also Gereth Reeves, *T. S. Eliot: Virgilian Poet* (New York: St. Martin's, 1989), esp. chapter 4, "Empire and the Agrarian Ideal," 96–116.

95. Walter Benjamin, "Theses on the Philosophy of History," in *Illuminations,* trans. Harry Zohn, ed. Hannah Arendt (New York: Schocken Books, 1969), 256.

96. Constantine Cavafy, "Waiting for the Barbarians"; my translation. It is no accident that J. M. Coetzee invokes Cavafy's poem as the title of his great postcolonial novel *Waiting for the Barbarians.*

3. Vietnam and the Pax Americana

1. This initiative is evident in the work of such diverse late postmodern critics as Fredric Jameson, Michael Hardt, Paul Bové, Masao Miyoshi, Ronald Judy, and Wlad Godzich. But it is most succinctly and provocatively exemplified by Bill Readings in *The University in Ruins* (Cambridge, Mass.: Harvard University Press, 1996). I am in full agreement with Reading's critique of the nationalist localism of North American critical thinking in the present historical conjuncture and with his general recommendation that American critical inquiry be reconstellated into the global scene. Indeed, I would go further to say that only acute and rigorous attention to the planetary context will enable the realization of the full extent and depth to which the university and its inherited critical paradigms have been rendered virtually useless by the new transnational "reality" that these global transformations have produced. I am referring, above all, to the planetary triumph of "technological" thinking, a thinking that, in bringing the third, anthropological phase of the ontotheological tradition to its end (fulfillment), has compelled the adversarial cultures to think their opposition in terms of the logical economy of the triumphant imperial discourse. But there is, in Reading's recommendation for such a displacement, the implicit suggestion that new forms, languages, and forums abandon the "local" site of "America" in the process. This representation of the site of America as having been rendered obsolete by current historical events — the emergence of transnational capital as overdetermined site of inquiry — strikes me as an evasion, if this revisionary strategy does not involve the role "America," if not the United States of America, has played and continues to play in the post–Cold War period in shaping the global context Readings privileges. Reading's recommendation, I suggest, constitutes a circumvention of the historical specificity of the transformational history culminating in the overdetermination of the planetary scene. It thus inadvertently repeats the fateful forgetting of the question of being that has characterized the representation of history by the dominant, especially American, culture ever since the fall of Saigon in 1975. I mean, as I will show, the

systematic forgetting of the epochal disclosures vis-à-vis the American *episteme* precipitated by the Vietnam War.

2. There are, on the other hand, critics — the optimistically "progressive" critics referred to above — who interpret the professionalization of "theory" as evidence of the positive political impact that contemporary criticism has had not only in the academy but in the "world." See, for example, Bruce Robbins, *Secular Vocations: Intellectuals, Professionalism, Culture* (London: Verso, 1993).

3. Francis Fukuyama, "The End of History?" *National Interest* 16 (summer 1998): 3–18; and Fukuyama, *End of History and the Last Man* (New York: Free Press, 1993); hereafter cited in the text as *EH*. Basing his reading of Hegel on Alexander Kojève's interpretation of the dialectical history of the Absolute Spirit, Fukuyama attempts to overcome the weaknesses of the deterministic reading of Hegel (which he associates with a totalitarian — Hegelian Marxist — politics) by identifying it with "historicism" and "liberal democracy": "While Hegel may not have been the first philosopher to write about history, he was the first *historicist* philosopher — that is, a philosopher who believed in the essential historical relativity of truth. Hegel maintained that all human consciousness was limited by the particular social and cultural conditions of man's surrounding environment — or, as we say, by 'the times.' Past thought, whether of ordinary people or great philosophers and scientists, was not true absolutely or 'objectively,' but only relative to the historical or cultural horizon within which that person lived" (*EH*, 62). But Fukuyama insists on the "directionality" (*EH*, 55–70), the *progress*, of history toward an end understood as both termination and fulfillment (maturation) of an initial seminal potential, that, in other words, dialectically annuls its conflictual temporal character — negates its negativity. This qualification clearly betrays its reinscription in the Enlightenment (anthro-logical) version of metaphysics, an ontology of presence that *informs* the differential events of history, thus reducing them to a complicated matter of "mere" *appearance*: "Where Hegel differed from Fontenelle and from more radical historicists who came after him was that he did not believe that historical process would continue indefinitely, but would come to an end with an achievement of free societies in the real world. There would, in other words, be an *end of history*" (*EH*, 64). The complicity of this Hegelian dialectic with Eurocentrism and European imperialism is everywhere manifest in Hegel's *Philosophy of History*, trans. J. Sibree (New York: Dover, 1956): "At this point we leave Africa, not to mention it again. For it is no historical part of the world; it has no movement or development to exhibit.... What we properly understand by Africa, is the Unhistorical, Underdeveloped Spirit, still involved in the conditions of mere nature, and which had to be presented here only as on the threshold of the World's History" (99). "The History of the World travels from East to West, for Europe is absolutely the end of History, Asia the beginning" (103). It is the terrorism of this Hegelian dialectic, which reduces the being of peoples whose cultures it cannot accommodate to nonbeing, that haunts Fukuyama's thesis. For a powerful indictment of Hegel's dialectical philosophy of history as it pertains to the "immaturity" (*Umreife*) of the civilizations of pre-Columbian Latin America, see the chapter titled "Eurocentrism" in Enrique Dussel, *The Invention of the Americas: Eclipse of the "Other" and the Myth of Modernity* (New York: Continuum, 1995), 19–26.

4. Richard Haass, *The Reluctant Sheriff: The United States after the Cold War* (Washington, D.C.: Institute of Foreign Affairs, 1997). The very title of Haass's book, which invokes a variant of the metaphorics of Manifest Destiny that justified the United States's Westward expansionism in the nineteenth century, bears witness to the continuity of its ontologically ordained imperial project.

5. Michael Herr, *Dispatches* (New York: Vintage Books, 1991 [1977]), 71.

6. Robert McNamara, *In Retrospect: The Tragedy and Lessons of Vietnam* (New York: Random House, 1995), xvi.

7. On the twentieth anniversary of the fall of Saigon, CNN presented a two-hour reprise of the Vietnam War in which a number of "leading" participants, including the North Vietnamese commander General Giap, were interviewed. The structural arrangement of this ritualized media event and the perspective of the questions it posed to the actors in its narrative were clearly oriented to distance the war. Like all the other periodically staged ritual remembrances of the war, they were designed to convey to the American public the sense that it was finally over and thus to exorcise its ghost.

8. McNamara, *In Retrospect,* 203. After McNamara left the Johnson administration in 1968, he became director of the World Bank, where, in the name of ameliorating the conditions of "undeveloped" Third World nations, he brought this same dehumanized problem-solving thinking to the reorganization of this powerful global capitalist institution. One of the legacies of his directorship is the present economic, political, and ecological catastrophe that has overtaken many of the Third World countries of Southeast Asia. For a critical analysis of his directorship of the World Bank, see Susan George and Fabrizio Sabelli, *Faith and Credit: The World Bank's Secular Empire* (Boulder, Colo.: Westview Press, 1994), 37–57, 118ff.

9. The latest of these is the CD-ROM *The War in Vietnam: A Multimedia Chronicle,* produced by CBS News and the *New York Times* (New York: Macmillan Digital U.S.A., 1996), and the American media's programming of documentaries, interviews, and symposia commemorating the watershed year of the Vietnam War, 1968. See, for example, the C-Span 1998 symposium on the twentieth anniversary of the Tet Offensive moderated by Marvin Kalb, which included David Halberstam, Stanley Karnow, and Barry Zorthian, and the 1998 PBS documentary *1968: The Year That Shaped a Generation,* written and directed by Steven Talbot.

10. Sacvan Bercovitch, *The American Jeremiad* (Madison: University of Wisconsin Press, 1978): "I approach the myth [of 'America'] by way of the jeremiad, or *political sermon,* as the New England Puritans sometimes called this genre, meaning thereby to convey the dual nature of their calling, as practical and as spiritual guides, and to suggest that, in their church-state, theology was wedded to politics and politics to the progress of the kingdom of God. These sermons provide most of the evidence in my discussion of early New England. But I draw widely on other forms of the literature as well — doctrinal treatises, histories, poems, biographies, personal narratives — in order to place the jeremiad within the large context of Puritan rhetoric, and . . . the much larger context of American rhetoric, ritual, and society through the eighteenth and nineteenth centuries. . . . I argue that . . . the Puritans' cries of declension and doom were part of a strategy designed to revitalize the errand ['in the wilderness']." Bercovitch

adds tellingly: "Even when they are most optimistic [however] the jeremiads express a profound disquiet. Not infrequently, their affirmations betray an underlying desperation — a refusal to confront the present, a fear of the future, an effort to translate 'America' into a vision that works in spirit because it can never be tested in fact" (xiv). The American jeremiad, in other words, is a cultural mechanism designed to remember the American calling by forgetting its actuality, but what it represses in thus memorializing the calling always returns to haunt this memory. It is in this sense that Bercovitch's analysis of the American jeremiad can be applied to the amnesiac remembering of Vietnam in the post-Vietnam period.

11. For exemplary instances of this now-pervasive equation, see Allan Bloom, *The Closing of the American Mind: How Higher Education Has Failed Democracy and Impoverished the Souls of Today's Students* (New York: Simon and Schuster, 1987); Roger Kimball, *Tenured Radicals: How Politics Has Corrupted Our Higher Education* (New York: Harper and Row, 1990).

12. See, for example, Luc Ferry and Alain Renaut, *Heidegger and Modernity,* trans. Franklin Philip (Chicago: University of Chicago Press, 1990); Ferry and Renaut, *French Philosophy of the Sixties: An Essay on Antihumanism,* trans. Mary Schnackenburg Cattani (Amherst: University of Massachusetts Press, 1990); David Lehman, *Signs of the Times: Deconstruction and the Fall of De Man* (New York: Poseidon Press, 1991); David H. Hirsch, *The Deconstruction of Literature: Criticism after Auschwitz* (Hanover, N. H.: Brown University Press, 1991); Richard Wolin, *The Politics of Being: The Political Thought of Martin Heidegger* (New York: Columbia University Press, 1990); Wolin, ed., *The Heidegger Controversy* (New York: Columbia University Press, 1992) (the volume contested by Jacques Derrida for its inclusion of an unapproved translation of one of his pieces on Heidegger in a context patently intended to lend Derrida's authority to the sustained effort to delegitimize Heidegger's thought); Robert Holub, *Crossing Borders: Reception Theory, Poststructuralism, Deconstruction* (Madison: University of Wisconsin Press, 1992), esp. the chapter titled "The Uncomfortable Heritage," 148–201; Tom Rockmore, *On Heidegger's Nazism and Philosophy* (Berkeley: University of California Press, 1992); and John D. Caputo, *Demythologizing Heidegger* (Bloomington: Indiana University Press, 1993).

13. See *Vietnam in America: Ten Years after the Fall of Saigon,* a special issue of the *New York Times Magazine,* March 31, 1985.

14. This project is in process, tentatively titled *Representing Vietnam: The American Cultural Memory and the Forgetting of Vietnam.*

15. Virginia Carmichael, in *Framing History: The Rosenberg Story and the Cold War* (Minneapolis: University of Minnesota Press, 1993), has shown how the American culture industry exploits (re)narrativization to bring "undecidable" historical events — and the national anxiety they activate (the doubts about the legitimacy of power) — to closure. Her instance is the disturbing execution of Ethel and Julius Rosenberg as Soviet spies in 1953, which was motivated more by American Cold War ideology than by legal evidence. Understood in terms of this renarrativizing project, the Gulf War of 1991 was to the national trauma activated by the Vietnam War what the "tapes [allegedly acknowledging the Rosenbergs' contribution to the Soviet Union's production of its first atomic bomb] said to have been made by Khrushchev" was to the national trauma precipitated by the execution of the Rosenbergs.

16. As in *The Green Berets*, the enemy in virtually all the films, documentaries, and oral histories "remembering" the Vietnam War is invariably represented as a faceless abstraction — a "gook," "dink," "slope" (a metonymy that evokes the species "Oriental hordes"), or simply a "Charlie" (which suggests the ventriloquized puppet). They are also represented as male, despite the obviously dislocating fact that women played a significant part in the struggle of the Vietnamese people against the United States army. A significant exception to this frame of representational reference is Stanley Kubrick's *Full Metal Jacket*, a film in which the brief end, which discloses the faceless murderous Vietcong sniper to be a young girl, deconstructs the perennial self-representation of the American soldier as benign deliverer (of women and children) to reveal him as a racist male phallus-killer.

17. The self-parodic degree to which the representation of the "reality" of Vietnam in *The Green Berets* is determined by the (popular) American imaginary is measured by its structural similarity with the Hollywood western epic *The Alamo* (1960), produced and directed by John Wayne.

18. Not accidentally, the American soldier invariably referred to the combat mission that took him out of a "base camp" into the Vietnamese "wilderness" as a foray into "Indian country": "It is midafternoon. The company is strung out along the trail on the north bank of the river. There is no front in this war, but we are aware that we have crossed an undefined line between the secure zone and what the troops call 'Indian country' " (Philip Caputo, *A Rumor of War* [New York: Ballantine Books, 1977], 102). The genealogy of this pervasive locution has its origins, of course, in the discourse of the American frontier, which represents the space beyond the white settlements as a dark wilderness inhabited by savages. But it is also one that became common currency in the canonical racist/imperialist writing of nineteenth-century American historians of the period of the French and Indian Wars. See, for example, Francis Parkman, *The Conspiracy of Pontiac* (New York: Library of America, 1984 [1851]). In tracing the origins of Pontiac's "conspiracy," Parkman, for example, writes: "[S]oon after, a report gained ground that every post throughout the Indian country had been taken, and every soldier killed. Close upon these tidings came the enemy himself. The Indian war-parties broke out of the woods like gangs of wolves, murdering, burning, and laying waste; while hundreds of terror-stricken families, abandoning their homes, fled for refuge towards the older settlements, and all was misery and ruin" (494; see also 627, 637). Tellingly, the rhetoric Parkman, like virtually all the custodians of the American memory of the time, invariably uses to refer to Indian country is deeply inscribed by the Romans' inaugural identification of the barbarian with the (uncultivated) forest (*silvestris:* "savage," literally "of the woods [*silva*])": "To rescue [this history] from oblivion is the object of the following work. It aims to portray the American forest and the American Indian at the period when both received their final doom" (Parkman, preface to the first edition, 347).

19. Caputo, *Rumor of War*, 213. Tellingly, however, as the last line of the quotation suggests, Caputo here, and in his agonized confessional narrative that articulates his disillusionment about the war, draws the wrong conclusion from his insight into the American public's amnesiac longing. Caputo's "autobiography" is more politically suggestive than the numerous other projects of that moment to "remember" the war by way of "eyewitness" accounts against

the American public's "ideologically induced" will to forget it. Nevertheless, it goes far to reinscribe that form of re-presentation epitomized by John Wayne's *The Green Berets* and the numerous personal narratives about the war published in the 1980s. See note 21 below.

20. See William V. Spanos, *The End of Education: Toward Posthumanism* (Minneapolis: University of Minnesota Press, 1993), especially the chapter titled "The Violence of Disinterestedness: A Genealogy of the Educational 'Reform' Initiative in the 1980s," 118–61.

21. Bernard Edelman, ed., *Dear America: Letters Home from Vietnam* (New York: Pocket Books, 1985); Al Santoli, ed., *Everything We Had: An Oral History of the Vietnam War by Thirty-Three American Soldiers Who Fought It* (New York: Random House, 1981) (the Ballantine paperback edition of this book had gone through twenty-one reprintings as of May 1988); Santoli, ed., *To Bear Any Burden: The Vietnam War and Its Aftermath in the Words of Americans and Southeast Asians* (New York: E. P. Dutton, 1985); Mark Baker, ed., *Nam: The Vietnam War in the Words of the Men and Women Who Fought There* (New York: William Morrow, 1981); Wallace Terry, ed., *Bloods: An Oral History of the Vietnam War by Black Veterans* (New York: Ballantine Books, 1984); Philip Caputo, *A Rumor of War* (New York: Holt, Rinehart and Winston, 1977); and Ron Kovic, *Born on the Fourth of July* (New York: Pocket Books, 1977). The other Hollywood movies include the popular melodramatic action films starring Chuck Norris, *Missing in Action* (1984), *Missing in Action II* (1985), and *Missing in Action III* (1988). On the ideological stakes surrounding the MIA issue, see Bruce Franklin *MIA, or Mythmaking in America* (New Brunswick, N.J.: Rutgers University Press, 1993); and Elliot Gruner, *Prisoners of Culture: Representing the Vietnam POW* (New Brunswick, N.J.: Rutgers University Press, 1993).

22. Santoli, *Everything We Had,* xvi; Santoli's emphasis.

23. For a radically different, indeed, antithetical, version of this reversed *mis en scène,* in which the American soldier as Leatherstocking-figure fights a guerrilla war against his corrupted country, see Robert Stone's novel *Dog Soldiers* (New York: Penguin, 1987 [1974]). In this resonant "American" novel, the "errand" of the idealist American frontier hero (Ray Hicks), who has been utterly disillusioned by the America that is conducting the war in Vietnam ("You can't blame us too much. We didn't know who we were till we got here," his friend says. "We thought we were something else" [57]), is reduced to drug running against a decadent America symbolized by a corrupt FBI agent and his criminal deputies. In a deliberately staged symbolic reversal of the westward American narrative, which now moves from the Vietnamese East to the American West, Stone brings the American "adventure" of this contemporary Natty Bumppo to its end in the southern California desert, where, in a shoot-out, he comes to understand himself as a Vietcong doing battle with the massive American war machine:

I'm the little man in the boonies now, he thought.

The thing would be to have one of their SG mortars. He was conceiving a passionate hatred for the truck — its bulk and mass — and for the man who sat inside it.

The right side for a change. (296)

The Rambo trilogy thus could be understood as an ideological effort to revise Stone's earlier parodic representation of the Leatherstocking-figure by making him the last American patriot: the saving remnant. As such, this alienated Rambo-figure becomes the fictional precursor of the emergent paramilitary movement that, adopting the imagery (minutemen, militia) of the American Revolution, represents the monolithic United States government as the betrayer of "America," and that figure's devastation of the town becomes the precursor of the type of violence enacted by the Oklahoma City bombing. For a brilliant analysis of the "negative interpellation" that determines this reversal (and of which Rambo is a proleptic instance), see Donald Pease, "Negative Interpellations: From Oklahoma City to the Trilling-Matthiessen Transmission," *boundary 2* 23 (spring 1996): 1–33.

24. For a powerful early cultural/psychological analysis of this perennial American archetype, see the chapter titled "The Metaphysics of Indian-hating," in Herman Melville, *The Confidence-Man* (Evanston, Ill.: Northwestern University Press and Newberry Library, 1984), 144–51. It is from this chapter that Richard Drinnon draws the title of his inaugural cultural study of America's genocidal Westward expansionism, *Facing West: The Metaphysics of Indian-Hating and Empire Building* (Minneapolis: University of Minnesota Press, 1980).

25. Santoli, *To Bear Any Burden*, xviii; hereafter cited in the text as *BAB*.

26. Reported by the *New York Times,* January 9, 1991.

27. George Bush to a group of state legislators, reported in *Newsweek* 117, March 11, 1991: "By God, we've kicked the Vietnam Syndrome once and for all" (30). The phrase was omnipresent in the discourse of the Bush administration and of the media both before the American decision to go to war and after the war ended. See, for example, the issues of *Time* and *Newsweek* at that time. This post–Gulf War euphoria incumbent on the overcoming of the specter of Vietnam was not restricted to the media. For a representative "historical" version, see Mark Clodfelter, "Of Demons, Storms, and Thunder: A Preliminary Look at Vietnam's Impact on the Persian Gulf Air Campaign," *Looking Back on the Vietnam War: A 1990's Perspective on the Decisions, Combat, and Legacies,* ed. William Head and Lawrence E. Grinter (Westport, Conn.: Greenwood Press, 1993), 145–60.

28. For extended critiques of this negative representation of the emergence of national self-questioning in the Vietnam decade and after, see William V. Spanos, "*boundary 2* and the Polity of Interest: Humanism, the Center Elsewhere, and Power," in *On Humanism and the University I*, special issue of *boundary 2* 12, no. 3 and 13, no. 1 (spring/fall 1984): 173–214; Spanos, "Destruction and the Critique of Ideology: A Polemic Meditation on Marginal Discourse," in *Repetitions: The Postmodern Occasion in Literature and Culture* (Baton Rouge: Louisiana State University Press, 1987), 277–313; and Spanos, *End of Education*, 243–44.

29. See Lauren Barritz, *Backfire: A History of How American Culture Led Us into Vietnam and Made Us Fight the Way We Did* (New York: William Morrow, 1985), 105. The latest version of this reactionary agenda to "forget" Vietnam in behalf of recuperating "our national pride" and the "promise" of America is articulated by the politically reformist American pragmatist Richard Rorty in his aptly titled *Achieving Our Country: Leftist Thought in Twentieth-*

Century America (Cambridge, Mass.: Harvard University Press, 1998): "One consequence of that disastrous war was a generation of Americans who suspected that our country was unachievable — that the war not only could never be forgiven, but had shown us to be a nation conceived in sin, and irredeemable. This suspicion lingers. As long as it does, and as long as the American Left remains incapable of national pride, our country will have only a cultural Left, not a political one" (38).

30. See William V. Spanos, "Rethinking 'Rethinking SUNY': The Costly Ideology Informing 'Cost Efficiency,' " *Crossings: A Counter-disciplinary Journal of Philosophical, Cultural, and Literary Studies* 1 (spring 1997): 164–77.

31. I am invoking here the rhetoric of Page duBois, *Torture and Truth: The New Ancient World* (New York: Routledge, 1991). In this provocative but quite unevenly argued book, duBois attempts to show, by way of analyzing a number of classical Greek texts (including Plato's), the absolute complicity of Western truth discourse (the quest for the concealed) with the practice of torture *(basanos)*. Her book provides historical textual evidence for my claim that Occidental ontology — its reification of being (to Being) and its representation of the ineffable truth of being in terms of a violently forced movement from darkness into light — finds its ultimate fulfillment in a willful practice of power epitomized by the phrase "search and destroy." Unfortunately, duBois's ideological agenda in this genealogical project is to implicate Martin Heidegger's "concept" of truth (*a-letheia*) with Nazi practice. As I understand it, Heidegger's "truth" (*a-letheia*) constitutes an effort to free itself from a certain Platonic impulse in post-Socratic thinking that would reduce being to *eidos* (one taken over and codified by the Roman *veritas*). Taking her point of departure from Victor Farias's *Heidegger et le nazisme* (1987), duBois, on the other hand, reads Heidegger's *a-letheia* as a continuation of Greek Platonism. Like many recent humanists who have grasped at the opportunity afforded by Farias's book to recuperate the ground humanism lost to postmodern theory since the Vietnam War, duBois thus misrepresents Heidegger's understanding of the relationship between thinking and political practice by viewing it within the traditionalist humanist problematic that restricts politics to the binary opposition between democracy and totalitarianism. This willful misreading of Heidegger's text is epitomized by duBois's failure to note that the Greek thinker Heidegger invokes above all to think being against a certain metaphysical Plato, the post-Socratics, and the Romans is the pre-Socratic Heraclitus: precisely the philosopher, according to duBois, whose thought, in opposition to the "totalitarianism" of Plato's, lends itself to democratic practice.

32. Following Hegel's modern interpreter Alexandre Kojève, Francis Fukuyama, in fact, antedates the end of history to the Enlightenment, specifically to the Battle of Jena (1806). It is a "developmentalist" reading that allows him to represent the seventy-year hegemony of communism as an ancillary agent of liberal democracy — a historical detour that, in its forceful immediacy ("at the time"), obscured the emergent larger historical pattern, retarding the recognition of the final triumph of liberal democracy: "The center of Kojève's teaching was the startling assertion that Hegel had been essentially right, and that world history, for all the twists and turns it had taken in subsequent years, had effectively ended in the year 1806. . . . [B]ehind this seemingly odd conclusion is the thought that the principles of liberty and equality that emerged from the French

Revolution, embodied in what Kojève called the modern 'universal and homogeneous state,' represented the end point of human ideological evolution beyond which it was impossible to progress further. Kojève was of course aware that there had been many bloody wars and revolutions in the years since 1806, but these he regarded as essentially an 'alignment of the provinces.' In other words, communism did not represent a *higher* stage than liberal democracy, it was part of the *same* stage of history that would eventually universalize the spread of liberty and equality to all parts of the world. Though the Bolshevik and Chinese revolutions seemed like monumental events at the time, their only lasting effect would be to spread the already established principles of liberty and equality to formerly backward and oppressed peoples, and to force those countries of the developed world already living in accordance with such principles to implement them more completely" (Fukuyama, *End of History,* 66). The analogy with the fate of the actual history of the Vietnam War under the ruthless commanding eye of this Hegelian/Kojèvian historiographic perspective should not be overlooked.

33. Raymond Williams warned against this structuration of being quite some time ago in *Marxism and Literature* (New York: Oxford University Press, 1977): "In the transition from Marx to Marxism, and then in the development of expository and didactic formulations, the words used in the original arguments were projected, first, as if they were precise concepts, and second, as if they were descriptive terms for observable 'areas' of social life. The main sense of the words in the original arguments had been relational, but the popularity of the terms tended to indicate either (a) relatively enclosed categories or (b) relatively enclosed areas of activity. These were then correlated either temporally (first material production, then consciousness, then politics and culture) or in effect, forcing the metaphor, spatially (visible and distinguishable 'levels' or 'layers' — politics and culture, then forms of consciousness, and so on down to the 'base'). The serious practical problems of method, which the original words had indicated, were then usually in effect bypassed by methods derived from a confidence, rooted in the popularity of the terms, in the relative enclosure of categories or areas expressed as 'the base,' 'the superstructure.'

"It is then ironic to remember that the force of Marx's original criticism had been mainly directed against the *separation* of 'areas' of thought and activity (as in the separation of consciousness from material production) and against the related evacuation of specific content — real human activities — by the imposition of abstract categories" (77–78).

But Williams's warning against this separation and spatialization of "conscious existence," which is especially applicable to the analysis of the Vietnam War and the advent of the New World Order, has not been heeded — perhaps because it has not been understood — either by Marxists or New Historicists.

34. Karl Marx, *The German Ideology, Part One, with Selections from Parts Two and Three, together with Marx's "Introduction to a Critique of Political Economy,"* ed. C. J. Arthur (New York: International Publishers, 1977), 47. Of course, Marx's rhetoric in *The German Ideology* circulates around the base/superstructure nexus and thus contributed massively to the eventual sundering of this resonant oxymoron in the discourse of "Marxism." But his overdetermination of this rhetoric is motivated not by a Transcendental Signified, but by the historically specific circumstances of the German occasion, specifically the primacy of the (Young) Hegelians' "Word": their positing of

"consciousness" as external to and determinative of the "actual life-process" of men and women.

35. John Hellman, *American Myth and the Legacy of Vietnam* (New York: Columbia University Press, 1986). The quotation is from a review of *The Quiet American* by A. J. Liebling in the *New Yorker,* April 7, 1956, 148–54. Some sense of the utter blindness of American intellectuals at that time to the ideological implications of Greene's satirization of the American national identity in the figure of Alden Pyle can be gleaned from the flippantly vacuous style and content of the following passage from this review: "I should perhaps explain here [after interrupting his account of the 'main incident of the book' (the 'messy explosion in downtown Saigon') to tell his readers that he had decided to finish the novel in order to 'kill the two last deadly hours' of his flight to Idlewild so that he 'could give it to the hostess, a brunette from Rye, New York'] that the book begins with Pyle in the morgue. That is the big gag: A Quiet American. It then goes on to the events that led up to his arrival there. The trouble that starts immediately and keeps on happening is known technically as Who Cares?" (149). The massive pertinence that *The Quiet American* came to have in the United States, as its deepening involvement in Vietnam increasingly exposed the abyssal gap between its self-representation and its actual practice, constitutes a terrific irony that should not be overlooked at this post–Cold War conjuncture. The reviews of Greene's novel published by the American culture industry at the outset of America's intervention in Southeast Asia were intended to bury it. But this resonant text has risen from its grave to haunt its grave-diggers.

36. Graham Greene, *The Quiet American* (New York: Penguin, 1977), 94–95.

37. Jacques Derrida, "Structure, Sign, and Play in the Discourse of the Human Sciences," in *Writing and Difference,* trans. Alan Bass (Chicago: University of Chicago Press, 1978), 279.

38. Herman Rapaport, "Vietnam: The Thousand Plateaus," in *The Sixties without Apologies,* ed. Sohnya Sayres et al. (Minneapolis: University of Minnesota Press, 1984), 138.

39. Alan W. Watts's account of the Taoist *wu-wei* constitutes a remarkable verification of the analogy I am drawing: "[C]oupled with the doctrine of Tao is the teaching of *wu-wei,* the secret of mastering circumstances without asserting oneself against them.... Actually it is the principle underlying *ju-jutsu* ..., the principle of yielding to an on-coming force in such a way that it is unable to harm you, and at the same time changing its direction by pushing it from behind instead of attempting to resist it from the front. Thus the skilled master of life never opposes things; he never yields to their full force and either pushes them slightly out of direct line or else moves them right round in the opposite direction without ever encountering their direct opposition. This is to say, he treats them positively; he changes them by acceptance, by taking them into his confidence, never by flat denial. Perhaps *wu-wei* can best be understood by contrast with its opposite, *yu-wei.* The character for *yu* is composed of two symbols — hand and moon — thus signifying the idea of clutching at the moon — as if it could be seized and possessed. But the moon eludes all attempts at grasping, and can never be held still in the sky anymore than circumstances can be prevented from changing by conscious striving. Therefore while *yu* is trying to

clutch what is elusive (and Life as Tao is essentially elusive) *wu* is not only *not* clutching but also the positive acceptance of elusiveness and change. . . . It is the principle of controlling things by going along with them, of mastery through adaptation" (*The Spirit of Zen: A Way of Life, Work, and Art in the Far East* [New York: Grove Press, 1958], 37). I am indebted to Jeannette McVicker for alerting me to this analogy: "In martial arts, the point is to anticipate your enemy's move, and *let it happen,* because it is your enemy who is expending his energy. You let his energy put him into a position of vulnerability so that you can thus take advantage of it — to 'fight without violence.' Americans interpreted the Vietnamese insurgents' mode of fighting the war as feminine, passive, and cowardly weakness; rather, it was a subtle harmonizing strategy of great insight that utilized nature and the earth all directed toward the 'goal' of letting the Americans defeat themselves through their arrogant indifference to the land (*Xa*) and disrespect for 'the Way' " (letter, July 7, 1998).

40. See Tom Englehardt, *The End of Victory Culture: Cold War America and the Disillusioning of a Generation* (New York: Basic Books, 1995).

41. See the epigraph to this section from Martin Heidegger's "What Is Metaphysics?" trans. R. F. C. Hull and Alan Crick, in *Existence and Being,* ed. Werner Brock (Chicago: Henry Regnery, 1949), 336; see also *Being and Time,* trans. John Macquarrie and Edward Robinson (New York: Harper and Row, 1962), 231–32 and 393ff. It has been one of my abiding concerns as a literary critic to draw attention to the appropriatability of Heidegger's distinction between the dread that has no thing and the fear that has some thing as its object to the project of tracing the genealogy of the privileged status of narrative in the Western literary tradition back to the foundation of the idea of the Occident and demonstrating its complicity with the imperial will to power over the Other. See chapter 1 above. Here, I am extending this restricted focus to include its appropriatability to the genealogy of the metanarratives privileged by the Occident in general and America in particular.

42. Caputo, *Rumor of War,* 107; hereafter cited in the text as *RW*.

43. O'Brien, *Going after Cacciato* (New York: Dell, 1989 [1978]), 240; hereafter cited in the text as *GC*.

44. As I suggested in chapter 2, the map, the sine qua non of the imperial project, is endemic to the anthropological (Enlightenment) phase of the onto-theological tradition. Not accidentally, an acute awareness on the part of the American Military Mission of the utter ineffectuality of the map was pervasive in the discourse of the Vietnam War. One of the most consciously articulated instances of this awareness is to be found in John M. Del Vecchio's Melvillian *The 13th Valley* (New York: Bantam, 1982). In this novel the incommensurability of the (Ahabian) narrative quest (to find and destroy an NVA headquarters and communications center) with the appended visual maps that represent its "progress" (toward the final catastrophe) becomes the structural principle of the narrative. Michael Herr's meditations on the Vietnam War in *Dispatches* are instigated by this destructive relation between the being of Vietnam and the imperial map: "If dead ground could come back and haunt you the way dead people do, they'd have been able to mark my map [of Vietnam under French rule] *current* and burn the ones they'd been using since '64, but count on it, nothing like that was going to happen. It was late '67 now, even the most detailed maps didn't reveal much anymore; reading them was like trying to read

the faces of the Vietnamese, and that was like trying to read the wind" (1; see also 92–93).

45. Tim O'Brien, *The Things They Carried* (New York: Penguin, 1991), 228–29; see also O'Brien, *Going after Cacciato*, 77.

46. See also Caputo, *Rumor of War*, 55.

47. Herr, *Dispatches*, 95.

48. Del Vecchio, *13th Valley*, 381.

49. Gustav Hasford, *The Short Timers* (New York: Harper and Row, 1979), 73.

50. To retrieve my discussion of the peripatetic Herodotus in the preceding chapter, this decentering and demolecularizing strategy of invisibility practiced by the Vietnamese insurgents is proleptically theorized in his remarkable account of the bafflement and eventual withdrawal of Darius's more formidable invading Persian army due to the guerrilla tactics of the nomadic (barbarian) Scythians, who lived on the margins of the *oikoumene*. Herodotus prefaces this account in the following way: "The Scythians, however, though in most respects I do not admire them, have managed one thing, and that the most important in human affairs, better than anyone else on the face of the earth: I mean their own preservation. For such is their manner of life that no one who invades their country can escape destruction, and if they wish to avoid engaging with an enemy, that enemy cannot possibly come to grips with them. A people with fortified towns, living, as Scythians do, in wagons which they take with them wherever they go, accustomed, one and all, to fight on horseback with bows and arrows, and dependent for their food not on agriculture but upon their cattle: how can such a people fail to defeat the attempts of an invader not only to subdue them, but even to make contact with them?" (*The Histories*, trans. Aubrey de Selincourt and A. R. Burn [Harmondsworth, England: Penguin, 1972], 286). For an extended analysis of Herodotus's account of the Scythians' defeat of the invading Persian army that focuses on this baffling nomadic strategy, see the aptly titled chapter "The Hunter Hunted: Poros and Aporia," in François Hartog, *The Mirror of Herodotus: The Representation of the Other in the Writing of History*, trans. Janet Lloyd (Berkeley: University of California Press, 1988), 34–60.

51. The American strategy of attrition (the body count) was nothing more than an allotrope, indeed, the fulfillment of the trope informing the traditional European concept of warfare — that is, the table, which, to be effective, must reduce the differential otherness of the Other to calculative quantity: "Once the [casualty] reports were filed, I brought Colonel Wheeler's scoreboard up to date. Covered with acetate and divided into vertical and horizontal columns, the board hung behind the executive officer's desk, in the wood-framed tent where he and the colonel made their headquarters. The vertical columns were headed, from left to right, KIA, WIA, DOW (died of wounds), NON-HOST, VC-KIA, WIA, and VC-POW. The horizontal columns were labeled with the numerical designations 1/3 for 1st Battalion. 3d Marines, 2/3 Battalion, and so forth. In the first four vertical columns were written the number of casualties a particular unit had suffered, in the last three the number it had inflicted on the enemy. After an action, I went into the colonel's quarters, erased the old figures and wrote in the new with a grease pencil. The colonel, an easy going man in most instances, was adamant about maintaining an accurate scoreboard: high-ranking

visitors from Danang and Saigon often dropped in unannounced to see how the regiment was performing. And the measures of a unit's performance in Vietnam were not the distances it had advanced or the numbers of victories it had won, but the number of enemy soldiers it had killed (the body count) and the proportion between that number and the number of its own dead (the kill ratio). The scoreboard thus allowed the colonel to keep track of the battalions and companies under his command and, quickly and crisply, to rattle off impressive figures to visiting dignitaries. My unsung task in that statistical war was to do the arithmetic. If I had been an agent of death as a platoon leader, as a staff officer I was death's bookkeeper" (Caputo, *Rumor of War,* 159–60).

52. Herr, *Dispatches,* 71.

53. John Duffet, *Against the Crime of Silence: Proceedings of the International War Crimes Tribunal,* with an introduction by Bertrand Russell and a preface by Noam Chomsky (New York: Simon and Schuster, 1968). The American Mission did not, needless to say, represent this undiscriminating military initiative in terms of genocide. It felt, characteristically, that "saving Vietnam" from communist totalitarianism at any cost was logically justified by the universal principles of liberal democracy. Only when critics of the war such as Jean-Paul Sartre and Bertrand Russell began referring to America's conduct of the war as genocidal did the "gap" between the ontological principles justifying the intervention and the indiscriminate violence of America's conduct of the war begin to manifest itself. It was only after these critics began comparing American aggression in Vietnam to Nazi genocide that the word came to assume a resonant significance in the debates over the question of the culpability of those conducting the war in Vietnam. (See, for example, General Telford Taylor, *Nuremberg and Vietnam: An American Tragedy* [Chicago: Quadrangle Books, 1970].) It was, I suggest, the specter of that terrible contradiction that brought the war to its shuddering end. And it is the disclosure of the relationship between the two that the official memory has tried to forget. It is this relationship that a posthumanist discourse has to remember.

54. Television interview, quoted in Emile de Antonio's documentary video, *The Day of the Pig* (1968). Later in the interview, in response to a question about the quality of the "Vietcong" soldier, Clark adds, "Oh, there's no question about it. They're willing to die readily, as all Orientals are. And their leaders will sacrifice them and we won't sacrifice ours." This typically grotesque racist/political view of the Asian Other was entirely shared by General Curtis Lemay: "Our every American instinct makes us want to jump in with both feet to get an unpleasant job over with as soon as possible. But traditional Oriental patience makes them willing to carry on the struggle into generation after generation if necessary. We're fighting a war over there with a commodity most precious to us and held far more cheaply by the enemy: the lives of men." What is especially telling is that this formulaic ideological relay was not restricted to politically reactionary militarists, then euphemistically called "hawks." It was also essential to the "liberal" discourse of all-too-many so-called liberal doves. Thus, for example, Tounsend Hoopes, the undersecretary of the Air Force who became a leading advocate of withdrawal after the Tet Offensive, wrote: "We believe the enemy can be forced to be 'reasonable,' i.e., to compromise or even capitulate, because we assume he wants to avoid pain, death, and material destruction. We assume that if these are inflicted on him with increasing severity,

then at some point in the process he will want to stop suffering. Ours is a plausible strategy — for those who are rich, who love life and fear pain. But happiness, wealth, and power are expectations that constitute a dimension far beyond the experience, and probably beyond the emotional comprehension, of the Asian poor." To this Noam Chomsky replies: "Hoopes does not tell us how he knows that the Asian poor do not love life or fear pain, or that happiness is probably beyond their emotional comprehension. But he does go on to explain how 'ideologues in Asia' make use of these characteristics of the Asian hordes. Their strategy is to convert 'Asia's capacity for endurance in suffering into an instrument for exploiting a basic vulnerability of the Christian West.' They do this by inviting the West 'to carry its strategic logic to the final conclusion, which is genocide. . . .' At that point we hesitate, for, remembering Hitler and Hiroshima and Nagasaki, we realize anew that genocide is a terrible burden to bear. Thus by their willingness to die, the Asian hordes, who do not love life, who fear no pain and cannot conceive of happiness, exploit our basic weakness — our Christian values which make us reluctant to bear the burden of genocide, the final conclusion of our strategic logic. Is it really possible to read these passages without being stunned by their crudity and callousness?" ("On War Crimes," in *At War with Asia* [New York: Pantheon, 1970], 298–99).

55. Frances FitzGerald, *Fire in the Lake: The Vietnamese and the Americans in Vietnam* (New York: Vintage Books, 1998), 433.

56. Herr, *Dispatches,* 106–7. Herr is acutely conscious of both the polyvalent leveling power of the Mission's "American" narrative and its contradictory consequences: the terrible absurdity of its beginning-middle-end logic. His account of what the American Mission and the culture industry in the United States represented as a Dien Bien Phu overlaid with the heroic image of the Alamo and called "The Battle of Khe Sanh" or "The Siege of Khe Sanh" ends as follows: "A token American force was kept at Khe Sanh for the next month, and the Marines went back to patrolling the hills, as they had done a year before. A great many people wanted to know how the Khe Sanh Combat Base could have been the Western Anchor of our Defense [as General Westmoreland has narrativized the occasion] one month and a worthless piece of ground the next, and they were simply told that the situation had changed. A lot of people suspected that some kind of secret deal had been made with the North; activity along the DMZ all but stopped after Khe Sanh was abandoned. The Mission called it a victory, and General Westmoreland said that it had been 'a Dien Bien Phu in reverse' " (163). I made this point about the narrative-obsessed American structure of consciousness in an essay written during the Vietnam War titled "The Detective and the Boundary: Some Notes on the Postmodern Literary Imagination," *boundary* 2 1, no. 1 (fall 1972): 147–68; reprinted in *Repetitions,* 13–49, and in *Early Postmodernism: Foundational Essays,* ed. Paul Bové (Durham, N.C.: Duke University Press, 1995), 17–39. There, I invoked the representation by the then secretary of defense in the Nixon administration, Melvin Laird, of the well-"rehearsed" (*New York Times*) and "perfectly executed" (*Time*) American rescue mission staged against the Son Tay prisoner of war camp in North Vietnam, which ended in finding no one there: "Despite this mockery 'of our contrived finalities' [Iris Murdoch], these revelatory glimpses into the horror, the secretary, . . . like the detective in his "Retrospective,' was driven to declare reiteratively in the aftermath that the Son Tay affair was a successfully com-

pleted operation. It is this metamorphosis of the absurd into manageable object, into fulfilled objective, into an accomplishment — this deus ex machina, as it were — that is especially revealing. For the obvious incommensurability between the assertion of successful completion and the absurd and dreadful non-end constitutes a measure of the intensity of the need that the power complex and the people that depend on it feel for definite conclusions. Returning to the ontological level, it is a measure of modern Western man's inscribed need *to take hold of the Nothing* that, despite or perhaps because of his technic, is crowding in on him" (165).

57. Frank Lentricchia, *Ariel and the Police: Michel Foucault, William James, Wallace Stevens* (Madison: University of Wisconsin Press, 1988), 20–21.

58. This postmodern literary genre, I suggest, was, in part, instigated by the Vietnam War or related modern wars bearing witness to the wholesale slaughter of the "criminal" Others unleased in the name of the West's self-appointed task to win their hearts and minds.

59. See especially Donald E. Pease, *Visionary Compacts: American Renaissance Writing in Cultural Context* (Madison: University of Wisconsin Press, 1987); and Pease, "New Americanists: Revisionary Interventions in the Canon," in Pease, ed., *New Americanists,* a special issue of *boundary 2* 17 (spring 1990): 1–37.

60. Herman Melville, *Moby-Dick or The Whale,* ed. Harrison Hayford, Hershel Parker, and G. Thomas Tanselle (Evanston, Ill.: Northwestern University Press and the Newberry Library), 184. Melville's insight into this productive relay between a meta-physical ontology that reduces "all" to one (*monos*) and an obliterating practice taking the form of a technological weapon that is identified metaphorically with the human heart (see the passage below from Philip Caputo's *Rumor of War*) is not accidental. This is made clear by the fact that Melville repeats and amplifies this insight later in the chapter: "Ahab's full lunacy subsided not, but deepeningly contracted; like the unabated Hudson, when that noble Northman flows narrowly, but unfathomably through the Highland gorge. But, as in his narrow-flowing monomania, not one jot of Ahab's broad madness had been left behind; so in that broad madness, not one jot of his great natural intellect had perished. That before living agent, now became the living instrument. If such a furious trope may stand, his special lunacy stormed his general sanity, and carried it, and turned all its concentrated cannon upon its own mad mark; so that far from having lost his strength, Ahab, to that one end, did now possess a thousand fold more potency than ever he had sanely brought to bear upon any one reasonable object" (185). For a full amplification of this reading of Melville's novel, see William V. Spanos, *The Errant Art of Moby-Dick: The Canon, the Cold War, and the Struggle for American Studies* (Durham, N.C.: Duke University Press, 1995). In working out the continuity of American history from the Puritans' ontologically justified New Adamic errand in the wilderness through the devastating expansionism legitimated by Manifest Destiny to the "imperial"/genocidal practice of "America" in Vietnam, I have relied heavily on Sacvan Bercovitch's important, if also disablingly flawed, book, *The American Jeremiad;* John Hellman's *American Myth,* which extends Bercovitch's analysis of American cultural history to the Vietnam period; and Richard Drinnon, *Facing West.*

61. See also 301. That this symptomatic testimony is at the heart of Caputo's

memoir is made clear by his summation of its progress in the prologue: "At times, the comradeship that was the war's only redeeming quality caused some of its worst crimes — acts of retribution for friends who had been killed. Some men could not withstand the stress of guerrilla-fighting: the hair-trigger alertness constantly demanded of them, the feeling that the enemy was everywhere, the inability to distinguish civilians from combatants created emotional pressures which built to such a point that a trivial provocation could make these men explode with the blind destructiveness of a mortar shell" (xix).

62. The violence inflicted on the truth in the name of (American) truth by the military court martial is epitomized by the ironies informing the defense strategy of Caputo's lawyer:

"I don't want you to get bitter. I want you to do well on the stand today. I can tell you that I admire you for the way you've borne up under all this. Don't mess it up now. Really, I would've cracked long ago."

"Well, I don't break, Jim. That's one thing I'm not going to do. I broke once and I'm never going to break again."

"Hell, when did you ever break?"

"That night. The night I sent those guys out there. I just cracked. I couldn't take it anymore. I was frustrated as hell and scared. If I hadn't broken, I would've never sent those guys out."

"Oh, that. We've been over that a dozen times. No drama, okay? This is the real world. We've been over that, over and over. You told them to capture those Vietnamese and to kill them if they had to. You didn't order an assassination. That's what you'll say on the stand and you'll say it because it's the truth." (*Rumor of War*, 307)

63. Herr, *Dispatches*, 2.

64. The specter of the genocide of the natives of North America and of the abduction and enslavement of millions of Africans has, of course, haunted the Occidental epistemic memory ever since the period of the Enlightenment, the period in which the achievement of global domination by the West is represented simultaneously as its moral triumph. But these specters have been kept at bay by the West's (especially America's) interpretation of these horrors as aberrations in the epistemic logic of the Occident that have been corrected. Similarly, it could be said that the epistemic break I am attributing to the period of the Vietnam War, in fact, occurred earlier in this century. I am referring to World War II, when Nazi Germany called the differential nothing that allegedly threatened the identity and peace of Europe "the Jews" and, in the name of Europe and according to its logic, undertook "the final solution": the systematic extermination of this Other — spectral — people. As Philippe Lacoue-Labarthe has said: "In the Auschwitz apocalypse, it was nothing less than the West, in its essence, that revealed itself — and that continues, ever since to reveal itself" (*Heidegger, Art and Politics,* trans. Chris Turner [London: Blackwell, 1990], 35). But because the other Western democratic nations — Great Britain, France, the United States — were allied against fascist Germany in what they represented as a just war being fought in the name of the fundamentally benign principles of Western civilization, this epochal revelation was occluded until it exploded into view as unmistakable in the course of the Vietnam War, that is, when the logic of liberal democracy ended in a genocidal practice that, according to many serious

thinkers at the time, was *in essence* the same as the genocidal practice enabled by the logic of German Nazism.

65. Fukuyama, *End of History,* 45. It is not my concern in this essay to specify what the end-of-history discourse means by "liberal democracy." It will suffice, paraphrasing Fukuyama's representative definition, that it involves the integral relationship between the "liberal" rational drive to satisfy material desires (capitalism) and the "aristocratic" emotional drive for recognition (*thymos*) (a relationship in which Fukuyama would give more weight to the aristocratic *megalothymia* in order to counter the enervating effect of liberal equalitarian *isothymia*) and that this definition itself poses problems that preclude easy assent. What does concern me immediately — in the context of my retrieval of the history of America's intervention in Vietnam — is where Fukuyama locates this political formation: namely, at a moment of modern history that, in being represented as "the end of the Cold War" or the "triumph of liberal democracy over communism," occludes a history the witness of which would destroy — disclose the delegitimating aporia in — such a triumphal representation.

66. I am thinking of Milan Kundera's *The Book of Laughter and Forgetting,* trans. Michael Henry Heim (New York: Alfred A. Knopf, 1980), in which he foregrounds the literal practice of this tactic of forgetful remembering in communist Czechoslovakia enabled by a totalizing Universal History: "In February 1948, Communist leader Klement Gottwald stepped out on the balcony of a Baroque palace in Prague to address the hundreds of thousands of his fellow citizens packed into Old Town Square. It was a crucial moment in Czech history — a fateful moment of the kind that occurs once or twice in a millennium.

"Gottwald was flanked by his comrades, with Clementis standing next to him. There were snow flurries, it was cold, and Gottwald was bareheaded. The solicitous Clementis took off his own fur cap and set it on Gottwald's head.

"The Party propaganda section put out hundreds of thousands of copies of a photograph of that balcony with Gottwald, a fur cap on his head and comrades at his side, speaking to the nation. On that balcony the history of Communist Czechoslovakia was born. Every child knew that photograph from posters, schoolbooks, and museums.

"Four years later Clementis was charged with treason and hanged. The propaganda section immediately airbrushed him out of history and, obviously, out of all the photographs as well. Ever since, Gottwald has stood on the balcony alone. Where Clementis once stood, there is only bare palace wall. All that remains of Clementis is the cap on Gottwald's head" (1).

67. Noam Chomsky, *Deterring Democracy* (New York: Hill and Wang, 1992).

68. Herr, *Dispatches,* 219.

69. Ibid., 50. "Straight history, auto-revised history, history without handles, for all the books and articles and white papers, all the talk and the miles of film, something wasn't answered, it wasn't even asked. We were back-grounded, deep, but when the background started sliding forward not a single life was saved by the information. The thing had transmitted too much energy, it heated up too hot, hiding low under the fact-figure crossfire there was a secret history, and not a lot of people felt like running in there to bring it out" (ibid., 49–50).

4. "Theory" and the End of History

1. It is the fundamental claim of this chapter that the periodic but insistent violence that has characterized the American way of life, in both the domestic and international spheres, from its beginning in the Puritan errand in the wilderness to the Vietnam War, is not, as it is always claimed by its ideological apparatuses, a lapse from or betrayal of America's benign, exceptionalist ideals, but is inherent in its liberal/humanist democratic (onto)logic. What Derrida says in general about the ontologic of Marxist history by way of thinking a "new International" "based" on a "certain spirit of Marx" applies as well — and needs to be thematized more than it has been — to Western, and especially American, liberal democracy: "Whatever one may think of this event [the promised International of this particular spirit of Marx], of the sometimes terrifying failure of that which was thus begun, of the techno-economic or ecological disasters, and the totalitarian perversions to which it gave rise (perversions that some have been saying for a long time are precisely not perversions, that is, they are not pathological and accidental corruptions but the necessary deployment of an essential logic present at the birth of an originary dis-adjustment — let us say, for our part, in a too-elliptical fashion and without contradicting this hypothesis, they are the effect of an *ontological* treatment of the spectrality of the ghost) [the transformation of 'spirit' into 'Spirit']" (Jacques Derrida, *Specters of Marx: The State of the Debt, the Work of Mourning, and the New International,* trans. Peggy Kamuf [New York: Routledge, 1994], 91). This was not only the lesson of Stalinism; it was also the lesson of the Vietnam War. Adversarial Americanist criticism must cease once and for all to think the violence perpetrated by America in terms of perversions, accidents, and betrayals. To continue to think opposition in this way is to succumb to the disabling ruse of "reformism," which leaves the source of the violence intact. A recent case in point is Richard Rorty's call, against the new "cultural Left" precipitated by the Vietnam War, for the rehabilitation of "national pride" and the traditional "reformist Left," which "dated back to the Progressive Era" (1900–1964) and "struggled within the framework of constitutional democracy" (*Achieving Our Country: Leftist Thought in Twentieth-Century America* [Cambridge, Mass.: Harvard University Press, 1998], 43).

2. See William V. Spanos, "The Intellectual and the Posthumanist Occasion: Toward a Decentered Paideia," in *The End of Education: Toward Posthumanism* (Minneapolis: University of Minnesota Press, 1993), 187–221.

3. See William V. Spanos, "The Indifference of *Différance:* Retrieving Heidegger's Destruction," in *Heidegger and Criticism: Retrieving the Cultural Politics of Destruction* (Minneapolis: University of Minnesota Press, 1993), 81–131. See also Edward W. Said, "Reflections on American 'Left' Literary Criticism," in *The World, the Text, and the Critic* (Cambridge, Mass.: Harvard University Press, 1983), 158–77; and Michael Sprinker, "Textual Politics: Foucault and Derrida," *boundary 2* 8 (spring 1980): 75–98.

4. Jürgen Habermas, *The Philosophical Discourse of Modernity: Twelve Lectures,* trans. Frederick Lawrence (Cambridge, Mass.: MIT Press, 1987). See especially Terry Eagleton, *The Illusions of Postmodernism* (Oxford: Blackwell, 1996); Christopher Norris, *Truth and the Ethics of Criticism* (Manchester,

England: Manchester University Press, 1994); and Timothy Bewes, *Cynicism and Postmodernity* (London: Verso, 1997).

5. This is not to say that this end-of-history discourse has been avoided by oppositional criticism. It is to say, rather, that oppositional criticism has been blind to the enormous power with which recent history, aided and abetted by the media, has endowed it. On the one hand, there are those English Marxists like Fred Halliday ("An Encounter with Fukuyama," 89–95), Michael Rustin ("No Exit from Capitalism," 96–107), and Ralph Miliband ("On Socialist Democracy," 108–13), who, in a symposium on Francis Fukuyama's *The End of History* published in *New Left Review* 193 (June 1992), cull from Fukuyama's admittedly neocapitalist end-of-history discourse a certain progressive thrust that, in its appeal to "universal analytic and moral criteria," which is to say, in its resistance to postmodern indeterminacy, is amenable to appropriation by a progressive Marxism. On the other hand, there are the New Historicists, who, in their triumphant historical localist disdain of the "old" "grand historical narratives," are blinded to the resonantly effective historicity of Fukuyama's "pop" theoretical representation of the post–Cold War world. See Louis Montrose, "New Historicisms," in *Redrawing the Boundaries: The Transformation of English and American Literary Studies,* ed. Stephen Greenblatt and Giles Gunn (New York: Modern Language Association, 1992), 410. See also Aijaz Ahmad, "Reconciling Derrida: 'Spectres of Marx' and Deconstructive Politics," *New Left Review* 208 (November/December 1994): 88–106. This last is a Marxist-oriented critical commentary on the section, primarily on Fukuyama, of *Specters of Marx* published in *New Left Review* 205 (May/June 1994): 31–58. In this critique, Ahmad says that "the section where Derrida offers a deconstructive reading of Fukuyama's much-publicized book does not much interest me.... Coming so much later, Derrida's treatment of Fukuyama strikes me as conventional" (90). Virtually overlooking/repressing Derrida's insight into the recuperated foundations of the renewed hegemony that has "buried" Marx and "Marxism," Ahmad predictably — and conventionally — chooses rather to demonstrate the complicity of deconstruction with the right-wing in the death of Marxism (91–101) and to show that, despite his avowal of his Marxist inheritance, little in Derrida's "reconciliation" with Marx would indicate a radical overcoming of that complicitous tendency.

6. Derrida, *Specters of Marx,* 53.

7. I put quotation marks around the name of the most distinguished and innovative contemporary Marxist thinker to emphasize that my critique is directed not so much against Jameson as such as to a certain reductive reading of Jameson's understanding of postmodernism that now prevails not simply in discussions of the term, or in cultural studies in general, but also in the discourse of the media — print and visual — where its identification with commodification is epitomized by its abbreviation to the acronym "POMO." Nevertheless, I also do not want to obscure Jameson's role in providing a context for this "Jamesonian" discourse on the postmodern.

8. This relationship was clearly articulated in a paper titled "Empire" delivered by Michael Hardt at Binghamton University in the spring of 1996; forthcoming in Michael Hardt and Antonio Negri, *Empire* (Cambridge, Mass.: Harvard University Press).

9. For Jameson, high modernism is to be distinguished from postmodern-

ism by its self-conscious adherence to historical depth and affect in the face of the late capitalist project to transform historicity into a global spatial surface or hyperspace of simulacra. In order to justify this distinction, which is necessary to the representation of postmodernism as the cultural dominant of the late capitalist period, Jameson is compelled to overlook entirely the fundamental modernist impulse to spatialize time, not simply that of Anglo-American modernism but that of European modernism at large (e.g., the art and architecture of the Viennese postsecessionists [Gustave Klimt, Otto Wagner, and so on] [see Carl Schorske, *Fin de Siècle Vienna: Politics and Culture* (New York: Vintage, 1986)]). This oversight is epitomized by Jameson's and his followers' omission of any reference to the decisively enabling influence of modernist painters, sculptors, and architects (Pablo Picasso, Amedeo Modigliani, Piet Mondrian, Wyndham Lewis, Henri Gaudier-Brezska, Jacob Epstein, Constantin Brancusi, Le Corbusier, for example) on modernist literary artists (and theoreticians) such as T. E. Hulme, Wyndham Lewis, Ezra Pound, T. S. Eliot, W. B. Yeats, Virginia Woolf, James Joyce, and the New Critics. I am referring to those whose art, like that of Byzantium, Africa, ancient Egypt, preclassical Greece, and the Orient, according to Wilhelm Worringer and his modernist English popularizer T. E. Hulme, was compelled by the "urge to abstraction": the impulse to spatialize and thus annul by rising above — gaining aesthetic distance from — the dread of time. See Worringer, *Abstraction and Empathy*, trans. Michael Bullock (New York: International University Press, 1953); and Hulme, especially, "Modern Art and Its Philosophy," in *Speculations*, ed. Herbert Read (New York: Harcourt, Brace, n.d.), 75–109. Instead, Jameson chooses to represent high modernism by the example of Edvard Munch: "Edvard Munch's painting *The Scream* is, of course, a canonical expression of the great modernist thematics of alienation, anomie, solitude, social fragmentation, and isolation, a virtually programmatic emblem of what used to be called the age of 'anxiety' " (*Postmodernism, or The Cultural Logic of Late Capitalism* [Durham, N.C.: Duke University Press, 1991], 11). The characteristics of Munch's painting enumerated by Jameson are those I take to be the essential existential — and antimodernist — traits of the protopostmodern. As I read Munch's *The Scream* — so profoundly different from, say, a painting by Modigliani or a sculpture by Epstein or a building by Le Corbusier — it exists to deconstruct *both* traditional bourgeois realism (and its post-Enlightenment urge to empathize with time) and modernist spatial form (and its urge to abstraction). By transforming the stylized angularity of the urge to abstraction and spatialization to the dynamic flow of temporal flux and by foregrounding and juxtaposing the dread-struck woman with the complacent indifference of the two backgrounded bourgeois men who have just passed her, Munch's painting breaks down our inscribed urge to (patriarchal) narrative or aesthetic closure and compels us to engage or confront (in the sense of an *Auseinandersetzung*) the corrosive ("feminine" and "barbaric") dynamics of temporal/historical existence. This, of course, is hardly an adequate response to Jameson's powerful displacements, but it should at least suggest that his definition of postmoderism may be the end of what Althusser has called, against a certain Marxist reading of Marx, doing history in the "future anterior" and finally in the "Hegelian" mode.

10. Jameson, *Postmodernism*, 16.

11. Ibid., 6.

12. Guy Debord, *The Society of the Spectacle,* trans. Donald Nicholson-Smith (New York: Zone Books, 1994).

13. Jameson, *Postmodernism,* 17.

14. Michel Foucault, "Nietzsche, Genealogy, History," in *Language, Counter-memory, Practice: Selected Essays and Interviews,* ed. Donald F. Bouchard, trans. Donald F. Bouchard and Sherry Simon (Ithaca, N.Y.: Cornell University Press, 1977), 160–61; my emphasis. Foucault's Nietzschean concept of parody is intended to address the question of the identity of the European national state, but it is easily translatable to the postcolonial context.

15. Edward W. Said, *Culture and Imperialism* (New York: Alfred Knopf, 1993), 323–24. Said's representation of modern imperialism as essentially "incorporative" is fundamental to his analysis and critique and constitutes an important emphasis in the face of the now-pervasive representation of the contemporary symbolic order in terms of a period of fragmentation. (The latter is also the view of Gerald Graff in his analysis of the profession of English in *Professing Literature: An Institutional History* [Chicago: University of Chicago Press, 1987].) But Said's enabling ontological center is also assumed rather than theorized. He fails to make explicit the ontological grounds that constitute the condition of possibility for the discourse and practice of this seductive, late capitalist (neo)imperialism.

16. Antonio Gramsci, *Selections from The Prison Notebooks,* ed. and trans. Quintin Hoare and Geoffrey Nowell Smith (New York: International Publishers, 1971), 12.

17. Derrida, *Specters of Marx,* 51–52.

18. Ibid., 10.

19. Ibid., 53–54.

20. For a telling example of what a "Jamesonian" representation of postmodernism can be turned into by liberal humanists, see V. R. Berghahn's review of *Forever in the Shadows of Hitler: Original Documents of the Historikerstreit, the Controversy concerning the Singularity of the Holocaust,* trans. James Knowlton and Truett Cates (Atlantic Highlands, N.J.: Humanities Press, 1993) and of Christopher Browning's *The Path to Genocide* (Cambridge: Cambridge University Press, 1993) in the *New York Times Book Review,* April 18, 1993, 3, 33. Berghahn writes: "To be sure, the articles and essays by those who pursue the normalization of the German past are considerably more subtle than the crude denials of the radical right. Written in the mood of a conservative post-modernism, they point out, often with an air of cynical innocence, that history after all is constantly being revised and that it would be constantly pernicious to impose a ban on the scholarly freedom to ask questions. Had [Enrst] Nolte done any more than to claim this freedom for himself?" (33). Berghahn's source may be Jürgen Habermas's well-known identification of Derrida's and Foucault's poststructuralist discourse with "neoconservatism." Nevertheless, his overdetermination of the undecidability of postmodernism — which he identifies with the reactionary German revisionist historians' effort to normalize the Nazi period "within the larger context of modern German history" — is basically the same as the "Jamesonian."

21. Hardt and Negri, *Empire.* See also Masao Miyoshi, *The Culture of Globalization* (Durham, N.C.: Duke University Press, 1998); Wlad Godzich, "L'Anglais mondiale et les stratégies de la diglossie," *boundary 2* 26 (summer

1998): 31–44; Ronald Judy, "Some Notes on the Status of Global English in Tunisia," *boundary* 2 26 (summer 1998): 2–29. For a more extended interrogation of this "transnational capitalist" view of "global English," see William V. Spanos, "American Studies in the 'Age of the World Picture': Thinking the Question of Language," in *The Future of American Studies,* ed. Donald Pease and Robyn Wiegman (Durham, N.C.: Duke Univesity Press, forthcoming).

22. Bill Readings, *The University in Ruins* (Cambridge, Mass.: Harvard University Press, 1997): "Global 'Americanization' today (unlike during the period of the Cold War, Korea, and Vietnam) does not mean American national predominance but a global realization of the contentlessness of the American national idea, which shares the emptiness of the cash nexus and of excellence" (35).

23. "Interview with Edward Said," in *Edward Said: A Critical Reader,* ed. Michael Sprinker (Cambridge, Mass.: Blackwell, 1992), 239–40.

24. W. B. Yeats, "The Second Coming," in *The Collected Poems of W. B. Yeats* (New York: Macmillan, 1956), 184.

25. Terry Eagleton, "The Crisis of Contemporary Culture," *New Left Review* 196 (November–December 1992): 33.

26. Michel Foucault, *Discipline and Punish: The Birth of the Prison,* trans. Alan Sheridan (New York: Pantheon, 1977), 30–31. The Foucault I am invoking is not the Foucault of the New Historicists. In his effort to rehabilitate the marginalized against all forms of totalization (including the Marxist), this latter Foucault, as Brook Thomas has shown in a critique of Stephen Greenblatt (which does assume the latter's reading of Foucault to be the right one), attributes "equal significance to all social practices" (renders difference the same), that is, represents power as ubiquitous. In thus championing everything marginal, Foucault paradoxically reinscribes his discourse in a "totalizing vision" "from which [he] would break." In his breaking of boundaries, in short, Foucault (and his New Historical ephebes) "risks defusing attempts at organized resistance": "The Foucauldian aspect tries to avoid perpetuating the play of domination by exposing what power has repressed. In continually calling attention to the costs involved in instituting any discursive system, this strategy has a certain moral attraction as it tries to avoid any positive statements that would make it part of the existing power structure. But one thing that it seems to avoid asking is: what are the costs involved in its own mode of discourse? An obvious one for excluded groups, who want to seize or at least share power, is that by positioning itself on the margins, it virtually guarantees its failure" (Brook Thomas, *The New Historicism and Other Old-Fashioned Topics* [Princeton, N.J.: Princeton University Press, 1991], 46–47). I cannot here articulate the Foucault I am invoking. (For my version, see "Heidegger and Foucault: The Politics of the Commanding Gaze," in *Heidegger and Criticism,* 132–80.) Suffice it to say in general that I am of that company (which includes Gilles Deleuze, Edward Said, and Paul Bové) who, Thomas anticipates, will accuse him of "misreading Foucault, who has been celebrated precisely because he works against Marxism's totalizing sense of history" (46). The Foucault I am invoking is the Foucault who always differentiates power relations, not according to metaphysically established boundaries, but, like a certain Marx (especially the Marx of *The German Ideology*), according to historically constructed and therefore contingent divisions.

27. Paul Bové, introduction to *In the Wake of Theory* (Hanover, N.H.: Wesleyan University Press, 1992), 10.

28. The liberal humanist attacks on Heidegger's and "Heideggerians'" "antihumanist" thought afforded by Victor Farias's *Heidegger et le nazisme* (Paris: Éditions Verdier, 1987) are by now legion. But see especially Luc Ferry and Alain Renaut, *Heidegger and Modernity* (Chicago: University of Chicago Press, 1990); Richard Wolin, ed., *The Heidegger Controversy: A Critical Reader* (New York: Columbia University Press, 1991); and Tom Rockmore, *Heidegger's Nazism and Philosophy* (Berkeley: University of California Press, 1992). What is always left unsaid in this growing body of criticism is that its ideological project is not simply to identify "Heideggerian" thought with fascism, but to recuperate and relegitimize the discourse and practice of the ontotheological tradition, especially its last, anthropological, phase. This is the tradition that "Heideggerian" theory has called into question and that, in exposing the violence latent in its benign *logos,* self-destructed during the Vietnam War. This criticism thus lends itself in a fundamental way to the project of authorizing the post–Cold War end-of-history discourse.

29. Said, *Culture and Imperialism,* xx–xxi. Said is everywhere extremely critical of identity politics — "the Archimedean perspective that is subject neither to history nor to a social setting" (32) — whether it takes the form of Afrocentrism or "negritude" or "nativism" or nationalism or Islamic fundamentalism or feminism. Indeed, his rejection of essentialism is the fundamental point of departure of his oppositional critical project. Curiously, however, Said, like other postcolonial or cultural critics, refuses to theorize this ontological site and thus leaves unfocused the indissoluble relationship between the imperialism of the meta-physical or logocentric center/periphery and the imperialism of the Metropolis (the measuring as well as the mother city)/provinces, and the degree to which the latter (including its cultural allotrope) is dependent for its legitimacy on the former. As the frequent references to his equivocal attitude toward humanism suggest, this theoretical uncertainty strikes me as the most vulnerable aspect of Said's otherwise powerfully persuasive project. See Benita Parry, "Overlapping Territories and Intertwined Histories: Edward Said's Postcolonial Cosmopolitanism," in *Edward Said: A Critical Reader,* ed. Michael Sprinker (Cambridge, Mass.: Harvard University Press, 1993), 30.

30. See Ernesto Laclau and Chantal Mouffe, *Hegemony and Socialist Strategy: Towards a Radical Democratic Politics* (London: Verso, 1985), 7–46.

31. Compare this oxymoron with Gayatri Spivak's proposal of a "strategic essentialism" in response to a certain complaint that deconstruction means the demise of the subject, and thus the annulment of the identity without which there can be no practice of resistance against a dominant culture: "I think it's absolutely on target not to be rhetorically committed to it [essentialism], and I think it's absolutely on target to take a stand against the discourses of essentialism, universalism as it comes in terms of the universal — of classical German philosophy or the universal as the white upper-class male... etc. But *strategically* we cannot. Even as we talk about *feminist* practice, or privileging practice over theory, we are universalizing.... Since the moment of essentializing, universalizing, saying yes to the onto-phenomenological question, is irreducible, let us at least situate it at the moment, let us become vigilant about our own practice and use it as much as we can rather than make the totally counter-productive

gesture of repudiating it. One thing that comes out is that you jettison your own purity as a theorist. When you do this you can no longer say my theory is going to stand against anyone else's because in this sense the practice really norms the theory, because you are an essentialist from time to time. So, from that point of view the universal that one chooses in terms of the usefulness of Western high feminism is the clitoris. *The universalism that one chooses in terms of anti-sexism is what the other side gives us, defining us genitally.* You pick up the universal that will give you the power to fight against the other side, and what you are throwing away by doing that is your theoretical purity. Whereas the great custodians of the anti-universal are obliged therefore simply to act in the interest of a great narrative, the narrative of exploitation, while they keep themselves clean by not committing themselves to anything. In fact they are actually run by a great narrative even as they are busy protecting their theoretical purity by repudiating essentialism" (Spivak, "Criticism, Feminism, and the Institution," in *The Post-colonial Critic: Interviews, Strategies, Dialogues* ed. Sarah Harasym [New York: Routledge, 1990], 11–12; my emphasis). If Spivak's emphasis in the italicized sentence falls on "what the other side gives us," the meaning of "strategic essentialism" would be something like the meaning I am attributing to "identityless identities."

32. Derrida, *Specters of Marx,* 29.

33. Thomas Pynchon, *Gravity's Rainbow* (New York: Viking Press, 1973), 556.

5. Thinking in the Interregnum

1. Martin Heidegger, "The Age of the World Picture," in *The Question concerning Technology and Other Essays,* trans. William Lovitt (New York: Harper and Row, 1977), 129–30.

2. Martin Heidegger, "The Question concerning Technology," in *The Question concerning Technology:* "Everywhere everything [under the dispensation of the 'enframing' of technology] is ordered to stand by, to be immediately at hand, indeed to stand there just so that it may be on call for further ordering. Whatever is ordered about in this way has its own standing. We call it the standing-reserve [*Bestand*]" (17). As *The Pentagon Papers* make appallingly clear, it was this dehumanized and dehumanizing American instrumentalism that characterized the thinking of the policy makers — "the best and the brightest," as they were called — who planned and conducted the Vietnam War from the distance of the Pentagon. See Richard Ohmann's brilliant, but now forgotten, analysis of the deadly "cost/benefit" logic informing these memoranda in *English in America: A Radical View of the Profession* (New York: Oxford University Press, 1976), 190–206.

3. Francis Fukuyama, *The End of History and the Last Man* (New York: Free Press, 1992), 45.

4. Martin Heidegger, "Hölderlin and the Essence of Poetry," trans. Douglas Scott, in *Existence and Being,* ed. Werner Brock (Chicago: Henry Regnery, 1968), 313.

5. Martin Heidegger, "What Is Metaphysics?" trans. Davis Farrell Krell, in *Martin Heidegger: Basic Writings,* revised and expanded edition (New York: Harper and Row, 1993), 96.

6. Heidegger, "Age of the World Picture," 152.

7. Ibid., 135; my emphasis.

8. Martin Heidegger, "Language in the Poem: A Discussion on Trakl's Poetic Work," in *On the Way to Language*, trans. Peter D. Hertz (New York: Harper and Row, 1977), 159–98; hereafter cited in the text as "LP."

9. Heidegger makes it clear that by *geistlich* he does not mean something essential: " 'Ghostly' means spiritual, but not in the narrow sense that ties the word to 'spirituality.' This opposition [between 'ghostly' understood as 'of the spirit' and materiality] posits a differentiation of two separate realms and, in Platonic-Western terms, states the gulf between the suprasensuous *noeton* and the sensuous *aistheton*. 'Of the spirit' so understood — it meanwhile has come to mean rational, intellectual, ideological — together with its opposites belongs to the world view of the decaying kind of man [*verwesenden Geschlechtes*]. But the 'dark journey' of the 'blue soul' [in Trakl's poem 'In Hellbrun'] parts company with this kind. The twilight leading toward the night in which the strangeness goes under deserves as little to be called 'of the spirit, intellectual,' as does the stranger's [*Der Abgeschiedene's*] path. *Apartness is spiritual* [geistlich], *determined by the spirit* [Geist], *and ghostly, but it is not 'of the spirit' in the sense of the language of metaphysics*" (178–79). My interpretation of Heidegger's *Abgeschiedene* is indebted to Jacques Derrida's reading of Heidegger's essay on Trakl in *Of Spirit* (Chicago: University of Chicago Press, 1993), but it also contests it.

10. Jacques Derrida, *Specters of Marx: The State of the Debt, the Work of Mourning, and the New International*, trans. Peggy Kamuf (New York: Routledge, 1994), 99–103. In putting this inversion in this way, Derrida intends to activate consciousness of the etymology of these terms (Latin: *videre*, "to see"), that is, to evoke the metaphorics of vision that inform and enable Western imperialism.

11. Edward W. Said, *Culture and Imperialism* (New York: Alfred A. Knopf, 1993), 332–33; my emphasis.

12. I want to make it clear that I am invoking the strategy of the NLF, *not* the Vietnam of the post–Vietnam War period, as a model of the postmodern *polis* any more than I would Bosnia. For, of course, the Vietnamese, in the aftermath of the war, did not organize their national polity in terms of the differential ontological wisdom that allowed them to defeat the United States. Rather, they reverted to an essentialist nationalism grounded precisely in the kind of ontological — and imperial — identity from which they fought to free themselves. Is it possible to distinguish the postwar polity envisioned by the original insurgents, the NLF (better, if misleadingly, known as the Vietcong) from that of North Vietnam?

13. Sacvan Bercovitch, afterword to *Ideology and Classic American Literature*, ed. Bercovitch and Myra Jehlen (Cambridge: Cambridge University Press, 1986): "The option [for American critics] is not multiplicity or consensus. It is whether to make use of the categories of the culture or to be used by them" (438). For a decisive critique of Bercovitch's reformist mode of dealing with problems confronting the Americanist seeking alternatives to the consensus-producing imperatives of the American jeremiadic discourse, see Paul Bové, "Notes toward a Politics of 'American' Criticism," in *In the Wake of Theory*, 52–60. See also Richard Rorty, *Achieving Our Country: Leftist Thought in Twentieth-Century America* (Cambridge, Mass.: Harvard University Press,

1998). In his highly mediatized book, Rorty castigates the "New Left" that emerged during the Vietnam War for its disparagement of the positive social and political potentialities of American democratic institutions, indeed, for its blatant anti-Americanism. And he calls for "a moratorium" on the theory that, he claims, has nourished negativity into a fully fledged defeatist doctrine of original sin (91) and for a resurgence of "national pride" within a revitalized Leftist politics that has its origins in the "civic religion" (15, 38, 101) of Walt Whitman, John Dewey, and William James and its practical allotrope in the "progressivist" initiatives of such social reformers as Eugene Debs, A. Philip Randolph, John L. Lewis, and Lyndon Baines Johnson. For an amplified critique of Rorty's reformist recommendations, see William V. Spanos, "American Studies in the 'Age of the World Picture': Thinking the Question of Language," in *The Future of American Studies,* ed. Donald Pease and Robyn Wiegman (Durham, N.C.: Duke University Press, forthcoming).

14. The most recent and politically suggestive effort of these postmetaphysical theorists to think positively the specter that haunts the metaphysical "Spirit" of the New World Order is that of Jacques Derrida in *Specters of Marx.* The parallel between his call for a new "spectral" International "grounded" in "a certain spirit of Marx" and Said's concluding call for a community of exiles, for whom, like the perfect person envisaged by the twelfth-century Saxony monk Hugo of St. Victor, " 'the entire world is as a foreign place' " (*Culture and Imperialism,* 335), is striking. Given the conditions of the academy, however, it is unlikely that this parallel will be thought.

15. Edward W. Said, "Travelling Theory," in *The Text, the World, and the Critic* (Cambridge, Mass.: Harvard University Press, 1983), 226–47.

16. William V. Spanos, *The Errant Art of* Moby-Dick: *The Canon, the Cold War, and the Struggle for American Studies* (Durham, N.C.: Duke University Press, 1995).

17. Herman Melville, *Moby-Dick or The Whale,* ed. Harrison Hayford, Hershel Parker, and G. Thomas Tanselle (Evanston, Ill.: Northwestern University Press and the Newberry Library, 1988), 184. See Spanos, *Errant Art,* 270.

18. Herman Melville, *Pierre; or The Ambiguities,* ed. Harrison Hayford, Hershel Parker, and G. Thomas Tanselle (Evanston, Ill.: Northwestern University Press and the Newberry Library, 1971), 204, 208. As in "Bartleby the Scrivener," the spectral silence that haunts the discourse of America is confined to the national context in *Pierre.* But in *Israel Potter* (as in *Moby-Dick*), which retrieves the forgotten or preterited voice of a common American soldier of the Revolution, it is globalized. It should be remembered in the context of Melville's canonization that in his lifetime the custodians of the American Cultural Memory went all out to annul his witness against America. As one eminent contemporary American critic put this general project, Melville's "impious" attack on "the foundations of society" justified "turn[ing] our critical Aegis upon him, and freez[ing] him into silence" (George Washington Peck, review of *Pierre,* by Herman Melville, *American Whig Review* 16 [November 1852]; reprinted in Brian Higgins and Hershel Parker, eds., *Herman Melville: The Contemporary Reviews* [Cambridge: Cambridge University Press, 1995], 443). The canonization of Melville following the "revival" of the 1920s was a continuation of this silencing by other means: the "Americanization" of his witness.

19. What I have said about Melville's relationship to American thinking can

also be applied to Henry Adams, the other American writer whose radically exilic condition instigated both a global perspective on the American nation-state and an awareness of the need to overcome American thinking. See Paul Bové's inaugural meditations on Adams, "Reclaiming Criticism: Willful Love in the Tradition of Henry Adams," in *Mastering Discourses: The Politics of Intellectual Culture* (Durham, N.C.: Duke University Press, 1992), 168–86; Bové, "Abandoning Knowledge: Disciplines, Discourse, Dogma," *New Literary History* 25 (summer 1994): 601–19; Bové, "Giving Thought to America: Intellect and *The Education of Henry Adams*," *Critical Inquiry* 23 (autumn 1996): 80–108; and Bové, "Policing Thought: On Learning to Read Henry Adams," *Critical Inquiry* 23 (summer 1997): 939–46.

20. Jacques Derrida, "The Ends of Man," in *Margins of Philosophy*, trans. Alan Bass (Chicago: University of Chicago Press, 1982), 109–36.

21. Hannah Arendt, *The Life of the Mind* (New York: Harcourt Brace, 1978), 3–4. See also Arendt, *Eichmann in Jerusalem: A Report on the Banality of Evil* (New York: Penguin, 1963), 276.

22. Derrida, *Specters of Marx*, 56–57; see also 63–65.

23. Michael Herr, *Dispatches* (New York: Vintage, 1991), 71. The terrible banality of the American colonel's response should not be understood as either unique or confined to the American military leaders. On the contrary, it reflects the thinking of the American cultural army that planned the Vietnam War that the military executed by way of the indiscriminate strategy of the body count. As Richard Ohmann's brilliant analysis of the appallingly banal inhumanity of the language of *The Pentagon Papers* demonstrated a quarter of a century ago — only to be forgotten — the policy makers in the Pentagon relied on an unrelenting "problem-solving" rationality: the fulfilled allotrope of the American pragmatist tradition. They based their futural projections on a pre-preestablished but unacknowledged narrative scenario that was informed by a purely quantitative measure absolutely stripped of any consciousness of particularity, especially human particularity. It is a mistake to read the dehumanizing logic of these memoranda as simply a *conscious* strategy, cynical or otherwise, intended to render the conduct of the war more efficient by obliterating from view the particularities of that occasion that would complicate and impede the progress of the war. On the contrary, the logic of these Pentagon thinkers — they were "the best and the brightest" — was the logic of common sense taken to its end. Those who practiced it were not unique conspirators, evil men in the conventional sense of the word; they were Americans whose thought was consonant with the truth as most Americans understood it. That is the real horror of these inhuman documents that routinize killing: they show no evidence of their authors' consciousness of the reality they were indiscriminately obliterating. As Ohmann says, "The main point to make [in the context of the terrible effects of this "cost/benefit" rhetorical framework of this problem-solving thinking] is that since the suffering of the Vietnamese didn't impinge on the consciousness of the policy-makers, it had virtually no existence for them" (Ohmann, *English in America*, 202).

24. Enrique Dussel, *Philosophy of Liberation*, trans. Aquilina Martínez and Christine Morkovsky (Maryknoll, N.Y.: Orbis Books, 1985), 14.

Index

Abrams, M. H., 86

Achebe, Chinua: *Things Fall Apart*, 105–6

Adams, Henry: and Rome, 94; and American thinking, 271–72n. 19

Adanson, Michel, 43; and the classificatory table, 46; *Cour d'histoire naturelle*, 223n. 78

Adorno, Theodor, 100, 189; *Minima Moralia*, 191, 198–200; and the negative, 195

Aeneas: as culture-bringer, 101; in Eliot (T. S.), 112–15; as seed-bearer, 101–2; in Sir Philip Sidney, 101–2; story of, in European history, 240n. 62; and violence, 159. *See also Aeneid*; Virgil

Aeneid: Aeneas's shield and, 86–87; as classic, 113–15; and correction of Homer, 100–102, 108–11; and Dido, 235n. 47; and the fate of Turnus, 159; as founding myth of the West, 21, 27, 88–90, 94, 98–102, 240n. 62; prophecy/fulfillment structure of, 21, 27, 99, 110–13, 235n. 47. *See also* Aeneas; Virgil

Agrippa, 69

Ahmad, Aijaz: "Reconciling Derrida: 'Spectres of Marx' and Deconstructive Politics," 264n. 5

Aidoo, Ama Ata: *Anowa*, 244n. 80

Alatas, S. H., 105

Alberti, Leone Battista, 34, 79, 233n. 34

Alembert, Jean Le Rond D': *Preliminary Discourse to the Encyclopedia of Diderot*, 44–45

Alexander the Great, 2, 80; and "Indography," 225n. 87

Algeria, 187

Althusser, Louis, 2, 95, 185, 202–3; "From *Capital* to Marx's Philosophy," 227–28n. 7; and the future anterior mode of philosophy, 216n. 31, 265n. 9; and Heidegger, 226n. 96, 227–28n. 7; "Ideology and Ideological State Apparatuses (Notes toward an Investigation)," 223n. 93; and the interpellated subject, 50–51, 83; and the problematic, 67, 227–28n. 7; and the visible/invisible binary, 195, 227–28n. 7; "On the Young Marx," 216n. 31

America: and the "Age of the World Picture," 194–95; "Ahabism" of, 160–64, 166–67, 256n. 44; and the banality of instrumentalist discourse, 130–31, 144, 192, 203–4, 272n. 23; and the captivity narrative, 139; cultural memory of, 128, 131–42, 165, 194, 202; and the culture industry, 128–44, 155–56, 249n. 15; and the doomed Indian, 41, 207n. 2, 222n. 73; and the end of history, 96, 99, 129–30, 166–69; "exceptionalism" of, xv, xviii, xx, 22, 128–29, 146, 159, 160, 166, 170, 184, 185, 191, 197, 202; and the frontier, xvii, 139, 146–47, 163–64, 175, 250n. 18; and gender, 156; and genocide, xx, 44, 130, 155, 165, 168, 194, 258n. 53, 261n. 64; global "errand of," xvii, 99, 139, 143–44, 146, 191, 201, 260n. 60; and globalism, 126–27, 167, 177–80, 184–85, 191–93, 201; and the jeremiad, xvii, 99, 132, 136, 240n. 64, 248–49n. 10, 260n. 60; and liberal capitalist democracy, 149; and Manifest Destiny, xvii, 22, 99, 166, 175, 260n. 60; and narrative, 154–60, 259–60n. 56; and the New World Order, xvi–xviii, xix, 59–63, 130, 146, 159, 166; and the "Old World," xviii, 128, 146–49, 191; ontological principles of, 144–64, 159; planetary triumph of, 129–30, 166–69, 179–80, 191–93, 198, 204–5; promised end of, 142–43, 157–58; and race, 156, 250n. 16, 258–59n. 54;

WILLIAM V. SPANOS is the founding editor of *boundary 2* and the author of several books, including *The End of Education: Toward Post-humanism* and *Heidegger and Criticism: Retrieving the Cultural Politics of Destruction,* both published by the University of Minnesota Press. He is also the author of numerous articles on modernist and postmodernist literature, culture, and theory.